The
BERKSHIRE
Book
A Complete Guide

Judith Monachina

THE
BERKSHIRE
BOOK
A Complete Guide

FOURTH EDITION

Jonathan Sternfield
AND
Lauren R. Stevens

Berkshire House Publishers
Lee, Massachusetts

The Berkshire Book: A Complete Guide
Copyright © 1986, 1991, 1994, 1997 by Berkshire House Publishers
Cover and interior photographs © by credited photographers

Library of Congress Cataloging-in-Publication Data
Sternfield, Jonathan
    The Berkshire book : a complete guide / Jonathan Sternfield and Lauren R. Stevens. — 4th ed.
        p.   cm. — (Great destinations series)
    Includes bibliographical references and index.
    ISBN 0-936399-88-0
    1. Berkshire Hills (Mass.)—Guidebooks. I. Stevens, Lauren R., 1938- . II. Title. III. Series.
F72.B5S831997
917.44'10443—dc20   96-44796
                                                                      CIP

ISBN: 0-936399-88-0
ISSN: 1056-7968 (series)

Editor: Deborah Burns. Managing Editor: Philip Rich. Original design for Great Destinations™ series: Janice Lindstrom. Cover design: Jane McWhorter.

Berkshire House books are available at substantial discounts for bulk purchases by corporations and other organizations for promotions and premiums. Special personalized editions can also be produced in large quantities. For more information, contact:

Berkshire House Publishers
480 Pleasant St., Suite 5; Lee, Massachusetts 01238
800-321-8526

Manufactured in the United States of America
First printing 1997
10 9 8 7 6 5 4 3 2 1

No complimentary meals or lodgings were accepted by the author or reviewers in gathering information for this work.

The GREAT DESTINATIONS Series

The Great Destinations™ series features regions in the United States rich in natural beauty and culture. Each Great Destinations™ guidebook reviews an extensive selection of lodgings, restaurants, cultural events, historic sites, shops, and recreational opportunities, and outlines the region's natural and social history. Written by resident authors, the guides are a resource for visitor and resident alike. The books feature maps, photographs, directions to and around the region, lists of helpful phone numbers and addresses, and indexes.

Contents

CHAPTER ONE
From the Glaciers to the Present
HISTORY
1

CHAPTER TWO
Getting Here, Getting Around
TRANSPORTATION
17

CHAPTER THREE
The Keys to Your Room
LODGING
28

CHAPTER FOUR
What to See, What to Do
CULTURE
81

CHAPTER FIVE
Pleasing the Palate
RESTAURANTS & FOOD PURVEYORS
140

CHAPTER SIX
For the Fun of It
RECREATION
206

CHAPTER SEVEN
Fancy Goods
SHOPPING
257

CHAPTER EIGHT
Practical Matters
INFORMATION
290

Acknowledgments

"This was a real nice clambake. . . ."

With many fine minds and so rich a culture, Berkshire presents a cultural carousel, full of choice and variety. Fortunately, many exceptional Berkshire friends and colleagues came along for the ride on this fourth edition. First of all, the card-carrying Berkshire County Mealmen — J. Peter Bergman, Ellen Joy Bernstein, Wendy Webster Coakley & Michael Coakley, Kim Cushman, Karen Davis, Ted Davis, Andrew Howitt, Joyce Monachina, Judith Monachina, Paul Monachina, Seth Rogovoy, Jean J. Rousseau, Barbara Rudd, Eric Rudd, Katherine Myers, Gerard Smith, Jonathan Sternfield, Lauren R. Stevens, Edith M. Stovel, and Jack A. Stovel undertook the *Restaurants* chapter, updating old eateries' descriptions and adding new ones. And among them, special notice to Jerry Smith, who knew whom to tap for this exclusive organization. Maryjane Fromm researched and rewrote the *Shopping* chapter. Mary Osak and Gail King helped review the Night Life. Mary Grace Butler checked the facts, Deborah Burns edited the manuscript, Judith Monachina updated the photographs and commented on the manuscript. Mary Osak reviewed the manuscript once again before it went to press. I appreciated all the help and the good grace with which it was offered, but any errors remain mine.

Thanks go to Jean Rousseau, president and publisher of Berkshire House, and his staff: Mary Osak, Liz Rousseau, and Philip Rich, managing editor. They continued to return even the telephone calls they must have dreaded. Finally, thanks to Jonathan Sternfield and David Emblidge, who first concocted this special guide to a special place, now seemingly so many years ago, and especially Jonathan, who continues to power it.

". . . and we all had a real good time."

— L.R.S.

Introduction

Like vintage wine, we hope we're only getting better with age, maturing in our flavors, marrying all the separate ingredients we were given at the start. Coming into our fourth edition, over a decade old, *The Berkshire Book* brings all the elements of the larger picture hereabouts to an up-to-the-minute pulse of Berkshire that we trust will keep you close to the action.

In order to swing to the current Berkshire beat, writer Lauren R. Stevens has roved the county and gathered a crew to freshen the vision of Berkshire life. Whether you gorge on Berkshire's delights or only occasionally graze at her splendid banquet, we trust *The Berkshire Book* will continue to guide you to the good stuff.

We have completely revamped the restaurant section, with reviews that are generally shorter. In addition, to help you sort out the breakfast and lunch type places from the dinner spots, we've opened up a new breakfast-lunch section, with a quick lowdown on where to get those meals, lighter fare, and snacks.

"Art combined with Nature," that is the essence of Berkshire life, an essence that led novelist Henry James to write of his visits to Lenox novelist Edith Wharton: "This renews the vision of the Massachusetts Berkshire, land beyond any other in America today. . . ." Ever since the 19th-century influx of artists and art patrons, Berkshire culture has had a ripe medium in which to flourish. The legacy for us today is an almost unbelievably rich cultural life, from soaring symphonies at Tanglewood to breathtaking dance artistry at Jacob's Pillow; from the folksy characters of Norman Rockwell's paintings to the elegant austerity of Shaker ways and means; from the dramatic heights of acclaimed theatrical stars at Williamstown Theatre Festival and Berkshire Theatre Festival in Stockbridge to the great theatrical moments at Shakespeare & Co. in Lenox. Berkshire is home to great museums, too, like the Clark and the Williams College museums in Williamstown, the Berkshire Museum in Pittsfield, and the Norman Rockwell Museum outside Stockbridge.

The cultural brilliance doesn't set with the sun. Pop music comes to life after dark, from guitar-strumming folksingers to blues and jazz groups, from hard rockers to new wavers, all playing at a variety of pubs, clubs, taverns, bars, restaurants, and boogie joints.

There is lodging to suit every taste here, from the baronial "cottages," such as Wheatleigh and Blantyre, to the rusticity of dozens of quaint houses offering a simple bed and breakfast. For those who prefer to sleep closer to nature, the county's state parks are a camper's delight. Berkshire has its own restaurants, too — hundreds of them — from haute cuisine to home cookin', with true winners in every category.

> *Berkshire, by common consent, is not only a good place to be born in, but a good place to live in, and a good place to die in, as well. It is also prominently recognized as a good place to go out from, and an equally good place to come back to. A Berkshire birth is something to be proud of, a Berkshire sojourn a delight, a rest, a recreation, a circumstance of pleasant memory, ever after; and a Berkshire residence a rich and enjoyable life experience.*
>
> The Book of Berkshire, 1887

In recreation the region gets its greatest attention from skiers, drawn by the county's fine downhill and cross-country ski runs. For hikers, the Appalachian Trail traverses the entire county. And in warmer weather, Berkshire golf courses, tennis courts, and lakes come alive with sportspeople, eager to play.

The work of contributing authors and editors has been mentioned in the Acknowledgments (see page ix). Other chapters remain the work of the principal authors.

As in previous editions, the *Culture* chapter, "What to See and What to Do," is based on the events themselves; on insider's information; on personal interviews with public relations and artistic directors; art gallery owners, and artists; and finally on book research, including histories, biographies, and letters. For the fourth edition, all of Berkshire's perennial cultural attractions, and some new ones, were visited and reviewed. Where space permitted, comments about performances or shows occurring since the third edition were included.

For the *Restaurants* chapter, every restaurant reviewed in the last edition was revisited, many newly opened establishments sampled for the first time. The editorial budget paid for all meals; we were in no way indebted to any restaurant, and we never announced our visit or our intention. During the meals, we often had extensive conversations with waiters, managers, and sometimes the chefs themselves.

Recreational opportunities were studied again, and transportation alternatives reviewed. And the *Information* chapter has been brought up to date.

From start to finish, we have aimed to create a comprehensive, reliable guide for one of America's premier places to live or vacation. We wish you every pleasure as you come to know the Berkshires better, and we hope our *Berkshire Book* continues to serve you as a trusted friend.

Jonathan Sternfield
South Egremont, Massachusetts

THE WAY THIS BOOK WORKS

ORGANIZATION

Entries are located by subject in the appropriate chapters. Among the chapters, arrangements vary to suit the needs of subject matter. Most material is arranged in three geographical groupings, with *__South County__* offerings first, followed by those in *__Central County__*, and finally *__North County__* A few nearby listings that are located *__Outside the County__* are given, as well.

Within these geographic groupings, listings are arranged alphabetically — first by town or topic, and then by establishments' names. Some entries, such as those in *Shopping,* are arranged by type; hence all the craft shops appear together. Each chapter has its own introduction, and the specific arrangement of that chapter is spelled out there.

Factual information was researched at the latest possible time before publication, but be advised that chefs and innkeepers come and go, hours change, shops appear and disappear. When in doubt, phone ahead.

Specific information (such as address and location, telephone number, hours of business, and a summary of special features or restrictions) is presented in the lefthand column or is otherwise shown separately, adjacent to descriptions of various entries throughout the book.

LIST OF MAPS

Berkshire County
Berkshire Topography
Berkshire Access
Berkshire Recreational Sites
Town maps: Great Barrington, Stockbridge, Lenox, Pittsfield,
    Williamstown, North Adams

PRICES

With few exceptions, specific prices are not given. Because pricing is constantly changing, generally we have noted price ranges.

Lodging prices are on a per-room rate, double occupancy, in the high season (summer, fall foliage, and ski months). Low-season rates are likely to be 20–40% less. We urge you always to phone ahead for updated prices and other information and for reservations.

Restaurant prices indicate the cost of an individual's meal, which includes appetizer, entrée, and dessert but does not include cocktails, wine, tax, or tip. Restaurants with a prix fixe menu are noted accordingly.

Price Codes

	Lodging	*Dining*
Inexpensive	Up to $65	Up to $10
Moderate	$65 to $100	$10 to $20
Expensive	$100 to $175	$20 to $35
Very Expensive	$175 or more	$35 or more

Credit Cards are abbreviated as follows:

AE — American Express   DC — Diner's Club
CB — Carte Blanche   MC — Master Card
D — Discover Card   V — Visa

AREA CODE

There is one telephone area code for all of Berkshire County: **413**.

INFORMATION BOOTHS

Volunteers in several Berkshire towns staff tourist Information Booths in the summer and early fall. Often information is available at the site even when volunteers aren't. Year-round tourist information can be obtained from the *Berkshire Visitors Bureau*, Berkshire Common, bottom level, Hilton Hotel, West St., Pittsfield (413-443-9186). The bureau is open Mon.–Fri., 8:30–4:30.

Great Barrington Information Booth: 362 Main St.; 413-528-1510.
Lee Information Booth: Main St. at the park; 413-243-0852.
Lenox Chamber of Commerce Information Office: Lenox Academy, 75 Main St.; 413-637-3646.
Massachusetts Turnpike: at Burger King, Eastbound Mile Marker 8, Lee; 413-243-4929.
Northern Berkshire Chamber of Commerce: Main office, 40 Main St., Holiday Inn, N. Adams; 413-663-3735. Open Mon.–Fri., 9–5. Tour booth located on Union St.; open 7 days, 10–4.
Pittsfield Information Booth: Bank Row. Open Mon.–Thurs., 9–5; Fri.–Sat., 9–8; Sun. 10–2.
Stockbridge Information Booth: Main St. 413-298-5200; Self-service, open 7 days. Lodging information 413-298-5327.
West Stockbridge Information Booth: Rte. 102, Albany Rd. near Shaker Mill Tavern. Self-service, open 24 hrs.
Williamstown Information Booth: Rte 7; 413-458-4922. Attended or self-service, year-round, 24 hrs.

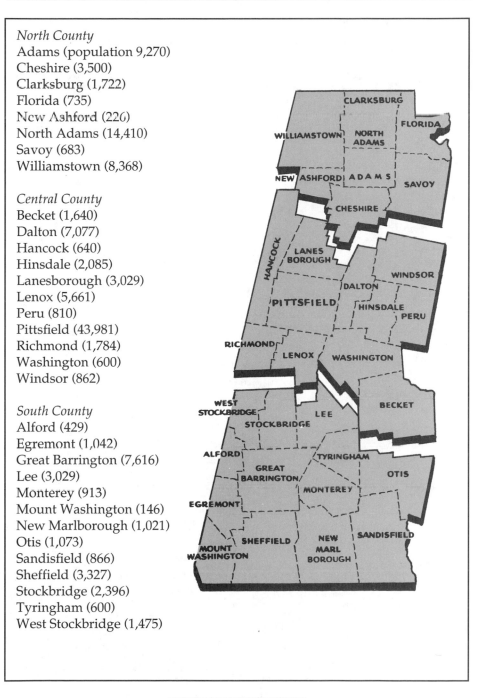

North County
Adams (population 9,270)
Cheshire (3,500)
Clarksburg (1,722)
Florida (735)
New Ashford (226)
North Adams (14,410)
Savoy (683)
Williamstown (8,368)

Central County
Becket (1,640)
Dalton (7,077)
Hancock (640)
Hinsdale (2,085)
Lanesborough (3,029)
Lenox (5,661)
Peru (810)
Pittsfield (43,981)
Richmond (1,784)
Washington (600)
Windsor (862)

South County
Alford (429)
Egremont (1,042)
Great Barrington (7,616)
Lee (3,029)
Monterey (913)
Mount Washington (146)
New Marlborough (1,021)
Otis (1,073)
Sandisfield (866)
Sheffield (3,327)
Stockbridge (2,396)
Tyringham (600)
West Stockbridge (1,475)

BERKSHIRE TOWNS

The
BERKSHIRE
Book
A Complete Guide

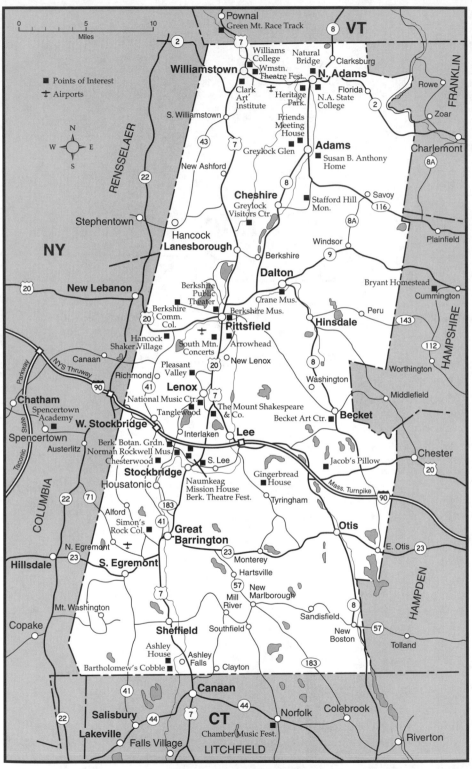

BERKSHIRE COUNTY

CHAPTER ONE
From the Glaciers to the Present
HISTORY

To the hard-working Berkshire settlers, much of what we prize as beauty — these rolling hills — was at the least unproductive, and at most an absolute impediment to making a living. Jeremiah Wilbur, who in 1767 at the age of 14 began farming on the sides of Mount Greylock, could not have had a lot of time to admire the view. This prodigious worker built a carting road over the Notch between Ragged Mountain and Greylock into Adams, built a road to near the summit of

Judith Monachina

The Housatonic River runs through the southern half of Berkshire County, continuing to Long Island Sound in Connecticut. Here, just outside of the village of Housatonic, is a quiet spot on the river.

Greylock (the forerunner of today's Notch Road), cleared enough land to grow and cut 100 tons of hay in a year, tapped enough maples to produce 1,800 pounds of sugar in a year, protected his herd of free-roaming cattle from wolves, maintained the best sheep herd in the county, built a cider mill, a grist mill, and a sawmill on Notch Brook, increased his holdings to 1,600 acres, and died in 1813 a relatively wealthy man. Water power may have lured this early farmer out of the valley and onto the wildest land around, but that same water was a constant threat to his road, wild animals threatened to destroy his livelihood, and the steep terrain was hard to negotiate and tough to plow.

We're fortunate to know a bit about Wilbur. One eyewitness was Timothy Dwight, who toured upstate New York and New England in 1800, after retiring from the presidency of Yale College, and published *Travels in New England and New York* in 1822. At the time people traveled to settle, trade furs, convert Indians, survey boundaries, or fight wars. The concept of taking a recreational spin through remote and unsettled places was unheard of. Dwight may, in

fact, have been America's first tourist. Our good fortune is that he was an intel-
ligent, observant, literate man.

When Dwight rode into Williamstown in October, he looked up Ebenezer
Fitch, president of Williams College, who had written about Wilbur's remarkable sheep farm, and suggested a trip up Mount Greylock. Fitch led the way to
Wilbur's home, partway up the mountain. Wilbur not only allowed the men to
cross his land, but he accompanied them up the road he had built to carry salt
to his cattle.

"We alighted from our horses within 20 feet of the summit," Dwight wrote,
"and found our path better than a great part of the town and country roads
throughout the hill country of New England." The summit of Mount Greylock
was covered with trees; no one, as yet, had built a tower there. So to obtain a
view, the farmer and the two college presidents each picked out a wind-bat-
tered fir tree, and shinnied up.

"The view was immense and of amazing grandure," Dwight recalled. "You
will easily suppose that we felt total superiority to all the humble beings who
were creeping on the footstool beneath us. The village of Williamstown shrunk
to the size of a farm; and its houses, church, and colleges appeared like the
habitation of martins and wrens."

Dwight recognized the Adirondacks, the Green Mountains, Mount
Monadnock, Mount Tom, and the Catskills. He discovered the joy of the third
dimension — height — which we, who so easily drive over hills or fly above
them, take for granted. To Dwight's generation and those to follow, Mount
Greylock was spectacular, as most people did not visit higher peaks; just as
Bash Bish Falls, at the southwest corner of Berkshire, inspired awe in the days
when few had seen Niagara.

Berkshire, The Berkshires, The Berkshire Hills

What is the name of this place, anyway? The original Berkshire is in England,
south of Oxford. There it's pronounced "Bark-shuh." "Shire" refers to an Anglo-
Saxon administrative district.

Purists refer to the "Berkshire Hills," meaning specifically what this book calls
the southern Taconics, including peaks in New York State. The logic of calling all
hills in Berkshire County the Berkshire Hills seems to be gaining acceptance.

Berkshire residents — and visitors — refer to the area variously as "Berkshire
County," as simply "Berkshire," and as "the Berkshires," actually a 20th-century
term created to publicize the area. This book does likewise.

Forty-four years later, when writer/naturalist Henry David Thoreau
climbed past the old Wilbur homestead, Mount Greylock was still wild country, still an adventure. He exchanged a few words about reaching the summit
that night with Smith Wilbur, Jeremiah's son. Thoreau used the trip to over-
come his grief over his brother's death, his disappointment at being rejected as

Foresters examine an old-growth specimen on Mt. Greylock.

Lauren R. Stevens

a suitor by a cousin, his remorse at having accidentally burned 300 acres of woodlands in Concord, and his need to find his own Transcendental vision. All these things, he implies, he put behind him on his walk up Greylock, awakening the next morning to an inspiring sunrise above the clouds. The trip was his preparation for Walden, pond and book.

(Thoreau must have read Dwight, for he made the same mistake of identifying Williamstown from the summit. Can't be done: Mount Prospect is in the way. Thoreau admitted, in his account of the trip in *A Week on the Concord and Merrimack Rivers*, that he had only a very quick view out before the sun set.)

What Dwight began, and 19th-century writers and painters continued, was to instruct hard working, practical folk like farmer Wilbur in the appreciation of the landscape. For a farmer occupied with the daily grind of producing food for his family, someone had to say — as Thoreau did more than once — slow down, enjoy, observe the values nature maintains without any human labor.

Thus the Hudson River School of painters created large, inspiring landscapes and toured them through the towns and cities. "Look what we have here!" they exclaimed to frontierspeople who had seen little beyond the back forty. Furthermore, these artists transformed the religious view of the landscape. When the Puritans arrived on these shores, they saw the woods as dark, evil, aligned with the devil. When Thoreau described his July sunrise or Thomas Cole painted the sun breaking through the clouds, we realize that it is really heaven that is in cahoots with the trees, fields, and falling water around us. Thoreau came to terms with his own problems on Greylock, but he also taught his readers to appreciate the marvels of this godly place.

Building on this tradition, excelling and expanding in their seasons, the arts in Berkshire are still teaching residents and visitors to pay attention to our magnificent surroundings.

NATURAL HISTORY

Tell me your landscape and I will tell you who you are.

— Ortega y Gasset

Erosion gentled the Berkshire landscape in much the same way that culture has smoothed the rough edges of its people — whom Edith Wharton once called her "granite outcroppings." Artists taught us to appreciate this gentled landscape.

Six hundred million years ago this area was flatter, covered by a shallow sea. Lapping waves built up beaches that turned to sandstone, which in turn metamorphosed into quartzite — the erosion-resistant backbone of many county ridges. Shelled marine animals built coral reefs, which calcified over eons into limestone. Deposits of this alkaline agent, which are mined on the side of Mount Greylock today, buffer the area against the worst ravages of acid precipitation. Some of the limestone recrystallized into marble, snowy chunks of which grace hiking trails and can be examined at Natural Bridge, in North Adams. Offshore, muddy sediments settled to form shales and then schists, crystalline rocks that fracture into clean layers. All of these rocks are still present in Berkshire County.

Then at a speed of an inch a year over 150 million years, the land masses that would one day be North America, Africa, and Europe moved toward each other, closing the proto-Atlantic Ocean. Several arcs of offshore volcanic islands were shoved onto the continent in a series of slow but cataclysmic collisions known as the Taconic Orogeny (orogeny means "mountain building"). The entire continental shelf was squeezed into a series of enormous folds, the monumental forerunners of the Appalachian Mountains. Then, slowly, the continents began to pull apart, as they are still doing.

Even as the mountains were rising, to several miles in elevation, the process of erosion began. Rain fell, forming streams that raged through a landscape mostly free of vegetation. Over the eons, water and wind tamed the rugged landforms and sculpted the hills of Berkshire.

Less than two million years ago, the first in a succession of four ice sheets ground down in response to a cooling climate. These mile-high glaciers deposited debris, gravel, and rocks around the relative nubbins of mountains that remained. Glacial lakes covered Great Barrington, Tyringham, and the basin from Williamstown to Adams, and when they drained left gravel beaches on the mountainsides. But the glaciers did not create these mountains; they only iced the Berkshire cake. The great work of diminution had begun — and continues — through everyday erosion. Two great landslides on Mount Greylock in the summer of 1990 were simply more dramatic instances. The Hoosic, Housatonic, and Westfield river valleys remained largely the same as

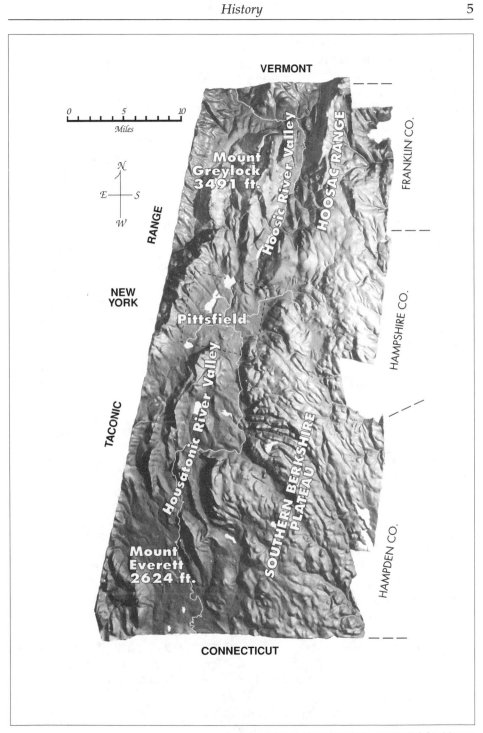

From the relief map by Bartlett Hendricks, courtesy Berkshire Museum they had been before the glaciers, although glacial debris forced the Farmington River to swing north to the Connecticut.

As the region warmed, as recently as 11,000 years ago, vegetation returned and further tempered the climate. From boggy marshlands the evergreen forest moved north, lingering now only on the tops of the highest ridges. In its place the broad-leaved deciduous forest moved in, characterized by oak and its associated species in South County and the sugar maple farther north.

As the glaciers withdrew, animals returned — and humans arrived. Perhaps a few of the earliest North Americans, whose ancestors had boated or walked across the land bridge from Asia, were in Berkshire to watch the glacial lakes drain. The first Americans in the region were foragers, but after developing tools they crafted weapons and became hunters. In South Egremont not long ago were found the remains of a 12,000-year-old mastodon and, around it, arrowheads of the same age.

Seen from above, Berkshire County presents its ridges as north-south-running folds: the Taconics along the New York boundary, the Green Mountains protruding south from Vermont, the Hoosacs filling the northeast quadrant, and the Southern Berkshire Plateau in the southeast. Tributaries of the two major Berkshire rivers, the Housatonic and the Hoosic, nearly meet at Brodie Mountain and then flow in opposite directions to form the extended north-south valley that U.S. Route 7 now follows. The Greylock massif stands as a peninsula, as indeed it was when glacial Lake Bascom filled the Hoosac Valley to the 1,300-foot elevation. Greylock rises 3,491 feet, the highest point in southern New England, visible from most of the county. Mount Everett is the 2,264-foot sentinel of South County. It is possible to see the one from the other.

The rocky steepness of the county does not lend itself to leisurely flowing water and big lakes. With the exception of the southern reach of the Housatonic River, which meanders through Sheffield, Berkshire rivers rush to their destinations. With the exception of Stockbridge Bowl, we owe the county's present-day lakes to 19th-century industrialists, who either dammed small ponds to make them larger, as with Otis, Pontoosuc, and Onota, or created reservoirs out of rivers, as with Cheshire Reservoir. They wanted a supply of water available to turn the mill wheels in low water times.

The two branches of the Housatonic River rise in the Greylock range and in Washington, the northernmost part of the Southern Berkshire Plateau. They meet in Pittsfield and flow south to enter Long Island Sound at Stratford, Connecticut. The Hoosic River flows north from Cheshire Reservoir (a.k.a. Hoosac Lake) through Adams, joins with its North Branch in North Adams, and passes through Williamstown and Vermont on its way to the Hudson River above Albany. The Westfield River forms in the Hoosac Plateau, joining the Connecticut River in Westfield, while the Farmington River forms in the Southern Berkshire Plateau, mostly in Otis Reservoir, the largest recreational body of fresh water in the Commonwealth.

Although settlement and deforestation of the county once drove off the larger animals, today they are returning. One hundred years ago the county was 75 percent cleared. Now, as the farms grow in, it is 75 percent wooded, providing habitat for deer, black bear, red and gray fox, coyotes, bobcats, beavers, mink, and the occasional moose. Tales of eastern cougar sightings are making the rounds; the last cougar in these parts was thought to have been shot in Vermont 100 years ago. Berkshire hosts rare salamanders who thrive only in these wetlands because of the area's high lime content. Wild turkey flap about in the woods, while an occasional bald eagle wings over from Quabbin Reservoir or the Hudson Valley. Giant blue herons, with wings six feet across, can be seen here on isolated ponds; ruffed grouse and quail occupy the woods.

Although formal gardens at historic homes are beautiful, so are the ephemeral spring flowers at Bartholomew's Cobble and the delicate boreal blooms on Greylock. A gentled, cultivated Berkshire awaits your exploration.

This geology follows Lauren R. Stevens's *Hikes & Walks in the Berkshire Hills*, for which Williams College geologist Paul Karabinos consulted. The pamphlet *A Canoe Guide to the Housatonic* comments on the local ecology. Berkshire Sanctuaries Director René Laubach, in his *Guide to Natural Places in the Berkshire Hills*, invokes the flora, fauna, geology, and ecology. The Berkshire Museum, the county's center for natural history study, displays Bartlett Hendricks's wall-sized raised relief topographic map of the country. For field trips, try any of the "Outdoor Sites" (see Chapter Six, *Recreation*). And in the summer the Appalachian Mountain Club runs excellent nature study programs at sky-high Bascom Lodge atop Mt. Greylock.

SOCIAL HISTORY

History is to the community what memory is to the individual.

— Shaker saying

As recent archeological digs in South County have confirmed, American Indians settled and farmed this area before the time of Europeans. The words *housatonic* and *hoosic* have a similar linguistic root, which may have meant "beyond-place," beyond the Hudson. The Mahican Indians entered the area from the Hudson Valley by way of the Green and Hoosic rivers to hunt and fish, in prehistory. They fished for shad, herring, and salmon in the springtime. The Mahicans built weirs to trap fish in Housatonic tributaries and also fished with hand nets from dugout canoes on the river. They gathered mussels from the rocky river bottoms and smoke-cured them, together with their surplus fish, for winter storage. They hunted duck and geese, and they maintained gardens in the river's floodplain, which was fertilized annually by the spring flood.

After the Dutch established a fur-trading outpost at Fort Orange (now Albany, N.Y.) in 1624, the Mahicans fell into conflict and then went to war with the neighboring Mohawks over the valuable fur trade. By 1628, the Mahicans had been driven to the east of the Hudson, some settling in Berkshire.

In 1676, the first European of record set foot in Berkshire, when Major John Talcott overtook a raiding band of about 150 Indians "neare onto Ousatunick" (Great Barrington) and won the last significant battle of King Philip's War. Smallpox brought by the Europeans dramatically reduced Mahican ranks by the late 17th century.

As the numbers of Indians shrank, a few Dutch settlers came from the Hudson Valley to what is now the town of Mount Washington. Dutch town names such as Van Deusenville (in Great Barrington) still exist in South County, and traces of Dutch architecture linger in the square gable ends of certain old buildings.

In 1724, a small band of Mahicans led by chiefs Konkapot and Umpachenee sold their lands along the Housatonic River, including what is now Sheffield, Great Barrington, Egremont, Mount Washington, Alford, and parts of Lee, Stockbridge, and West Stockbridge. The price: £460, 3 bbls. of cider, and 30 qts. of rum." While the first land-buyers were speculators from the Bay Colony (Massachusetts), the first settlers tended to come from Connecticut, because it was easier to move north along the river valleys than from east to west over the mountains.

English settlers moved to the Sheffield grant, building the first homesteads at some distance from the Housatonic, on the second river terrace. This allowed the fertile floodplain to be used for agriculture and kept homes away from the malarial lowlands and safely distant from floods. In the mid-1730s, the Rev. John Sergeant came from Yale College to proselytize and educate the hundreds of Mahicans who lived around *W-nahk-ta-kook* ("Great Meadow"), later called Indian Town and then Stockbridge. He learned their language and won their respect.

In 1744, Berkshire was opened to cross-country travel for the first time, when the "Great Road" was laid out between Boston and Albany, crossing the county at Great Barrington. Five years later, John Sergeant died, and two years after that, Rev. Jonathan Edwards came to Stockbridge. With his fiery preaching style, Edwards had stirred up the "Great Awakening," a religious revival that swept New England. His zeal, however, had offended parishioners at his previous pulpit in Northampton, resulting in his dismissal. Exiled to Stockbridge, he got along less well with the Indians than Sergeant had. One of America's earliest religious philosophers, Edwards published *Freedom of the Will*, Berkshire's first book, in 1754.

After the British victory over the French at Quebec marked the end of the French and Indian Wars in 1759, western Massachusetts was less vulnerable to Indian attack and considered safer for settlement. The county was created as a political entity on July 1, 1761, when the royal governor, Sir Francis Bernard, struck off a section from the already-existing Hampshire County and declared this one "Berkshire," after his home county in England. The county's boundaries corresponded in an unusual degree to its geology (although the boundary with New York wasn't settled until the 1790s).

In early 1773, a group of townspeople and lawyers met in the Sheffield study of Colonel John Ashley. There, in one of the earliest public assertions of American freedom, they drafted "The Sheffield Declaration," stating to Great Britain and all the world that "Mankind in a State of Nature are equal, free, and independent of each other. . . ."

During the following year, ferment against the British intensified in the county. In July, a county convention met under the chairmanship of Colonel Ashley. From this meeting the "Stockbridge Non-Intercourse Articles" of 1774 were drafted, complaining that "whereas the Parliament of Great Britain have of late undertaken to give and grant away our money without our knowledge or consent, . . . we will not import, purchase, or consume" any British goods.

British oppression mounted. On August 16, 1,500 Berkshire citizens staged a peaceful sit-down strike around the Great Barrington Courthouse, preventing the royal judges from meeting. It was the first open resistance to British rule in America.

In April 1775, a regiment of Berkshire Minutemen under Colonel John Paterson of Lenox started out for Cambridge to aid in the Revolutionary effort. And in May, former Sheffield resident Ethan Allen led his Green Mountain Boys, with 57 Berkshire men, in a successful surprise attack on Fort Ticonderoga on Lake Champlain. That winter (1776), General Henry Knox with Continental troops and over 100 oxen dragged captured Ticonderoga cannon through Berkshire to General George Washington in Cambridge. With the help of this additional weaponry, Washington was able to drive the British from Boston.

After the Revolution Daniel Shays led a revolt of Western Massachusetts veterans disappointed in their lot. In 1786 they closed court houses and released debtors from jail. An attempt to take the Springfield arsenal the following January failed. Most of the Regulators were killed or captured. Mum Bett, then employed by the Sedgwicks, hid the family silver during the fighting.

With peace and prosperity, the 1790s saw the beginnings of a number of long-term county institutions. The Shakers established colonies in Hancock and Tyringham, and marble quarrying started in West Stockbridge. Williams College's faltering beginnings in 1793 led, eventually, to its position as one of the finest liberal arts colleges in the U.S.

The Native American community in Berkshire had meanwhile collapsed socially and economically. As Konkapot's tribe dwindled to fewer than 400 members, in 1771 at age 94 he had stepped down as chief of the rechristened "Stockbridge Indians" — Mahicans plus the remnants of several other tribes. Beginning in 1784 the Stockbridge were forced into westward migration, leaving only their Housatonic legends — and a Bible — behind them. Their descendants returned to the Mission House for the Bible 200 years later.

Two Presidents Say Cheese

The farmers of Cheshire pooled the entire town's milk production for one day in 1801. Together they produced the Great Cheshire Cheese, a 1,235-pound, barrel-shaped cheddar that was hauled by oxen to Albany and then by boat to Washington, for presentation to President Jefferson. Wrote the citizens:

We believe the Supreme Ruler of the Universe, who raises up men to achieve great events, has raised up a Jefferson at this critical day to defend Republicanism and baffle the arts of aristocracy. . . . The cheese was procured by the personal labor of freeborn farmers with the voluntary and cheerful aid of their wives and daughters, without the assistance of a single slave. It is not the last stone of the Bastille, nor is it an article of great pecuniary worth, but as a free-will offering we hope it will be favorably received.

It was. Jefferson delighted in his gargantuan Cheshire Cheese, personally eating the delicacy often and sharing it with his cabinet members and visiting dignitaries. Every White House servant received a wedge. Then Jefferson cut a generous slab of the cheese and returned it to Berkshire, that the residents of Cheshire might enjoy the product of their own labor.

Along with the slice, President Jefferson sent $200 to the town in payment for the Great Cheese, at the going rate of 16 cents a pound. Accompanying this unsolicited payment, the president sent the following note:

I receive with particular pleasure the testimony of good will with which your citizens have been pleased to charge you. It presents an extraordinary proof of the skill with those domestic arts which contribute so much to our daily comfort. . . . To myself, this mark of esteem from freeborn farmers, employed personally in the useful labors of life, is particularly grateful. . . .

In 1993, residents of the town of Cheshire pooled some of their milk to create another wheel of Cheshire cheese, this time for President Bill Clinton. The president sent a thank-you note to this tiny Berkshire town for their wheel of Cheshire cheese, this time 21 pounds.

"Please extend my thanks to everyone involved with this gift, especially the Cornstalkers 4-H Club," wrote President Clinton. "Your thoughtfulness and generosity are deeply appreciated."

Elkanah Watson introduced Spanish Merino sheep — and, incidentally, the agricultural fair — into Berkshire in 1807, tethering two of the animals on the Pittsfield common. Their wool, spun into fine worsted yarn and woven into Berkshire broadcloth in the county's state-of-the-art mills, was fashioned into President Madison's inauguration suit in 1807. Shortly thereafter, the first stage route in the county was established, running from Greenfield to North Adams, Williamstown, and Albany.

"Americans! Encourage your own manufactories
and they will improve. Ladies, save your RAGS."
The 1801 ad that started the Crane Paper empire.

Americans !

*Encourage your own Manufactories,
and they will Improve.*

LADIES, save your RAGS.

A S the Subscribers have it
in contemplation to erect a PA-
PER-MILL in *Dalton*, the ensuing
spring ; and the business being very ben-
eficial to the community at large, they
flatter themselves that they shall meet with
due encouragement. And that every woman, who has the good of her country,
and the interest of her own family at
heart, will patronize them, by saving her
rags, and sending them to their Manu-
factory, or to the nearest Storekeeper—
for which the Subscribers will give a generous price.

HENRY WISWALL,
ZENAS CRANE,
JOHN WILLARD.

Worcester, Feb. 8, 1801.

The mill on the farm became the mill in the town. Driven by plentiful water power, industry took a firm hold in Berkshire when Zenas Crane began paper production in Dalton and David Estes opened the first textile mill in North Adams.

Writers and painters arrived soon after. William Cullen Bryant spent a year at Williams College and then practiced law in Great Barrington, attempting simultaneously to divine the art of poetry. His friend Catherine Sedgwick published her first novel, *A New England Tale,* in 1820 to critical acclaim. Hudson River School artist Thomas Cole painted Mount Greylock over Pontoosuc Lake, while others depicted the lower Housatonic and Bash Bish Falls. Alexis de Tocqueville visited the Sedgwicks by stagecoach in Stockbridge in 1831. Not long after, trains huffed into the hills, one of them carrying Mr. and Mrs. Henry Wadsworth Longfellow to honeymoon in Pittsfield. Dr. Oliver Wendell Holmes, "the autocrat of the breakfast table," built a home on family property at Canoe Meadows in order to spend his summers in Berkshire. Nathaniel Hawthorne moved from Salem to Lenox and took up residence at a property he called Tanglewood. Then in 1850 Herman Melville bought Arrowhead Farm in Pittsfield. David Dudley Field introduced Melville to Hawthorne on the occasion of a climb up Monument Mountain; the two great writers' imaginations were entwined thereafter.

In 1851 construction began on the Hoosac Tunnel between the Berkshire towns of Florida and North Adams, a project that was to take 24 years and cost 195 lives. At 4.75 miles it was the longest railroad tunnel in America and the one in which nitroglycerine was used for the first time.

Before those explosions were silenced, shells were fired in hate in the Civil War. Five days after the Confederate forces opened fire on Fort Sumter, Berkshire militiamen were on their way south to defend the Republic. Those

Hawthorne and Thoreau

Nathaniel Hawthorne was one of 19th-century Berkshire's greatest admirers. During his year-and-a-half residence in the "Red Cottage" at "Tanglewood," overlooking Stockbridge Bowl, he kept a journal that recorded the fullness of his affection for the landscape.

October 16, 1850

A morning mist filling up the whole length and breadth of the valley, betwixt here and Monument Mountain; the summit of the mountain emerging. The mist reaches to perhaps a hundred yards of our house, so dense as to conceal everything, except that, near its hither boundary, a few ruddy or yellow tree-tops emerge, glorified by the early sunshine; as is likewise the whole mist cloud.

Henry David Thoreau shared Hawthorne's reverence for these hills, praising Williams College's position at the foot of Greylock — or anyone's willingness to learn from nature.

It would be no small advantage if every college were thus located at the base of a mountain, as good at least as one well-endowed professorship. ... Some will remember, no doubt, not only that they went to college, but that they went to the mountain.

first county recruits stayed three months and saw little action, but other Berkshire regiments took their place, fighting through 1865 as far south as the state of Florida.

After two unsuccessful attempts, in 1866 Cyrus Field of Stockbridge and his engineers laid a cable across the Atlantic Ocean, connecting America with Europe. A year later in America's leading paper town, Lee, paper fabrication from wood pulp rather than rags was demonstrated for the first time in the United States.

Industry was booming in the Berkshires, with textile and paper plants lining the rivers. Fueled by the county's abundant forests, iron smelters, railroads, and other heavy industries cut deep into the Berkshire woodland. Before long nearly 75 percent of the county's timber was gone, and the hills were nearly bald.

In 1875 the Hoosac Tunnel was finally completed, opening North County to interstate commerce. Shortly thereafter, in 1879, Crane & Co. of Dalton obtained an exclusive contract with the federal government involving a lot of money — producing U.S. currency.

In 1886, William Stanley installed the world's first commercial electric system, lighting 25 shops along Main Street in Great Barrington. The General Electric Company visited Stanley in his Pittsfield workshop and, soon after, moved nearby. Five years later, an electric trolley system was introduced in Pittsfield, running from Park Square to Pontoosuc Lake. Soon this quiet, reliable transport would connect most of the towns in the county, and the county with the region.

The 1880s ushered in Berkshire's Gilded Age during which millionaires came to the hills to play and to build their dream "cottages." Mrs. Searles had

Home of Crane Paper Company founder Zenas Crane. This paper company still makes the U.S. currency as well as all of its other personal and business paper products at its Dalton facility. This building now houses administrative offices. The Crane Paper Museum is nearby.

Judith Monachina

just completed her $2.5 million castle in Great Barrington; Anson Phelps Stokes had spent nearly as much in completing the largest home in America just then, his 100-room Shadowbrook in Stockbridge. A mile away, the 33-room Italianate palazzo called Wheatleigh was being finished, a gift of H. H. Cook to his daughter on the occasion of her marriage to Count Carlos de Heredia. The 50-room Elm Court was nearby in Lenox, built by rug magnate W. D. Sloane; and across town, Giraud Foster had erected his multimillion-dollar likeness of the French Petit Trianon at his estate, Bellefontaine. In Stockbridge was Naumkeag, Ambassador Choate's homey mansion, along with sculptor Daniel Chester French's splendid Chesterwood. Soon Robert Paterson constructed Blantyre and Edith Wharton built The Mount, both in Lenox. In all, some 75 extraordinary mansions graced the Berkshire landscape. European and urban tastes had arrived in the hills.

The Mount, home of Edith Wharton, now owned by the Edith Wharton Restoration and the home of Shakespeare & Company.

Steven Ziglar, courtesy Edith Wharton Restoration

Yet William C. Whitney, secretary of the Navy under Grover Cleveland, acquired more land than all of these. In 1896 Whitney established an 11,000-acre game preserve in the Berkshire town of Washington and stocked it with buffalo, moose, Virginia deer, and elk. The estate later became October Mountain State Forest, a giant reserve in the center of the county. Two years later North Adams industrialists donated 400 acres at the top of Mount Greylock to the Commonwealth, creating the first state reservation.

In North Adams a "Normal School" or teachers' college was established in 1894. Over the following century it became North Adams State College, with a focus on liberal arts.

President James Garfield was assassinated on his way to his 25th Williams College reunion, so his vice president, Chester A. Arthur, took over. Both men had taught in the same one-room school in Pownal, Vermont, in the 1850s. In the fall of 1902, President Theodore Roosevelt visited Berkshire, sustaining minor injury after his coach overturned near the Pittsfield Country Club. That next summer, both ex-president Grover Cleveland and humorist Mark Twain summered in Tyringham. Eight years later, as Pittsfield observed its gala 150th anniversary on July 4, 1911, President Taft spoke before a crowd of 50,000 at the railroad station. Later that same year, Edith Wharton's novella *Ethan Frome* was published, a critical and popular success that derived many of its dramatic and scenic details from life in the Berkshires.

Railroad Street, Great Barrington, around the turn of the century.

Courtesy of the Snap Shop

The 20th century in Berkshire has been marked by events principally in industry and the arts. Since 1903 General Electric has played a significant role in the county's industry. In 1914, GE established a high-voltage laboratory in Pittsfield, and seven years later, the lab made electrical history by producing a million-volt flash of artificial lightning. While GE developed a large transformer business and produced naval armaments, Sprague Electric met the country's enormous need for capacitors during World War II and expanded to occupy former mills in North Adams. Both manufacturers were to decline significantly in the second half of the century.

In the arts, the Stockbridge Playhouse (now the Berkshire Theatre Festival) opened in 1928 with Eva LeGallienne in *Cradle Song*. Ted Shawn established a School of Dance at Jacob's Pillow in Becket in 1932. The 1930s heard the first Berkshire Symphony Festival concerts, a prelude to Tanglewood.

Downhill skiing debuted in Berkshire in 1935 as Bousquet opened runs in Pittsfield and arranged "ski trains" from New York City. Then the Thunderbolt Trail on Greylock, carved by the Civilian Conservation Corps, became the scene of Eastern downhill ski championships, before and after World War II. Soon half a dozen mountains in the county were crisscrossed by trails.

The 1950s saw the arrival of artist Norman Rockwell in Stockbridge and the creation of the Sterling and Francine Clark Art Institute in Williamstown, with its collection and library of international import. The Williamstown Theatre Festival began performances, enlivening all of Berkshire with star-studded drama. In the 1960s, two more colleges joined Williams and North Adams State: Berkshire Community College in Pittsfield, the first in a series of state junior colleges; and Simon's Rock Early College in Great Barrington, a progressive school that is now part of Bard College. Arlo Guthrie, scion of a folk legend and former student at Stockbridge School, wrote a song about littering, the draft, and a community of friends living in Stockbridge.

The last Shaker sisters left their "village" in Hancock in 1960. A group of visionary citizens led by Amy Bess Miller managed to purchase their property and turn it into a living museum, today one of the county's premier attractions.

In the mid-'60s, General Electric made another breakthrough, this time in plastics, and the company subsequently developed a new family of polymers that diversified the corporation. In the 1990s Lockheed Martin purchased the defense systems, and soon after they were purchased by General Dynamics Defense Systems, which is now developing liquid propellant technology for military and civilian use.

The great estates of the past have been recycled since mid-century (and increasingly in recent years), turning Berkshire's fiefdoms into public domain. The arts have blossomed gloriously at The Mount, now owned by Edith Wharton Restoration, Inc., with Shakespeare & Co. presenting plays by the Bard and others on stages indoors and out. Bellefontaine has become a sophisticated spa, Canyon Ranch. In the Glendale section of Stockbridge, the gracious Linwood estate was transformed into the new home of the Norman Rockwell Museum. Looking back toward Tanglewood from this splendid site, the visitor obtains a fresh view of unspoiled 19th-century Berkshire.

Tanglewood has expanded, creating the $10 million Seiji Osawa Hall, where 1,200 music lovers can enjoy both intimacy and acoustic fidelity. A different type of music will be celebrated near the center of Lenox, where the National Music Foundation has selected Springlawn for its new National Music Center. Spearheaded by rock and roll's godfather, Dick Clark, the facility will include a residence for musicians and radio people, a performing arts center, museum, library, and educational facility.

Now some of North County's abandoned mills are experiencing new life, giving innovative artists large spaces in which to work. The Massachusetts Museum of Contemporary Art in North Adams attracts film-makers and artists in music, theater, dance, and the visual arts to mills abandoned by Sprague.

Mass MoCA ground-breaking. Plans are underway at the old Sprague Electric Company in North Adams to make this plant the home of one of the largest contemporary art museums in the country.

Mark Rondeau

Berkshire citizens discuss the changes in their county: condos, shopping malls, bypasses, and the Greylock Glen sustainable development project. The Wal-Marting of Berkshire has begun, first up in North Adams and then in Pittsfield. Some say Wal-Marts create jobs and bring low prices; others point out that the successful Berkshire Mall has drained life from downtown Pittsfield.

Environmental issues are being addressed head-on. A variety of ecologically aware groups are mobilizing to clean up Berkshire's principal river, the Housatonic. In the fall of 1996, the Hoosic River appeared to be on its way to be cleansed of PCBs for good.

The Berkshire Natural Resources Council and other environmental protection groups guard and preserve the splendor of the landscape. With the gradual shrinking of industry here, and with tourism becoming among the most stable of Berkshire businesses, protecting the rolling hills makes economic and aesthetic sense. Once the hills were decimated, shaved bald by paper and lumber mills and charcoal manufacturers. Now the hills are once more alive, fully forested and soothing to the eye.

CHAPTER TWO
Getting Here, Getting Around
TRANSPORTATION

The astonishing Pittsfield train station, around 1905.

Although bus lines bring some visitors to and from Berkshire County, and the B Bus (Berkshire Regional Transit Authority) carries some through the county, most people rely on automobiles. Travel was more colorful, if less comfortable, in the past.

First we walked or rode horseback on county roads that were choked with dust, buried in snow, or clogged with bottomless mud, depending on the season. The Hudson and Connecticut rivers carried passengers toward Berkshire aboard sailing ships and, after 1825, steamboats. Both Albany and Hartford were connected to New York City by regular steamboat runs. The upper Connecticut River was outfitted with an elaborate system of locks to bypass the rapids.

With the harnessing of steam for riverboat power, it wasn't long before the iron horse galloped into the Berkshire Hills. The Housatonic Railroad brought visitors from New York City and southern New England. Two lines competed to the west: the Albany-West Stockbridge Line and the Hudson and Berkshire Line.

From Boston, construction of the Western Railway up from Springfield was reportedly "delayed by competition between Stockbridge and Pittsfield for fixing of the route through their town. After surveys, Pittsfield won." During the summers of 1840–41, workers made deep cuts in the hills and built many bridges. When the lines were completed, Berkshire was nine hours by train from Boston and about three hours from Albany. Many who had come to work on the railroads never took the train back. Hundreds of Irish rail laborers from cities east and west stayed on.

Sons of these rail workers may have labored on a remarkable system of electric trolley track and overhead wires running from Williamstown east to North Adams and south through Adams, Pittsfield, Lenox, Lee, Great Barrington, and Sheffield. Quiet and reliable, this Berkshire Street Railway grew so popular that opulent parlor cars were constructed and put into service, running till 1932. When automobiles and buses were refined, the possibilities for public transport changed: paved roads were improved, and unpaved ones were surfaced. Passenger rail and trolley service to and within the Berkshires withered.

PRESENT POSSIBILITIES

If a car is available, the roads to Berkshire are smooth and scenic, and automobiles are useful to explore the back roads and byways. Buses run regularly from New York, Hartford, Boston, and Albany. If you're in a hurry to get to these hills, you can fly in, but, alas, only by private or charter plane to Great Barrington, Pittsfield, or North Adams. Major airlines with regular service fly into Bradley International near Hartford and the Albany County Airport; from there, car rentals or limousine and bus service are available. The future of Amtrak's once-a-day service to Pittsfield is questionable. For your convenience, a host of details about Berkshire transportation follows; none of it as up-to-date as your telephone call, however.

GETTING TO THESE HILLS

BY CAR

From Manhattan: Take the Major Deegan Expressway or the Henry Hudson Parkway to the Saw Mill River Parkway, then proceed north on one of the most beautiful roadways in the world, the Taconic State Parkway. For southern Berkshire, exit the Taconic at "Hillsdale, Claverack, Rte. 23" and follow 23 east, toward Hillsdale and on to Great Barrington. For Stockbridge, Lee, and Lenox, proceed up Rte. 7. For Pittsfield and northern Berkshire, exit the Taconic at Rte. 295, following Rte. 22 to Rte. 20 for Pittsfield or to Rte. 43 through Hancock to Williamstown and North Adams.

BERKSHIRE ACCESS

Using Tanglewood (on the Stockbridge-Lenox line) as the Berkshire reference point, the following cities are this close. (Newly increased speeds on the interstates bring Berkshire somewhat closer to the rest of the world than this table indicates.)

CITY	TIME	MILES
Albany	1 hr	50
Boston	2.5 hrs	135
Bridgeport	2 hrs	110
Danbury	1.75 hrs	85
Hartford	1.5 hrs	70
New Haven	2.5 hrs	115
Montreal	5 hrs	275
New York City	3 hrs	150
Philadelphia	4.5 hrs	230
Providence	2.5 hrs	125
Springfield	.75 hr	35
Waterbury	1.5 hrs	75
Washington, DC	7 hrs	350
Worcester	1.75 hrs	90

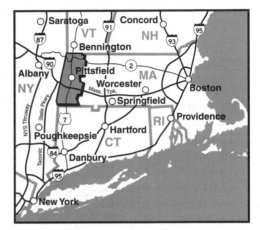

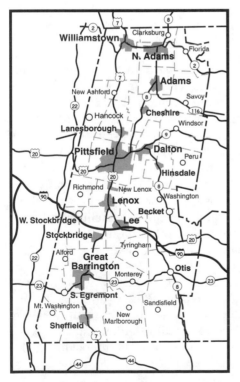

Berkshire County is 56 miles in length from Sheffield to Williamstown, and, depending on the season and the weather, normally takes 1.5 hours to drive along Rte. 7. Because of the mountain ranges that also run north to south, east-west travel across the county remains more difficult. All of the county's east-west routes (2 in the north; 9, midcounty; and 23 in the south) are tricky drives in freezing or snowy weather. Back roads in particular vary tremendously in condition and type, ranging from smooth macadam to rough dirt. On these back roads especially, drivers should keep an eye out for bicyclists, horseback riders, hikers, joggers, roller-bladers — and deer, bear, moose, and bobcat.

From New Jersey, Pennsylvania and south: If local color is high on your list or you'd rather ramble northward, Rte. 22 north is a good choice, and you can pick it up as far south as Armonk or Bedford in Westchester County, New York. Rte. 22 is a road still proud of its diners: of particular note is the Red Rooster in Brewster, just north of I-684's end. Further upstate on Rte. 22, turn right at Hillsdale on Rte. 23 east toward Great Barrington, Rte. 20 to Pittsfield, and Rte. 43 to Williamstown. For the most direct route from New Jersey, Pennsylvania, and south, take the New York Thruway to I-84 east; at the Taconic Parkway, turn north, following instructions "From Manhattan."

From Connecticut and/or the New York metro area: Rte. 7 north was an early stagecoach thoroughfare to Berkshire, and you join the same trail at Danbury, via I-684 and I-84. Driving up Rte. 7, you'll wend your way along the beautiful Housatonic River, north through New Milford, Kent, and Canaan and into Massachusetts through Ashley Falls (an especially good ride for picnics and antiques). To arrive in southeastern Berkshire, Rte. 8 is a quick and scenic drive as it follows the Farmington River north.

From Boston and east: The scenic Massachusetts Turnpike is the quickest and easiest route west to south Berkshire and Pittsfield. From Boston, there's no better bet, especially as tolls at the western end have been dropped. For the best route to Otis Ridge, Butternut Basin, and Catamount ski areas, you can leave the turnpike at Exit 3 west of the Connecticut River, take Rte. 202 south to Rte. 20 west, and pick up Rte. 23 west at Woronoco. Most people stay on the turnpike right into the Berkshires, exiting either at Lee or West Stockbridge.

A less rapid but more colorful route westward from Boston is Rte. 20, which cuts across southern Massachusetts, connecting with Lee. If you're coming west to the Berkshires from more northern latitudes, Rte. 9 from Northampton is a splendid drive, a high road with long lovely vistas and few towns. Still farther to the north, eastern entry to Berkshire County can be gained by driving the spectacular Mohawk Trail, originally an Indian byway. Also known as Rte. 2, this is the most direct way to North Adams, Williamstown, and the ski slopes at Jiminy Peak and Brodie Mountain.

From Hartford: The quickest route is I-91 north to the Massachusetts Turnpike west. Then proceed as in the directions for Massachusetts Turnpike travel from Boston. A slower but more pleasant drive is Rte. 44 west, up through Avon, Norfolk, and Canaan, where you take Rte. 7 north into Berkshire County.

From Montreal and Albany: Leaving Canada, take I-87 (known as "the Northway") south to Albany. Exit at either Rte. 7 to Rte. 2 toward Williamstown or Rte. 20 to Pittsfield; or continue on I-87 south to I-90 east, which becomes the Massachusetts Turnpike. Exit at either Canaan, N.Y., or Lee. (There is no eastbound exit from the Mass Pike at West Stockbridge.)

BY BUS

McClelland's Pharmacy in Lee is the Grand Central Station of south Berkshire. All interstate buses, east/west- or north/southbound, stop here, where tickets are sold and an old-fashioned soda fountain shortens the wait. The building across the way is Memorial Hall, built to honor local men who fought in the Civil War.

Judith Monachina

From Manhattan (3.5 hours): Bonanza (800-556-3815) serves the Berkshires out of New York City's *Port Authority Bus Terminal* (212-564-8484) at 40th St. between 8th and 9th Aves. Tickets may be purchased at the Greyhound ticket windows (800-231-2222), near 8th Ave. Several buses a day. Boarding is down the escalators at the center of the terminal, and then to the right, usually at Gate 13. Berkshire locales marked with an asterisk (*) are Flag Stops, where you must wave to the bus driver in order to be picked up.

Berkshire Phone Numbers for New York Buses

Canaan, CT	Canaan Pharmacy, Main St.	860-824-5481
Gt. Barrington	Bill's Pharmacy, 362 Main St.	413-528-1590
Hillsdale, NY	*Junction Rtes. 22 & 23	800-556-3815
Lee	McClelland Drugs, 43 Main St.	413-243-0135
Lenox	Lenox News & Variety, 39 Housatonic St.	413-637-2815
New Ashford	*Entrance to Brodie Mt. Ski Area, Rte. 7	800-556-3815
Pittsfield	Bus Terminal, 57 S. Church St.	413-442-4451
Sheffield	*Bank of Boston, Rte. 7	800-556-3815
S. Egremont	*Gaslight Store	800-556-3815
Stockbridge	Information Booth, Main St.	800-556-3815
Williamstown	The Williams Inn, 1090 Main St.	413-458-2665

From Boston (3.5 hours): *Bonanza* and *Greyhound* serve the Berkshires from Boston out of the *Greyhound Terminal* at 10 St. James Ave. (800-231-2222). *Peter Pan/Trailways* runs daily to Pittsfield and North Adams-Williamstown out of the Trailways Terminal at South Station. Berkshire-bound passengers change buses at Springfield. Call 800-343-9999 for prices and schedules.

Berkshire Phone Numbers for Boston Buses

Lee	McClelland Drugs, 43 Main St.	413-243-0135
Lenox	Lenox News & Variety, 39 Housatonic St.	413-637-2815
Pittsfield	Bus Terminal, 57 S. Church St.	413-442-4451
Williamstown	The Williams Inn, 1090 Main St.	413-458-2665

From Hartford (1.75 hours): The *Greyhound Line* runs two buses to Pittsfield daily, at 11:15 a.m. and 4:20 p.m., from the *Greyhound Terminal* at 409 Church St., Hartford (860-522-9267).

From Montreal (6 hours): *Greyhound* runs south to the Albany Greyhound Terminal. Connect to Pittsfield as noted below.

From Albany (1 hour): *Bonanza* runs two buses daily from Albany to Pittsfield. *Greyhound* runs one bus daily.

BY TRAIN

From Manhattan: You can ride at the commuter rate, a fraction of the regular, if you get off at Dover Plains, NY. *Amtrak* (800-USA-RAIL or 800-872-7245) can also help you get to the Berkshires. Their turboliner from Grand Central Station runs frequently and smoothly along the Hudson River, a splendid ride. For southern Berkshire, stay aboard till Hudson, NY, a river town recently restored; for northern Berkshire, carry on to Rensselaer, NY. For travel connections from Dover Plains, Hudson, or Rensselaer to the Berkshires, see "By Taxi or Limousine."

From Boston: Amtrak may continue to run a single train daily through the Berkshires, starting from Boston's South Station. To find the Pittsfield shelter: take West St. west past the Hilton; at the first light, turn right onto Center St.; take the next right onto Depot St.; the shelter is on the left. Anyone boarding the train in Pittsfield must purchase tickets on the train. The round-trip ticket prices vary, depending on time of travel and seat availability. Private compartments are available.

From Montreal: Amtrak runs one train daily from Montreal through Albany. There is no same-day train connection from this run to the Berkshires; see "By Limousine or Taxi"; or see "By Bus."

From Albany: Amtrak may continue a single daily Pittsfield-bound train from the Albany/Rensselaer Depot on East St. (2 miles from downtown Albany), stopping at Pittsfield's Depot St. shelter (see directions above under "From Boston").

BY PLANE

If you own a small airplane or decide to charter one, you can fly directly to the Berkshires, landing at Gt. Barrington, Pittsfield, or N. Adams airports.

From New York City: Feeling rich, traveling high with some friends, or riding on the corporate account? There are several charter air companies in the metropolitan New York area that will fly you from La Guardia, JFK, or other airports near New York to any of the Berkshire airports. Charters currently flying these routes include:

Aircraft Charter Group	800-553-3590
Chester Charter, Chester, CT	800-752-6371
Long Island Airways	800-645-9572

and from Westchester County:

Panorama (White Plains airport)	914-328-9800
if calling from New York City:	718-507-9800
Richmor Aviation	800-331-6101 or
	518-828-9461

From Boston: There are several charter flight companies that fly from Beantown to Berkshire. Some of those you can try are:

Bird Airfleet	508-372-6566
Wiggins Airways	617-762-5690 Ext. #251

From Hartford: Bradley Airport in Hartford handles numerous domestic and international airlines, so you can fly to Bradley from nearly anywhere. From there, charter air service to the Berkshires is available through the companies listed under "From Boston" or through the Berkshire County companies listed below.

From Albany: Albany is terminus for a substantial volume of domestic jet traffic and, being less than an hour from the Berkshires by car, is the closest you can get to these hills by jet. Charter connector flights from Albany to the Berkshires are available through Signature Flight Support (518-869-0253) or through the Berkshire County companies listed below.

In Berkshire County: There are two aviation companies in Berkshire County which operate air taxi service to just about any other northeastern airport.

Berkshire Aviation	Gt. Barrington Airport	413-528-1010 or
		528-1061
Esposito Flying Service	Harriman & West Airport,	
	N. Adams	413-663-3330

BY LIMOUSINE OR TAXI

If you're with a group or want to pamper yourself, a limousine direct to Berkshire is the smoothest approach. There are many limousine services that will whisk you away from urban gridlock to the spaciousness of this hill country.

From New York and its Airports:

Kabot	718-545-2400
Esquire	212-935-9700

From Boston and Logan Airport:

Cooper	617-482-1000 or 800-343-2123
Fifth Avenue	617-286-0555

From Hartford and Bradley Airport:

Carey Elite Limousine	860-666-9051 or 800-RE:LIMOS (735-4667)
Ambassador	860-633-7300 or 800-395-LIMO (395-5466)

From Albany, Albany Airport and Rensselaer:

AAA Limousine Service	518-456-5030
Diamond Limousine	518-283-8000

To northern Berkshire (by reservation only):

Norm's Limousine Service	413-663-8300 or 413-663-6284

From Hudson, NY and its Amtrak Station:

Star City Taxi	518-828-3355

GETTING AROUND THE BERKSHIRES

Note: Individual town maps of Great Barrington, Stockbridge, Lenox, Pittsfield, North Adams, and Williamstown can be found at the back of this book.

Sign Near Otis.

> You are entering God's country.
> Don't drive through like hell.

Rte. 7 is Berkshire County's main roadway, connecting cities and towns from south to north. Driving in winter, you'll certainly need snow tires. In summer, the cruising is easy; but on certain weekends during Tanglewood season and fall foliage, temporary traffic delays in popular villages are likely. Whenever possible, park and walk. Friendly but firm traffic police will suggest outlying parking areas. And motorists beware: state law requires a full stop for pedestrians in crosswalks.

BY BUS

Berkshire County is no longer served by the electrified Berkshire Street Railway, but the *"B,"* a public bus system, has in some ways filled the gap. The buses run from early in the morning to early in the evening. Information can be obtained from the *Berkshire Regional Transit Authority* (413-499-2782 or, from Massachusetts phones, 800-292-2782). Fares vary by distance. If you're visiting without a car, the *"B"* will provide plenty of access to other communities, but Sunday service is not available.

BY RENTED CAR

Car rental agencies abound in Berkshire. Most will not deliver cars — you must first go to their place of business to do the paperwork. Two exception are *Enterprise* and *Ugly Duckling.* Their drivers will pick you up from the train, bus, or wherever, and then drive you back to the office to complete the paperwork. Berkshire car rentals are available through the following agencies:

Canaan, CT	Ugly Duckling	
	(new and used)	800-824-5204 or 800-843-3825
Cheshire	Bedard Brothers Auto	413-743-0014
Gt. Barrington	Caffrey Ford	413-528-0848 or 800-698-0848
	Condor Chevrolet	413-528-2700 or 528-2260
	Larkin's Car Store	
	(used only)	413-528-2156
Lee	R.W.'s, Inc.	413-243-0946
Pittsfield	Enterprise Rent-a-Car	413-433-6600 or 800-325-8007
	Hertz Rent-a-Car	413-499-4153 or 800-654-3131
	Johnson Rent-A-Car	413-443-6437 or 800-825-FORD
	Pete's Rentals	413-443-1406 or 800-696-7383
	Rent-A-Wreck	413-447-8117
N. Adams	Mohawk Car Rentals	413-663-3729
Williamstown	B & L Service Station	413-458-8269

BY TAXI OR LIMOUSINE

Numerous taxi and limo companies serve Berkshire County. The following is a listing by town, with notations indicating if they have only taxis (T), only limos (L), or both (B).

Gt. Barrington	Taxico	413-528-0911 or 528-0567 (T)
Lee	Abbott's Limousine	
	& Livery	413-243-1645 (L)
	Park Taxi	413-243-0020 (T)
Lenox	Alston's	413-637-3676 (L)
	Tobi's Limousine Service	413-637-1224 (L)

N. Adams	Berkshire Livery Service	413-662-2609 or
		800-298-2609 (L)
	Norm's Limousine Service	413-663-8300 or
		663-6284 (B)
Pittsfield	Aarow Taxi	413-499-8604 (T)
	Airport & Limousine	413-443-7111 (L)
	Rainbow Taxi	413-499-4300 (T)
Stockbridge	Stockbridge Livery	413-298-4848 (T)

BY BICYCLE

Bicycling in the Berkshires gives an exciting intimacy with the rolling land-scape. Depending on your willingness to bundle up, biking from town to town is possible nearly year around. Bike rental prices vary widely, with bikes available through:

Canaan, CT	The Bike Doctor	860-824-5577
Lenox	Main Street Sports	413-637-4407 or
	& Leisure	800-952-9197
Pittsfield	Plaine's Bike, Golf, Ski	413-499-0391
Williamstown	Spoke Bicycle & Repair	413-458-3456

ON FOOT

The Appalachian Trail enters southern Berkshire in the town of Mount Washington and runs over hill and dale, past Great Barrington, through Monterey, and down into Tyringham Valley, then up through the town of Washington, through Dalton and Cheshire, over Mt. Greylock, and toward Vermont. If you've got the time, we've got the trail. See "Hiking" in Chapter Six, *Recreation*.

Many Berkshire towns are small enough for walking exploration, and three in particular are well suited to visiting without a vehicle: Stockbridge, Lenox and Williamstown. All are lovely villages, with good accommodations, fine dining, interesting shopping, and first-rate cultural attractions within easy walking distance.

NEIGHBORS ALL AROUND

Although we tend to think of the Berkshires as a place apart, the county and its people have close ties to their neighboring communities, counties, and states. Travelers as well will want to connect with these neighbors, for Berkshire is surrounded by areas of extensive natural beauty. Many nearby towns are loaded with good restaurants, old inns, and cultural attractions.

TO THE SOUTH

The Litchfield Hills of northwest Connecticut are gentler than the Berkshire Hills, but they still make for good hiking. There is lovely architecture in this area, with many stately homes in Salisbury, Lakeville, Sharon, Litchfield, and Norfolk. And there are music festivals as well, such as the ones at Norfolk and at Music Mountain in Falls Village. See "Music" in Chapter Four, *Culture.*

TO THE EAST

Halfway across the Berkshire highlands between the Housatonic River valley and the Connecticut River lies the jagged eastern county border, shared with Franklin, Hamden, and Hampshire counties. Besides its natural splendor, this eastern area boasts an attractive array of cultural possibilities. The "Five College Area" of Amherst, South Hadley, and Northampton offers all the aesthetic and academic action anyone could want, with Amherst, Hampshire, Mt. Holyoke, and Smith colleges and the University of Massachusetts.

TO THE NORTH

The Green Mountains of Vermont offer great skiing, hiking, and camping. The town of Bennington makes an interesting stopover with The Bennington Museum (featuring Grandma Moses paintings), a fine college (Bennington), and Robert Frost's grave behind the historic Old Bennington Church. There is also the extraordinary Bennington Pottery, where you can both buy and dine on the handsome stoneware. Rte. 7 continues north as the spine of the Green Mountains. A ride to architecturally stunning Manchester is worth the time, even if you decide to dawdle along old Route 7 (7-A).

TO THE WEST

The farms and small towns of Columbia County, in New York State, hold treasures for antiques and "untiques" hunters. Berkshire is not far from the Hudson Valley, an area rich with history and with vineyards worth visiting. Then there's Albany, which offers big-city cultural entertainment such as the touring New York Metropolitan Opera, performing at the capital city's structurally unique theater, The Egg. A bit farther north is Saratoga with its spas, its springs, its own summer arts festival (known as SPAC), and its elegant and justly famous racecourse.

CHAPTER THREE
The Keys to Your Room
LODGING

Courtesy the Red Lion Inn

The gracious porch of the Red Lion Inn

As stagecoach travel through the Berkshires developed in the 18th century, the need for roadside lodgings grew; and of those original inns still welcoming wayfarers today, the *New Boston Inn* in Sandisfield was probably the first. Built in 1737, this recently restored inn is about as authentic an early American lodging experience as you can find in New England. Close in age and attention to period detail is the *Old Inn on the Green* (1760) in New Marlboro. This inn served as tavern, store and, later, post office; today it has a small number of authentically Colonial rooms and a superlative restaurant. Next came the *Red Lion Inn* (1773) in Stockbridge, which hosted pre-Revolutionary political activists eager to communicate their grievances to Britain. More than 200 years later, the Red Lion is still the best-known stopover on the Berkshire trail.

Many other 18th-century Berkshire inns still offer warmth, hospitality, and a good night's sleep, often in a four-poster bed. These include *River Bend Farm*, built as a tavern in 1770; the *Village Inn* (1771) in Lenox, originally a farmhouse; the *Egremont Inn* (1780) and the *Weathervane Inn* (1785) in South Egremont, the *Elm Court Inn* (1790) in North Egremont, and the *Williamsville Inn* in West Stockbridge, originally a farmhouse dating from 1797.

Is the 19th century's sumptuous Gilded Age more your cup of tea? Berkshire can offer you, among other possibilities, an Italian palazzo called *Wheatleigh* and a Tudor castle called *Blantyre*, both in Lenox. Strikingly different in style, these palatial estates-turned-hotels can satisfy even the most refined of tastes and do so with panache.

About 300 Berkshire lodgings exist today, some shorter perhaps on romance but more reasonably priced than others. Berkshire Visitors Bureau Executive Director William R. Wilson, Jr., estimates that 4,000 pillows are available for guests to the county. The number of guest houses is growing, both in town and out, and many offer bed and breakfast ("B&B"); there are simple inns where precious quiet is an everyday experience; and there are modern hotels and all grades of motels for those on a budget or with little concern for country charm.

Since we cannot adequately describe them all, we have tried to present a representative sampling, in terms of price, geography and architecture. To evaluate lodgings, we place a high value on hospitality, the personal attention and sincere care that can turn a visit into an unforgettable sojourn. We also assign value and significance to the architectural qualities of a property; to its history and traditions; to its care in furnishing and use of antiques or other art; to the views and the natural beauty right at its doorstep. As always, we would appreciate hearing about pleasant surprises — or unhappy disappointments.

BERKSHIRE LODGING NOTES

Rates

Rate cards are generally printed early in the spring and will change slightly from year to year. Reminder: Price codes are based on a per-room rate, double occupancy, during the high seasons (summer, fall foliage, skiing). Off-season rates are usually a few dollars lower. (For some, ski season is _the_ season.) Many establishments have mid-week rates as well.

Inexpensive	Up to $65
Moderate	$65 to $100
Expensive	$100 to $175
Very Expensive	Over $175

These rates exclude required room taxes or service charges that may be added to your bill.

Minimum Stay

Many of the better lodgings require a minimum stay of two or three nights on summer or autumn weekends. For a single night's stay in Berkshire at such times, the B&Bs or motels are the best bet. During the off season, minimum-stay requirements relax and in most instances no longer apply.

Deposit/Cancellation

Deposits are usually required for a confirmed reservation. Policies regarding deposits, cancellations, and refunds vary. It is always wise to inquire about these in advance. In the high season, including college graduation weekends in late May and early June, demand for lodgings can exceed supply, so reservations for the more popular places need to be made months or even years ahead.

Special Features

Wherever pertinent, we mention special features of lodgings, along with any caveats, e.g., restrictions on smoking or pets. We also suggest the ages of children for whom the inn might be appropriate, based on information provided by the establishments themselves. This is intended as a general guide only, and it is always best to call and inquire, as policies are often flexible and subject to change according to the season.

Other Options

For last-minute or emergency lodging arrangements in Berkshire, here are some numbers to phone.

Berkshire Visitors Bureau: 413-443-9186
Berkshire Bed and Breakfast Reservation Service: 413-268-7244

Information Booths

For single-night stays in the high season or spur of the moment arrangements at other times, visit any of the tourist information booths listed in the Introduction.

LODGING SOUTH COUNTY

Egremont

North Egremont

ELM COURT INN
Managers: Urs & Glee Bieri.
413-528-0325.
P.O. Box 95, N. Egremont,
 MA 01252.
227 Rte. 71, in the center of
 N. Egremont.
Price: Moderate.
Credit Cards: AE, MC, V.
Special Features: No pets.

Three immaculate, comfortable rooms above one of the more popular restaurants in South Berkshire invite the traveler. One room has a private bath; the other two share a bath. They reside in the center of a quaint, quiet hamlet.

South Egremont

BALDWIN HILL FARM B&B
Owners: Richard & Priscilla Burdsall.
413-528-4092; 888-528-4092.
121 Baldwin Hill Rd. N/S, Gt. Barrington, MA 01230.
From Taconic Parkway, Rte. 23 E. to S. Egremont, left on Baldwin Hill Rd., 1 1/2 miles to inn on left.
Price: Moderate.
Credit Cards: AE, D, MC, V.
Special Features: Pool; No smoking; No pets; Children over 12.

Baldwin Hill, with an unusual 360-degree view of its magnificent surroundings, includes an 1820s farmhouse turned B&B and barns galore. Peace, quiet, and tranquility abound on 500 acres perfect for hiking, cross-country skiing, or simply observing the wildlife. Guests enjoy reading by the fieldstone fireplace in winter or on the screened porch in summer. Four rooms, two with private bath, have views across fields to the mountains beyond. Full breakfast, from a menu with numerous choices, is served by friendly innkeepers, who take pride in this farm that has been in the family since 1910.

THE EGREMONT INN
Owner: Steven Waller.
413-528-2111.
Old Sheffield Rd., S. Egremont, MA 01258.
Side street off Rte. 23 in center of village.
Price: Moderate to Expensive.
Credit Cards: AE, D, MC, V.
Special Features: Pool, 2 tennis courts.

Coziness, low ceilings, fireplaces, broad porches, 20 delightful rooms furnished with antiques: these set the tone for this historic 1780 stagecoach inn nestled on a quiet side street in the heart of a classic old village. Scenery ranges from lovely to gorgeous. Pool and tennis courts for guests' use. Tavern and fine restaurant located on main floor.

TRAIL'S END GUESTS
Owner: Anne Hines.
413-528-3995.
678 S. Egremont Rd., Gt. Barrington, MA 01230.
On Rte. 23, just E. of S. Egremont.
Closed: Nov.–Apr.
Price: Moderate.
Credit Cards: None.
Special Features: No smoking; No pets.

This large modern Colonial is neat and trim inside and out. Set back from Rte. 23, it has three rooms, all with private bath, air conditioning, and TV. Continental breakfast served, with fruit and cereal. Look for the handsome sleigh on the porch. In summer the large screened porch is a popular spot for reading. Children are welcome.

THE WEATHERVANE INN
Owners: Anne & Vincent Murphy.
413-528-9580.
Box 388, S. Egremont, MA 01258.
Rte. 23, just E. of the village.
Closed: Thanksgiving and Christmas.
Price: Expensive; MAP on weekends.
Credit Cards: AE, D, MC, V.
Handicap Access: Limited.
Special Features: Pool; No Pets; Children over 7.

This is a comfortable, clean, and very well-run operation set within a 1785 farmhouse; all 12 rooms have private baths, air conditioning. Your hosts are skilled at their trade and provide their version of Colonial lodging and fine dining in their cheery restaurant. Location is convenient to some of the best antiques shopping in the Berkshires, including one shop just behind the inn. Note that weekends in July and August have a three-night minimum.

WINDFLOWER INN
Owners: Liebert & Ryan families.
413-528-2720.
684 S. Egremont Rd., Gt. Barrington, MA 01230.
Rte. 23, just E. of S. Egremont.
Price: Expensive (MAP).
Credit Cards: AE.
Handicap Access: Limited.
Special Features: Pool; No pets.

One of the prettiest locations in South Berkshire complements the soothing, comfortable interior of this gracious and respected inn. Antiques furnish the common rooms as well as the bedrooms. All 13 rooms have private bath and six have fireplaces. Please note that MAP price includes full breakfast for two. The inn and its restaurant are available for special dinners or occasions.

Great Barrington

COFFING-BOSTWICK HOUSE
Proprietors: Diana & William Harwood.
413-528-4511.
98 Division St., Gt. Barrington, MA 01230.
Corner of Rte. 41 & Division St. 2 mi. N. of Gt. Barrington.
Price: Moderate.
Credit Cards: None.
Special Features: No pets.

It's hard to imagine now, but the sleepy village of Van Deusenville was once a bustling town with mills and factories. Little remains except this large 1825 mansion belonging to Mr. Van Deusen himself, now a six-room bed and breakfast. The guest rooms are spacious and well appointed, as are the public rooms. The Harwoods are hard at work renovating the exterior of the main house. Breakfasts prepared by Diana, a local caterer, are sumptuous. Just down the street is the church where Alice of "Alice's Restaurant" fame lived, now owned by Arlo Guthrie.

GREENMEADOWS
Owners: Frank Gioia & Susie Kaufman.

A rural setting on a quiet country road in what is still a farming area, although only 1.5 miles out of Great Barrington. The rooms have had a

413-528-3897.
117 Division St., Gt.
 Barrington, MA 01230.
1 ¹/₂ mi. N. of Gt.
 Barrington, ¹/₄ mi. W.
 of Rte. 41
Closed: Mar. & Apr.
Price: Moderate.
Credit Cards: AE, MC, V.
Special Features: No
 smoking; No pets.

**LITTLEJOHN MANOR
 B&B**
Co-owners: Herbert
 Littlejohn, Jr., &
 Paul A. DuFour.
413-528-2882.
Newsboy Monument Lane,
 Gt. Barrington, MA
 01230.
On Rte. 23, W. of town, en
 route to S. Egremont.
Price: Moderate.
Credit Cards: None.
Special Features: No pets;
 Children over 12.

**SEEKONK PINES INN
 B & B**
Owners/Innkeepers:
 Lefkowitz Family.
413-528-4192.
142 Seekonk Crossroad, Gt.
 Barrington, MA 01230.
Rte. 23, between S.
 Egremont & Gt.
 Barrington.
Price: Moderate to
 expensive.
Credit Cards: MC, V.
Special Features: Pool;
 Bicycles; No smoking;
 No pets.

THORNEWOOD INN
Owners/Innkeepers: Terry
 & David Thorne.
413-528-3828; 800-854-1008.
453 Stockbridge Rd., Gt.
 Barrington, MA 01230.
Rte. 7, just N. of Gt.
 Barrington.

recent face-lift and include cable color TV and air conditioning. A suite in the former carriage house has a large deck overlooking pastoral fields, plus a full kitchen. The owners serve full breakfast.

This turn-of-the-century Victorian home is run in a very friendly way and partially furnished with antiques. One of the four bedrooms has a working fireplace and all share two baths. A full English breakfast is complemented by afternoon tea served in the sitting room. To assure the freshest of homemade scones and shortbreads, reservations are necessary for tea. Delightful flower and herb gardens.

Surrounded by meadows and well-groomed acreage, this 150-year-old house, originally the main house for a large estate, keeps getting better and better. Furnished in country antiques and collectibles, the six guest rooms, all with private baths, are filled with personal touches. A recently added guest pantry has a refrigerator, hot water dispenser, and sink, with complimentary beverages available. There are a swimming pool for hot summer days and formal gardens for walking or reading. A hearty breakfast is served.

Creativity and imagination are evident throughout this marvelous inn. Several years ago the owners purchased an old, run-down but handsome Dutch Colonial and restored and expanded it to create 10 lovely guest rooms, all with private bath, and four delightful public rooms. The antiques used throughout include canopy beds, pier mir-

Price: Moderate to
  Expensive.
Credit Cards: AE, D, MC, V.
Special Features: Pool; No
  pets; designated
  smoking; Children
  welcome; in July–Aug.,
  children over 11.

TURNING POINT INN
Owners: Irving Yost.
  Managers: Monica
  Cleveland & Adam
  Gudeon
413-528-4777.
3 Lake Buel Rd., Gt.
  Barrington, MA 01230.
Rte. 23, E. of town.
Price: Moderate to
  Expensive.
Credit Cards: AE, MC, V.
Special Features: No
  smoking; No pets;
  Children welcome.

WAINWRIGHT INN
Innkeepers: Anne & David
  Rolland.
413-528-2062.
518 S. Main St., Gt.
  Barrington, MA 01230.
Rte. 7, one block S. of
  intersection with Rte. 23
  west.
Price: Moderate to
  Expensive.
Credit Cards: AE, MC, V.
Handicap Access: Full.
Special Features: No
  smoking; Dining room
  reserved for guests;
  dinner Sat.; Children
  welcome, crib available.

Housatonic

BROOK COVE
Managers: Clifford &
  Barbara Perreault.
413-274-6653.
30 Linda Lane, Housatonic,
  MA 01236.

rors, and original sinks. The carriage house, refurbished in 1992, has two rooms and is especially convenient for families. The restaurant has a view of the Berkshire Hills, and the full breakfast might include strawberry-stuffed French toast or apple pancakes. The inn enjoys hosting banquets and weddings.

Very well-regarded lodging in a handsome brick and clapboard former stagecoach inn that's over 200 years old. Informal atmosphere. Full vegetarian breakfast served to guests in the eight inn rooms (four with private baths). A separate two-bedroom cottage is perfect for families. The popular Butternut Basin ski area is ¹/₃ mile down the road.

A gracious year-round inn, this beautiful gabled house, built by Peter Ingersoll in 1766, was the Tory Tavern and Inn until 1790, when it became the private home of the Wainwright family. David and Anne bought it in 1993 and have remodeled it as a guest house. The eight guest rooms/suites have private baths, some with fireplaces. One guestroom has been renovated to be entirely wheelchair-accessible.

Definitely not your typical guest house. The Perreaults have one large ground-floor apartment with full kitchen, which they rent by the night. The apartment sleeps four, with more beds available. Since the country property meanders

Off Rte. 41., 5.7 mi. from
    Exit #1 Mass. Pike.
Price: Moderate.
Credit Cards: None.
Handicap Access: Yes.
Special Features: No
    smoking.

CHRISTINE'S GUEST HOUSE B&B

Innkeepers: Steve &
    Christine Kelsey.
413-274-6149.
325 N. Plain Rd.,
    Housatonic, MA 01236.
Rte. 41 about 4 mi. N. of Gt.
    Barrington.
Price: Expensive.
Credit Cards: MC, V.
Special Features: Gift Shop;
    No smoking; No pets;
    Children over 11.

Lee

(See also South Lee)

APPLEGATE

Owners: Nancy & Rick
    Cannata.
413-243-4451; 800-691-9012.
279 West Park St., Lee, MA
    01238.
Off Rte. 20, between Lee &
    Stockbridge.
Price: Moderate to Very
    Expensive.
Credit Cards: MC, V.
Special Features: Pool; No
    pets; Children over 12.

BEST WESTERN BLACK SWAN INN

Manager: Peter Conkling.
413-243-2700; 800-876-
    SWAN.

down to the Williams River, the setting seems ideal for longer stays. The room price is for two, with an $8 charge for each additional person. No breakfast served.

A little jewel (three rooms, all with private bath), off the beaten path between Great Barrington and West Stockbridge. The rooms and the innkeepers are delightful. One room is decorated in white wicker, one has a queen canopy bed, and the other a four-poster. All are filled with antiques. Full breakfast. Occasional wine tastings. Those who book for a holiday weekend should prepare for a bonus experience: decorations, often a special rates package, and usually a favor (fathers take home a bag of homemade chocolate chip cookies on Father's Day and mothers a bouquet of flowers on Mother's Day).

This magnificent white-pillared Colonial is special in every way. From the gracious and delightful hosts — he a pilot and she a flight attendant — to the detailed attention they have lavished on their inn, a stay at Applegate will be a cherished treat. Public rooms are large, with fireplaces and bay windows. Inn dolls Martha, Heather, and Claudia observe the activity from their antique rockers. Breakfast is served by candlelight. Guests are greeted in their rooms by crystal decanters filled with brandy and Godiva chocolates. Six large guest rooms all have private bath and two have fireplaces; one even boasts a sauna/shower. The house has central air conditioning. From the screened porch filled with wicker furniture, the view across the pool, enclosed by a low rock wall, to the six landscaped acres beyond is tranquility itself. If anyone wishes to go farther afield, the Cannatas will loan bicycles.

From the outside, this 52-room "inn" looks decidedly like a motel, but its location on placid Laurel Lake, its private balconies, Colonial decor, and friendly hospitality provide an innlike atmos-

435 Laurel St. (Rte. 20W),
Lee, MA 01238.
On Laurel Lake, N. of Lee.
Price: Moderate to Very
Expensive.
Credit Cards: AE, D, DC,
MC, V.
Handicap Access: Yes.
Special Features: Pool;
Exercise room and sauna;
No pets.

phere. Lovely restaurant, swimming pool, and exercise room with sauna. There are boat rentals for boating on the lake. Close to Tanglewood, hiking trails, countless other Berkshire amenities. Conference facilities available. In the summer, meals not included; in winter a continental breakfast may be.

Chambéry Inn in Lee, once a school, still has chalkboards in the guest rooms on which visitors write and draw to express gratitude.

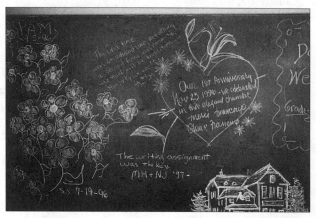

Judith Monachina

**CHAMBÉRY INN:
SCHOOLHOUSE
SUITES**
Owners: Joe & Lynn Toole.
413-243-2221; 800-537-4321.
199 Main St., Lee, MA
01238.
On Main St. (Rte. 20) in Lee.
Price: Moderate to Very
Expensive.
Credit Cards: AE, D, MC, V.
Handicap Access: Yes.
Special Features: No
smoking; No pets;
Children over 15.

Joe Toole is an unabashed romantic, and we all are allowed to benefit. The Chambéry Inn began life as a schoolhouse in 1885, when five nuns arrived from France to teach the youngsters of St. Mary's Parish in Lee. Joe's grandfather was in the first class. Concerned that it was scheduled for the wrecker's ball and enchanted by its history, Joe took on the gargantuan task of moving the schoolhouse to its present location. He left the proportion of the rooms as they were, which is BIG, with 13-foot ceilings and massive windows. There are nine rooms (seven are suites with fireplaces); all have large private baths with whirlpools and king or queen beds. One room and its bath are fully handicapped-equipped. The furniture, including canopy beds, is Amish handcrafted cherry. All the rooms have central air conditioning, telephones, and color cable TV. Breakfast is delivered to the room. In the suites are the original blackboards, a charming feature. Joe invited former students and teachers to share their remembrances of school life at St. Mary's. It's probably a "one-of-a-kind" in the United States.

DEVONFIELD
Owners/Managers: Sally & Ben Schenck.
413-243-3298.
85 Stockbridge Rd., Lee, MA 01238.
Off Rte. 20 just outside village of Lee.
Price: Moderate to Very Expensive.
Credit Cards: AE, D, MC, V.
Special Features: Heated pool; Tennis; Bicycles; Children over 10 in July–Aug.

No expense was spared in renovating this 1800s house, built by a Revolutionary War soldier and initially restored by George Westinghouse in the early 1900s. The small estate became the 1942 summer sanctuary for Queen Wilhelmina of the Netherlands, her daughter Princess Juliana, and granddaughters Beatrix and Irene. The house is secluded, with ten air-conditioned rooms, all with private bath. Full breakfast.

INN ON LAUREL LAKE
Owners: Thomas and Heidi Fusco.
413-243-1436.
615 Laurel St., Lee, MA 01238.
Rte. 20, 2 mi. W. of Lee.
Price: Moderate to Very Expensive.
Credit Cards: AE, D, MC, V.
Handicap Access: Limited.
Special Features: Private beach; Tennis; Sauna; No smoking.

On the shore of Laurel Lake, this 97-year-old country property has attracted a loyal following with its 19 comfortable bedrooms and two sitting rooms filled with an impressive collection of record albums, books, and games. The tennis court, sauna, and private beach add to guests' playtime possibilities. Breakfast buffet served; picnic can be held in backyard. Proximity of major highway should be noted.

AUNTI M'S BED & BREAKFAST
Owner: Michelle Celentano.
413-243-3201.
60 Laurel St., Lee, MA 01238.
Rte. 20, W. of Lee.
Price: Moderate to Expensive.
Credit Cards: None.
Special Features: No smoking; No pets; Children over 15.

Aunti M's (for Michelle) is a restored Victorian within walking distance of historic downtown Lee. There are five comfortable rooms, all with period furnishings, floral wallpapers and borders, and oak floors. One has a private bath and the others share two baths. There is a homey feeling here. In winter, guests can stay around the stove, and in summer they can swing on the "lemonade-type porch" with its wicker furniture. A piano in the foyer is the focal point for after-breakfast camaraderie. The breakfasts always include a home-baked goodie.

THE MORGAN HOUSE INN
Innkeepers: Lenora and Stuart Bowen.

A full-service inn, with some changes in place and others underway. The Morgan House, built in 1817 and a stagecoach stop beginning in 1853, has a

413-243-0181.
33 Main St., Lee, MA 01238.
Town center, .8 mi. from
  Exit 2, Mass. Pike.
Price: Moderate to
  Expensive.
Credit Cards: AE, D, DC,
  MC, V.
Special Features: No pets;
  Children welcome.

bustling and convenient in-town location and 12
comfortable rooms in a variety of shapes and sizes,
some with private bath, some shared. The Bowens
have 20 years' experience in the innkeeping and
restaurant business. Lenora has the distinction of
being owner/chef. The dining room has been
spruced up, and the new menu features New
England cuisine with a contemporary flair; light fare
is available in the tavern. Morgan House hospitality
begins in the small lobby, where the "wallpaper" is
actual pages from 19th-century guest registers —
look for U.S. Grant and Charles Dickens.

PROSPECT HILL HOUSE
Managers: Marge & Chuck
  Driscoll.
413-243-3460.
100 S. Prospect St., Lee, MA
  01238.
Just off Park St.
Closed: Nov.–May.
Price: Moderate.
Credit Cards: None.
Special Features: Children
  over 12.

This Cape Colonial on one acre at the end of a
street offers a quiet setting near the golf course.
Three rooms; shared baths; all air conditioned.
Common room has fireplace. Home-baked breakfast served.

*Federal House: the ambience
of classic Americana.*

Jonathan Sternfield

South Lee

THE FEDERAL HOUSE INN
Owners: Robin & Kenneth Almgren.
413-243-1824; 800-243-1824.
1680 Pleasant St., S. Lee, MA 01260.
Just E. of Stockbridge on Rte 102.
Price: Moderate to Expensive.
Credit Cards: AE, D, MC, V.
Special Features: Restaurant; No pets.

This brick Federal house, built in 1824, has been beautifully restored. In this historic property, the seven guest rooms sit above a respected restaurant. Graceful and charming rooms feature antique furnishings. All have private bath and air conditioning. Full breakfast included. Owned and operated by a dynamic couple who combine good taste and culinary talents.

HISTORIC MERRELL INN
Owners: Faith & Charles Reynolds. Innkeeper: Pam Hurst
413-243-1794; 800-243-1794.

Those who walk through the massive door of this striking brick inn, built in 1794, will find themselves transported back in time. For years it served as a stagecoach stop on the busy Boston-Albany Pike. It lay idle and boarded up for over

Colonial antiques highlight the entry at the historic Merrell Tavern Inn.

Paul Rocheleau, courtesy Merrell Tavern Inn

1565 Pleasant St., S. Lee, MA 01260.
Rte. 102, just E. of Stockbridge.
Closed: Christmas Eve & Christmas.
Price: Moderate to Expensive.
Credit Cards: MC, V.
Special Features: No smoking; No pets; Inquire about children.

100 years until purchased by the Reynoldses in late 1980. Now lovingly and carefully restored, the inn is listed on the National Register of Historic Places. The nine bedrooms, completely redecorated in 1992, are furnished with four-poster and canopy beds, and all have private baths, air conditioning, and telephones; three have fireplaces. The Old Tavern Room features the original circular Colonial bar. A groomed lawn in back leads to the banks of the Housatonic River, where there is a screened gazebo. A full breakfast is served from a menu.

OAK N' SPRUCE LODGE

Manager: Paul DiCroce.
413-243-3500; 800-424-3003.
P.O. Box 237, Meadow St., S. Lee, MA 01260.
Off Rte. 102, on Meadow St., N. of village.
Price: Moderate to Expensive; MAP.
Credit Cards: AE, MC, V.
Handicap Access: Yes.
Special Features: Indoor and outdoor Pools; Tennis; Golf; Health Club; No pets.

A full-service but by no means fancy resort. For rent are 57 hotel rooms and 130 time-share condominiums. Restaurant and bar in main building. Function and meeting facilities. Beautiful natural scenery offsets the hodgepodge architecture and interiors. Very casual atmosphere. Modified American plan provides breakfast and dinner.

New Marlborough

THE OLD INN ON THE GREEN AND GEDNEY FARM

Innkeepers: Bradford Wagstaff & Leslie Miller.
413-229-3131.
Star Rte. 70, New Marlborough, MA 01230.
Rte. 57, in center of village.
Price: Expensive to Very Expensive.
Credit Cards: AE, MC, V.
Special Features: Restaurant; No pets.

A beautiful village rich in unaffected nostalgia is the setting for this 18th-century inn. The five rooms in the inn, each with private bath, have been lovingly restored and furnished in a simple American country style. Gedney Farm, a short walk from the inn, has 13 guest rooms, mostly two-level suites, carved out of a Normandy-style barn, which was built around 1900 as a showplace for Percheron stallions and Jersey cattle. All suites feature fireplaces in the living rooms, large bedrooms, and whirlpool tubs in the master baths. The restored second horse barn serves as space for weddings, parties, meetings, an art gallery, concerts, and, in summer, the Gallery Cafe. The restaurant in the inn is one of the finest in the Berkshires.

RED BIRD INN

Managers: Don & Joyce
  Coffman.
413-229-2433.
Box 592, Gt. Darrington,
  MA 01230.
Adsit Crosby Rd., Rte. 57,
  New Marlborough.
From Gt. Barrington, Rte.
  23 E. to Rte. 57.
Price: Expensive.
Credit Cards: AE.
Handicap Access: Limited.
Special Features: No
  smoking; No pets;
  Children over 12.

A former stagecoach stop, the 18th-century Red Bird Inn is located on 10 ten acres on a quiet country road. The seven rooms, four with private baths, are furnished with antiques, decorated with Ralph Lauren and Laura Ashley, and retain their original wide plank floors, fireplaces, and old iron-work. A separate suite has one huge room with a queen-size bed, two twins, a sitting area, and private bath. The large screened porch is a popular feature with warm-weather guests. A full breakfast is served.

Otis

GROUSE HOUSE

Managers: The Goulet
  Family.
413-269-4446.
Rte. 23, Otis, MA 01253.
Near Rte. 8, on Rte. 23.
Price: Inexpensive.
Credit Cards: AE, MC, V.
Special Features: No Pets.

Next door to Otis Ridge Ski area, Grouse House offers six rooms, all with shared baths. Reduced rate on lift tickets for guests of the house. Guests can get breakfast at the ski lodge, as no breakfast is served at Grouse House. In summer, there are horseshoes and volleyball.

JOYOUS GARDE B&B

Owner: Joy Bogen.
413-269-6852.
Olde Quarry Rd./PO Box
  132, Otis, MA 01253.
From Rte. 8 in the center of
  Otis village to Rte 23E;
  almost 1 mi. to left onto
  Gibbs Rd., continue to
  fork in road; go left and
  follow signs.
Price: Expensive to Very
  Expensive.
Open: Year-round.
Credit Cards: AE, DC, MC,
  V.
Handicap Access: Yes, one
  room; ramp to breakfast
  room.
Special Features: No
  Smoking; No pets;
  Children over 11 welcome;
  call about younger ages.

In Arthurian legend, Joyous Garde was the name of Launcelot's castle retreat, and the Berkshires' own Joyous Garde — a hideaway down a country road — is just as magical. In two adjacent farm-houses and a cabana, the common areas and bed-rooms are a charming mix of elegant and casual, old-fashioned and up-to-date. Nine cozy bedrooms offer big beds dressed up with lush linens, striped and floral wallpaper and curtains, and whimsical accent pieces, many antique. Each bedroom has an updated private bath (one is just across the hall-way). In the first house is also a serve-yourself breakfast alcove for early risers, a wicker-filled sunporch, and second-floor sitting areas, inside and out, across from an enormous stone chimney. Out back is a cabana/sauna, Jacuzzi, and swimming pool. The second house, also a vintage farm building with arched stonework, includes a formal living room and dining room, where a full breakfast is served. Just beyond are a tennis court and trails for woodland hiking or cross-country skiing.

Owner Joy Bogen — once an opera and concert singer and the only student of Lotte Lenya — says she goes out of her way to provide extra services for her guests, such as making appointments for massage therapy or tennis instruction. Though the inn has no restaurant, Joy will make up picnics or light dinners and provides snacks for concert- or theater-goers returning in the evening for fireside socializing. She can also stage a full gourmet meal for special occasions. There's an antique shop on the premises for guests, and many of the prints, paintings, and other pieces throughout the rooms are for sale, too.

Sandisfield

DAFFER'S MOUNTAIN INN
Owner: John Field.
413-258-4453.
212 Sandisfield Rd.,
    Sandisfield MA 01255.
Price: Inexpensive.

Mostly a restaurant (closed Mondays), but with seven rooms upstairs that share several baths. Congenially run to cater effectively to their guests' needs. In fall, the large sign reads "Hunters Welcome." Very informal. Friendly groups return year after year. A full breakfast is included during deer season.

NEW BOSTON INN
Innkeeper: Paula McCarthy
    Tatko.
413-258-4477.
Rtes. 8 & 57W, 101 N. Main
    St., Sandisfield, MA
    01255.
Jct. Rtes. 8 & 57,
    Sandisfield. In the village
    of New Boston.
Price: Moderate.
Credit Cards: AE, D, MC,
    V.
Handicap Access: Yes.
Special Features: 1737 pub.

Built in 1737, this remarkable old stagecoach inn, listed on the National Register of Historic Places, underwent a painstaking renovation in 1984, and the owners continue to make improvements. The eight guest rooms are, true to the period, snug. Low ceilings, wide-board floors, and multi-paned windows hark back to the 18th century and, in most cases, are original. All rooms feature private baths and are decorated with early pine furniture and stenciling. All closets are cedar-lined.

Our favorite space at the inn is the second-floor ballroom. After wandering through the cozy bedrooms, you enter the spacious ballroom, now called The Gathering Room, complete with an antique billiards table and a barrel-vaulted ceiling. The sense of openness, grace, and the continued presence of the past is romantic, especially the matching fireplaces at either end.

Another historic delight is the taproom, now open as a pub, that adjoins the low-ceilinged dining room. The 22-inch-wide oak boards on the wall are called "king's wood" because they were illegally retained by the colonists after the deputies of the king of England went about marking trees for masts for the

Royal Navy. In this room as throughout the inn, the wooden molding, plaster walls, slanted floors, venerable windows and doorways (there is hardly a right angle in the place) provide a powerful charm and sense of history. What's more, the New Boston Inn has a resident ghost. She is real enough to have been reported in *Yankee* magazine: an Irish maiden, dressed in bridal black, who was shot by a scorned suitor in an upstairs room.

Breakfast included.

Sheffield

CENTURYHURST ANTIQUES & BED & BREAKFAST
Managers: Ronald & Judith Timm.
413-229-8131.
Box 486, Sheffield, MA 01257.
Main St., Rte. 7.
Price: Moderate.
Credit Cards: AE, MC, V.
Special Features: No smoking; No pets; Children over 11.

This grand 1800 home, nestled among towering trees, is listed on the National Register of Historic Places. The inn features four guest rooms that share two baths. The rooms are named for previous owners of the home. Visitors enjoy an "all-you-can-eat continental breakfast," in Judith's words. A new post-and-beam barn behind the house serves as an antiques shop, specializing in antique American clocks, early 19th-century furniture, and Wedgwood.

IVANHOE COUNTRY HOUSE
Managers: Carole & Dick Maghery.
413-229-2143.
254 S. Undermountain Rd. (Rte. 41), Sheffield, MA 01257.
On Rte. 41, 4 mi. S. of Rte. 23; 10 mi. N. of Lakeville, CT.
Price: Moderate.
Credit Cards: None.
Special Features: Pool; No young children July–Aug. wknds.

Set along one of the most scenic roads in South Berkshire, the Ivanhoe provides nine comfortable rooms, all with private bath, at reasonable prices. Continental breakfast served at your door. Take a dip in the pool before dinner, play the piano if you wish, enjoy the fire in the chestnut-paneled public room, and select from the many fine local restaurants for your evening meal. At the base of Race Mountain, traversed by the Appalachian Trail, 20 wooded acres hug this 1780-vintage country house. Golden retrievers are raised on the property, and guests are welcome to bring their own dogs (no cats!), for an additional $10.

ORCHARD SHADE
Owners: Debbie & Henry Thornton.
413-229-8463.
Box 669, Sheffield, MA 01257.
On Maple Ave., off Main St. (Rte. 7) N. of Christ Church, Sheffield.

This venerable 1840 house has operated as a bed and breakfast since 1888. Furnished with antiques, the public rooms have two spacious fireplaces to ward off the chill on cooler evenings. Some of the eight bedrooms have private baths. The large screened-in porch is perfect for relaxing

Price: Moderate to
Expensive.
Credit Cards: AE, D, MC,
V.
Special Features: Pool; No
smoking; No pets;
Children welcome.

RACE BROOK LODGE
B&B
Innkeeper: David
Rothstein.
413-229-2916.
864 S. Undermountain
Rd./Rte. 41, Sheffield.
Two miles S. of Berkshire
School.
Price: Moderate to
Expensive.
Open: Year-round.
Credit Cards: AE, MC, V.
Handicap Access: Ground-
level entry to many
rooms.
Special Features: Smoking
restricted; Well-behaved
pets accepted; Children
welcome.

after a busy day of Sheffield antiquing. So are the
10 acres and gardens.

This rustic lodge beside Race Brook has its own
trail leading to a state forest with waterfall,
ravine, and the Appalachian Trail. A large rambling barn, dating from the 1790s and recently renovated, embraces rooms and suites in what were
once haylofts, with exposed original beams, stenciling, nooks and alcoves, and windows and stairs in
unexpected places. The variety of bedroom, bathroom, and entrance arrangements can work for
couples, family groups, or friends traveling
together. Having converted a garage into the
Meeting House, the lodge emphasizes team-build-
ing retreats for organizations.

The interiors have been specifically designated a
"chintz-free zone" to maximize informality. More
rooms and suites, available seasonally, are in
nearby cottages. (There are 14 rooms in the winter,
20 in the summer and fall, all with private baths.)

In the lofty common rooms at the heart of the barn
are tables, a TV corner, and a horseshoe bar run on the honor system. The
lodge will produce lunches and suppers for groups, on request. A hearty continental breakfast is served. A popular feature here is the dynamic Third Sunday
Jazz Series.

RAMBLEWOOD INN
Owners: Martin & June
Ederer.
413-229-3363.
Box 729, Sheffield, MA
01257.
Rte. 41, 5 mi. S. of Gt.
Barrington.
Price: Moderate to
Expensive.
Credit Cards: MC, V.
Handicap Access: Limited.

Up a short hill off scenic Rte. 41, this Alpine
structure at the edge of the woods has an attractive rustic look, with all the comforts of home
including central air conditioning. The Ederers offer
six guest rooms (four with private bath) and a
ground-floor suite with full kitchen, bedroom, living
room, and bath. June, an English teacher, has named
each room for a character in *Canterbury Tales*. The
Miller's Room on the first floor has its own deck
and, not surprising, the Wife of Bath's Room on the
second floor is the largest in the house. New to the
inn is a piece of pondfront property across the road,
where guests may swim, canoe, and fish.

A full gourmet breakfast is served. The Berkshire School, site of the Berkshire Choral Institute (see the "Music" section in Chapter Four, *Culture*), is a mile down the road.

STAGECOACH HILL INN
Innkeeper: Sandra MacDougall.
413-229-8585.
854 South Under Mountain Rd., Sheffield, MA 01257.
On Rte. 41, several mi. N. of Lakeville, CT.
Price: Inexpensive to Moderate.
Credit Cards: AE, MC, V.
Handicap Access: Limited.
Special Features: Pool; Supervised children 10 and over welcome.

A time machine. Nostalgia for bygone eras (especially Colonial times as evident in the decidedly English pub and restaurant) plus charm and comfort greet the fortunate visitor to this ideally situated hostelry. Choice of 11 rooms in the main house or cottage, nine with private bath. Meals separately priced. There is access to the Appalachian Trail from the property.

STAVELEIGH HOUSE
Owners: D. Marosy & M. Whitman.
413-229-2129.
Box 608, Sheffield, MA 01257.
Just S. of village, on Rte. 7.
Price: Moderate.
Credit Cards: None.
Special Features: No smoking; No pets; Children over 12.

This vintage 1821 house is set in the heart of Sheffield. Your hostesses believe in old-fashioned hospitality and have succeeded in creating a warm and comfortable interior, with hooked rugs and patchwork quilts in the five guest rooms (one with private bath; four share two baths). A full breakfast, with imaginative specialties, is featured. The grounds feature perennial beds, an herb garden, and a place to sit under the trees. There are two resident cats.

Stockbridge

ARBOR ROSE BED & BREAKFAST
Owner: Christina Alsop.
413-298-4744.
Box 114, Stockbridge, MA 01262.
8 Yale Hill Rd., off E. Main St. (Rte. 102).
Price: Moderate to Expensive.
Credit Cards: AE, MC, V.
Special Features: No smoking; No pets; Children welcome.

The first thing you hear on entering the driveway to Arbor Rose is the soothing sound of rushing water. The house sits on a hill overlooking an early 1800s sawmill and millpond. The large white house has five guest rooms, some with fireplaces, all with private bath. A new one has been opened in the mill. The charming decor is highlighted by colorful paintings by the owner's mother, Suzette Alsop, a noted local artist. There are family pets — dog, cat, and horse.

Full breakfast includes magnificent muffins. A downstairs room has recently been converted into a gift shop.

BERKSHIRE THISTLE

Owners: Gene & Diane
Elling.
413-298-3188.
9 East St., Box 1227,
Stockbridge, MA 01262.
Rte. 7, N. of village.
Price: Moderate to
Expensive.
Credit Cards: None.
Special Features: Pool; No
smoking; No pets;
Children 8 and older.

CONROY'S B&B

Owners: James and Joanne
Conroy.
413-298-4990.
Box 191, Stockbridge, MA
01262.
On Rte. 7, about 1.5 mi. N.
of village.
Price: Expensive.
Credit Cards: AE, MC, V.
Special Features: No
smoking; No pets;
Special events catering;
Deposit in advance and
two weeks' notice of
cancellation.

THE INN AT STOCKBRIDGE

Innkeepers: Alice & Len
Schiller.
413-298-3337.
Box 618, Stockbridge, MA
01262.
On Rte. 7, about 1 mi. N. of
village.
Price: Moderate to Very
Expensive.
Credit Cards: AE, D, MC,
V.
Handicap Access: Limited.
Special Features: Pool; No
smoking; No pets;
Children over 12.

The owners of one of the truly impressive homes on Rte. 7 have had years of training in the bed and breakfast business, filling in for Gene's parents at their B&B. This location, midway between Lenox and Stockbridge, is unbeatable. Although the house is a recently built Colonial, it is comfortable and beautifully sited, with a wraparound deck to take advantage of the views. All five rooms have private baths and air conditioning. Easy access to theater, Tanglewood, and great hiking trails. Swimming pool and picturesque pasture with grazing horses.

Located just off Route 7 north of Stockbridge village in a handsome 1830s Federal-style house, Conroy's B&B is close to, but acoustically quite insulated from, the Mass. Pike. As such, it is perfectly situated for just about all of the mid-summer cultural attractions. Owner/proprietors Joanne and Jim Conroy serve in the same capacities at the justly famous Cactus Cafe Mexican restaurant in downtown Lee. The dining and lounging rooms are located in a spacious addition behind the original house, so period charm is not compromised by lack of space or conveniences. The Conroys offer five double rooms in various configurations, some with private baths, some shared. Check to see how they can accommodate the size and shape of your group.

A marvelous, secluded inn run by friendly, professional people. The large, white-columned house is decorated with impeccable taste, featuring priceless antiques and many thoughtful touches. All 12 rooms have private baths and are air-conditioned. One room and bath are fully handicapped-accessible. The four newest rooms have their own fireplaces. Wine and cheese are served in the living room (warmed by a fire in chilly weather) and breakfast in the formal dining room is incredible. The breakfast pastries are all homemade, with croissants, French toast, and cinnamon buns as possible offerings. Special private dinners can be arranged on request.

The fireplace at the Red Lion Inn has served to warm generations of guests during the colder months of the year.

Courtesy the Red Lion Inn

THE RED LION INN
General Manager: Brooks
  Bradbury.
413-298-5545.
30 Main St., Stockbridge,
  MA 01262.
Village center, Rtes. 7 &
  102.
Price: Moderate to Very
  Expensive.
Credit Cards: AE, D, DC,
  MC, V.
Handicap Access: Yes.
Special Features: Pool;
  Exercise Room; Massage
  Therapist.

In Colonial America, three years before the States became United, the Red Lion Inn first opened its doors to travelers on the stagecoach route linking Albany, Hartford, and Boston. Today, over two centuries later, the Red Lion continues to welcome visitors and locals, and still with consummate Colonial charm. The present inn, rebuilt in 1897 after a fire in 1896, is an icon of the Berkshires, representing graceful country lodging at its best.

Antique furniture and a fine collection of china teapots adorn the lobby. Each private room is decorated with unique period appointments, carefully coordinated by the inn's owner, Jane Fitzpatrick, also owner of Country Curtains. Recent improvements have concentrated on creating larger rooms and increasing the number of suites (bedroom plus living room), consistent with guest requests.

The atmosphere is faithful to the rhythms of a simpler, slower time while providing all contemporary comforts. Sipping a cool drink on a hot summer's day on the famous porch of the Red Lion, or meeting a companion in front of the cheery fireplace in the lobby in winter, is to beat with the heart of the Berkshires.

Throughout the inn, the loving attention to detail is evident in every aspect of its operation. It's easy to feel at home here because all the inn's top quality services are offered by a vibrant, eager-to-please staff. In summer, porch or courtyard company may be an actor or actress of note, who spends evenings nearby on the boards of the Berkshire Theatre Festival.

The Red Lion Inn is not, however, a particularly tranquil place. The main building is full of activity and people, and the street right outside (Rtes. 7 & 102) is sometimes noisy with traffic. There's a conviviality and gaiety about the lobby that some folks love and others don't. If you're in the latter category, take heart: there are several sweet Red Lion cottages that form a complex around the inn: the Stafford House, the O'Brien House, the yellow cottage, the Stevens House (just up the street), the Fire House (Elm St.), and McGregor House. Soon to be added will be Anderson House (Maple and Elm Sts.).

Reservations should be made in advance at this popular inn, especially in the summer. The rooms have many fine complements: an excellent formal dining room; the Lion's Den, a pub featuring nightly entertainment; a courtyard for summer meals under the trees, surrounded by bushels of impatiens; the Pink Kitty, an outstanding gift shop; and a Country Curtains retail store.

THE ROEDER HOUSE
Innkeepers: Vernon &
    Diane Reuss.
413-298-4015.
Box 525, Stockbridge MA
    01262.
Rte. 183, just S. of Glendale
    village center.
Price: Expensive to Very
    Expensive.
Credit Cards: AE, D, MC,
    V.
Special Features: Pool; No
    smoking; No pets;
    Children over 9.

A delightful hideaway, in a small village far from the crowds but close to summer attractions and just three-quarters of a mile from the new Norman Rockwell Museum. Awaiting lucky house guests are seven large, exquisitely furnished air-conditioned rooms, all with private bath and filled with antiques and four-poster queen-sized beds. The owners also run an antiques shop, and the entire house reflects their impeccable taste. A full breakfast is served on tables set with china, silver, and crystal on the charming screened-in porch, weather permitting.

TAGGART HOUSE B&B
Owners: Hinckley & Susan
    Waitt.
413-298-4303.
18 Main St., Stockbridge
    01262.
Price: Very Expensive.
Credit Cards: AE, CB, D,
    DC, MC, V.
Special Features: No
    smoking; No pets;
    Inquire about children.
    Golf and tennis available.

A stunning array of art and antiques in the richly detailed architectural setting of a 19th-century mansion, with a fireplace around just about every corner, a billiards room, a paneled library, a music room, and three secluded acres of gardens and field: the description of a romantic country manor house in a Victorian novel. Actually, the Taggart House is right on Main Street in Stockbridge, where resident owners Hinckley and Susan Waitt have transformed fiction into reality. Their personal collection of antique furnishings and artwork, with dramatic choices of color and texture, artfully blend elegance and whimsy, opulence and coziness.

Throughout the downstairs living rooms and the upstairs bedrooms are a variety of fabulous faux effects painted on walls and ceilings, including bois and tortoiseshell finishes. In the butler's pantry, trompe-l'oeil painting merges a real garden scene with an illusory one. The abundance of imaginative details also includes fabrics and wallpaper with William Morris designs, a birchbark canoe suspended from a frescoed ceiling over the billiards table, curtains drawn back with antlers, a collection of Native American artifacts in the library, and a pillowed nook halfway up the stairs. The cavernous music room has hosted chamber concerts from Bach to Gershwin — and an 18-foot Christmas tree. The four bedrooms feature rich and restful color themes, fireplaces, and luxurious antique beds, as well as air conditioning; each room's private bath is equally sumptuous, with antique furnishings, heated towel racks, and even bath salts. Morning brings gourmet breakfasts, and there are some self-serve options, too. Afternoon tea can be provided, as well as early evening hors d'oeuvres.

Tyringham

THE GOLDEN GOOSE
Innkeepers/Owners: Lilja & Joe Rizzo
413-243-3008.
Box 336, Tyringham, MA 01264.
On main st. of village, across from town hall.
Price: Moderate to Expensive.
Credit Cards: AE, D, MC, V.
Special Features: No pets; Children in the studio only.

The town itself is worth the trip. Beautiful, surprising, and secretive, Tyringham is a gift. The Golden Goose is a white Colonial hideaway with six cozy rooms, four with private bath, and one studio apartment (with bath) in a setting of absolute peace and quiet. The deck and picnic tables watch over the Appalachian Trail, so it's a perfect stopping place for Trail hikers. Afternoon wine and cheese, and hot cider in season, are served in the antique-furnished, fireplaced common rooms. Breakfast is a hearty continental, including homemade biscuits and jam.

West Stockbridge

CARD LAKE COUNTRY INN
Innkeepers: Ed & Lisa Robbins.
413-232-0272.
29 Main St., W. Stockbridge, MA 01266.
Main St., center of village.
Price: Moderate to Expensive.
Credit Cards: AE, MC, V.
Special Features: No pets.

The inn offers eight guest rooms featuring brass and iron beds. All have private bath. Village shops across street are artsy-craftsy. Guests may want to ask for a room at the back of the inn, to avoid traffic noise. Restaurant and tavern on the premises.

KASINDORF'S
Managers: Shirley & Meyer Kasindorf.

A lovely contemporary home set on five parklike acres. There are three rooms, one with private

413-232-4603.
Box 526, W. Stockbridge,
 MA 01266.
Price: Moderate.
Credit Cards: None.
Special Features: No
 smoking; No pets;
 Children over 13.

MARBLE INN
Owners: Yvonne & Joe
 Kopper.
413-232-7092.
4 Stockbridge Rd., W.
 Stockbridge, MA 01266.
Rte. 102, near ctr. of village.
Price: Moderate to
 Expensive.
Credit Cards: MC, V.

SHAKER MILL INN
Owner: Jonathan Rick.
413-232-8596.
Box 521, W. Stockbridge,
 MA 01266.
On Rte. 102 in village.
Price: Expensive to Very
 Expensive (2-bdrm.
 suite).
Credit Cards: AE, MC, V.
Special Features: Children
 and pets welcome.

bath. Full breakfast and complimentary afternoon beverages.

The house that is Marble Inn was built in 1835 during the expansion of marble quarries and limestone works in the area. In a cozy country atmosphere guests will find four rooms, all with private bath, furnished with antiques and fluffy terry robes. A full breakfast is served from a menu, with as many as seven entrée choices every day. The inn's homemade jams are for sale to take home.

While the fate of the restaurant is uncertain, guests are still fortunate to stay at the inn. Nine enormous, modern deluxe rooms (all but one with a deck or balcony) with king- or queen-sized beds come complete with small kitchens. The suite has two full bedrooms, two full baths, large, fully equipped kitchen, living room, two TVs, laundry, and just about anything else you might want. All accommodations are in a converted barn.

The colonial charm of the 18th-century Williamsville Inn.

Jonathan Sternfield

THE WILLIAMSVILLE INN
Owners: Gail & Kathleen Ryan.
413-274-6118.
P.O. Box 138, W. Stockbridge, MA 01266.
On Rte. 41, 5 mi. N. of Gt. Barrington.
Price: Expensive to Very Expensive.
Credit Cards: AE, MC, V.
Special Features: Pool; Tennis; Children welcome.

The gracious, white Colonial home was built in 1797 and retains the charm of a bygone era. There are 10 guest rooms in the main house, two with fireplaces. Two cottages and four more units, all with woodstoves, in the converted barn, bring the room total to 16. All rooms have private bath and air conditioning. Fine restaurant on main floor, pool, and clay tennis court give the inn added dimension. Summer guests will enjoy the sculpture garden, with changing exhibits. In winter there are Sunday evening storytelling programs. The inn is available for meetings and conferences.

LODGING CENTRAL COUNTY

Becket

LONG HOUSE B & B
Owners: Roy & Joan Simmons.
413-623-8360.
155 High St., Box 271, Becket, MA 01223.
Off Rte. 8, Becket.
Price: Moderate.
Credit Cards: AE, MC, V.
Special Features: No smoking; No pets; Children welcome.

The Simmonses have been welcoming bed and breakfast guests since 1966. Their charming 1820 country home, listed on the National Register of Historic Places, has four cozy rooms, one with private bath. Convenient to Jacob's Pillow, hiking and nature trails. Full breakfast offered. In summer, a weekly plan can be arranged.

Dalton

THE DALTON HOUSE
Hosts: Gary & Bernice Turetsky.
413-684-3854.
955 Main St., Dalton, MA 01226.
Price: Moderate to Expensive.
Credit Cards: AE, MC, V.
Special Features: Pool; No smoking; No pets; Children over 6.

The rooms in the Main House and Carriage House, 11 altogether, all have private baths. Set in a small New England village, the house has been partially furnished with antiques. Summer guests enjoy air conditioning, the pool, extensively landscaped lawn and flower gardens, and a picnic area. Breakfast is served.

Hancock

HANCOCK INN
Managers: Ellen & Chester
   Gorski.
413-738-5873.
102 Main St., Hancock, MA
   01237.
On Rte. 43, between
   Williamstown and
   Stephentown, NY.
Price: Moderate.
Credit Cards: AE, D, MC, V.
Special Features: No
   smoking; No pets;
   Children under 12 free.

Exceptionally cozy Victorian inn set in a village
that seems unaware of the 20th century's
arrival. A tastefully furnished, family-run establishment, the inn has the charm of a delightful, for-
gotten keepsake discovered one day in your grand-
mother's attic. Six comfortable rooms, all with
private baths and air conditioning, above a
respected and well-managed restaurant. A full
breakfast is included.

JIMINY PEAK, THE
   MOUNTAIN RESORT
General Manager: Paul
   Maloney.
413-738-5500; 800-882-8859
   (outside Mass.)
Brodie Mountain/Corey
   Rd., Hancock, MA 01237.
Between Rtes. 7 & Rte. 43,
   10 mi. N. of Pittsfield.
Price: Very Expensive.
Credit Cards: AE, D, DC,
   MC, V.
Handicap Access: Yes.
Special Features: Pool;
   Tennis; Health Club;
   Trout Fishing; Alpine
   Slide; Downhill skiing;
   No pets.

This relatively new full-service resort truly has it
all. In the Country Inn, all 105 units are suites
featuring kitchen, living room with queen-sized
sofa bed, bath with powder room, and master bedroom with king-sized bed. Most of the units can be
rented for two nights. There are also one- and two-
bedroom condominiums for rent and time-sharing.
Add to that several restaurants, tennis, swimming,
health club, trout fishing, an Alpine Slide for summer, and — best of all — great downhill skiing,
and you've got one of the Berkshires' most complete resorts. Conference facilities are available.
Meals are not included. Jiminy is building a new
set of condos as we go to press.

Hinsdale

MAPLEWOOD B & B
Innkeepers: Charlotte &
   Bob Baillargeon.
413-655-8167.
435 Maple St., Box 477,
   Hinsdale, MA 01235.
On Rte. 143.
Price: Inexpensive to
   Moderate.
Credit Cards: None.
Special Features: No
   smoking; No pets.

Country setting; country style. The house is set
on six acres with a small pond and has three
rooms, one with private bath. Full breakfast might
feature fresh trout caught by Bob or corn pancakes
with fresh, locally made maple syrup; special diets
can be accommodated. Antiques in many rooms.
Guests have a separate common room and entrance.

Lanesborough

THE TUCKERED TURKEY
Managers: Dan & Marianne Sullivan.
413-442-0260.
30 Old Cheshire Rd., Lanesborough, MA 01237.
From Rte. 7, turn E. on Summer St., then N. on Old Cheshire Rd.
Price: Moderate.
Credit Cards: None.
Special Features: No smoking; No pets.

A restored 19th-century Colonial farmhouse, set on close to four acres, with spacious views. Three antique-furnished rooms share baths. Guests are welcome to bring their children to play with the owner's younger two. Full breakfast served, along with a great sense of humor.

Lenox

AMADEUS HOUSE
Owners/Innkeepers: Marty Gottron & John Felton.
413-637-4770; 800-205-4770.
15 Cliffwood St., Lenox, MA 01240.
Off Main St. in Lenox.
Price: Moderate to Expensive.
Credit Cards: AE, D, MC, V.
Special Features: No smoking; No pets; Children over 6.

John Felton, a writer and former journalist, and Marty Gottron, an editor, met when both worked for *The Congressional Quarterly*. Their interests and hospitable ways make a stay at Amadeus House a comfortable and relaxing experience, steps away from the busy main street of Lenox.

Each of the seven rooms (plus the third-floor apartment, available by the day, week, or month) is named for a composer. Two rooms share a bath; the rest have private baths. The Mozart Room on the first floor has a sitting area, a wood-burning stove, and its own front porch. All the rooms are comfortable and pretty, with a number of antiques and quilts. Guests are welcome to choose from a collection of several hundred compact discs in the common room, or take a book from the upstairs library shelves and spend the day on the wraparound porch. A full breakfast, complete with vegetarian hot entrée is served, as well as complimentary afternoon tea with fresh-baked cookies, tea cakes, or scones.

THE APPLE TREE INN
Owners: Sharon Walker & Joel Catalano.
413-637-1477.
10 Richmond Mtn. Rd., Lenox, MA 01240.
On Rte. 183, W. of Tanglewood Main Gate.

Magically set, the Apple Tree Inn is indisputably the lodging that lies closest to the front gates of Tanglewood. The guest rooms in the main house are down-comforter dainty, some with antique brass beds and fireplaces, two with shared baths. A separate unit with 21 additional rooms is less charming, though the rooms are convenient

Price: Moderate to Very
Expensive.
Credit Cards: AE, CB, D,
MC, V.
Special Features: Pool;
Tennis; No pets; Children
over 10.

and clean, bringing the total number of units to 35.

The Apple Tree would be worth a visit for the views alone: a magnificent Berkshire panorama from the south rooms, from poolside, or from the gazebo, which now serves as a restaurant. There is also dining on the deck. The downstairs parlor is thoughtfully appointed and very comfortable; the bar has rich wood paneling, stained glass windows, and a huge hearth. A crowning touch is the landscaping, boasting hundreds of varieties of roses set among the apple trees — truly a visual feast throughout late spring and summer.

BIRCHWOOD INN
Innkeepers: Joan, Dick,
Anne, & Dan Toner.
413-637-2600; 800-524-1646.
Box 2020, 7 Hubbard St.,
Lenox, MA 01240.
On corner of Main and
Hubbard.
Price: Moderate to Very
Expensive.
Credit Cards: AE, CB, D,
DC, MC, V.
Special Features: Massage
therapy; No smoking; No
pets; Children over 12.

Elegant 1767 mansion high on the hill overlooking the charm of Lenox. The Toner family has owned the inn since June 1991. They are gradually renovating the rooms and recently have added telephones, as well as new carpeting in the corridors. There are ten rooms in the main house, eight with private bath, and two suites in the carriage house. A magnificent library extends along one side of the house, with books, magazines, and games galore. The wicker-furnished front porch is a popular spot in summer. A full gourmet breakfast, plus wine and cheese in the afternoon, is included.

Frank Packlick, courtesy Blantyre

Stately Blantyre.

BLANTYRE
Manager: Roderick
Anderson.

Regally set amidst 85 conscientiously groomed acres of lawns, trees and hedges, Blantyre

413-637-3556
(Winter: 413-298-1661).
16 Blantyre Rd., Lenox, MA
01240.
Off Rte. 20, 3 mi. N.W. of
Lee (and Mass. Pike).
Closed: Nov.–mid-May.
Price: Very Expensive.
Credit Cards: AE, DC, MC,
V.
Handicap Access: Limited.
Special Features: Pool;
Tennis; Croquet; Exercise
Room; Sauna; Hot Tub;
No pets; No Smoking;
Children over 12.

offers its guests attentive and even ingenious service, great natural and architectural beauty, palatial furnishings, and magnificent vistas.

Built by New York City businessman Robert Paterson in 1902, a replica of his wife's ancestral home in the Scottish village of Blantyre, east of Glasgow, Blantyre went through several hands in mid-century and fell into disrepair. In 1980 Jack and Jane Fitzpatrick bought the property and with their daughter, Ann, restored it to its present excellent condition: a baronial yet hospitable place — massive but comfortable, grand yet delicately appointed.

A member of the prestigious Relais et Châteaux, Blantyre was awarded the Relais et Châteaux Gold Medal in 1989, bestowed on the hotel that receives the highest number of complimentary guest comments. The five original suite-size bedrooms, with four-poster beds, fireplaces, and magnificent bathrooms, are the true "jewels" in Blantyre's crown. There are three other rooms on the same floor, created in the "nanny's wing" on a different scale, smaller but just as elegant. Twelve more rooms are neatly tucked away in the original Carriage House. There are also two cottages on the grounds, both cozy, endearingly whimsical, and brilliantly situated.

In addition to its superb accommodations, Blantyre has a magnificent gourmet dining room. The hotel maintains four Har-Tru tennis courts and two tournament-size bent-grass croquet courts. A delightful exercise room fashioned out of a former potting shed provides a sauna and hot tub. Nearby is a lovely, landscaped swimming pool. Tanglewood is a mere three miles to the west. Conferences and small meetings are welcome. (Please note that the grounds and buildings are not open to the public for casual viewing.)

BROOK FARM INN
Owners/Innkeepers: Joe &
Anne Miller.
413-637-3013; 800-285-POET.
15 Hawthorne St., Lenox,
MA 01240.
Just off Old Stockbridge Rd.
Price: Expensive.
Credit Cards: D, MC, V.
Special Features: Pool; No
smoking; No pets.

The Millers bought this inn in January 1992 and have continued the special poetry feature started by the previous owners. A 1,400-volume library is supplemented by 75 poets on tape, and a reading takes place every Saturday at 4 p.m., accompanied by tea and scones. A buffet breakfast and afternoon tea are served daily to guests; on Sunday mornings musicians from the nearby Tanglewood Institute perform during breakfast. Twelve antique-furnished rooms, all with private bath, are offered in this large Victorian home, close to many Berkshire attractions. Several of the rooms have been renovated, with special attention lavished on the two large rooms at the front of the house, both with four-posters, sitting areas, and new bathrooms.

CANDLELIGHT INN
Managers: Rebecca & John Hedgecock.
413-637-1555.
35 Walker St., Lenox, MA 01240.
On corner of Walker & Church sts., near village center.
Price: Moderate to Expensive.
Credit Cards: AE, MC, V.
Special Features: No pets; Children over 9.

This comfortable, antique-furnished inn has eight large guest rooms, all with private bath, some retaining their original fixtures. Like the rooms, a small upstairs lounge is furnished in period style. Centrally located in the heart of historic Lenox Village, the inn features a charming restaurant on the main floor. Beside that is a storied wooden bar, once part of the former Curtis Hotel and prior to that, scorched in a fire that destroyed a famous old Boston hotel. Delightfully and professionally run by friendly hosts.

CLIFFWOOD INN
Owners/Managers: Scottie & Joy Farrelly.
413-637-3330.
25 Cliffwood St., Lenox, MA 01240.
Just off Main St., in village.
Price: Expensive to Very Expensive.
Credit Cards: None.
Special Features: Pool; No smoking; No pets; Children over 12.

This special inn, on a quiet, residential street, was built for an ambassador to France in the early 1890s. The elegant public rooms have tall ceilings, polished inlaid hardwood floors, and grand fireplaces. The seven guest rooms have private baths and air conditioning; six come with their own fireplaces. In summer, a continental breakfast is served on the spacious veranda overlooking the gardens and pool. On winter mornings, breakfast is served by a warming fire in the oval dining room with its ornate wood-carved fireplace mantel. Wine, hors d'oeuvres, and friendly conversation served early evening.

CORNELL INN
Manager: David Rolland.
413-637-0562; 880-637-0562.
209 Main St., Lenox, MA 01240.
On Rte. 7A, just N. of center of town.
Price: Expensive to Very Expensive.
Credit Cards: AE, DC, CB, D, MC, V.
Handicap Access: Yes.
Special Features: Spa (sauna, steam room, Jacuzzi); No pets.

The Cornell Inn just keeps getting better. It began life in 1888 as a large, well-built Victorian, and the owners keep making all the right improvements. Each of the ten bedrooms in the main house has its own bath and is furnished with brass or four-poster beds; several have wood-burning fireplaces. There are four additional rooms in the converted carriage house and ten in the adjacent McDonald House, which has recently been renovated. The McDonald House rooms have fireplaces and whirlpool tubs. European plan or MAP.

CRANWELL RESORT AND GOLF CLUB
General Manager: Joe Corso.
413-637-1364; 800-272-6935.

Cranwell is a 380-acre estate high on a hill with one of the finest views of the Berkshire Hills. The 1893 Tudor mansion is surrounded by lawns, gardens, and a par-71 championship golf course.

55 Lee Road, Lenox, MA
01240.
Rte. 20 S. of Lenox center, 3
½ mi. from exit 2 Mass.
Pike.
Price: Expensive to Very
Expensive.
Credit Cards: AE, D, DC,
MC, V.
Handicap Access: Yes.
Special Features: Pool;
Tennis; Golf; No pets.

Guest rooms are in the Mansion (Cranwell Hall); Beecher's Cottage (the farmhouse built on the property in 1853 by Henry Ward Beecher); the Carriage House; and a group of one-bedroom cottages (totaling 64 units). The most luxurious bedrooms in the Mansion are spacious and individually decorated in the Victorian style, with private marble baths. In the various outbuildings, accommodations are slightly simpler and more contemporary, but some have the advantages of wet bar, refrigerator, and/or galley kitchens. Two dining rooms, a lounge, and numerous conference rooms complete the full-service offerings of this property.

**THE PONDS AT
  FOXHOLLOW**
Manager: Linda Syriac.
413-637-1469.
Route 7, Lenox, MA 01240.
Price: Expensive.
Credit Cards: AE, D, MC, V.
Special features: Pools,
  sauna, outdoor sports;
  No pets; Security deposit.

The property was once owned by George Westinghouse, who put in the canoe ponds and stone bridges in the 1890s, and later by Mrs. Alfred G. Vanderbilt. In her day the grounds hosted the forerunner of Tanglewood. Forty-eight condominium units, half with one bedroom, half with two, face onto the ponds. The modern and attractive units are available for two-night visits (full week minimum in July and Aug.) Unlike spending the night in a motel, visitors are staying in someone else's vacation home, using someone else's furniture; hence the security deposit. The units come complete with fully equipped kitchens, including place settings for six to eight persons. "All you have to bring is your food and your clothes," according to Assistant Manager Eileen Lagerwall. For those who want to go first class: color television, VCR, stereo, AC, access to pool and exercise equipment.

EASTOVER
Managers: Susan & Bob
  McNinch & Ticki
  Winsor.
413-637-0625; 800-822-2386.
430 East St., Lenox, MA
  01240.
From Rte. 7 in Lenox, take
  Housatonic St. E., then
  left onto East St. for 1 mi.
Price: Moderate AP; wkly
  rates also.
Credit Cards: AE, D, MC, V.
Special Features: Indoor &
  outdoor pools; Tennis;

Eastover makes no bones about it. Informality is the key! It is a picturesque, amiable place, admirably free of pretension. What would William Fahnestock, the original owner, say? As another of the celebrated Lenox "cottages," this grand Gilded Age house is obviously living out of character but seems to be thriving. The sprawling grounds present tennis, swimming, biking, volleyball, sauna, exercise room, horseback riding, and all sorts of winter activities, including short downhill and cross-country skiing, and the longest tobogganing run in New England.

Exercise room; Sauna; Driving range; Miniature golf; Horseback riding; Mountain biking; Downhill skiing; XC skiing; Toboggan run; No pets; Inquire about children.

Inspired by the remarkable spirit of the late founder, George Bisacca, the staff is up for anything as long as it's fun. To add to the festivities, there is dancing to live music during happy hour and again later in the evening. No liquor license here, so it's BYOB, but the band can play into the wee morning hours. This is not the place for the shy, the reclusive, or those who don't quite feel dressed without a jacket and tie or a skirt and heels. For the good sport, the incurably casual, or the curious, Eastover means relaxation, silliness, and whatever the weekend's theme may be. Special weekends are organized for couples, singles, and families. Prospective guests should call ahead. Eastover has some fun planned.

While wandering the grounds, guests may glimpse the American buffalo, geese, burros, and other pets of the singular Bisacca. The founder's collection of Civil War artifacts and the museum in the "Heritage Room" will fascinate history buffs. The rooms are large in the main house and of various sizes elsewhere.

THE GABLES INN
Manager: Frank Newton.
413-637-3416.
81 Walker St., Lenox, MA 01240.
In center of village.
Price: Moderate to Very Expensive.
Credit Cards: D, MC, V.
Handicapped access: Limited.
Special Features: Pool; Tennis; No Pets; Children over 12.

Charming 1885 home where Edith Wharton summered while her "cottage," the Mount, was being built. Visitors can stay in her room or her husband, Teddy's. He stayed there until 1928, long after she'd taken off. Manager Frank Newton discusses the Whartons knowledgeably. The inn is fully air conditioned. Television, VCR. As it is located in the center of the village, it is within walking distance of almost everything, including Tanglewood. There are 18 bedrooms, all with private baths; nine with fireplaces. A handsome house. Full breakfast.

GARDEN GABLES INN
Owners: Mario & Lynn Mekinda.
413-637-0193.
Box 52, 141 Main St., Lenox, MA 01240.
Price: Moderate to Expensive.
Credit Cards: AE, D, MC, V.
Special Features: Pool; No pets; Children over 11.

Since purchasing this inn in 1987, the Mekinda family has brought it new life. All 18 rooms have been upgraded to include private baths (three have whirlpools); eight rooms have fireplaces; some have private porches; and some have TV. The five acres of landscaped grounds include the largest outdoor pool in Berkshire County. Walking distance to Lenox shops and restaurants, and even to Tanglewood for the hardy. Breakfasts are extra special.

GATEWAYS INN
Owners: Fabrizio and
Rosemary Chiariello.
413-637-2532.
51 Walker St., Lenox, MA
01240.
Just off Main St., in center
of village.
Price: Very Expensive.
Credit Cards: AE, CB, D,
DC, MC, V.
Special Features: Tennis
(nearby public court); No
smoking; No pets;
Children over 12.

This Berkshire "cottage" was built in 1912 by
Harley Procter of Procter and Gamble fame.
Up a graceful, skylighted mahogany staircase from
an award-winning restaurant are 12 spacious, elegant rooms, each with bath, three with fireplaces, a
four-poster here, a canopy there, and peace and
quiet everywhere. Arthur Fiedler stayed here when
performing at Tanglewood, and the "Fiedler Suite"
is especially lovely, with two fireplaces and a
Jacuzzi. Television and telephone in each room.

THE HILLTOP INN
Owner: Vito Perulli.
413-637-1746.
174 Main St., Lenox, MA
01240. In the center of
town.
Price: Expensive to Very
Expensive.
Credit Cards: AE, D, DC,
MC, V.
Handicap Access: Limited.
Special Features: No
smoking; No pets;
Children over 11.

An upscale guest house opened in June 1993 by
the owner of Gateways, with six elegant guest
rooms and splendid public areas. This attractive
Victorian, at the crest of Main St. across the street
from Kennedy Park, has a wraparound porch and a
handsome sitting/breakfast room overlooking the
back lawn. The bedrooms are air-conditioned, and
each has a private bath with period fixtures and
decor, fireplace (many with the original Victorian
tiles), and cable TV. Duvets and cutwork linens add
a romantic touch. The Norman Rockwell suite has a
canopy bed, a sitting room with sofabed, and an
especially splendid bathroom.

THE KEMBLE INN
Owners: Richard & Linda
Reardon.
413-637-4113; 800-353-4113.
2 Kemble St., Lenox, MA
01240.
Rte. 7A in Lenox.
Price: Expensive to Very
Expensive.
Credit Cards: D, MC, V.
Handicap Access: Yes.
Special Features: No
smoking; No pets;
Children over 12.

The newest luxury bed and breakfast inn in Lenox
is named for the actress Fanny Kemble, who
once lived on the street named for her. It occupies yet
another Berkshire "cottage" — this one the Georgian
mansion built by Chester Arthur's secretary of state,
Frederick T. Frelinghuysen, in 1881. Richard
Reardon, a contractor, has supervised the complete
renovation of the house, which included adding several bathrooms. Each of the 15 guest rooms has a private bath and air conditioning, and the furnishings
throughout the house are period reproductions. The
Master Suite has a bedroom with fireplace and a
bathroom with Jacuzzi and another fireplace. The
most impressive features of the inn are the elegant
and spacious common spaces on the ground floor — foyer, reception room, dining room, and back porch — all with magnificent Adam-style paneling — and
the views of the mountains to the back and historic Trinity Church to the front.

**PINE ACRES BED &
   BREAKFAST**
Manager: Karen Fulco.
413-637-2292.
137 New Lenox Rd., Lenox,
   MA 01240
Price: Moderate.
Credit Cards: None.
Special Features: No
   smoking; No children.

A bed and breakfast on a quiet back road, close to all the Berkshire highlights. Three rooms, shared bath, have a pleasant Colonial decor. In summer, a continental breakfast is served on the sun porch.

ROOKWOOD INN
Owners: Amy Lindner-
   Lesser and Stephen
   Lesser.
413-637-9750; 800-223-9750.
11 Old Stockbridge Rd.,
   P.O. Box 1717, Lenox,
   MA 01240.
Just off Main St. in center of
   town.
Price: Expensive to Very
   Expensive.
Credit Cards: AE, MC, V.
Handicap Access: Limited.
Special Features: No
   smoking; No pets.

The Lesser family purchased the inn in the fall of 1996. It's a grand, 166-year-old Victorian lady on a quiet street in back of the Town Hall. All 19 rooms have private bath and eight include fireplaces. The two-level turret room is a marvelous secluded aerie, and the three rooms in the new addition at the back of the house are particularly comfortable.

Stephen Lesser, a gourmet chef, will prepare breakfasts. The Lessers have two children and are delighted to accept well-supervised children as guests. Babysitting can be arranged.

SEVEN HILLS INN
Owners: Jim and Patty
   Eder.
413-637-0060; 800-869-6518.
40 Plunkett St., Lenox, MA
   01240.
At the junction of rtes. 7 &
   20, just beyond The
   Mount.
Price: Moderate to Very
   Expensive.
Credit cards: AE, D, MC, V.
Handicapped Access: Yes.
Special Features: Fireplaces
   in many rooms; Pets
   accepted; Pool.

In 1993, after years in the financial world, the Eders purchased a Berkshire Cottage that formerly belonged to Emily Spencer. It had been a summer house, on 27 well-landscaped acres. They kept the lovely main building largely intact and gutted and redid the Terrace House to make it more useful as an inn. All 52 rooms in both buildings have private baths — to be sure, some in the main house are quite small. Each comfortable and welcoming room is imaginatively decorated in a different style, and all look out on the wooded scene that surrounds Edith Wharton's The Mount. Patty Eder kept much of the original furnishings and traveled to auctions to pick up the rest.

When we visited the stucco inn, it was entertainingly decorated for the holidays with stuffed creatures between the bannister rails. Jim said the tone was less formal than Wheatleigh or Blantyre. As well as the attractive dining room on the first floor of the main building, public spaces include a banquet room suitable for weddings and other functions and a bar from which wafts music on summer evenings. A full breakfast is included in the room rent for a night's stay or guests may choose other combinations of meals and lodgings.

SUMMER HILL FARM
Owners: Sonya Chassell
  Wessel & Michael
  Wessel.
413-442-2057; 800-442-2059.
950 East St., Lenox, MA
  01240.
Off Rtes. 7 & 20 at Holmes
  Rd.; right on Chapman
  Rd. (becomes East St.) to
  red farmhouse on left.
Price: Moderate to
  Expensive.
Credit Cards: AE, MC, V.
Handicap Access: Yes.
Special Features: No pets;
  Children under 1 and
  over 4.

Stay on a working farm. Here is a piece of the old Berkshires, before the days of the grand "cottages" and the influx of New York society. The historic 1770s farmhouse has seven rooms, with a one-bedroom suite recently added in a cottage behind the house. All the rooms have private baths, color TVs, and air conditioning (some have fireplaces), and are furnished with Wessel family antiques. Michael is English, and Sonya lived in England for 36 years, which makes for an appealing cosmopolitan atmosphere. Twenty acres of peaceful countryside at the foot of October Mountain, at the northern edge of Lenox, provide a peaceful stopping place away from the busy village. Wildflower walks, horseback riding, canoeing, cross-country skiing, and bicycling are just a few of the possible pastimes in the area. Horse Sense, a riding school run by the Wessels' daughter, shares the farm. Country breakfast included.

The Village Inn by moonlight.

Bruce MacDonald, courtesy the Village Inn

THE VILLAGE INN
Proprietors: Clifford
  Rudisill & Ray Wilson.
413-637-0020; 800-253-0917.
Box 1810, 16 Church St.,
  Lenox, MA 01240.
Off Walker St. in the center
  of town.

Innkeepers Cliff Rudisill and Ray Wilson are cultivated, hospitable hosts whose personal warmth complements this old, highly respected hostelry. Their pride in restoration and furnishings is evident in their renovations. There are 32 guest rooms, all with private bath and telephone. Six rooms have

Price: Expensive; suite:
Very Expensive.
Credit cards: AE, CB, D,
DC, MC, V.
Handicapped Access: Yes.
Special Features: No
smoking; No pets;
Children over 6.

fireplaces, and there is one suite with a kitchenette. All guest rooms are nonsmoking, as are the public rooms.

The inn was built in 1771 as a farmhouse; four years later, its original owner started to put up weary travelers arriving by horse-drawn coach. By 1815, he had sold his surrounding land, and it is surmised that he was by then exclusively an innkeeper.

Among the nice culinary touches offered today are the hearty breakfasts served on the sunny all-season porch and the English afternoon tea for which the Village Inn is justly famous (neither is included in the summer or fall room rate). There is a full-scale restaurant as well as a downstairs tavern featuring English ales.

WALKER HOUSE

Innkeepers: Peggy &
Richard Houdek.
413-637-1271.
64 Walker St., Lenox, MA
01240.
Price: Moderate to Very
Expensive.
Credit Cards: None.
Handicap Access: Limited.
No smoking.

Comfortable, well-furnished, 1804-vintage Federal house operated by two friendly people. The three acres of garden and woods behind the house are gorgeous. Eight rooms all have private baths; five have fireplaces. The decor in each is an impression of the composer for whom the room is named. Have the Houdeks explain. Sitting rooms offer an impressive collection of music and books, and a new feature is the 7-foot video screen in the Library Theatre, wonderful for opera, films, and sports events. Generous continental breakfast. Within walking distance of Tanglewood, Lenox shops, and restaurants.

WHEATLEIGH

Owners: Susan & Linfield
Simon.
Manager: Francois Thomas.
413-637-0610.
Box 824, Hawthorne Rd.,
Lenox, MA 01240.
From Rte. 183 in Lenox, left
on Hawthorne Rd. to
Wheatleigh sign.
Price: Very Expensive.
Credit Cards: AE, DC, MC,
V.
Special Features: Pool;
Tennis; Fitness Room; No
pets; Children over 9.

Wheatleigh is pure romance. An estate built for heiress Georgie Bruce Cook, wife of "Count" Carlos de Heredia, it encourages flights of imagination. The grounds and setting are absolutely captivating. From the broad terrace, the manicured lawns slope down to a grassy stairway and then to a fountain. Straight ahead is an awesome view of the Stockbridge Bowl with the Berkshire hills in the distance. The heated pool is hidden away in a knoll surrounded by trees, and the tennis court is off in another direction.

Owners Linfield and Susan Simon have preserved the expansive luxury of the interior space and decorative details in this turn-of-the-century mansion. The approach is by way of a winding dri-

Courtesy Lenox Library

veway, then through an enclosed courtyard with a circular drive — reminiscent of a 16th-century private palazzo in the hills outside Florence. Once inside, the Great Hall is impressive with magnificent Tiffany windows lining the grand staircase, newly added antique furnishings, and original brass chandelier. The dark-wooded Conservatory with its cooling breezes is perfect for summer dining.

The 17 guest rooms, completely redecorated in 1993, are baronial in size. Nine still have their working fireplaces. All have television, VCR, personal portable telephones. The bathrooms are splendid, several with original fixtures. Wheatleigh contains an award-winning prix-fixe restaurant, complemented by an award-winning wine list. The premises are available for business meetings, weddings, and parties.

The music room at Whistler's Inn.

Jonathan Sternfield

WHISTLER'S INN
Managers: Richard & Joan
   Mears.
413-637-0975.
5 Greenwood St., Lenox,
   MA 01240.

Charming, much-admired guest house created within an 1820s English Tudor summer estate. Cultivated, accommodating hosts (Richard is an author; Joan is an artist) will put you at ease. The inn is furnished with antiques, chandeliers, and

On corner of Rte. 7A &
  Greenwood St.
Price: Moderate to Very
  Expensive.
Credit Cards: AE, D, MC,
  V.
Special Features: No pets.

Persian rugs, resulting in an Old-World Victorian atmosphere. The interior is full of pleasant surprises, including an extensive library. The 12 bedrooms, all with private bath, are quaint and cozy. From the stone-walled terrace it's possible to walk among seven acres of gardens and woodland. Full breakfast is provided. Afternoon tea is served in the library.

Note: See also Canyon Ranch under "A Luxury Spa" in Chapter 6.

Peru

CHALET D'ALICIA
Managers: Alice & Richard
  Halvorsen.
413-655-8292.
East Windsor Rd., Peru,
  MA 01235.
Off Rte. 8, 3 mi. on Rte. 143,
  then left on E. Windsor
  Rd., 3 mi.
Price: Inexpensive.
Credit Cards: None.
Special Features: No
  Smoking; No Pets.

Remote location in the wilds of the Berkshire hilltowns. Congenial home with three rooms, one with private bath. Full country breakfast. Ideal for nature buffs, cross-country skiers, hunters, or simply for those seeking solitude. Ponds are available for swimming. Hot tub and sauna for total relaxation.

Pittsfield

**CROWNE PLAZA
BERKSHIRE /
BERKSHIRE HILTON
INN**
General Manager: Donald
  Bruce.
413-499-2000.
Berkshire Common, West
  St., Pittsfield, MA 01201.
Off Park Square.
Price: Expensive to Very
  Expensive.
Credit Cards: AE, D, DC,
  MC, V.
Handicap Access: One unit.
Special Features: Indoor
  pool; Sauna; Jacuzzi.

As we went to press, the Berkshire Hilton Inn announced a new affiliation with **Crowne Plaza Hotels** starting in summer 1997. It had been a Hilton for many years.

As a Hilton, this inn has always been far above the average. VIP rooms have a New England flair with prints on the walls, English-style furniture, and chintz. Even the corridor carpeting is classy. A pub-like casual restaurant, the Park Square Grille, with photos of Pittsfield's old Park Square for decoration, complements the more formal Rockwell's. For business people, there is extensive meeting space, from a grand ballroom to small meeting rooms. The top floor of the inn feataures function rooms.

WHITE HORSE INN
Innkeepers: Joe & Linda
  Kalisz.
413-442-2512.
378 South St., Pittsfield, MA
  01201.
Rtes. 7 & 20, S. of town
  center.
Price: Moderate to
  Expensive.
Credit Cards: All.
Special Features: No
  smoking; No pets.

An attractive 1907 Colonial Revival set back from the busy main street, south of the center of Pittsfield. All eight rooms have private baths and air conditioning and have been totally redecorated with pretty linens and wallpapers. Several rooms have fireplaces. There is a kitchenette for guests on the second floor, as well as a small sitting room. A full breakfast is served in the dining room, where guests have individual tables, or on the deck in summer. Perennial gardens and a picnic table complete the picture.

Richmond

**A BED & BREAKFAST IN
  THE BERKSHIRES**
Manager: Doane Perry.
413-698-2817.
Dublin Rd., Richmond, MA
  01254.
Rte. 20 to Rte. 41S, then S.
  on Dublin Rd.
Price: Moderate to
  Expensive.
Credit Cards: AE, MC, V.
Handicap Access: Limited.
Special Features: No
  smoking; Well-behaved
  children & pets welcome.

Serene valley views and personal attention are the hallmarks of this special home, just 3 1/2 miles from both Tanglewood and Hancock Shaker Village. Its serene setting on 3 1/2 acres includes magnificent perennial gardens, a wildflower meadow, an orchard complete with hammock and bluebirds, and in winter, cross-country skiing out the back door. The three guest rooms have private baths, hand-made quilts, antiques, down pillows and comforters, and fresh flowers. In summer, the full country breakfast is served on the spacious porch; there is also complimentary afternoon tea or sherry.

**BERKSHIRE HILLS
  COUNTRY INN**
Owner: Ann Meyer.
413-698-3379.
673 Dean Hill Rd.,
  Richmond, MA 01254.
Off Rte. 41.
Closed: Nov.–May.
Price: Inexpensive.
Credit Cards: None.
Special Features: No
  smoking; No pets;
  Children over 17.

Great view of the Berkshires from this 147-acre hilltop property." It's really marvellous," Ann admits. Three comfortable rooms share a bath. Another has a private bath. Continental breakfast served. Tanglewood and Hancock Shaker Village, just a hop, a skip, and a jump.

**ECHEZEAUX, A
  COUNTRY BED &
  BREAKFAST**
Proprietors: Ronald Barron
  & Ina Wilhelm.

Delightful country retreat, owned by a member of the Boston Symphony Orchestra and frequently rented to other BSO members, this house often fills the surrounding hills with music. The

413-698-2802 (winter 617-
965-3957).
Cheever Rd., Richmond,
MA 01254.
2 ¹/₄ mi. N. on Swamp Rd.
(from W. Stockbridge),
then rt. on Cheever to
end.
Closed: Labor Day–last
wkend. in June.
Price: Moderate.
Credit Cards: None.
Special Features: Pool; No
smoking; No pets.

main house has three antique-furnished rooms,
sharing a bath. An elegant continental breakfast is
served. Guests are just two miles from the front
gate of Tanglewood.

Washington

BUCKSTEEP MANOR
Manager: Domenick Sacco.
413-623-5535.
Washington Mtn. Rd.,
Washington, MA 01223.
Off Rte. 8 N. from Becket.
Price: Inexpensive to
Moderate.
Credit Cards: AE, D, MC,
V.
Handicap Access: Yes.
Special Features: XC ski
center; No Pets; Children
welcome.

Deep in the Washington woods, a cross-country
skier's paradise. Of the 22 rooms, several in
the inn share baths and are comfortably furnished.
Fourteen rooms in the lodge have private baths. In
the summer nine cabins plus campgrounds
increase the number of accommodations and add
to the rustic feeling of the property. Hiking, biking,
and birding opportunities abound. Pool and hot
tub. There's a Memorial Day rock concert on the
lawn. At other times, private parties, weddings,
and conferences gather there. Good vibes, funky
buildings, and that mellow, laid-back feeling predominates.

Windsor

WINDFIELDS FARM
Owners: Carolyn & Arnold
Westwood.
413-684-3786.
154 Windsor Bush Rd.,
Cummington, MA 01026.
Off Rte. 9, outside W.
Cummington, 1.7 mi. N.
on Bush Rd. in Windsor.
Closed: Mar. & Apr.
Price: Inexpensive to
Moderate.
Credit Cards: None.
Special Features: No
smoking; No pets;
Children over 12.

Up in one of the hill towns, this country farmhouse offers a friendly welcome. Two rooms
with shared bath are furnished comfortably with
contemporary and antique furnishings. Guests
have the use of a living room with a fireplace, a
guest refrigerator, and a separate entrance. The
property adjoins the Windsor State Forest,
Windsor Jambs waterfall is within walking distance, and there are a swimming pond and miles of
trails for hiking or skiing. Hearty breakfast.

LODGING NORTH COUNTY

Adams

Bascom Lodge, atop Mount Greylock.

Lauren R. Stevens

BASCOM LODGE
Managers: Candy Merritt,
Appalachian Mtn. Club.
413-443-0011 (9–5 daily).
Summit Road, Adams, MA
01220.
From Rte. 7 take North
Main St. to Rockwell Rd.,
or Notch Road from N.
Adams, to the summit of
Mt. Greylock.
Closed: Mid-Oct.–mid-
May.
Price: Inexpensive.
Credit Cards: MC, V.
Handicap Access: Yes.
Special Features: rustic
lodge, extraordinary
view.

Bascom Lodge, atop Mt. Greylock, is a marvel of dramatic beauty, adventure, and good food. Operated by the Appalachian Mountain Club and owned by the Massachusetts Department of Environmental Management, the lodge at the 3,491-foot summit of the state's highest peak was built of stone and wood by the Civilian Conservation Corps during the Depression. Generations of hikers, birders, and canny travelers have celebrated the accommodations, returning often.

The stone fireplace and hand-cut oak beams cultivate a sense of adventure, which the magnificent hills and trails confirm. This is lodging for the hearty, or at least the sporting. Though linen is supplied, you might want to bring a sleeping bag or extra blanket. The guest rooms are private or dormitory style, with bathrooms down the hall; plan accordingly. Breakfast and dinner are served family style at a set time.

Workshops and field trips on topics ranging from birdwatching and backpacking to geology and photography are offered throughout the hiking season. Appalachian Trail through hikers, campers from Sperry Road Campground, naturalists, and tourists rub elbows in a friendly way. The price is cheap. It is even possible to exchange trail-clearing labor for a five-day stay.

North Adams

BLACKINTON MANOR
Hosts: Dan & Betsy
    Epstein.
413-663-5795; 800-795-8613.
1391 Massachusetts Ave.,
    N. Adams, MA 01247.
One block off Rte. 2,
    minutes from
    Williamstown.
Price: Expensive.
Credit Cards: None.
Special Features: Pool;
    Chamber music; Hiking;
    No smoking; No pets;
    Children over 7.

This handsome Federal mansion offers the most elegant and romantic bed and breakfast experience in North Berkshire County. Reopened in 1993 after a complete renovation by new owners, the 1829 house is notable for its French-Italianate features — including intricate wrought-iron balconies, floor-to-ceiling pocket windows, and a spacious bay window. The five bedrooms, all with private baths and air conditioning, have furnishings, fabrics, and wallpaper appropriate to the period. A full gourmet breakfast is served in the formal dining room or, in summer, on the screened porch or pool patio. Ironed linen.

Dan is pianist for the Raphael Trio and Betsy is an opera singer and invested cantor, so house concerts and chamber music workshops are a regular part of life at Blackinton Manor. Hiking weekends are also a specialty, since the Appalachian Trail is out the back door.

**HOLIDAY INN
    BERKSHIRES**
General Manager: Edward
    Bassi.
413-663-6500.
40 Main St., N. Adams, MA
    01247.
Price: Moderate.
Credit Cards: AE, CB, D,
    DC, MC, V.
Handicap Access: Yes.
Special Features: Indoor
    pool; Sauna; Jacuzzi;
    Fitness center; No pets.

Centrally located in the heart of town and convenient to numerous area attractions, the completely renovated former North Adams Inn calls itself "the newest full-service hotel in the Berkshires." The 87 air-conditioned rooms, all with private bath, color TV, and telephones, are large and decorated in soft tones of purple and mauve. Due Baci, a full-service restaurant, serves breakfast, lunch, and dinner. Conference and meeting facilities are available, and tours are welcome.

TWIN SISTERS INN
Manager: Anthony
    Zappone.
413-663-6933.
Box 1013, 1111 S. State St.,
    N. Adams, MA 01247.
Rte. 8, 2 mi. S. of North
    Adams city hall.
Price: Inexpensive.
Credit Cards: None.
Handicap Access: Limited.
Special Features: No pets;
    Children welcome.

Set on 10 lovely acres, this former carriage house now serves guests as a bed and breakfast. "They come back," Zappone says. Four rooms share two baths. All have televisions. The large living room has a fireplace. The porch has a great view of the eastern Hoosac range, looking toward the Mohawk Trail. Continental breakfast served.

Williamstown

FIELD FARM GUEST HOUSE
Managers: Jean & Sean Cowhig.
413-458-3135.
554 Sloan Rd.,
Williamstown, MA 01267.
From jct. Rtes. 43 & 7, 1 mi. on right.
Price: Moderate.
Credit Cards: None.
Handicap Access: Limited.
Special Features: Pool; Tennis; Hiking trails; No pets.

A property of The Trustees of Reservations, Field Farm comprises 296 acres of land, excellent for hiking and cross-country skiing, and a house built in 1948 in the American Modern style. Five guest rooms all have private bath, two have working fireplaces, and three have sun decks. A swimming pool and tennis courts are added attractions. Country living with views of Mt. Greylock and the Taconic Range, just minutes from the attractions of Williamstown. Sean is an experienced chef, so the breakfasts are to admire — and eat.

GOLDBERRY'S
Hosts: Bev & Ray Scheer.
413-458-3935.
39 Cold Spring Road,
Williamstown, MA 01267.
Rtes. 7 & 2, near Williams Inn.
Price: Moderate.
Credit Cards: None.
Special Features: No smoking; No pets; Children over 3.

J.R.R. Tolkien fans will recognize the name. Hobbits are welcome. This bed and breakfast opened in 1991 in an ideal location, within three blocks of the Williams College campus, the Williamstown Theatre Festival, and the Clark Art Institute. The 1830s house is comfortably furnished with antiques and appropriate companion pieces, and guests are invited to use the living room, dining room, sun porch, and back porch overlooking the perennial gardens. The three bedrooms have private baths. Bev Scheer's gourmet breakfast might include lemon ricotta or pumpkin pancakes and always lots of fresh fruit. This is a popular stopping place for Williams College alumni and parents.

THE HOUSE ON MAIN STREET
Innkeepers: Phyllis, Bud, & Regina Riley.
413-458-3031.
1120 Main St.,
Williamstown, MA 01267.
Near jct. Rtes. 2 & 7, W. of Williams Inn.
Price: Moderate.
Credit Cards: MC, V.
Handicap Access: Limited.
Special Features: No smoking; No pets; Children welcome.

Once known as Victorian Tourist & Antique House, this bed and breakfast has been taking guests since the 1930s. The Rileys became innkeepers in 1991 and are proud of the comment of one satisfied guest: "You have achieved a great combination of Victorian charm and modern comfort."

This home began in the 18th century, with a major Victorian addition in the 1870s. The six guest rooms are light and spacious, with accents of antique furnishings, pretty country prints, and braided rugs. A healthful and hearty breakfast — fruits in season and eggs or pancakes — is served in the country kitchen. Guests may use the parlor and the wicker-laden screened porch. The congenial Rileys are well versed on the attractions of Williamstown, all within walking distance.

LE JARDIN
Manager: Walter Hayn.
413-458-8032.
777 Cold Spring Rd.,
Williamstown, MA
01267.
On Rte. 7 a few mi. S. of
town.
Price: Moderate.
Credit Cards: AE, MC, V.
Special Features: No pets.

Just south of the heart of Williamstown, on a wooded hillside above Rte. 7, Le Jardin offers six cozy rooms, all with private bath, in a large country farmhouse. Well-known restaurant on the first floor.

THE ORCHARDS
Owner: Sayed M. Saleh.
413-458-9611.
222 Adams Rd.
Williamstown, MA
01267.
On Rte. 2, E. of town center.
Price: Expensive to Very
Expensive.
Credit Cards: AE, CB, DC,
MC, V.
Handicap Access: Yes.
Special Features: Pool;
Exercise Center with
sauna, environmental
chamber, and whirlpool;
No pets.

This small luxury hotel, a member of Preferred Hotels & Resorts Worldwide, is reminiscent of an English country inn. Antique furnishings, complimentary afternoon tea, and enormous guest rooms featuring four-poster beds with down pillows are just a few of the amenities. Many rooms have wood-burning fireplaces and bay windows. The Orchards' award-winning restaurant features a menu that reflects New England's heritage and the chef's distinctive international talents. In summer al fresco patio dining is available overlooking the pond in the nicely landscaped inner courtyard. Chocolate chip cookies are a regular bedtime treat. Private conference and meeting rooms.

RIVER BEND FARM
Owners: David and Judy
Loomis.
413-458-3121.
643 Simonds Rd.,
Williamstown, MA
01267.
Rte. 7, $^3/_4$ mi. N. of jct. of
Rtes. 7 & 2 in town
center.
Price: Moderate.
Credit Cards: None.
Closed: Nov.–Mar.
Special Features: restored
1770 tavern.

A stay at River Bend Farm, an authentic 1770 home listed on the National Register of Historic Places and featured on PBS's "This Old House," comes as close to an 18th-century lodging experience as one can have, but with heat and water. The house was built by Colonel Benjamin Simonds as a tavern. Thanks to the Loomises' painstaking work, the original features are intact — wide pine floorboards, magnificent paneling, corner cupboards, and a central chimney containing five separate fireplaces, two ovens, and an attic smoking chamber. Furnishings, accessories, and fabrics used throughout the house are from the period or appropriate to it. Four guest rooms share two very large bathrooms (one was the buttery of the house and its walls are lined with crocks, paddles, and other implements). Breakfast (homemade breads, jams, granola, and River Bend's own honey) is served in the keeping room at the back of the house, and the former tap room is a guest parlor In summer, lawn furniture and a hammock are placed among the perennial and herb gardens, which feature a variety of 18th-century plants.

STEEP ACRES FARM
Owners: Mary & Marvin Gangemi.
413-458-3774.
520 White Oaks Rd., Williamstown, MA 01267.
From Rte. 7, E. on Sand Springs Rd., N. on White Oaks Rd.
Price: Moderate.
Credit Cards: None.
Special Features: Pond for swimming, boating, and fishing; Hiking trails; No smoking; Children 5 and up; No pets.

Two miles from the center of Williamstown, Steep Acres offers country lodging up a long, gravel drive. The 1900 stone and shingle house sits on a hilltop on the Vermont state line, overlooking Mount Greylock. The Gangemis' 50 acres include a 1.5 acre pond for canoeing, trout fishing, and swimming (there are a diving board and raft), and trails for hiking and cross-country skiing. A patio off the sunporch — great for summer breakfasts or reading - - seems to be perched at the top of the world. The house features an attractive decor combining late Victorian oak, wicker, and handsome fabrics. Two of four possible guest rooms available, depending on preference of party; three baths. A full gourmet breakfast and afternoon refreshments are included.

UPLAND MEADOW HOUSE
Owners: Alfred and Pam Whitman
413-458-3990
1249 Northwest Hill Rd., Williamstown, MA 01267
3 mi. from junction of Bulkley St. and Rte. 7 N.
Price: Moderate
Credit cards: None
Handicap access: Yes
Special features: Panoramic view of mountains. No smoking; No pets; Children.

Situated on the eastern slope of the Taconic Range, this modern house and 150 acres of fields and woods reveal a wrap-around view of the Green Mountains, Hoosacs, and Taconics. The land adjoins 2,000 acres of Hopkins Forest, which Williams College makes available to the public for hiking and cross-country skiing. Two downstairs rooms are available, sharing a bath; one room has a private entrance. The Whitmans serve a full breakfast, with fresh fruit in season and jam made from local berries.

Follow gravel Northwest Hill Rd. N.W. from top of Bulkley St. 2.3 mi. The Whitman house is up a long driveway to the left. Call ahead in case of snow or mud. The least expensive of Williamstown B&Bs listed.

WILLIAMS INN
Owners: Carl and Marilyn Faulkner.
413-458-9371.

The generous Faulkners are much respected for making their inn a hub of town activities. Though its architecture is not exactly in keeping

On the Green,
 Williamstown, MA
 01267.
On Main St., junction of
 Rtes. 7 & 2.
Price: Expensive.
Credit Cards: AE, CB, D,
 DC, MC, V.
Handicap Access: Yes.
Special Features: Indoor
 pool; Sauna; Dogs
 permitted.

with the classic Williamstown, The Williams Inn and its staff please a great many North County travelers — and take the hassle of being an interstate bus stop as well. Vast and modern, the facility offers an indoor pool, sauna, and whirlpool, perfect for those cold or rainy days. The Faulkners are energetic about organizing special events, such as horse-drawn wagon rides. Sunday brunch is highly regarded. On weekend nights there is live entertainment — guitar on Friday nights and jazz on Saturdays — in the tavern. Nearby are two of America's fine museums and the renowned Williamstown Theatre Festival. There is no charge for children under 14 in parents' room and pets are welcome in ground-floor rooms.

**THE WILLIAMSTOWN
 BED AND BREAKFAST**
Owners: Kim Rozell &
 Lucinda Edmonds.
413-458-9202.
30 Cold Spring Rd.,
 Williamstown, MA
 01267.
Just off the circle where
 Rtes. 2 & 7 join.
Price: Moderate.
Credit Cards: None.
Special Features: No
 smoking; No pets;
 Children over 10.

Open for business since 1989, the Williamstown Bed & Breakfast credits its success to a central, in-town location and a high proportion of returning guests. This spacious and airy Victorian has been completely renovated and tastefully furnished with a mixture of antiques and comfortable sofas and chairs. Each of the four guest rooms has its own bath and is individually decorated in period oak, maple, or mahogany furniture. Guests have exclusive use of the living room, dining room, and broad front porch. Lingering around the table after Kim Rozell's popular breakfasts — featuring homemade breads, muffins, scones and always a hot entrée — is standard operating procedure at Williamstown B&B. Summer guests enjoy the perennial gardens and two hammocks for lazy afternoons.

LODGING OUTSIDE THE COUNTY

Salisbury, Connecticut

UNDER MOUNTAIN INN
Owners: Peter & Marged
 Higginson.
860-435-0242.
482 Undermountain Rd.
 (Rte. 41), Salisbury, CT
 06068.

Have you been longing for a quiet day in the English countryside? Save the airfare and drive to the Under Mountain Inn, a 1730s Colonial set on three acres on a picturesque country road. Owner Peter Higginson, retired from the British

4 mi. N. on Rte. 41 from center of Salisbury.
Price: Expensive to Very Expensive (MAP).
Credit Cards: MC, V.
Special Features: No pets; No smoking; Children over 6.

Merchant Navy, has recreated his heritage in Connecticut.

The menu in the dining rooms, warmed by a fire in winter, features such English staples as steak and kidney pie, bangers and mash, and shepherd's pie. The seven rooms in the inn are partially furnished with antiques, and all have private baths. Hartley and Gibson sherry in the rooms, afternoon tea, and Gilchrist & Soames soaps all add to the British atmosphere. A wealth of British books, audiotapes, and videos in the parlor invite a quiet afternoon far removed from the hectic city. Tally ho!

THE WHITE HART INN
Owner/Managers: Terry & Juliet Moore.
860-435-0030.
The Village Green, Box 385, Salisbury, CT 06068.
At intersection of Rtes. 41 & 44, in center of town.
Price: Moderate to Very Expensive.
Credit Cards: AE, CB, DC, MC, V.
Handicap Access: Yes.
Special Features: Pets in some rooms; Children welcome; Senior Citizen Discount.

Those indomitable restaurateurs Terry and Juliet Moore have restored this landmark inn to polished perfection. The oldest portions of the inn were built sometime prior to 1810, when records indicate the farmhouse was converted to a tavern. The public spaces display an air of country elegance and comfort. Twenty-six charming guest rooms (three suites) all offer private baths, air conditioning, phones, and cable TV. Meals are not included in the rate but breakfast, lunch, and a light dinner are served in the Garden Room and in the historic tavern. The American Grill is a popular destination for dinner and Sunday brunch. Whether planning a wedding reception, business meeting, romantic weekend, or escape from city pressures, the White Hart has it all.

Averill Park, New York

THE GREGORY HOUSE
Owners/Innkeepers: Bette & Bob Jewell.
518-674-3774.
Box 677, Rte. 43, Averill Park, NY 12018.
Price: Moderate.
Credit Cards: AE, CB, D, DC, MC, V.
Handicap Access: Limited.
Special Features: Pool; No smoking; No pets.

The Gregory House has a clean, sophisticated country look. Twelve guest rooms, all with air conditioning and private baths, have stenciled walls and attractive country furnishings. A continental breakfast is served to guests, and the cozy bar and the restaurant are open for dinner Tuesday–Sunday. Averill Park is convenient to Williamstown attractions and North County ski areas as well as to the Saratoga Performing Arts Center.

Berlin, New York

THE SEDGWICK INN
Innkeeper: Edie Evans.
518-658-2334.
Rte. 22, Box 250, Berlin, NY
 12022.
Price: Moderate to
 Expensive.
Credit Cards: AE, CB, D,
 DC, MC, V.
Special Features: Gift shop;
 Smoking, Pets, and
 Children in annex only.

A 1791 house with restaurant and small motel unit (the annex) attached, set on 12 acres in the country. Privately owned and operated, this quaint, well-kept property offers comfortable rooms and proximity to Berkshire attractions. Rooms in the main house are preferred.

Hillsdale, New York

AUBERGINE
Owner: David Lawson.
518-325-3412.
Box 387, Hillsdale, NY
 12529.
At junction of Rtes. 22 & 23.
Price: Moderate to
 expensive.
Credit Cards: MC, V.
Special features: No
 smoking; Call ahead
 about pets.

This Federal-period brick house, reflecting New York State's Dutch Colonial heritage, strikes a noble profile above a busy intersection in a small upstate New York village. Four delightful, large rooms, two with private bath, are thoughtfully furnished. The owner/chef, a Minnesotan, operates an extraordinary restaurant on the ground floor. A "high continental" breakfast is available to residents for an additional $10.

**SWISS HUTTE
 COUNTRY INN**
Owners: Gert & Cindy
 Alper.
518-325-3333; 413-528-6200.
Rte. 23, Hillsdale, NY.
 12529
2 mi. E. of Hillsdale on
 MA-NY border.
Price: Moderate to
 Expensive.
Credit Cards: MC, V.
Handicap Access: Yes.
Special Features: Pool;
 Tennis.

At the entrance to the popular South County ski area, Catamount, this property boasts several tennis courts, a pool, lovely gardens, and, of course, an inviting downhill slope in its front yard. Fifteen comfortable, well-furnished rooms are split between the original wooden chalet and a newer building. An award-winning restaurant completes the picture (See Chapter Five, *Restaurants & Food Purveyors*). A modified American plan is available. Breakfast is not included with the basic room rate.

New Lebanon, New York

**CHURCHILL HOUSE
 BED & BREAKFAST**

Churchill House was built in 1797 for Rev. Silas Churchill and remained in the Churchill

Hosts: Michele & Michael Arthur.
518-766-5852; 800-532-2702
Rte. 22 & Churchill Rd., P.O. Box 252, New Lebanon, NY 12125.
Rte. 22, 0.25 mi. S. of Rte. 20.
Price: Moderate.
Credit Cards: D.
Special Features: Hiking trails; No smoking; No pets; Children welcome.

family until 1965. The Arthurs bought the property, which includes 18 acres of land, in 1991. Churchill House has four guest rooms with private baths. Two can have an additional bed in the room. There is a charming room under the eaves, with trails of ivy stenciled by Michele. Each room has bathrobes, and the beds are mounded high with featherbeds. The living room and wraparound front porch with views of the Taconic Hills are for the guests' use. A full breakfast is served on weekends, with dietary restrictions accommodated. Away from the madding crowds but handy to all Berkshire attractions.

Stephentown, New York

THE MILL HOUSE INN
Innkeepers: Frank Tallet and family.
413-738-5348.
Box 1079, Hancock, MA 01237.
Rte 43, E. Stephentown, NY (on the state line).
Price: Moderate to Expensive.
Credit Cards: AE, MC, V.
Handicap Access: One unit.
Closed: Mar. 15–May 15; Sept. 1–Oct. 1.
Special Features: Pool; No smoking; No pets.

O ld-World touches in a former sawmill enhance this cozy, well-regarded country inn, with refurbishing ongoing. Furnished with antiques, the rooms are warm and whimsical. A living room with fireplace offers warm comfort. Seven rooms and five suites, several with fireplaces of their own; all have private baths, air conditioning, and telephones. Set on three peaceful, rural acres with formal gardens, stone walls, garden paths, and a pool, it's the perfect romantic escape — a touch of country with a European flair. Afternoon tea and continental breakfast are served; a full breakfast is available à la carte.

MOTELS

South County

Barrington Court Motel (413-528-2340; 400 Stockbridge Rd., Rte. 7, Gt. Barrington, MA 01230; on Rte. 7, N. of Gt. Barrington) Price: Moderate to Very Expensive. AE, MC, V. Handicap access. 21 motel units and 2 suites, refrig., coffee makers in every room. Suites have kitchenettes; Jacuzzi; pool.

Briarcliff Motor Lodge (413-528-3000; 506 Stockbridge Rd., Gt. Barrington, MA 01230; on Rte 7, N. of town) Price: Inexpensive to Moderate. AE, D, DC, MC, V. Handicap access. 16 units on spacious landscaped grounds, with view of Monument Mtn.

Days Motor Inn (413-243-0501; Rte. 102, Box 426, Lee, MA 01238; between

Stockbridge and Lee) Price: Moderate to Expensive. AE, D, DC, MC, V. 26 units in convenient location to Tanglewood, Berkshire Theatre Festival, Jacob's Pillow, and other South County attractions. Color cable TV; air conditioning.

Gaslight Motor Lodge (413-243-9701; Rte. 20, Greenwater Pond, Lee, MA 01238; 5 mi. E. of town) Price: Inexpensive to Moderate. MC, V. 8 units on pond with own swimming, paddle boats, row boats, ice skating, cross-country skiing and hiking, as the Appalachian Trail crosses property. Refrig. in every room, complimentary coffee or tea in morning.

Lantern House Motel (413-528-2350; Stockbridge Rd., Box 97, Gt. Barrington, MA 01230; on Rte. 7, 1 mi. N. of Gt. Barrington) Price: Moderate (3-night weekend min. in summer). D, MC, V. Handicap access. Pool. Refrig., phones, and color cable TV in the 14 rooms.

Laurel Hill Motel (413-243-0813; Box 285, Rte. 20, Lee, MA 01238; Laurel St. N. of Lee) Price: Moderate to Expensive. AE, CB, D, DC, MC, V. 20-unit motel with pool and view.

Monument Mountain Motel (413-528-3272; 249 Stockbridge Rd., Gt. Barrington, MA 01230; on Rte. 7, just N. of Gt. Barrington) Price: Moderate to Expensive. AE, CB, D, DC, MC, V. Far above an ordinary motel. Color cable TV, heated pool, lighted tennis courts, picnic tables, 20 acres that border the Housatonic River, spectacular flower gardens. No pets.

Mountain View Motel (413-528-0250; 304 State Rd., Gt. Barrington, MA 01230; Rte. 23, E. of town) Price: Moderate to Expensive. AE, D, MC, V. 17 units. Color cable TV, in-room phones, and coffee. No pets. 1 mi. Butternut.

Pilgrim Motor Inn (413-243-1328; 165 Housatonic St., Lee, MA 01238; on Rte. 20, E. of Lee) Price: Expensive. AE, D, DC, MC, V. 34 units. Color cable TV in every room. Pool.

Pleasant Valley Motel (413-232-8511; Rte. 102, W. Stockbridge, MA 01266; sandwiched between Exit 1, Mass. Pike & Rte. 102) Price: Inexpensive to Expensive. AE, D, MC, V. Handicap access. Color cable TV in every room. Pool. Continental breakfast included summer weekends.

Sunset Motel (413-243-0302; 150 Housatonic St., Lee, MA 01238; on Rte. 20, in town) Price: Inexpensive to Expensive. AE, CB, D, DC, MC V. 22 units with AC, color cable TV, pool. Convenient to Mass. Pike, but may be noisy.

Super 8 Motel (413-243-0143; 170 Housatonic St., Lee, MA 01238; just off Mass. Pike on Rte. 20) Price: Inexpensive to Moderate. AE, D, DC, MC, V. Handicap access. Non-smoking rooms, free coffee & paper. VCRs for rent. This two-level motel, next to a Burger King and conveniently close to the Mass. Pike, has 49 attractive rooms, decorated in cranberry and gray, all with private baths. Some come with king-sized bed and others with two doubles. Color cable TV.

Central County

Berkshire North Cottages (413-442-7469; 121 S. Main St., Lanesborough, MA 01237) Price: Inexpensive to Moderate. MC, V. 5 cottages, 3 with full kitchens, 2 with refrigerator and hot plates only. Color cable TV. Closed Nov. mid May.

Econolodge International Choice Hotel (Pittsfield-Lenox Rd., Lenox) Not reviewed at press time; scheduled to open late summer 1997 on the site of the former Golden Key Motel.

Heart of the Berkshires Motel (413-443-1255; 970 W. Housatonic St., Pittsfield, MA 01201; on Rte. 20, W. of town) Price: Inexpensive to Moderate. AE, D, MC, V. 16 units with color cable TV & AC in all rooms. Outdoor pool.

Holiday Inn Express. Operating at press time as the **Mayflower Motor Inn** (see below), this inn is scheduled to be renovated, enlarged, and reopened as a Holiday Inn in late 1997 or early 1998.

Huntsman Motel (413-442-8714; 1350 W. Housatonic St., Pittsfield, MA 01201; on Rte. 20, W. of town) Price: Moderate. AE, MC, V. 14 units plus a suite with kitchen. All units have color cable TV.

Inn at Village Square (413-684-0860; 645 Main St., Dalton, MA 01226) Price: Moderate. AE, D, MC, V. Handicap access. A 16-unit motel, with a restaurant attached. Color cable TV.

Lamp Post Motel (413-443-2979; Rte. 7, Box 335, Lanesborough, MA 01237; on Rte. 7, N. of Pittsfield) Price: Inexpensive to Moderate. AE, D, MC, V. 10 units, all with efficiency kitchens. Pool available. Color cable TV.

Lanesborough Mountain Motel (413-442-6717; Rte. 7, Box 335, Lanesborough, MA 01237) Price: Inexpensive to Moderate. Special mid-week rates. AE, D, MC, V. 10 rooms with in-room phones. 5 mi. to Jiminy and Brodie.

Lenox Motel (413-499-0324; Rtes. 7 & 20, Box 713, Lenox, MA 01240; N. of Lenox) Price: Expensive. AE, D, DC, MC, V. 17 units with AC, color cable TV, and coffee in rooms. Pool.

Mayflower Motor Inn (413-443-4468; Rtes. 7 & 20, Box 952, 474 Pittsfield Lenox Rd., Lenox, MA 01240; N. of Lenox) Price: Moderate to Expensive. AE, CB, D, DC, MC, V. Color cable TV. Swimming pool, some views. 20 rooms. This will become the **Holiday Inn Express** in late 1997 or early 1998, with renovations and added rooms.

Mountain View Motel (413-442-1009; 499 S. Main St., Lanesborough, MA 01237) Price: Inexpensive to Moderate. AE, D, MC, V. Color cable TV. 13 rooms in motel. Efficiency cottages available year-round.

Pittsfield City Motel (413-443-3000; 150 W. Housatonic St., Pittsfield, MA 01201; on Rte. 20, W. of town) Price: Moderate to Expensive. AE, MC, V. 38 recently refurbished units with AC, color cable TV and direct-dial phones in rooms. Pool.

Pittsfield Travelodge (413-443-5661, 800-578-7878; 16 Cheshire Rd., Pittsfield, MA 01201; at junction of Rtes. 8 & 9) Near Berkshire Mall. Price: Moderate to Expensive. AE, CB, D, DC, MC, V. Handicap access. 47 units with color cable TV.

Quality Inn (413-637-4244; 800-442-4201; 130 Pittsfield Rd., Rte. 7, Lenox, MA 01240) Price: Expensive. AE, D, DC, MC, V. Outdoor pool, tennis court. Restaurant & lounge. Color cable TV, refrigerators, and coffee makers in each room.

Susse Chalet Motor Lodge (413-637-3560; 800-2CHALET; 194 Pittsfield Rd., Lenox, MA 01240; on Rtes. 7 and 20, N. of town) Price: Expensive. AE, D, DC, MC, V. 59 units all with AC, color cable TV. Pool.

Howard Johnson Motel (413-442-4000; 462 Pittsfield Rd., Lenox, MA 01240; on Rtes. 7 & 20, N. of town) Price: Moderate to Very Expensive. AE, D, DC, MC, V. 44 units with AC, color cable TV; some with Jacuzzis. Pool.

Wagon Wheel Motel (413-445-4532; 484 Pittsfield Rd., Box 808, Lenox, MA 01240; 3 mi. N. of Lenox center) Price: Moderate to Expensive. AE, D, MC, V. 17 units with color cable TV.

The Weathervane Motel (413-443-3230; 475 S. Main St., Lanesborough, MA 01237; on Rte. 7, S. of town) Price: Moderate. AE, CB, D, MC, V. 17 units. Pool.

The Yankee Home Comfort (413-499-3700; 461 Pittsfield Rd., Lenox, MA 01240; on Rtes. 7 & 20, near Pittsfield town line) Price: Moderate to Very Expensive. AE, D, DC, MC, V. Handicap access, color cable TV. This stylish, 61-unit motel has a heated pool with rock waterfall in center, 12 rooms with fireplaces; some queen-sized beds, four-poster beds, and manicured grounds. Three-night minimum.

North County

Berkshire Hills Motel (413-458-3950; Rte. 7, Williamstown, MA 01267; on Rtes. 7 & 2, 2 mi. S. of Williamstown) Price: Inexpensive to Moderate. D, MC, V. Brick, 2-story motel, spacious, landscaped grounds, heated pool, generous continental breakfast buffet, charming rooms, and gracious, friendly innkeepers who display their collection of more than 200 teddy bears. Non-smoking rooms and king-size beds available. Color cable TV.

Best Western Springs Motor Inn (413-458-5945; Rte. 7, New Ashford, MA 01237; halfway between Pittsfield and Williamstown on Rte. 7) Price: Moderate to Expensive. AE, D, DC, MC, V. This is a well-run motel, conveniently located near several winter ski resorts. 40 standard motel rooms, complemented by two small chalets with fireplaces. Color satellite TV; coffee-maker in every room. Pool, tennis court. The Springs Restaurant across the street.

Carriage House Motel (413-458-5359; Rte. 7, New Ashford, MA 01237) Price: Inexpensive to Moderate. AE, CB, D, DC, MC, V. Partial handicap access. Owned by Brodie Mtn., this grey & yellow motel with 14 units sits high on a hill, behind a respected restaurant. Guests have access to a pool, indoor tennis & racketball, woods, brook, and trails.

Chimney Mirror Motel (413-458-5202; Rte. 2, Williamstown, MA 01267; just E. of town) Price: Moderate. AE, MC, V. 18 units. AAA-approved. Color cable TV; continental breakfast included in summer.

Cozy Corners Motel (413-458-8006; 284 Sand Springs Rd., Williamstown, MA 01267, but actually Rte. 7 N. of town center) Price: Inexpensive to Moderate. AE, D, MC, V. 12 units across from convenience store at gateway to Vermont.

Dublin House Motel (413-443-4752; Rte. 7 at Brodie Mtn., New Ashford, MA 01267; near Lanesborough town line) Price: Moderate. AE, D, DC, MC, V. Owned by Brodie Mtn. Ski Resort. 21 units with convenience over charm, but right at the base of the slopes.

Dug Out Motel (413-743-9737; 99 Howland Ave., Adams, MA 01220; on Rte. 8, going N. out of town) Price: Inexpensive. AE, D, MC, V. Several units have handicap access. Color cable TV; air conditioning. Basic motel unit on road between Adams and N. Adams.

1896 Motel Brookside (413-458-8125; 910 Cold Spring Rd., Rte. 7, Williamstown, MA 01267) Price: Moderate. AE, D, DC, MC, V. As close to a country inn as a motel can get, the 16 attractive rooms have knotty pine, Waverly papers and fabrics, and vintage maple furniture. Scenic Hemlock Brook at the front door. Access to pool at 1896 Pondside. Remote color cable TV. Generous continental breakfast (as well as in-room coffee and tea).

1896 Motel Pondside (413-458-8125; 910 Cold Spring Rd., Rte. 7, Williamstown, MA 01267, just north of 1896 Brookside) Price: Moderate. AE, D, DC, MC, V. Twelve rooms (each 3with 2 queen-size beds) and 1 efficiency suite have Cape Cod curtains and Waverly papers and fabrics in soft colors. Pool. Remote color cable TV. Danish and coffee (as well as in-room coffee and tea).

Four Acres Motel (413-458-8158; 213 Main St., Rte. 2, Williamstown, MA 01267; on Rte. 2) Price: Moderate. AE, CB, D, DC, MC, V. Handicap access. 30 units with color cable TV. Garden area with pool; meeting rooms. Continental breakfast.

Green Valley Motel (413-458-3864; Rte. 7 N., 1214 Simonds Rd., Williamstown, MA 01267; on Rte. 7, N. of town) Price: Moderate. AE, MC, V. 18 units with color cable TV, telephones. Pool. Continental breakfast.

Jericho Valley Inn (413-458-9511 or 800-JERICHO; Rte. 43, Box 239, Williamstown, MA 01267; 9 mi. S. of Williamstown, then 5 mi. W. on Rte. 43) Price: Moderate. AE, MC, V. Heated pool, on 350 mountain acres with spectacular views, fireplace lounge. Near Jiminy Peak and Brodie Mtn. Satellite color TV. Also has suites and cottages. Pets allowed in cottages.

Kerry House Motel (413-443-4753; Rte. 7 at Brodie Mtn., New Ashford, MA 01267; near Lanesborough town line) Price: Moderate. AE, D, DC, MC, V. Owned by Brodie Mtn. Ski Resort, this new 8-unit motel is located on the slopes of Brodie Mtn. Some efficiency apartments are available. Cable TV.

Maple Terrace Motel (413-458-9677; 555 Main St., Williamstown, MA 01267; on Rte 2, just E. of town green) Price: Moderate. AE, D, DC, MC, V. Pool with mountain views. 17 units. Spacious grounds well off the highway. Color cable TV.

New Ashford Motor Inn (413-458-8041; Rte. 7, New Ashford, MA 01237; 1 mi. N. of Brodie Mtn.) Price: Inexpensive to Moderate. AE, MC, V. 16-unit motel made for the skier and traveler who does not insist on old-world charm. Four channels of TV.

Northside Motel (413-458-8107; 45 North St. Williamstown, MA 01267; on Rte. 7, N. of town) Price: Inexpensive. AE, D, DC, MC, V. Handicap access. 33 units with coffee shop for breakfast. Pool. Color cable TV.

Villager Motel (413-458-4046; 953 Simonds Rd, Rte. 7 N. of town) Price: Inexpensive. D, MC, V. 13 AAA country rooms, on main road but set back. Expanded continental breakfast. Color cable TV, air conditioning, in-room phones. Pets OK in two rooms.

Wigwam & Western Summit Cottages (413-663-3205; Rte. 2, Mohawk Trail, Box 7, North Adams, MA 01247) Price: Moderate. AE, D, MC, V. 5 units at the top of the Trail, east and up from the town center. Color TV. Porch with fantastic view of Mt. Greylock. Gift shop. Open late May to mid-Oct.

The Willows Motel (413-458-5768; 480 Main St., Williamstown, MA 01267; on Rte. 2 E. of town) Price: Inexpensive to Moderate. AE, MC, V. 16-room above-average motel. Heated pool. Color cable TV.

CHAPTER FOUR
What to See, What to Do
CULTURE

To glorify God's grandeur by gracefully combining Art and Nature: this was the expressed goal of the Stockbridge Laurel Hill Society in 1853. This mission combined a new appreciation of nature with a well-developed Berkshire cultural awareness that dated from Colonial times, when the earliest schools, churches, and newspapers were the centers of cultural activity. By the early 19th century, artists came to Berkshire to absorb the

Judith Monachina

The Paul Taylor II company, part of Jacob's Pillow's "Inside/Out" series, draws an overflow crowd on a rain-threatened night. In good weather this series is held outdoors prior to mainstage productions.

beauty and to teach its appreciation. By mid-century the tradition of a Berkshire cultural bounty had taken hold.

The county's artistic abundance is out of proportion to its size and population. In music, dance, theater, and other art forms, Berkshire has long had a cultural calendar of astonishing excellence and variety — especially for a mountainous area once thought of as remote.

There are good reasons for this legacy. Summers in the crowded eastern cities were not only unpleasant but frequently unhealthy. Improvements in transportation opened this area while the more dramatic mountain regions of the country remained inaccessible. Even in the mid-1800s a few families of taste, talent, and money were setting the tone of cultural sophistication still found here today. If you have come to Berkshire to escape the city, you are part of a grand old tradition.

A local intelligentsia developed around Stockbridge and Lenox in the early 19th century, and no single family was more dynamic than the convivial and civic-minded Sedgwicks of Stockbridge. Novelist Catherine Sedgwick shares honors with poet William Cullen Bryant as Berkshire's, and America's, first native-born, published writers in their fields. The Sedgwick house and family still grace Stockbridge today.

Herman Melville and Nathaniel Hawthorne lived in Berkshire in the 1850s, along with the even more popular Oliver Wendell Holmes, who returned to his roots by summering in Pittsfield. Edith Wharton came and created an opulent European lifestyle and the novels to go with it. The list of famous artistic residents is lengthy and impressive. Our bibliography (in Chapter Eight, *Information*) cites several engaging books that tell the fascinating story.

When the Berkshires became the "Inland Newport" during the late 19th-century Gilded Age, culture rode into Berkshire along with big money: architectural indulgences, furnishings, musical instruments and people to play them, paintings, chefs with their foreign cuisines, and landscape gardeners. A number of Berkshire estates have become cultural centers, such as Tanglewood for music and The Mount for theater. And yet, as if to remind us that beauty need not be ornate or expensive, Hancock Shaker Village is also a Berkshire cultural legacy of remarkable value and vitality.

Furthermore, leading Berkshire families have always been patrons of the art and the landscape. The Crane family of Crane Paper Co. of Dalton started the Berkshire Museum; Francine and Sterling Clark created the Art Institute in Williamstown; and the Tappan family gave Tanglewood to the Boston Symphony Orchestra. There are hosts of others. We owe them all our thanks.

Many artists drawn to the Berkshires have lived here seasonally, like Edith Wharton, or year-round, like Norman Rockwell. Thousands more have come just to perform or exhibit. But on each, Berkshire has left its mark. When asked what the Berkshires and Tanglewood meant to him, Seiji Ozawa, music director of the Boston Symphony Orchestra, replied: "Tanglewood has an absolutely special connotation for me. It was the first place I ever saw in America since I came to Tanglewood as a student in 1960 at the invitation of Charles Munch. For me and the orchestra, Tanglewood represents an opportunity to appreciate both the beauty of the Berkshires, and of the music we make here."

Art combined with nature, up and down the county, from the fine woodwork in colonist John Ashley's study at Ashley Falls to the nation's four founding documents in Williams College's Chapin Library; from dioramas and Egyptian mummies at the Berkshire Museum in Pittsfield to beautiful flowers and shrubs at the Berkshire Botanical Garden in Stockbridge. In performance halls, museums, libraries, theaters, nightclubs, and historic homes, Berkshire is rich in art beyond measure.

The following descriptions will provide many ideas of where to go and what to do in Berkshire, but they cannot say what's currently playing or showing.

For the larger seasonal schedules, such as Tanglewood and other concert series, Jacob's Pillow, the museums, and the theaters, it's best to write for information. We provide many addresses for you. Tanglewood issues its summer schedule by March 15; other arts organizations soon follow. With that information in hand you can plan a customized Berkshire festival. Telephoning is always a good idea for specifics. Sold-out performances are not uncommon. For information on cultural events as they happen, the *Berkshire Eagle* is the best bet. Especially comprehensive listings can be found in its Thursday magazine supplement, "Berkshires Week."

ARCHITECTURE

Those who enjoy roaming through New England in search of handsome buildings will find Berkshire County an inexhaustible delight. True, they won't find the architecture of the Deep South or the Southwest here. But they will find in Berkshire virtually all other styles popular in North America, from Colonial times to the present. Few counties anywhere can claim this much architectural variety.

The Round Stone Barn at Hancock Shaker Village, seen from the herb garden.

Courtesy Hancock Shaker Village

Berkshire is justly famous for the scores of mansions built during the opulent Gilded Age. Under "Historic Homes" in this chapter, in the chapters called *Restaurants* and *Lodging*, and elsewhere in this book, we describe several of the best surviving examples of these great "cottages," as they were called. But the saga of the sumptuous cottages isn't half the Berkshire building history.

Consider humbler examples: one-room schoolhouses or steepled churches, icons of America's simpler past. Still serving their original function in some Berkshire towns, adapted to alternative uses in others, these white clapboard structures are often handsome and always charming. Some of the best churches are the ones in Alford, Lenox, Lee, Washington, and Lanesborough (a stone structure, c. 1800).

Berkshire villages seem architectural set pieces, so artfully coordinated are their building styles and locations. The villages of Alford, New Marlborough, Stockbridge, and Williamstown have this look. There is a conspicuous absence of neon and plastic commercial clutter in these towns. Feelings of space and grace predominate. Yet also in each town arises the clear sense of the heart of a community where religion (churches), education (schoolhouses), government (town hall), domestic life (private homes), and the honor due the dead (cemeteries) all naturally fit together. People who live in cities or suburbs where all services are decentralized will find such Berkshire villages intriguing as well as architecturally beautiful. New Marlborough bears all of this out with its archetypal village green, surrounded in part by the Colonial-style *Old Inn on the Green* (1760), a fine Federal-style house (1824), and a Greek Revival-style *Congregational Church* (1839).

Berkshire farms have formed this landscape. Almost any country road leads past splendid examples of old farmhouses, with numerous outbuildings, including rugged barns. Some of the barns date to times earlier than the homes. Good rides for farm viewing include Routes 57 (New Marlborough); 41 (south from South Egremont or north from West Stockbridge); and 7 (north from Lanesborough). Dramatic Tudor-style barns from the Gilded Age are still in use at High Lawn Farm (on Lenox Rd., between Lee and Rte. 7, south of Lenox), but the most famous barn in Berkshire is the round stone barn at *Hancock Shaker Village*, described under "Museums" in this chapter.

South County towns have many impressive buildings, among them several interesting industrial sites. Rising above them all is the *Fox River Paper* (c. 1875; Rte. 183 in Housatonic, north of Great Barrington), with its handsome mansard slate roof. A similar mansard slate roof style is pushed to artful extremes on campus buildings at *Simon's Rock College of Bard* (Alford Rd., Great Barrington).

On its *Congregational Church* the village of Lee has the tallest wooden spire in the Berkshires. In South Lee (Rte. 102) is *Historic Merrell Inn*, a Federal-period building still functioning as an inn, exquisitely maintained by the Society for the Preservation of New England Antiquities.

Sheffield, architecturally lovely and filled with antique shops, appropriately prided itself on having preserved the *oldest covered bridge in Massachusetts* (1837). Unfortunately it recently burned, but townspeople hope to erect a duplicate. Otis, a Berkshire hilltown, is graced with *St. Paul's Church* (1829), a fine example of the Gothic Revival style.

Stockbridge dazzles. Architect Stanford White's turn-of-the-century work appears in impressive diversity here: a casino (now the *Berkshire Theatre Festival*; at Rte. 102 and Yale Hill Rd.); a mansion (*Naumkeag*; on Prospect Hill Rd.); a former railroad station (on Rte. 7 south of the village); and a church (*St. Paul's Episcopal*; center of town). We describe the *Mission House*, a Colonial "Historic Home," later in this chapter. Two other Stockbridge churches well worth a look are the red brick *Congregational Church* (Main St., next to Town

Hall); and the Chapel at the **Marian Fathers Seminary** (on Eden Hill, off Prospect Hill Rd.). Whereas the interior of the Congregational Church has a powerful beauty in its plainness, the Marian Fathers Chapel is beautiful for its finely crafted stone, woodwork, painting, and fabrics — much of it done by transplanted European artisans.

Three outlying sites in Stockbridge are worth a drive. The district originally called Curtisville, now known as Interlaken (Rte. 183, north of Rte. 102), boasts several strikingly pretty 18th- and 19th-century homes and a remarkable former tavern-inn, as well as **Citizens Hall** with its Victorian period Second Empire-style exterior details. Another building of note in rural Stockbridge is at Tanglewood's Lions' Gate (Hawthorne St., off Rte. 183), where the replica of Nathaniel Hawthorne's **"Little Red House"** overlooks Stockbridge Bowl and the distant mountains. The estate known as **Linwood** has opened to the public as the site of the new **Norman Rockwell Museum**. The new museum is an upscale New England town hall designed by Robert A. M. Stern, but Charles E. Butler's unpolished marble cottage, **Linwood** (1859), is the architectural highlight of this delightful Berkshire hilltop.

Finally, in South County, a ride out on the Tyringham Rd. (off Rte. 102, south of Lee) and then upland on Jerusalem Rd. will lead to **"Jerusalem,"** the remnants of a Shaker settlement dating from 1792. Five buildings remain, but none is open. Jerusalem Rd. begins in tiny Tyringham Village. Along the Tyringham Valley Rd. is the **Witch House**, a thatched-roof English cottage built by sculptor Henry Kitson in the late 1800s and known presently as **Tyringham Art Gallery**; see "Art Galleries," the next section in this chapter.

Central County abounds with notable architecture. In Dalton, a ride along Main St. (Rte. 9) provides views of the **Crane Paper Mills** (the Old Stone Mill, dating to 1844, is open as a museum in season) and several Crane family estates. In addition to other fine papers, Crane manufactures U.S. currency paper in these venerable mills. In 1816, Zenas Crane, company founder, built a dignified Federal-style house that still stands. There are also three 19th-century Richardsonian Romanesque churches on Main St. in Dalton proper.

In the hilltown of Hinsdale on Rte. 8 are some architectural surprises, vestiges of more prosperous, populous times when various mills were alive and well in the Berkshire highlands. The oldest (1798) Federal-style church in Berkshire is here. A Greek Revival town hall was built in 1848. The public library is in the high Gothic style, designed in 1868 by architect Leopold Eidlitz, who did St. George's Church in New York City and the New York State Capitol in Albany.

The only stone early Gothic Revival church in the county is **St. Luke's Chapel** in Lanesborough (on Rte. 7). Like many other buildings cited in this book, St. Luke's is listed in the National Register of Historic Places.

Equal to any other village in Berkshire as an impressive architectural set piece is stately Lenox. This town has recently seen a commercial revival on its back streets that has spruced up the neighborhood, though some folks fear that it will soon be so trendy and chic as to lose its old New England charm. Recommended viewing in the historic center of the village includes the *Lenox Academy* (Federal style, 1803); the irresistibly photogenic *Church on the Hill* (1805); the *Lenox Library* (1815; see "Libraries" in this chapter). All three buildings are on Main St. (Rte. 7A). The *Curtis Hotel*, dominating the center of town, is now restored and converted to an apartment complex. From the Gilded Age to recent times, the Curtis was one of Berkshire's most fashionable addresses for travelers. Not far from Lenox village, on Rte. 20 heading toward Lee, is the *Cranwell* cottage, once the Jesuit-run Cranwell School.

Pittsfield's architectural record is a distinguished though problematic one. Preservation and restoration nowadays receive good attention, as a walk around Park Square reveals. Several new buildings integrate quite well, with the ornate elegance of the old Venetian Gothic Athenaeum, with the two churches, with the bank buildings, and with the courthouse — all dating from the 19th-century.

The former *Berkshire Eagle* newspaper building (on Eagle St., off North St.) is a fine example of the Art Deco style. Set on a triangle, it looks like a miniature of Chicago's Flatiron Building. Another important business structure in Pittsfield is the General Electric Plastics House, a handsome and interesting experimental and display house in the Plastics Division's new world headquarters complex. Address? "Plastics Ave.," of course (between Merrill Rd. and Dalton Ave.).

North County provides stark contrasts in architecture and much variety in the stories buildings tell about social history. The cities of Adams and North Adams owe their expansion to industrial times that are now long past. Revitalization proceeds, as some of the abandoned textile mills are converted to other uses. The idle *Sprague Electric plant* is already in transition to become a mammoth museum of contemporary art (visual and performing), or "Mass MoCA." Although urban renewal hit the downtowns unkindly, Adams and North Adams have recently beautified their main streets. In North Adams, *Western Heritage Gateway State Park* celebrates a 19th-century architectural and engineering wonder, the *Hoosac Tunnel*. (See "Museums" in this chapter.) The spires of North Adams's many churches are a pretty sight when descending into the city from the west on Rte 2. In Adams, suffragettes will want to pass the *Susan B. Anthony Birthplace* (1814; a private home near the corner of East Rd. and East St.); and the *Quaker Meeting House* (1782; near the end of Friends St.), another National Register of Historic Places building.

Williamstown has more of a country feel. Homes from Colonial to contemporary, a college that has been adding buildings nearly since the country began, quaint shops, and two masterfully designed art museums (the *Clark Art Institute* and the *Williams College Museum of Art*, both described under "Museums") await you. *West College* (1790), *Griffin Hall* (1828), the oldest (1838) extant college observatory in the U.S., and the 1802 *President's House* at Williams are alone worth a guided tour of the campus (413-597-3131 for infor-

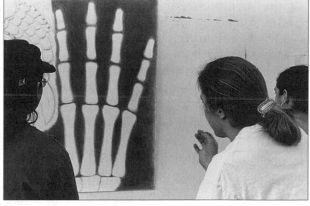

Williams College art students critique each other's work in the new Spencer Studio Art Building.

Judith Monachina

mation, or guide yourself via the large map in front of the main administration building, Hopkins Hall). The much photographed *First Congregational Church* (1869) is the replica of a Colonial one that burned in Old Lyme, Conn. The *Williamstown Public Library*, which houses the local history museum, faces the *1753 House*, built with authentic methods and materials for the town's bicentennial, on Field Park.

In Berkshire, a proud history still stands.

ARTS CLASSES

The world is turning interactive, and art in the Berkshires is part of the trend. Not content with simply looking at fine art and craft work in the multitude of galleries and museums in the county, many residents and visitors want to create art as well, and opportunities are growing apace. Art classes are offered from time to time by the Berkshire Museum, the Norman Rockwell Museum, and the YMCAs (call for their schedules), and several local institutions have made education the mainspring of their business.

BERKSHIRE CENTER FOR CONTEMPORARY GLASS
413-232-4666.
6 Harris Street, P.O. Box 377.
West Stockbridge.

Located just off Main Street opposite Truc and La Bruschetta restaurants, BCCG is a gallery, a glassblowing studio, and a school for glassblowers from beginner through accomplished. Founded and run by artist/sculptors Edward and Judy Bates Merritt, it incorporates the *All Fired Up Gallery* offering fine glass and other art craft work by local professionals. The glassblowing studio is available to qualified glassblowers and their students. Best of all, the Merritts offer an array of well-structured glassblowing workshops and classes for beginners and intermediates. Spend two hours at a Saturday Workshop morning and make your own paperweight; do a whole Glassblowing Getaway Weekend, or take a three-week mini-course or a full beginner course. A great way to entertain yourself and friends any time of year, but especially satisfying on a winter weekend.

INTERLAKEN SCHOOL OF ART
413-298-5252.
P.O. Box 1400.
Stockbridge, MA 01262.

Founded in 1992 by eminent handweaver and visionary Sam Kasten (see the "Fabrics and Weavers" sidebar, in Chapter 7, *Shopping*), Interlaken has developed into a full scale, year-round school of the arts. It is located midway between Stockbridge and Lenox in Interlaken village, in historic Citizens Hall on Hill Road, just off Route 183 via Trask Lane. Interlaken has something for everyone with an artistic inclination. It offers single classes, full semester courses, half-day to weekend workshops, and lectures in painting, drawing, ceramics, sculpture, metal, jewelry, and textiles of several sorts. There are programs in all categories for children as well as adults. The faculty draws both on the deep reservoirs of local artistic talent and on visiting teachers and lecturers of international repute. Call for a catalog and build the visual arts into your weekend, or your whole summer.

CINEMA

IMAGES CINEMA

North County's most dynamic movie house is flying high. Threatened by skyrocketing rents, Images pulled itself together in the summer of '89, with the help of Williamstown resident and actor Christopher Reeve — whose voice asks you not to put your feet on the seats. So Images lives on in refurbished modernity, for a fine future of feature films. Eclectic, exciting: the best from camp to classic. *Images Cinema:* 413-458-5612; 55 Spring St., Williamstown, MA 01267.

LITTLE CINEMA

This is the great little film festival in Berkshire, now featuring state-of-the-art projection and sound, and running year-round. Fine American and foreign films, downstairs in the Berkshire Museum.

Little Cinema: at Berkshire Museum, 413-443-7171; 39 South St., Pittsfield, MA 01201.

THE MAHAIWE

Reminding you of how movie palaces used to look, the Mahaiwe's ornate elegance survives. Now the spruced-up theater hosts special live concerts and occasional children's weekend movie matinees between conventional first-run movie offerings. More than the sum of its magnificent movies, the Mahaiwe is a local treasure. A multiplex has been added nearby (see below).
The Mahaiwe: 413-528-0100; 14 Castle St., Great Barrington, MA 01230.

OTHER CINEMA

South County

Mahaiwe Triplex (413-528-8885; 70 Railroad St., rear entrance, Great Barrington) Part of the Hoyts chain. Three modern theaters with Kintek stereo and surround sound, offering first-run films, refeshments.

Simon's Rock College of Bard (413-528-0771; Alford Rd., Great Barrington) Occasional classics and fun films, open to the public. Phone for information.

Central County

Berkshire Mall Cinemas (413-499-2558; Berkshire Mall, Rte. 8 and Old State Road, Lanesborough) 10 theaters with Dolby stereo, Kintek stereo, action, adventure, drama, comedy, popcorn. Part of the Hoyt chain.

Berkshire Community College (413-499-4660; Koussevitsky Arts Center, 1350 West St., Pittsfield) Series related to a theme.

Pittsfield Cinema Center (413-443-9639; Rte. 20, West Housatonic St., Pittsfield) Unlimited free parking and a choice of eleven (that's 11) different commercial flicks nightly.

Proposed: a downtown Pittsfield multiplex. Check it out.

North County

Hoyt's North Adams Cinema (413-663-5873; Rte. 8, Curran Highway) North County's multiplex, with six screens.

DANCE

JACOB'S PILLOW DANCE FESTIVAL
413-243-0745; winter
413-637-1372
Box 287, Lee, MA 01238.
Off Rte. 20, in Becket, 8 mi. E. of Lee.

America's first and oldest summer dance festival, Jacob's Pillow keeps step with the times, presenting the best in classical, modern, post-modern, jazz, and ethnic dance. Its schedule of offerings reads like a *Who's Who* of contemporary dance, featuring over the years Merce Cunningham, Dame

Bill T. Jones/Arnie Zane Dance Company at Jacob's Pillow.

Michael Mazzeo, courtesy Jacob's Pillow.

Season: Summer: Tues.–Sun.
Tickets: $10–$40.
Gift shop.

Margot Fonteyn, Peter Martins, Alicia Markova, Twyla Tharp, Alexander Gudunov, Martha Graham, Paul Taylor, Alvin Ailey, and the Pilobolus troupe, among many others.

High on a hillside in Becket is the farm that famed dancer Ted Shawn bought after successfully touring with his wife, Ruth St. Denis, and the "Denishawn" troupe in the 1920s. Here Shawn worked to establish dance as a legitimate profession for men, founding a world-class dance performance center and a school for dance. The school continues to flourish along with the festival, honoring its founder's heartfelt philosophy that the best dancers in the world make the most inspirational dance instructors. In addition to performing here, some of the Pillow's visiting dance luminaries stay on to teach master classes in the compound's rustic studios.

Drive up to the Pillow early to stroll among those studios where works are in progress and dancers are in development. Look through a window and watch choreography created before your very eyes. Walk down to the Pillow's natural outdoor theater, "Inside/Out," and watch avant-garde and experimental pieces in rehearsal and in performance. And after savoring that dance hors d'oeuvre, you might want to sup at the Pillow. Happily, here too there are several lovely options. You can dine at the Pillow Cafe, feasting under a brightly colored tent, or you can take your dinner over to the picnic area and possibly glimpse a dancer who will be performing later in the Ted Shawn Theatre.

Performances at the Pillow have included the Paul Taylor Company, the witty Mark Morris Dance Group, the jazzy Hubbard Street Dance Company, and the hot young troupe, Philadanco, among others. The Pillow's Studio/Theatre, seating 160, adds a separate 12-week schedule of new and emerging, offbeat companies, complementing the Ted Shawn Theatre's exciting dance schedule.

Everett Dance Company at Mass MoCA, in collaboration with Jacob's Pillow.

Judith Monachina

ALBANY-BERKSHIRE BALLET
413-445-5382.
51 North St., Pittsfield, MA 01201 (Mail).
Concerts at various theaters.
Season: Intermittently year-round.
Tickets: $12–$25; Discounts for seniors, children & groups.

The *New York Times* dance critic Jennifer Dunning put it positively in her review: "Berkshire Ballet can be counted on for impressively clear classical technique and fresh performing." Said the influential *Dance Magazine*: "Berkshire Ballet displays solid training, a distinctly soft, lyrical style, and a wide choreographic range. In short, it is a company with integrity and taste."

Performing frequently at Berkshire Community College's Koussevitzky Theatre, at the Consolati Art Center, and at the Palace Theatre in Albany and Symphony Hall in Springfield, the Albany-Berkshire Ballet also tours the Northeast. Lavish productions of *Cinderella* and *Giselle* have highlighted past seasons; one of our favorite Albany-Berkshire Ballet performances was the stunning *Arrow of Time*, by Laura Dean. Fall and winter concerts are capped with the traditional *Nutcracker*, staged at BCC around Christmastime.

OLGA DUNN DANCE CO., INC.
413-528-9674.
321 Main St., Gt. Barrington, MA 01230.
Season: Year-round.
Tickets: $5–$25.

Since its founding in 1977, the Olga Dunn Dance Company has enjoyed such success that it spawned two offspring: the Junior Company and the Olga Dunn Dance Ensemble. Performing a free mix of exuberant, witty jazz and ballet, frequently with live musicians, the Company has also toured area schools, exposing children to the creativity of dance and the excitement of movement. Their annual performances at theaters such as the Mahaiwe and at Great Barrington's Summerfest are highlights of the dance year. As noted dancer and

Berkshire resident Marge Champion put it: "The Olga Dunn Dance Company has become the radiating center of our experience in appreciating and participating in the art of dance."

OTHER DANCE

With Jacob's Pillow bringing the world's best dancers to the Berkshires, it's not surprising that quality dance troupes would spring up here and there throughout the county.

In *South County*, Great Barrington leads the dance. Many of the most innovative performances take place at the *Simon's Rock "ARC,"* the school's barntheater on Alford Rd. Simon's Rock (413-528-0771) has recently been offering two student-faculty dance programs during the school year, one in December, the other in May. These feature original music and choreography by members of the school's dance program. The *March Hare Dance Festival*, with area dancers and choreographers, hops into the Simon's Rock theater at the end of each winter. The *Barrington Ballet* (413-528-4963) gives classes and occasional performances. Eurythmy performances are sometimes given by the *Rudolf Steiner School* (413-528-4015) on West Plain Rd. There is also a flourishing country and contra dance network in the Berkshires. Check the newspapers and bulletin boards for listings.

In *North County*, the *Williams College Dance Department* (413-597-3131) sponsors an ongoing, energetic series with student and faculty choreography, and visiting notables. Chen & Dancers, a Chinese company, have recently been the artists-in-residence; the Chuck Davis African Dance Collective has also been seen and heard in Williamstown. Exciting Kusika, the college's own African dance company, which accompanies itself with drumming, often performs with the spirited Zambezi Marimba Band, usually inviting the audience to join in.

GALLERIES

Since the arrival in Berkshire of nationally recognized turn-of-the-century sculptors Daniel Chester French (who sculpted the Lincoln statue for the Lincoln Memorial) and Sir Henry Hudson Kitson (who did *The Minute Man* at Lexington), the county has been home to an increasing number of talented visual artists.

Much of the art on display in local galleries reflects the uplifting reality of the Berkshire landscape. Many artists focus on the undulating hills and their ever-changing light. Of course local galleries also show other themes and styles as well, from traditional still-life sketches to intriguing abstract paintings. Some galleries show Berkshire artists exclusively; others bring in works from artists the world over. Some are only regularly open in warm weather so, unless you're rambling, it's wise to call ahead.

The biggest news in the Berkshire gallery world is the emergence of Housatonic as the modern art capital of the county. Led by the dynamic and trend-setting *Spazi Contempory Art* at Barbieri's Lumber Mill, this tiny, sleepy village now boasts a number of galleries and artists' studios, making it a must stop on any Berkshire art tour.

View of Housatonic rooftops from the windows of Spazi Gallery. This village has become home to many galleries.

Judith Monachina

Emerging also is West Stockbridge, with its jampacked outdoor, riverside sculpture garden and several new, intriguing galleries. And artists are creating new excitement in former mills in North Adams, including Eric Rudd's recent Dark Ride project.

South County

SOUTH EGREMONT

Barbara Moran Fine Arts (413-528-0749; Main St., Rte. 23) Mostly contemporary artwork, but also offers antique country-style furnishings and accent pieces.

GREAT BARRINGTON

Berkshire Art Gallery (413-528-2690; Jenifer House Commons) 19th-century and current Berkshire paintings; some sculpture.

Birdhouse (413-528-0984; 87 Railroad St.) Folk art.

Frames on Wheels (413-528-0997; 84 Railroad St.) A custom framing and gift shop.

Galleria Arriba (413-528-4277; 87 Railroad St.) Contemporary Latin American art.

Kaolin & Co. Pottery (413-528-1531; 80 Rte. 71, near Great Barrington airport) Wheel-thrown and handbuilt ceramics, including sculptures of animals. Elegant home furnishings to whimsical conversation pieces. A richly colored palette; also specializing in black and white.

Lucien Aigner Studios (413-528-3610; 15 Dresser Ave.) Black and white photographs of Europe and the United States by the celebrated master photojournalist Lucien Aigner. Please call for appointment. A permanent public exhibit of some of Aigner's pictures may be viewed at the Great Barrington Town Hall, on the 2nd floor, on weekdays.

Mill River Studio (413-528-9433; 8 Railroad St.) Posters, hand-colored engravings, historic maps, and custom framing.

Simon's Rock of Bard College (413-528-0771; 84 Alford Rd.) Changing exhibits at various venues on campus.

Westenburg Gallery (413-528-9125; 268 Main St.) Johan Westenburg organizes shows by contemporary artists both at this site and at **The Annex** (Mahaiwe Triplex Building, Railroad St.).

HOUSATONIC

Front Street Gallery (413-274-6607; 129 Front St.) Co-op space is open on weekends and has the space to show large paintings.

Le Petit Musee (413-274-1200; 137 Front St.) Sherry Steiner's hole-in-the-wall gallery is so neat and so tiny (7 by 11) that it's made it into *Ripley's Believe It Or Not*. Shows miniatures, smalls, and itty bitties, all of substantial quality.

RiCA (413-274-0200; 395 Park St.) River Contemporary Art gallery (RiCA) schedules exhibits, videos, and performances.

S*A*S Gallery (413-274-0175; 1100 Main St.) Fine art photography, some sculpture.

Spazi Contemporary Art (413-274-3805, 410 Park St.) Leader of the Southern Berkshire pack in hip, contemporary art, this lofty gallery space has been the scene of great shows, avant-garde performance pieces, and outrageous openings.

Tokonoma Gallery Framing Studio (413-274-1166, 401 Park St.) Contemporary arts and crafts, much of it by area artists and artisans. Also hand-built furniture, pottery, jewelry, accessories, framed original Edward Curtis American Indian photographs, sculpture, and much more. Changing fine art shows, too.

LEE

Warehouse Gallery (413-243-8031; 154 West Park St.) Range of 20th-century intercultural work.

MONTEREY

Hayloft Gallery (413-528-1806; Rte. 23) Berkshire watercolors, including popular townscapes, by local artist Leonard Weber.

NEW MARLBOROUGH

Gedney Farm (413-229-3131) Gallery in the beautifully restored barn of an 18th-century inn.

SHEFFIELD

Ann Shanks Photography (413-229-7766; 50 N. Undermountain Rd., Rte. 41) Great classic photographs. By appointment.

Butler Sculpture Park (413-229-8924; 481 Shunpike Rd.) Open daily May–October and winter by appointment, the primary attraction is the outdoor exhibit of Robert Butler's welded sculpture — although smaller pieces are exhibited in his studio. New this year: an 18-acre section for monumental sculpture.

Loring Gallery (413-229-0110; Rte. 7, diagonal from Bradford's auction house) American art, sculpture, and turn-of-the-century posters.

SOUTH LEE

House of Earth Studio (413-243-1575; Rte. 102 east of town center) Contemporary oil, acrylic, and watercolor landscapes in a rammed earth studio.

STOCKBRIDGE

Dolphin Studio (413-298-3735, 11 West Main St.) Creations by the ffrench family, including ceramics, collages, jewelry.

Holsten Galleries of Stockbridge (413-298-3044; Elm St., summer only) Outstanding contemporary objects of art: glass, ceramics, jewelry, paintings, and wall-hangings. One of the world's leading showrooms for sleek, sculptural glass.

Image Gallery (413-298-5500; Main St.) Modern arts (such as the intense and buoyant paintings of Stockbridge teacher Leo Garel) and photography (usually by gallery-owner and master photographer Clemens Kalisher).

Reuss Audubon Galleries (413-298-4074; Pine and Shamrock Sts.) This 19th-century house features a rotating exhibit of the "double elephant folio" bird prints from Audubon's *Birds of America*. (Sales outlet in Great Barrington; see under "Antiques" in Chapter 7, *Shopping*.)

Ronrich (413-298-3556; Rte. 183, 2 mi. south of Tanglewood) Paintings and prints by American artists.

TYRINGHAM

Santarella (413-243-3260; the Gingerbread House, Tyringham Rd.) Originally called "The Witch House," the studio of Sir Henry Hudson Kitson, this structure has a unique rolling thatched roof inspired by the hills. Historic site and museum of Kitson and his work. Sculpture garden, paintings in mixed media.

WEST STOCKBRIDGE

All Fired Up Gallery — Berkshire Center for Contemporary Glass (413-232-4666; 6 Harris St.) Hand-blown contemporary glass, workshops, demonstrations. See also under "Arts Classes," above.

Hotchkiss Mobiles (413-232-0200; 8 Center St., the old farmer's market, near the old train station) Original and colorful mobiles for moving art, both indoors and out. Museum quality at country prices.

Waterside (413-232-7187; 32 Main St.) Contemporary outdoor sculpture garden and fine arts gallery.

Central County

HANCOCK

Beaverpond (413-738-5895; Rte. 43) Berkshire watercolors by owner Richard Heyer and others, custom framing, art classes.

BECKET

Becket Arts Center of the Hilltowns (413-623-6635; Rte. 8) Local shows and programs.

HINSDALE

John Stritch (413-655-8804; 526 Maple St.) Paintings, prints, and Tanglewood poster collection by popular Berkshire artist John Stritch, whose sculpture garden is open by appointment.

Sculptor John Stritch, at his Hinsdale Studio.

Warren Fowler.

LENOX

B.J. Faulkner (413-637-2958; 48 Main St.) Watercolors, oils, and reproductions by owner.

Clark Whitney (413-637-2126; 25 Church St.) Contemporary art.

Concepts of Art (413-637-4845; 65 Church St.) Handcrafted Judaica, photographs, and crafts, including glass, jewelry, pottery, and wood.

Ella Lerner (413-637-3315; 17 Franklin St.) 18th-, 19th-, and 20th-century paintings, American and European art, in one of the area's oldest galleries.

Hado Studio (413-637-1088; 70 Church St.; summer only) Contemporary paintings and sculpture.

The Hand of Man (413-637-0632; at the Curtis Shops, Walker St.) A wide range of appealing crafts, photographs, and paintings.

Hoadley (413-637-2814; 17 Church St.) Contemporary crafts, with a focus on ceramics and jewelry; also glass, wood, and wearable art.

Inspired Planet (413-637-2836; Brushwood Farm, Rtes. 7 & 20) Paintings, furniture, and artifacts from Asia, Africa, and the Americas.

Lenox Gallery of the Fine Art (413-637-2276; 69 Church St.) Paintings, drawings, watercolors by major Berkshire artists.

Stevens & Conron (413-637-0739; the Curtis Shops, 5 Walker St.) Watercolors and pastels, as well as traditional, contemporary crafts.

Towne (413-637-0053; 68 Main St.; downstairs below card shop) Regional paintings, graphics, sculpture, and crafts; framing. 19th-century Berkshire prints and maps.

Ute Stebich (413-637-3566; 69 Church St.) Outstanding international collection of art, from primitive African objects to sleek contemporary glass by Tom Patti; plus outstanding Berkshire-area painters. A must on any Lenox gallery hop.

PITTSFIELD

Berkshire Artisans (413-499-9348; 28 Renne Ave.; 1 block eastward off lower North St.) Exhibitions and workshops at the city's nonprofit municipal arts center. Also a gallery on North St. called **The Annex.**

Berkshire Community College, Koussevitzky Arts Center (413-499-4660; 1350 West St.) Changing exhibitions, 9–5 weekdays.

Pasko Frame & Gift Center (413-442-2680; 243 North St.) Berkshire oil paintings by Walter Pasko, prints and etchings by Pat Buckley Moss, prints and other graphics.

Potala (413-443-5568; 148 North St.) Fine art and crafts from Southeast Asia, Tibet, and Nepal.

Radius Art (413-445-7223; 137 North St.) Fine arts and crafts, often by local artists and craftspeople.

North County

ADAMS

The Alley (413-743-7707; 25 Park Street) Prints and sculpture.

Sylvia's (413-743-9250; 27 Park St., Rte. 8) Fine art and collectibles. Paintings, graphics, and drawings by modern artists.

NORTH ADAMS

Milltown Studios (413-662-2725; 51 Main St.) Works by local and regional artists. Folk singing, jazz, blues, other musical offerings on a regular basis.

Contemporary Artists Center (413-663-9555; 189 Beaver St.) Contemporary art.

WILLIAMSTOWN

1/2 Dozen or So, Mount Greylock Regional High School (413-458-9582; 1781 Cold Spring Rd.) Changing exhibitions open during school hours. Changes monthly.

Hip Pocket (413-458-2250; 181 Main St.) Changing exhibitions. No sign; shares space with Artists' Technical Services Framing Gallery.

Wilson Wilde, Williams College (413-597-3578; Spencer Studio Art Building) Changing student exhibits.

HISTORIC HOMES

ARROWHEAD
413-442-1793.
780 Holmes Rd., Pittsfield,
  MA 01201.
Off Rte. 7, (about 1.5 mi.)
  near Pittsfield-Lenox
  line.
Season: Memorial Day
  Weekend–Labor Day,
  open daily; Sept.–Oct.,
  closed Tues.–Thurs.;
  Winter by appointment.
Fee: Admission charged.
Gift shop.

In 1850, seeking to escape what he later called "the Babylonish brick-kiln of New York," Herman Melville gave in to his yearning "to feel the grass" and moved with his family to the Berkshires. He had already published two tales of his South Sea adventures, *Typee* and *Omoo*; at Arrowhead he took off on the grand literary whale hunt that was to be *Moby Dick*.

Arrowhead is the home of the Berkshire County Historical Society, which offers excellent guided tours through the house. In the second-floor study Melville wrote his great novel looking northward at the Mount Greylock range, its rolling form reminiscent of a giant whale. He dedicated his next novel, *Pierre*, to "Greylock's most excellent majesty." The

Herman Melville, at about the age he wrote Moby Dick.

Nellie Fink

implements of the writer's trade and duplicates of many important books in his library are right here.

The other thoroughly "Melville" room is the tavern, dominated by a grand stone hearth; the writer's brother inscribed the mantel with the opening of Melville's story, "I and My Chimney." Elsewhere is a collection of 19th-century period furnishings, fine arts, and textiles with Berkshire origins, several pieces of which belonged to Melville. The Ammi Phillips folk-art portraits are of particular interest.

Outside, the piazza, site of another story, is impressive, as are the extensive herb garden and a vintage cutting garden. Arrowhead is a lovely picnic spot.

The barn behind the house is the site of cultural programs such as literary readings and historical talks. A video about Berkshire literary figures and artists takes 20 minutes. Those hungry for more Melville can visit "The Melville Room" at the Berkshire Athenaeum on Wendell Ave., also in Pittsfield. (See the Berkshire Athenaeum entry under "Libraries" in this chapter.)

THE MOUNT

Edith Wharton Restoration, Inc.
413-637-1899.
Box 974, Lenox, MA 01240.
On Plunkett St., Lenox, near southern jct. of Rtes. 7 & 7A.
Season: May, Sat.–Sun. 9–2; Memorial Day weekend through October, 9–2; last tour at 2.
Fee: Admission charged.
Book/Gift shop.

In February 1901, the writer and heiress Edith Wharton arrived at the Curtis Hotel in Lenox for a week in the country. She had summered in the area for the preceding two years, and now, having found the "watering place trivialities of Newport" all but intolerable, sought a new site on which to realize the design principles incorporated in her book, *The Decoration of Houses*.

The Georgian Revival house was modeled on Christopher Wren's Belton House in Lincolnshire, England. At first, Wharton retained as architect her old associate, Ogden Codman. When his design fees grew exorbitant, she called upon Francis V. L. Hoppin to complete the job.

Wharton supervised creation of the gardens, orchards, and buildings while finishing her novel, *Disintegration*, writing as always in bed and tossing the pages on the floor for the staff to assemble. The Mount was elegant throughout, boasting marble floors and fireplaces and requiring 12 resident servants.

Judith Monachina

What does Edith Wharton think of what film critic, scholar, and writer Molly Haskell is saying about women in film?

Besides the 14 horses in their stables, the Whartons owned one of the earliest motorcars, a convenience that thrilled the visiting Henry James. In the fall of 1904, James and Wharton motored through Berkshire's autumnal splendor every day, enjoying social afternoons and evenings with visiting sophisticates.

"The Mount was to give me country cares and joys," she wrote, "long happy rides, and drives through the wooded lanes of that loveliest region, the companionship of a few dear friends, and the freedom from trivial obligations which was necessary if I was to go on with my writing. The Mount was my first real home . . . and its blessed influence still lives in me."

Happily, its blessed influence lives on for all of us, as its physical and spiritual restoration continue. Since 1980 Shakespeare & Co. has been performing Shakespeare and plays based on Wharton's years at The Mount, winning national critical acclaim. The National Trust for Historic Preservation bought The Mount to save it from commercial exploitation; the house is run today by Edith Wharton Restoration, Inc. (EWR).

EWR is now being guided by former fundraiser and theatrical producer Stephanie Copeland, who has strengthened The Mount as a locus for female energy, initiating the "Women on Women" lecture series.

In the summer, besides house and garden tours of The Mount, EWR and Shakespeare & Co. continue to offer plays centering on Wharton's life and writings. Among the recent standout presentations was an adaptation of Wharton's *Ethan Frome.*

NAUMKEAG
413-298-3239.
Box 792, Stockbridge, MA
   01262.
Prospect Hill Rd.,
   Stockbridge.

During the Gilded Age of the late 19th century, men and women of power played out their fantasies in Berkshire, dotting the hillsides with dream houses. A most livable example is the mansion of illustrious lawyer Joseph Choate, the summer "cottage" the Choate family came to call

*The Choate mansion,
"Naumkeag."*

Jonathan Sternfield

Season: Memorial Day
　Weekend–Columbus
　Day; Hours, 10–5.
Fee: Admission charged.
Gift Shop.

"Naumkeag" (an Indian word for "place of rest").

Here Joseph Choate found both a retreat from New York City life, as well as an enclave of great legal minds in Supreme Court justices Field, Brewer, and Brown — all Stockbridge residents!

In 1884, Choate bought the property from David Dudley Field and began construction. By the autumn of 1886, their 26-room, shingled, gabled, and dormered Norman-style house was complete, with architectural design by Stanford White and imaginative gardens by the landscaping pioneer, Nathaniel Barret.

The house eventually came into the hands of Choate's daughter, Mable, who added extensively to the gardens, under the direction of landscape architect Fletcher Steele. The Fountain Steps, framed by birches; the Afternoon Garden, an outdoor room; further southward, the Chinese Pagoda and Linden Walk; uphill, the brick-walled Chinese Garden, where mosses and stone Buddhas gather with carved lions and dogs, all shaded by ginkos; to the north, the topiary hedgework of the Evergreen Garden and the fragrance and color of the Rose Garden all reflect decades of inspired and distinctive garden design.

Now held by The Trustees of Reservations, Naumkeag still has its gardens, furnishings, and an extraordinary porcelain collection, much of it from the Far East. The tours are excellent. Often at Christmastime, Naumkeag sparkles with decorations and toys from the Choate era.

CHESTERWOOD
413-298-3579.
Box 827, Stockbridge, MA
　01262.
Off Rte. 183, in Glendale.
Season: May–Oct.; daily
　10–5.

At the age of 25, Daniel Chester French was commissioned by his hometown of Concord, Massachusetts, to create his first public monument, *The Minute Man*. Its lifelike pose and exquisite sense of surface modeling won the artist national acclaim. He had produced his first American icon.

Fee: Admission charged.
Gift Shop.

Years and scores of sculptures later, French sought a permanent country home to augment the New York City studio he maintained. In 1896, he and his wife, Mary, were shown the old Warner Farm and Boys School in the Glendale section of Stockbridge. After taking in the magnificent vista southward toward Monument Mountain, French pronounced it "the best dry view" he had ever seen and promptly arranged to buy the property. Thereafter, he and Mary spent half of each year in New York City, half in Glendale at Chesterwood. "[Glendale] is heaven," he said. "New York is — well, New York."

In Glendale he built a grand residence, studio, and garden complex, which are an enduring and eloquent tableau of his artistry. Here he created his masterpiece, the *Abraham Lincoln* that sits in the Lincoln Memorial in Washington. "What I wanted to convey," said French, "was the mental and physical strength of the great President. . . ." In his studio, filled with memorabilia, visitors can handle sculpting tools. Centerpieces in the studio are his marble *Andromeda*, an erotic work unknown to most Americans; and the fascinating "railway" that carried his works-in-progress out into the revealing daylight.

Hand studies in the Chesterwood studio of sculptor Daniel Chester French.

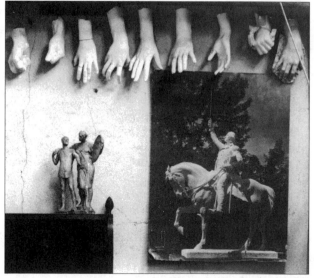

Jonathan Sternfield

French also designed magnificent gardens, maintained today by the National Trust for Historic Preservation. The grounds host an antique auto show in May, a flower show in July, outdoor sculpture July–Oct., Old House Fair in Sept., and Christmas decorations in Nov.

THE MISSION HOUSE
413-298-3239.
Box 792, Stockbridge, MA 01262.
On the corner of Main & Sergeant Sts., in Stockbridge.
Season: Daily, Memorial Day Weekend–Columbus Day; 10–5.
Fee: Admission charged.

In 1735, an earnest minister from Yale came to the Berkshire wilderness to preach to the Mahican Indians. John Sergeant learned the Indian language in which he preached two sermons every Sunday. In the springtime, he went out with the Indians to tap the sugar maples, writing the first account in English of this sugar production method. He frequently talked with the Indians for long hours in the back of his simple log cabin. Under Sergeant's leadership, the Stockbridge Mission flourished.

To please his wife, Abigail, Rev. Sergeant built what is now called Mission House, high on Prospect Hill. The tall and ornate "Connecticut Doorway," with panels representing the Ten Commandments, an open Bible, and St. Andrews' Cross, was carved in Westfield, Connecticut, and dragged by oxen 50 miles over rugged terrain to Stockbridge. This front door and the front rooms were Abigail's domain; in the back, a separate entry and long corridor allowed the Indians access to Sergeant's study.

When he died in 1749, the days of the Stockbridge Mission were numbered, too, even though eminent theologian Jonathan Edwards succeeded him. By 1785 the Indians had been displaced from Stockbridge, driven out for the most part by land speculators.

In 1927 Mabel Choate — the art collector and philanthropist who was heir to Naumkeag — acquired the Mission House. She moved it to its present Main St. position, close to the site of John Sergeant's first log cabin. Boston landscape architect Fletcher Steele, who had designed the gardens at Naumkeag, planted an orderly, symmetrical 18th-century herb, flower, and fruit garden beside the restored, relocated Mission House. There are today apple and quince trees; herbs such as lambs-ear, rue, and southernwood; bright flowers; a grape arbor; and a "salet garden" filled with garden greens.

The Trustees of Reservations maintain Mission House now. Tours of the house capture the 18th century's furnishings and kitchen implements and the feeling of humble domesticity around the dominant central hearth.

COLONEL ASHLEY HOUSE
413-229-8600.
Box 128, Ashley Falls, MA 01222.
On Cooper Hill Rd., Ashley Falls, off Route 7A.
Season: Sat. and Sun., Memorial Day through Oct. 14, plus Mon. holidays, 1–5.
Fee: Admission charged.

In his military role as colonel and as a political radical, John Ashley was destined to become as prominent a citizen as the Revolution would produce in Berkshire. He began his Berkshire life decades earlier, as a surveyor, trudging through the woods and swamps of Sheffield and mapping the wilderness with rod and chain.

Ashley loved what he saw. By 1735 he had built a handsome home on the west bank of the Housatonic River, the oldest extant house in Berkshire County. Framed of well-seasoned oak with chestnut rafters, it was the finest house in Sheffield. Woodworkers from across the colony came to carve paneling and to fashion the gracefully curved staircase. The craftsmanship of Ashley's study, with its broad fireplace and sunburst cupboard, inspires confidence. It was here that Ashley met with a group of his neighbors in early 1773 to draft "The Sheffield Declaration," stating to the world that all people were "equal, free and independent." In Ashley's study, they asserted their independence from Britain, some three years before Thomas Jefferson and associates did so in Philadelphia.

The Sheffield Declaration, 1773

Resolved that Mankind in a State of Nature are equal, free and independent of each other, and have a right to the undisturbed Enjoyment of their lives, their Liberty and Property.

Resolved that it is a well known and undoubted priviledge of the British Constitution that every Subject hath not only a Right to the free and uncontrolled injoyment and Improvement of his estate or property. . . .

Resolved that the late acts of the parlement of Great Britan expres porpos of Rating and regulating the colecting a Revenue in the Colonies; are unconstitutional as thereby the Just earning of our labours and Industry without Any Regard to our own consent are by mere power ravished from us.

Thanks to an excellent restoration and relocation (a quarter-mile from its original site) by The Trustees of Reservations, the Ashley House lives on. An herb garden flourishes outside while Colonial furnishings, a pottery collection, and the original wood paneling survive inside. A visit can complement viewing the extraordinary flowers at Bartholemew's Cobble or antique hunting in the Sheffield-Ashley Falls area.

THE BIDWELL HOUSE
413-528-6888.
Art School Rd., Monterey, MA 01245.
Off Tyringham Road, 1 mi.
Season: Memorial Day–Oct. 15, Tues.–Sun., holidays, 11–4.
Fee: Admission charged.

Bidwell is one of Berkshire's oldest homes, dating from 1750. Surrounded by 190 acres of pristine Monterey woodland, the house looks much as it might have back in the 18th century. We drive down Art School Road, then keep driving, back into the deep woods where the past still lingers. There rests the unassuming Bidwell house, simple, homey.

An active slate of lectures (such as "Fernside, the Shaker Village of Tyringham"), workshops (among them, cider pressing); and hikes (in the fall along historic Royal Hemlock Road) take place at the former home of Adonijah Bidwell.

THE WILLIAM CULLEN BRYANT HOMESTEAD
413-634-2244.
Off Rte. 9 on Rte. 112, South Cummington, MA 01026.
Season: Summer: Fri., Sat., Sun. & Holidays; Labor Day–Columbus Day: Sat., Sun. & Holidays; 1–5.
Fee: Admission charged.

William Cullen Bryant was born in 1794 in a small gambrel-roofed cabin of rough-hewn lumber, two miles from the frontier village of Cummington, on a farm of 465 acres. He went to Williams College, staying only eight months; shortly thereafter taking up the law. From 1816 on, Cullen, as he was called, practiced law in Great Barrington, where he wrote about 30 well-respected poems on such local themes as Monument Mountain's Indian legend, the Green River, and native waterfowl. With the influence of Catherine Sedgwick's brothers, Bryant became co-editor of the *New York Review* and *Athenaeum Magazine*, then editor at the *New York Evening Post* (one of America's oldest and most influential newspapers), and ultimately America's first popular and widely respected poet.

Bryant added substantially to his Cummington homestead; today it has 23 rooms. Visitors should read the poems first to capture the tour's fine points. Well managed by the Trustees of Reservations.

THE MERWIN HOUSE
413-298-4703.
14 W. Main St., Stockbridge, MA 01262.
In the center of Stockbridge.
Season: June 1–Oct. 15; Sat., Sun., 11–5.
Fee: Admission charged.

"Tranquility," a bit of 19th-century Berkshire refinement stopped in time, is the former home of Mrs. Vipont Merwin. This charming brick mansion, built about 1825, is filled with period antiques (mostly Victorian); both furnishings and collectibles reflect global travel and domestic dignity. Merwin House is maintained as a property of the Society for the Preservation of New England Antiquities. For Stockbridge strollers, evening views through the multipaned front windows give an inviting glimpse of an elegant world gone by.

SEARLES CASTLE

When Mark Hopkins, a founder and treasurer of the Central Pacific Railroad, died, his widow, Mary, consoled herself with the creation of a grand castle in Great Barrington. The 40-room castle was designed by Stanford White and constructed between 1882 and 1887 of locally cut blue dolomite stone. Upon its completion, Mary Hopkins married her interior decorator, Edward Searles, a man 20 years her junior. Searles had spared no expense on the castle's interior. Many of the major rooms feature massive carved wood or marble fireplaces, each one unique. More than 100 of the world's best artisans and craftsmen were brought on site to work with oak carvings, marble statues, atriums, columns, and pillars. The bills totalled $2.5 million.

With its Greek Revival temple, indoor pool, golf course, and tennis court, the

castle now serves as the home of the John Dewey Academy, a residential therapeutic high school. In 1982, Searles Castle was added to the National Register of
Historic Places. Usually closed to the public, the building and grounds are visible to pedestrians walking along Main Street. Several times a year — for an
Antiquarian Book Fair, for the Stockbridge Chamber Concerts, and at other special events — Searles Castle is open to the public, and well worth a visit.

Touring the Berkshire Mansions

For those who yearn to step back into Berkshire's Gilded Age, visits to
Naumkeag, The Mount, and Tanglewood, described in this chapter, will make an
excellent start. Other Gilded Age mansions are noted in the chapters on *Lodging*
and *Restaurants*. In addition, local historical societies and garden clubs arrange
occasional visits to some of the best mansions, normally off limits because they are
private homes.

You can also guide your own tour of the Gilded Age "cottages." Many are visible from the road and are well worth a look, respecting their owners' privacy, of
course. Carole Owens' book *The Berkshire Cottages* tells the stories of Berkshire's
Gilded Age in lively detail, bringing to life the business magnates, robber barons,
philanthropists, architects and designers, artists in residence, and squadrons of
domestic servants. Maps to guide the way are included. At most bookstores.

LIBRARIES

**BERKSHIRE
ATHENAEUM**
413-499-9480.
One Wendell Ave.
  Pittsfield, MA 01201.
Season: Year-round.
  Sept.–June: Mon.–Thurs.,
  9–9; Fri., 9–5; Sat., 10–5.
  Late June–Labor Day:
  Mon., Wed., Fri., 9–5;
  Tues., Thurs., 9–9; Sat.,
  10–5. Closed holidays.

The former Berkshire Athenaeum is a 19th-cen-
tury specimen of the Venetian Gothic style,
constructed next to the courthouse on Pittsfield's
handsome Park Square. Built of Berkshire deep
blue dolomite (a limestone) from Great Barrington,
along with red sandstone from Longmeadow,
Massachusetts, and red granite from Missouri, this
Athenaeum was once Berkshire's central library
and now serves as Pittsfield's court and the Central
Berkshire Registry of Deeds.

The new Athenaeum is a three-level brick and
glass facility featuring a tall and airy reading room
with natural clerestory lighting. An outdoor reading terrace serves adults and
another, children.

There is an outstanding dance collection, a Local Authors Room, and a Local
History Room. The jewel of the Athenaeum is its Herman Melville Room: a
trove of Melville memorabilia, from carved scrimshaw depicting the terror of
the Great White Whale to first editions of the author's works. Look for Moby

Dick in Japanese! Here also you'll find autograph letters from Melville, photos of his Pittsfield Farm, Arrowhead (see entry under "Historic Homes," in this chapter), and the desk on which he wrote his last haunting work, *Billy Budd*.

CHAPIN LIBRARY OF RARE BOOKS
413-597-2462.
Box 426, Williamstown, MA 01267.
On the 2nd fl. of Stetson Hall, on Williams College campus.
Season: Year-round: 10–12, 1–5, exc. weekends & holidays. Open July 4. Call for summer hours.

Chapin Library has one of the best-rounded collections of rare books and manuscripts in the world. On permanent display are the four founding documents of this country: *The Declaration of Independence*, owned by a member of the Continental Congress; *The Articles of Confederation and Perpetual Union*; *The Constitution of the United States*, annotated by George Mason; and the *Bill of Rights* (2 copies). The library owns General Greene's handwritten order for boats to cross the Delaware; on loan is George Washington's copy of *The Federalist Papers*. Every July Fourth, actors from the Williamstown Theatre Festival read the Declaration and the British Reply.

In 1923 Alfred Clark Chapin, Williams class of 1869 and mayor of Brooklyn, presented his alma mater with his magnificent library of first editions and manuscripts, specializing in historic literary and artistic masterworks. Other alumni have since given their collections.

Among other literary holdings are a Shakespeare First Folio and first editions of Pope, Swift, Fielding, Defoe, Richardson, Sterne, Johnson, Scott, Byron, Burns, Browning, Keats, Shelley, Thackeray, and Dickens. There is also a fine T. S. Eliot collection. Representing American literature are first editions by such writers as Crane, Melville, and Whitman. Scientific endeavor is represented by Tycho Brahe's *Astronomia* (1602), Harvey's *Anatomical Exercitations* (1653), Darwin's *Origins of the Species* (1859), and a double elephant folio of Audubon's *Birds of America*.

The Chapin frequently contributes documents to special exhibits at the Williams College Museum of Art and the Clark Art Institute.

SAWYER LIBRARY
413-597-2501.
Williams College, Williamstown, MA 01267.
In the center of Williams College campus.
Season: year-round; closed weekends when Williams is not in session.

At 725,122 volumes, 2,612 periodical subscriptions, 401,109 microtexts, 22,779 sound recordings including the Paul Whiteman Collection, 2,226 videos, 182 CD ROM discs, and 354,913 Federal documents, the Sawyer is a research resource unmatched within the county. Here we find a wide array of the latest periodicals, shelves of newly released books, and a library staff as helpful as they come. The public may use the facility, the stacks are open, and Sawyer is a pleasant place in which to work.

LENOX LIBRARY
413-637-0197.
18 Main St., Lenox, MA
01240.
Season:Year-round;
summer: Mon.–Sat. 10–5;
rest of year, Wed.–Sat.
10–5; Tues. and Thurs.,
open until 8.

Built in 1815 as the Berkshire County Court-house, when Lenox was still the "shire town," this classic Greek Revival building became the Lenox Library Association in 1873. It is listed on the National Register of Historic Places. You can enjoy the main reading room with its lofty illumi-nated ceiling and its amazing array of periodicals, or a lovely outdoor reading park. This is Old World reading at its best. A solid collection of about 75,000 volumes plus a music room are avail-able to the public. There is a closed collection of historical memorabilia, too, including the sled from the incident on which Edith Wharton based her novella *Ethan Frome*.

The Sled Ride

Though written after she completed her Berkshire life, Wharton's *Ethan Frome* is set in a Berkshire town that she calls Starkfield. In the climactic scene, soulmates Ethan and Mattie decide to take a suicidal sled ride rather than having to live apart, separated by Ethan's bitter wife, Zeena. The snowy downhill race toward obliteration was based on an actual sledding accident in turn-of the-century Lenox.

She waited while he seated himself with crossed legs in front of the sled; then she crouched quickly down at his back and clasped her arms about him. Her breath on his neck set him shuddering again, and he almost sprang from his seat. But in a flash he remembered the alternative. She was right: this was better than parting. He leaned back and drew her mouth to his. . . .

Just as they started, he heard the sorrel's whinney again, and the familiar wistful call, and all the confused images it brought with it went with him down the first reach of the road. Half-way down there was a sudden drop, then a rise, and after that another long delirious descent. As they took wing for this, it seemed to him that they were flying indeed, flying far up into the cloudy night, with Starkfield immea-surably below them, falling away like a speck in space. . . . Then the big elm shot up ahead, lying in wait for them at the bend in the road, and he said between his teeth: "We can fetch it; I know we can fetch it —"

As they flew toward the tree, Mattie pressed her arms tighter, and her blood seemed to be in his veins. Once or twice, the sled swerved a little under them. He slanted his body to keep it headed for the elm, repeating to himself again and again: "I know we can fetch it"; and little phrases she had spoken ran through his head and danced before him on the air. The big tree loomed bigger and closer, and as they bore down on it he thought: "It's waiting for us: it seems to know." But suddenly his wife's face, with twisted monstrous lineament, thrust itself between him and his goal, and he made an instinctive movement to brush it aside. The sled swerved in response, but he righted it again, kept it straight, and drove down on the black pro-jecting mass. There was a last instant when the air shot past him like millions of fiery wires; and then the elm. . . .

SIMON'S ROCK LIBRARY
413-528-0771, ext. 370.
Alford Rd., Gt. Barrington,
MA 01230.
Season: Year-round, hours
vary.

The Simon's Rock Library is one of the best in South County, the staff always attentive to one's research needs. The college it serves may be small, but this library's holdings are exceedingly well chosen. It is open to all visitors and to Berkshire County residents for borrowing. This is a library of half a dozen rooms, on two floors, in three interconnected pagoda-style buildings — all in a sylvan setting. With their big skylights, the reading rooms are highly recommended for naturally lighted wet-weather browsing. And fascinating art exhibits almost always grace the library's skylighted gallery.

STOCKBRIDGE LIBRARY AND HISTORICAL ROOM
413-298-5501.
Box 119, Stockbridge, MA
01262.
Main St., Stockbridge.
Season: Year-round,
Mon.–Fri. 9–5; Sat. 9–4;
Mon. and Fri. evenings
7–9; closed Sun. The
Historical Room:
Tues.–Fri. 9–5, Sat. 9–4.

Parts of the Stockbridge Library date to 1864, and the book-lined reading room is one the most felicitous anywhere — tall, stately, and obviously from another era. The children's collection is also first-rate.

Called W-nahk-ta-kook ("Great Meadow") by the Mahican Indians who settled there, the town of Stockbridge was incorporated by the English in 1739. A Colonial charter not only made the town official, but made it Indian property as well, and thereafter it was known as "Indian Town." The history of this great meadow and its town is displayed and explained in the Stockbridge Historical Room, a small museum in the basement of the library. Here are Indian artifacts, photos from the mid-1800s onwards, memorabilia from many famous residents and visitors to the village, and other intriguing historical bits that illuminate Stockbridge present.

WILLIAMSTOWN PUBLIC LIBRARY AND HOUSE OF LOCAL HISTORY
413-458-5369.
Main St., Williamstown,
MA 01267
Season: Year around;
Mon.–Fri., 10–5:30; Wed.
to 8; Sat. to 1:30.

The town is proud that a treasured resource now has a much roomier home, with ample parking. It complements the Sawyer Library (above) with strong holdings of children's books, fiction, local history, and popular music. The House of Local History (413-458-2160) moved with the library, now having room enough to display much of its holdings. Library and HLH each offer frequent programs.

MUSEUMS

Sharing the aesthetic, at Pittsfield's Berkshire Museum.

George Dimock, courtesy the Berkshire Museum

THE BERKSHIRE MUSEUM
413-443-7171.
39 South St., Pittsfield, MA 01201.
Season: Year-round; Tues.–Sat. 10–5, Sun. 1–5; open daily July–Aug: 10–5.
Fee: Adults $3; seniors and students $2; Children 12–18 $1; Members and children under 12 free.
Gift shop.

Cultural hub for the whole county, Berkshire Museum offers strong collections of art, science, regional and natural history, as well as offering an exciting calendar of lectures, films, concerts, classes, and field trips.

Founded in 1903 by Dalton paper maker and philanthropist Zenas Crane, the museum now shows the Hahn Collection of Early American Silver; the Gallatin Collection of Abstract Art; the Spalding Collection of Chinese Art; the Proctor Shell Collection; and the Cohn Collection of Minerals.

The collections are far-ranging: 19th-century glass made in the towns of Berkshire and Cheshire and pre-Christian glass bottles from Egypt; exhibits of shells and aquatic life, fossils, mushrooms, reptiles and amphibians, and "Uncle Beasley," the ten-foot-long model dinosaur who starred in the children's TV movie, *The Enormous Egg*. The Bird Room has a special section on Berkshire birds; the owl exhibit especially captivates. The Berkshire Animal Room presents native mammal specimens. A collection of beautiful dioramas by Louis Paul Jonas Sr. shows the animals of the world in one-tenth scale. An aquarium holds more than 100 species.

The Museum Theater, a 300-seat facility, is a site for lectures, plays, concerts, and the Little Cinema's admirable program of feature films. The theater now boasts state-of-the-art sound and projection and is visually enlivened by two Alexander Calder mobiles.

Upstairs, American portraiture is represented by works of Copley, Stuart, and Peale. The Hudson River School appears in works by Cole, Inness, and others. Two European galleries are devoted to the work of such English portrait painters as West and Reynolds, and European works by masters from the 15th to the 18th century. An ancient civilizations gallery includes "Pa-hat," the ever-popular Egyptian mummy, who lies resplendent amid a first-rate collection of ancient reliefs and artifacts.

In the museum's center is the lofty and skylit Ellen Crane Memorial Room, the museum's sculpture gallery, devoted to American and European pieces from the 19th and 20th centuries.

The museum has a year-round calendar of programs such as "Art for Lunch," events, lectures, and trips. Berkshire Museum also presents an unusual concert series, "Close Encounters with Music," a series of concerts combined with talks.

"At the Concert" (1880), by Pierre-Auguste Renoir, at the Sterling and Francine Clark Art Institute in Williamstown.

Courtesy the Clark Art Institute

STERLING AND FRANCINE CLARK ART INSTITUTE
413-458-2303.

Sterling Clark acquired his first Renoir in 1916; by the time he was finished, he owned 36. He and his French wife, Francine, bought what they liked, and the basis of this fine collection reflects

225 South St.,
Williamstown, MA
01267.
One mile south of junctions
of rtes. 7 & 2.
Season: Open Tues.–Sun.,
10–5, incl. Presidents'
Day, Memorial Day,
Labor Day, & Columbus
Day. Open Mondays in
July–Aug. Closed other
Mondays, New Year's
Day, Thanksgiving and
Christmas.
Fee: Free admission.
Gift shop, cafe.

their personal taste. Included with Impressionists are galleries filled with 19th-century American classics — by Winslow Homer, John Singer Sargent, and Frederick Remington — and a small but impressive collection of Old Masters.

The original 1950s building is elegant and efficient, a white Vermont marble neoclassic structure whose interior is finished in Italian marble, plaster, and natural-finish oak. Upon its opening the Clark was called by the editor of *Art News* ". . . very likely the best organized and most highly functional museum structure yet erected anywhere." The large red granite addition (1973) houses more galleries, a shop, and a serious art library. Substantial remodeling in 1996 added still more galleries and a cafe, and the selection of books offered in the museum's shop has been greatly enlarged, to include an extensive collection of art books and regional titles.

For most visitors, the centerpiece of the museum's collection is its gathering of French Impressionists, the Clarks' greatest artistic love. Among the standouts, besides Renoir, are works by Monet and Degas, the latter in both his racehorse and ballet dancer series. There are also prints, drawings, antique furniture, and silver. Almost every gallery has some form of natural light; many galleries offer not only splendid art on the walls but peaceful views of the Berkshire hills as well. All this, for free admission.

The Clark is beginning to host traveling exhibitions. Also an important art education center, it offers a broad spectrum of lectures open to the public, serving as classroom to a graduate program in art history run jointly with Williams College as well.

Besides its extensive art lecture series, the Clark presents chamber music and film programs. In its spare time, the Clark hosts mimes, puppeteers, one-person shows, poets, and storytellers, folk music, and popular outdoor band concerts in the summer.

**NORMAN ROCKWELL
MUSEUM**
413-298-4100.
Route 183, Stockbridge,
MA 01262.
Season: Open daily year-
round. May–Oct., daily
10–5; Nov.–April,
Mon.–Fri. 11–4, Sat.–Sun.
10–5. Closed Thanks-
giving, Christmas, New
Year's Day.

Whether we regard Norman Rockwell as illustrator or artist, the display of his life's work at the Norman Rockwell Museum resonates. A visit to this grand monument to his talents and insight is worth the crush of bus passengers — or we can go off-season.

Set on a gracious knoll overlooking the Housatonic River in the Glendale section of Stockbridge, the $4.4-million building designed by Robert A. M. Stern has a New England town hall look to it, with slate gables, clapboard siding, and fieldstone terraces. Inside,

Norman Rockwell in his Stockbridge studio, painting "Stockbridge Main Street at Christmas."

Louie Lamone, Courtesy the Norman Rockwell Museum

Fee: Adults $9; Children 6–18, $2; under 5, free. Family rate for 2 adults plus children $20. Gift shop.

spacious, well-lit galleries show permanent exhibits of Rockwell's paintings and changing exhibitions featuring Rockwell and other illustrators. The latter change three times a year.

At the core is the skylit gallery where Rockwell's *Four Freedoms* hang on permanent display. Created during the Second World War, they depict what we were fighting to uphold: Freedom of Speech; Freedom from Fear; Freedom of Worship; Freedom from Want. These four archetypal images constitute a shrine to America's hopeful image of itself.

Rockwell's long association with the *Saturday Evening Post* — forty-seven years — is well known, and the museum has many originals of his famous covers. In 1963, though, his relation with the *Saturday Evening Post* ended, and he signed on with *Look* and *McCall's*. His palette and cast of characters broadened. Where once he depicted white boys running from a prohibited swimming hole, now federal marshals lead a young black girl to school in Little Rock. From lovers and gossips, he moved on to Peace Corps volunteers and astronauts on the moon.

Outside stands Rockwell's studio, with a bucolic view of the Housatonic. The studio is a 19th-century carriage house, moved from the town to its present site in 1986. Inside it, we appreciate the light in which he loved to paint, the curious assemblage of painting props with which he liked to surround himself, and the modest space he felt was his "best studio yet." The studio is open daily from May through Oct.

The Rockwell Museum offers a variety of educational programs beyond its public exhibitions, including lectures, performances, special events, and art classes. Among our favorites is a sketch class taught by a succession of visiting artists. Special reference is made to Rockwell's work, as students are guided along in the development of the fine line.

HANCOCK SHAKER VILLAGE
413-443-0188.
Box 927, Pittsfield 01202.
Jct. rtes. 20 & 41, 5 mi. W. of Pittsfield.
Season: Main Season: late May–late Oct., 9:30–5:30 daily; Guided Tour Season: Apr. 1–late May and late Oct.–Nov., tours daily on the hour. Closed Thanksgiving.
Fees: Main Season: Adult $12.50, Ages 6–17 $5, 5 and under free; Family (2 adults and all children in immediate family under 18) $30. Tour Season: Adult $10, Ages 6–17 $5, 5 and under free; Family $25.
Museum shops, seasonal cafe and picnic area, walking tour brochures in English, French, German, Spanish, Japanese, and Braille.

The United Society of Believers in Christ's Second Appearing, later called Shakers, had their beginnings with a small group of English religious nonconformists in the mid-1700s. A young woman with strong religious convictions, Ann Lee, became their spiritual leader. In 1774, a small group of her followers joined "Mother Ann" in sailing to the new world. They landed in New York, near Albany, where the Shaker community Niskeyuna was later organized. A religious revival began in New England that spawned the formation of numerous villages throughout the region.

Shaker religion was also a way of life. Members joined into distinct communities isolated from the outside world. Men and women held equal status in daily life as well as leadership positions, but the genders were separated to support the Shaker commitment to celibacy. Communities were organized into families, brothers and sisters living separately in communal dwellings. Members also gave public confession of their sins.

A community was established in 1790 at Hancock. It was given the spiritual name City of Peace and prospered for more than 150 years. Residents at Hancock dedicated their labors to achieve heavenly perfection, resulting in products that have come to be known for their simple beauty and functionalism. Design of furniture, implements, and buildings was strictly functional, without the addition of deliberate ornaments. "Tis a gift to be simple" are words from a Shaker song, and such simplicity was a primary aim of both inner and outer life. "Beauty rests on utility" said their credo. Of great beauty, then, is Hancock's symbol, the stunning Round Stone Barn. As splendid as the structure is to the eye, how much more splendid that with such an efficient architecture, one farmhand at the center could easily and quickly feed an entire herd of cattle.

When the sect was at its peak during the mid-19th century, Hancock was one of 18 Shaker communities from Maine to Kentucky and had about 300 members. The agricultural base of the village was augmented by cottage industries, offering such items as cooperware, flat brooms, agricultural seeds, and dairy products to the World's People. But as religious ferment ceased, the Shaker population declined steadily until 1960, when the last of the Hancock Shakers moved away.

Since then, the village and its 1200 acres of meadows and woodlands have been a living museum to accommodate visitors who want to experience simple

Shaker ways. The City of Peace now acts as a center of re-created Shaker activities, including workshops, candlelight dinners, and evening tours. An important event the second weekend in July is the Americana artists and crafts show.

Visitors can tour 20 original Shaker buildings, to see Shaker furniture and tools, some of them attended by craftspeople working in the Shaker way: the chair maker, blacksmith, basketmakers, and spinners and weavers. Hancock's workshops teach how to create Shaker chair seats, oval boxes, natural herb wreaths, and a variety of other crafts. From the gardens, both herbal and vegetable, and from any of the village farm workers, visitors absorb the power of Shaker simplicity.

WILLIAMS COLLEGE MUSEUM OF ART
413-597-2429.
Main St. (Rte. 2),
Williamstown, MA
01267.
Across from Gothic chapel: set back from street.
Season: Year-round:
Tues.–Sat., 10–5, Sun. 1–5. Open: Memorial day, Labor Day, Columbus Day.
Closed: Thanksgiving, Christmas & New Year's.
Fee: Free.
Gift Shop.

One of the finest college art museums in the country, the Williams College Museum of Art is a 19th-century structure that has been strikingly revisited. Behind the original 1846 building, with its neoclassical octagonal rotunda, is an addition designed by Charles Moore, which opened in 1983. Combining wit and sophistication, Moore created a versatile, multileveled exhibition space in both old and new buildings, retaining the brick wall of the former as the stunning backdrop for a multilevel stair well. His design for the building's rear facade is a continuation of his lighthearted approach, featuring his "ironic columns" — there non-functionality revealed by the gap near the top.

Inside, the museum's permanent collection contains some 11,000 objects. Complementing the Clark Art Museum's collection of 19th-century European art, WCMA emphasizes early art, 20th-century art, and the art of Asia and other non-Western civilizations. Thanks to a recent $32 million gift by the widow of American impressionist Charles Prendergast, what was once a small, regional museum now houses the finest collection by both Charles and his talented brother, Maurice, and is now the leading center in the world for study of the Prendergasts' work.

A lively education program includes school programs and children's story/art hours. Several times a year, WCMA hosts popular free "family days" where children can try a range of art projects thematically linked to the collection, guided by enthusiastic Williams students.

Frequent loan exhibitions focus on a wide range of provocative subjects. Visitors should expect to be engaged, not soothed. Town residents ought to respond to the frequent tourist question, "Where's the museum?" with the answer, "Which museum?"

CRANE PAPER MUSEUM
413-684-2600.
30 South St., Dalton, MA
  01226.
Off Rte. 9, behind Crane
  office, Dalton.
Season: June to Mid-Oct.,
  Mon.–Fri., 2–5.
Fee: Free.

Ome of Berkshire's most important exports is money. Not the finished product but the rag paper on which every U.S. bill is printed. The Crane Paper Company makes it, these treasured notes circulate from Berkshire County to the nation and then the world.

While the mills themselves are not open to the public, the Crane Paper Museum, established in 1929, is open and tells a fascinating industrial tale. This magical, one-room brick museum — ivy covered and set in a garden — is really a restored 1844 paper mill building. The exhibits inside are mostly scale models, historical photographs, and paper samples. Crane produces only rag paper (nothing from wood pulp), and the exhibits show how the rags are soaked, softened, beaten to a pulp, and dried into paper stock. A 20-minute video on papermaking explains the process of watermarking, surface finishing (hard or soft), and anti-counterfeiting techniques. Also on display are historic documents, White House invitations, and U.S. and foreign currency, all printed on Crane paper. At the end of your visit, visitors may be offered an envelope of free Crane paper samples, including some of their luxurious stationery.

**WESTERN GATEWAY
HERITAGE STATE
PARK**
413-663-6312.
9 Furnace St. Bypass, N.
  Adams, MA 01247.
In N. Adams freight yard
  district.
Season: Year-round, 10–5.
  Closed New Year's Day,
  Easter, Thanksgiving,
  and Christmas.
Fee: Donations accepted.
Gift shop & Restaurant.

Nestled between long glacial ridges, Berkshire has always been separated from the rest of Massachusetts. In 1854, engineers and construction workers began an assault, drilling and blasting a 4.75-mile-long tunnel through the northeastern ridge. This Hoosac Tunnel was the first major tunneling work in the U.S. New methods were devised over the 20-year construction, at a cost of over $20 million and more than 195 lives. The building of the tunnel and related railroad development made North Adams the largest city in Berkshire in 1900. "We hold the Western Gateway," says the North Adams seal. At the turn of the century, more than half of Boston's freight came through the tunnel.

Western Gateway Heritage State Park now celebrates the former Boston and Maine Freight House and the Hoosac Tunnel, both of which are on the National Register of Historic Places. Inside, films, slide shows, models, written and visual histories of the railway and tunnel through the Hoosac barrier are presented. Outside, there are shops, the restored freight yard, the Freight Yard Pub restaurant, and the church-spired charm of North Adams.

**BERKSHIRE SCENIC
    RAILWAY MUSEUM**
413-637-2210.
Box 2195, Lenox, MA 01240.
10 Willow Creek Rd. at the
    end of Housatonic St.
Season: Memorial Day–
    Oct., weekends &
    holidays, 10–4.
Museum & Gift Shop: Free.
Short shuttle tickets: Adult
    $2; children, seniors $1.

Penned in by red tape and inter-railway dis-
putes, Berkshire Scenic has cut its cross-county
route to a short back-and-forth in front of Woods
Pond. While it's technically true that you get to
take a ride in their shined-up 1920s-vintage Erie
Lackawanna passenger coaches, the ride at present
is so brief as to be something of a tease. Things will
change, perhaps soon, and we'll once again be able
to tour southern Berkshire by rail.

For now, we can take the "Short Shuttle," check
out the model trains in the 1902 Lenox train station,
and admire lovely if polluted Woods Pond. And a
new exhibit is underway, as a 70-year-old B&O coach is being fixed up as
home for a Gilded Age exhibit.

OTHER MUSEUMS

Besides delving into fine art and rare books, the many museums in
Williamstown can take you in still other directions. You can go out at the
Hopkins Forest Museum (413-597-2346; *Hopkins Memorial Forest*, the
Rosenberg Center, and *Buxton Garden;* Northwest Hill Rd.), to such seasonal
events as sheepshearing and maple sugaring, while the museum itself exhibits
old photographs, farm machinery, and tools. And you can go up to the stars at
the 19th-century flintstone *Hopkins Observatory* (413-597-2188; Main St.) via
the projected shows at the *Milham Planetarium* (evenings Tues. and Thurs.
summer; Fri. during school year), or look at real pulsars and quasars through
the telescopes at Williams College.

Bennington Museum, 15 miles north of Williamstown on Rte. 7 in Vermont;
and *Historic Deerfield, Inc.,* east on Rte. 2 and south on Rte. 5, are fine daytrip
destinations.

MUSIC

TANGLEWOOD
413-637-1666 or
    413-637-1940.
Boston Symphony
    Orchestra, Tanglewood,
    Lenox, MA 01240.
Mail: 301 Massachusetts
    Ave., Boston, MA 02115.
On West St., Rte. 183, in
    Lenox.
Season: Summer.

Tanglewood remains *the* summer music festival
in New England, an incomparable facility for
all the world's musicians and music lovers.
Whether we picnic on the lawn or sit closer to the
BSO in the Shed, hearing music at Tanglewood is a
rare experience.

Critics assert that Tanglewood is too crowded,
too expensive, too predictable, and too lax in its
standards for music making or music listening, but

A moving bass passage through Tanglewood's parklike setting.

Courtesy the Boston Symphony Orchestra

Tickets: lawn (from $10) least expensive, then concert hall and shed; different events vary. Gift shops, restaurant.

this is belied by the powerful positive feeling it generates among musicians, students, and concert-goers alike. The sheer fun of seeing and hearing great music made in the great outdoors far out-weighs any criticisms. Tanglewood is the quintes-sential Berkshire entertainment.

Tanglewood began as the Berkshire Music Festival in the summer of 1934. Members of the New York Philharmonic were bused from Manhattan to the mountains and lodged in the area's hotels for the concert series. It was a sound success and repeated the following summer, but the New York orchestra withdrew. Then Serge Koussevitzky, the Russian-born conductor of the Boston Symphony Orchestra, was wooed and won. The BSO signed on for a series of three concerts on a single August weekend in 1936.

The popularity of this series was immense, nearly 15,000 people attending. And in the fall of that year, the Tappan family gave their Tanglewood estate on the Stockbridge-Lenox border to the BSO for a permanent summer home in the Berkshires. For the first two summers concerts were held in a large can-vas tent, but during one 1937 program, a torrential thunderstorm drowned out Wagner's *Ride of the Valkyries* and dampened instruments, musicians, and audience alike. During intermission, an impromptu fund drive raised pledges totaling $30,000 for the creation of a permanent "music pavilion." By the fol-lowing summer, through the combined architectural efforts of architect Eliel Saarinen and Stockbridge engineer Joseph Franz, the Shed was a reality.

Sensing the opportunity and the ideal setting, in 1940 Koussevitzky and the BSO added the Berkshire Music Center for advanced musicians, the only such school run by a major symphony orchestra. For the school's opening ceremony Randall Thompson composed his haunting *Alleluia* for unaccompanied chorus, which has been performed as the school's traditional opening music each sum-mer since.

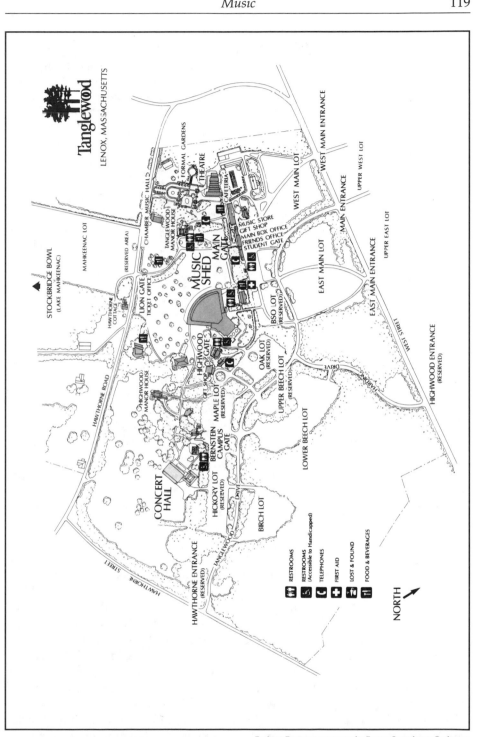

Tanglewood
LENOX, MASSACHUSETTS

STOCKBRIDGE BOWL
(LAKE MAHKEENAC)

MAHKEENAC LOT

(RESERVED AREA)

CHAMBER MUSIC HALL

FORMAL GARDENS

THEATRE

CAFETERIA

WEST MAIN ENTRANCE

WEST MAIN LOT

UPPER WEST LOT

TANGLEWOOD MANOR HOUSE

MUSIC STORE
GIFT SHOP
MAIN BOX OFFICE
FRIENDS OFFICE
STUDENT GATE

MAIN GATE

MAIN ENTRANCE

UPPER EAST LOT

HAWTHORNE COTTAGE

LION GATE
TICKET OFFICE

MUSIC SHED

EAST MAIN LOT

EAST MAIN ENTRANCE

BSO LOT
(RESERVED)

OAK LOT
(RESERVED)

WEST STREET

HIGHWOOD
GIFT SHOP GATE

HIGHWOOD MANOR HOUSE

UPPER BEECH LOT
(RESERVED)

DRIVE

HARDY

HIGHWOOD ENTRANCE
(RESERVED)

HAWTHORNE ROAD

BERNSTEIN CAMPUS GATE

MAPLE LOT
(RESERVED)

LOWER BEECH LOT

CONCERT HALL

HICKORY LOT
(RESERVED)

TANGLEWOOD DRIVE

BIRCH LOT

HAWTHORNE ENTRANCE
(RESERVED)

HAWTHORNE STREET

RESTROOMS

RESTROOMS
(Accessible to Handicapped)

TELEPHONES

FIRST AID

LOST & FOUND

FOOD & BEVERAGES

NORTH

Barbara Peterson, courtesy the Boston Symphony Orchestra

Where to Sit at Tanglewood

If you plan to picnic at Tanglewood before a performance in the Shed, it's best to arrive an hour or so in advance of concert time. Besides allowing time to eat before listening, arriving early affords a greater choice of spaces on the lawn, an important factor if you're to hear the music clearly. Although Tanglewood's amplification system is excellent and facilitates good listening from almost any lawn position, in our experience, places about 25 yards beyond the Shed-mounted speakers provide the best lawn listening.

Inside the Shed, the last series of back rows are good only for saying you were there, allowing only the most distant orchestra views and suffering greatly from much-diminished sound. At the optimum speaker sites on the lawn, the sound is far superior. If you're not picnicking and can afford to indulge (up to $60 tops), buy your way forward into the good seats where the sound is rich, sometimes robust and sometimes delicate, and you can really see classical music in the making.

Seiji Ozawa Concert Hall has its own lawn with seating for several hundred.

Regardless of where you sit, allow time for a walk in Tanglewood's beautifully groomed boxwood gardens. As the sun sets, on a clear day, you can see the hills in three states.

Each summer, the Tanglewood Music Center Orchestra is created from the year's crop of students; for their weekly concerts, this impressive group is usually led by a student conductor, but sometimes by the likes of Seiji Ozawa or Kurt Masur. So significant is this Tanglewood education that upwards of 20 percent of the members of America's major orchestras count themselves among Tanglewood Music Center alumni. Leonard Bernstein was a graduate, as are Seiji Ozawa and Zubin Mehta.

The $10 million, arched Seiji Ozawa Concert Hall opened in the summer of '94. Accommodating 1,200 inside, and an additional 700 on adjacent lawns, the new hall has sides that open, giving it flexibility and versatility as well as excellent acoustics. The hall is located on the Highwood section of Tanglewood, now designated as the Leonard Bernstein campus.

The Music Festival has evolved into a performance center of major proportions, with an annual attendance now of some 300,000 visitors. Pianists Emanuel Ax, Garrick Ohlsson, Peter Serkin, and Alicia de Larrocha, violinists Midori and Itzhak Perlman, and cellist Yo-Yo Ma return regularly. In addition to the regular Boston Symphony Orchestra concerts, Tanglewood presents weekly chamber music concerts in the smaller sheds, Prelude Concerts (Friday nights) and Open Rehearsals (Saturday mornings); the annual Festival of Contemporary Music; a Jazz Festival; and almost daily concerts by gifted young musicians at the Music Center. Some student concerts are free. The Boston Pops comes to play as well.

A favorite each season is "Tanglewood on Parade," an amazingly varied musical day lasting some ten hours and climaxing with booming cannon shots

---

Festivals-Within-the-Festival at Tanglewood

Not content merely to satisfy the classical music lover, Tanglewood offers mini-festivals and series featuring contemporary, jazz, and popular music.

Recent offerings in the Contemporary Music Festival have been an appropriately eclectic mix, including a performance by the California E.A.R. Unit, an eight-player ensemble from Los Angeles. If you find the free spirit in you is being kept too staid by the classicist in you, leave time this summer for a dose of Tanglewood's Contemporary Music.

Artistry of an even jazzier sort is showcased during Tanglewood's annual Jazz Festival, and songs of a slightly different sort are featured during Tanglewood's Popular Artist Series, which is sometimes announced after the Tanglewood summer schedule is published; keep an eye on local papers during the months of May and June.

---

and fireworks. But whatever the scale of the offerings, an evening at Tanglewood marks a high point in any summer.

Those staying in the Berkshires for a month or more and wanting to take in Tanglewood music frequently, should join the "Friends of Tanglewood" and enjoy ticket price reductions and other privileges.

SOUTH MOUNTAIN CONCERTS
413-442-2106.
Box 23, Pittsfield, MA 01202.
On rtes. 7 & 20, about 1 mi. S. of Pittsfield Center.
Season: Mid-Aug.–early Oct.
Tickets: Prices vary each concert.

South Mountain's concert hall in Pittsfield is called the Temple. Built in 1918, this colonial-style Temple of Music was the gift of Mrs. Elizabeth Sprague Coolidge, created to house the concerts of the Berkshire String Quartet. The acoustically splendid 500-seat auditorium, listed on the National Register of Historic Places, is set gracefully on its wooded South Mountain slope.

Past standout performers at the Temple have included Leonard Bernstein, Alexander Schneider, Leontyne Price, and Rudolf Serkin. Currently, a typical season features concerts by leading American string quartets such as the Guarneri, the Juilliard, and the Emerson, as well as other types of ensembles. A popular highlight of every season is the concert by the Beaux Arts Trio.

South Mountain Concerts frequently sell out — be sure to call ahead. Unlike Tanglewood, where watching the stars or basking in the sunshine may substitute for close listening to the music, South Mountain's more limited season and number of concerts are designed for the serious music lover.

ASTON MAGNA
413-528-3595; 800-875-7156.
Box 28, Gt. Barrington, MA 01230.

There's a great deal of historic preservation going on in the Berkshires, and none more artistic than the renaissance of Baroque, Classical, and early Romantic chamber music by Aston

Aston Magna.

Lincoln Russell, courtesy Aston Magna

In St. James Church, just S. of the town hall.
Season: July and Aug.
Tickets: $19 at the door; call for prices for seniors, students, and advance purchase.

Magna. Offering unique cross-disciplinary educational programs for professional musicians and a short run of superb summer concerts, Aston Magna has specialized in 17th-, 18th-, and early 19th-century music, always played on period instruments or reproductions. Hear Bach, Handel, Haydn, Mozart, Schubert, and their contemporaries as you might never have before, with festival director and virtuoso violinist Daniel Stepner, leading a distinguished roster of singers and instrumentalists.

Performances interpret the music as much as possible as the composer intended, hence the faithfulness to original instruments. Participants study the temperament and cultural milieu of the age and then make music that is buoyed with the period's sensibility as well.

Andrew Porter, writing in *The New Yorker*, has given this festival several reviews, noting that the string players are "probably as good as any in the world. The winds are in tune. The old self-consciousness has been replaced by confidence, by character and, beyond that, by something one might almost describe as a philosophy intelligently and joyfully embraced. For there is more to Aston Magna than authentic instruments, stylistic insights, and technical ability."

BERKSHIRE OPERA COMPANY
413-528-4420.
Box Office: 314 Main St., Gt. Barrington.
Performances: Koussevitzky Arts Center, Berkshire Com. Col., Pittsfield; Music Mountain, Falls Village, CT.

After nearly a decade, first under founder-director Rex Hearn and now conductor Joel Revzen, the Berkshire Opera seems stronger than ever. This talented group has won praise from both audiences and serious critics alike for their English-language renditions of chamber opera.

There are discoveries to be made here, and among them recently was Stockbridge resident

Season: July and August.
Tickets: $20–$50.

Maureen O. Flynn, whom Hearn initially heard singing at the First Congregational Church in Lee and who has since gone from the Berkshire Opera to the Metropolitan and a brilliant international career.

Recent offerings have included Carlisle Floyd's *Susannah*, and Mozart's *Don Giovanni*. "Mozart was well served," wrote the New York Times critic of the latter production. "The Berkshire Opera Company fills a needed role in the rich summer life of the region, offering artfully prepared chamber operas."

BERKSHIRE CHORAL FESTIVAL
413-229-8526.
Mail: 245 N. Undermountain Rd., Sheffield, MA 01257.
Concert Shed, Berkshire School, Rte. 41, Sheffield.
Season: July and August.
Tickets: $15–$18.

An experiment in mixing amateur, semi-pro, and professional singers into a makeshift chorus culminated in a single concert. Success there has led the Berkshire Choral Festival some 14 years later to evolve into a summer-long, professional quality chorus that can be counted on for stirring moments.

Each summer now brings a five-concert Berkshire celebration featuring 200 voices, powerful soloists and conductors, and the Springfield Symphony, at one of the loveliest preparatory schools in New England, the Berkshire School (Rte. 41, Sheffield; 413-229-8511). *Berkshire Eagle* critic Elsbet Wayne found the closing performance of a recent season "refreshingly boisterous," praising the chorus for its "beautiful diction." This is still something of a pick-up chorus, now being remade annually with a corps of 200 experienced amateurs and some professionals.

NATIONAL MUSIC CENTER
413-637-4718.
40 Kemble St., Lenox.
Season: Year-round concerts and workshops.
Prices and schedules to be announced.

The National Music Center, brainchild of aging rocker Joey Dee (whose big hits were "The Peppermint Twist" and "Shout") and spearheaded by the godfather of rock 'n' roll, the ageless Dick Clark, is the "campus" of the nonprofit National Music Foundation. Located on the outskirts of Lenox village, the Center has a twofold mission: "1. To educate the public about American music, in order to preserve our nation's musical heritage. 2. To provide for the retirement of professionals from the fields of music, radio and recording, with provision made for those who can't retire on their own."

Educational facilities will include an interactive museum, performance centers, a library and archive, a radio broadcast facility, and a recording studio. The center will offer workshops in every American music style, giving Berkshire a music balance unparalleled in modern country life.

Watch for the center's calendar of concerts, workshops, and lectures.

NORFOLK CHAMBER MUSIC FESTIVAL
860-542-3000; 203-432-1966 off season.
During season: Norfolk, CT 06058; Off season: 435 College St., New Haven, CT 06520.
Rtes. 44 & 272, in Norfolk.
Season: Mid-June–Mid-Aug.
Tickets: $9–$25.
Subscription for 5 concerts $34–$92.

From mid-June to mid-August at Norfolk, visiting virtuosos perform regularly, among them the Tokyo String Quartet and the Vermeer Quartet. Orchestral and choral works are also featured. Concurrent with this series of concerts, Yale's Summer School of Music runs a program of classes for its students and regularly schedules recitals by young professional musicians — recitals that are open to the public free of charge.

The setting is superb. Arrive early and you can picnic on the grounds of the elegant 75-acre estate on which the music center has grown. Norfolk's Music Shed is enclosed and beautifully crafted of acoustically resonant hardwoods. Some balcony seats along the sides may pose a viewing problem, but the sound is good everywhere, and the ticket prices are somewhat lower than at Berkshire County's more widely known music events.

Beginning in the fall of '93, Norfolk initiated a special series of Indian Summer concerts in October, effectively stretching their season over another month. In the southern foothills of the Berkshires, Norfolk is a quiet alternative to Tanglewood, offering chamber music at its finest.

MUSIC MOUNTAIN
860-824-7126.
Falls Village, CT 06031.
On Music Mountain Rd., off Rte. 7 opposite Housatonic Valley Regional High School.
Season: Early June to Labor Day.
Tickets: $18.

Founded in 1930 by Chicago Symphony concertmaster Jacques Gordon, Music Mountain is the oldest continuing chamber music festival in America. In the acoustically excellent, 325-seat Gordon Hall, set on a woody hilltop, concerts are given by the resident summer group, the Manhattan String Quartet, and by visiting guest artists.

OTHER MUSIC

In *South County*, the *Berkshire Bach Society* (413-528-9277) offers a fine series of concerts and lectures at various area churches, schools, and colleges. *Berkshire Friends of Music* (413-243-9744; P.O. Box 2397, Lenox, MA 01240) organizes chamber and orchestral concerts at Seiji Ozawa Hall, Tanglewood, and elsewhere, typically 5–7 concerts Sept.–June. (See also below, under Berkshire New Music Festival.) *Simon's Rock College of Bard* (413-528-0771; Alford Rd., Great Barrington) is one of the liveliest promoters of professional music in South County, with various events during the academic year. *The Curtisville Consortium* (413-698-2618) takes its name from the hamlet of Interlaken in Stockbridge, which was originally settled as Curtisville. The

Consortium is a group of Boston Symphony musicians and guest artists who present a five-week-long series of concerts each summer at the Congregational Church in Interlaken. And *Stockbridge Chamber Concerts* has likewise been a part of the South County musical scene.

In *Central County*, chamber music can be enjoyed at the *Armstrong Chamber Concerts*, held at Springlawn cottage on the grounds of the National Music Center in Lenox. Call the Lenox Chamber of Commerce (413-637-3646) for tickets. Still more chamber music is featured at the *Richmond Performance Series* at the Richmond Congregational Church, Rte. 41. Each of these chamber music series features professional symphony orchestra veterans, making intimate music in special settings. *Berkshire Community College* (413-499-4660; West St., Pittsfield) offers concerts year-round, many of them at *Koussevitzky Arts Center*; the summer *Koussevitzy Arts Festival*, June–Aug., offers opera, ballet, chamber music, drama, popular music, and more. Call BCC for information. The *Berkshire Museum*'s "Close Encounters with Music" series alternates between the Pittsfield home base and Great Barrington's St. James' Church, offering beautiful music and intriguing commentary by conductor/cellist Yehudi Hannani and guests. The *Berkshire Lyric Theatre*, under the direction of Robert Blafield, continues to play at a variety of county venues, including the Berkshire Museum and the Lenox Town Hall.

In *North County*, the *Williams College* music department supports concerts by the *Berkshire Symphony, Choral Society, Jazz Ensemble, Williams Trio, Kusika and the Zambezi Marimba Band*, the *Symphonic Winds*, and the *Group for 20th-Century Music. Thompson Concerts*, also under the music department's auspices, brings rising young professionals to campus, while the wholly independent *Griffin Hall* series presents harpsichord and organ music. New at Williams is the *Berkshire New Music Festival* (in conjunction with the Berkshire Friends of Music), performances of winning works from a national contest for college and high school composers. All college performance groups are involved in this festival scheduled for fall. (For information on Williams College musical events, call the concert manager's office, 413-597-2736, or the 24-hour Concertline, 413-597-3146.)

Elsewhere in Williamstown, the Clark Art Institute (413-458-9545) presents concerts, and the *Williamstown Chamber Concerts* (413-458-8273; P.O. Box 287, Williamstown, MA 01267) continues its winning ways. Over in North Adams, *North Adams State College* (413-662-5000) sponsors the *Smith House Concert Series*, usually professional musicians with local connections.

Just *Outside the County*, in the Berkshire hilltown of Charlemont (Rte. 2, Franklin County), the *Mohawk Trail Concerts* (413-625-9511; 75 Bridge St., Shelburne Falls, MA 01370) presents a season of informal classical concerts at the Federated Church. In nearby Columbia County, NY, *Tannery Pond Concerts* (518-794-7887; Box 446, New Lebanon, NY 12125) most recently hosted that very popular Canadian ensemble, the St. Lawrence String Quartet. In adjacent Spencertown, NY, the *Spencertown Academy*'s concerts (518-392-

3693; Box 80, Spencertown, NY 12165) are among the Berkshire region's neatest. Said the *Berkshire Eagle* of Spencertown, "Acoustically the hall is a little gem, and each featured artist, cognizant of these attractive surroundings, radiates a feeling of 'I am happy to be performing here.'"

NIGHTLIFE

Folk singer David Grover, nationally known for his children's songs and locally appreciated for his captivating style, plays at the Berkshire Museum.

Judith Monachina

When the sun sets on Berkshire, what was quiet becomes quieter — except at the dozens of clubs across the county. From videotheques to cabarets, from hard rock to softly sung madrigals, nightlife in the Berkshires will satisfy most and truly please many. But do be aware that places come and go quickly; check the local papers for current listings and for newer sites and sounds not listed in our highly selective list below.

Starting in **South County**, in Sheffield, the *Sheffield Pub/Cyber Bar* (413-229-8880; Rte. 7), often hosts karaoke nights, where you can sing your soul out, or just throw back a cold one. In Egremont, the *Egremont Inn* (413-528-2111; Old Sheffield Rd.), *Egremont Country Club* (413-528-4222; Rte. 23) and the *Old Egremont Club* (413-528-9712; 264 Hillsdale Rd.) schedule good live bands. In Great Barrington, the *Helsinki Tea Company* (413-528-3394; 284 Main St.) has jazz Thursday evenings during the summer and open-mike poetry readings on Mondays. At *Spencer's* (413-528-3828; Jct. of Rte. 7 and 183), owner David Thorne and his jazz trio play dance music on Friday and Saturday nights (and then do a jazz brunch on Sunday mornings!). Way out in New Boston, at the *Silverbrook Cafe* (413-258-4597), "The Best Little Honky Tonk West of the Clam River," a whole lotta shakin' goes on. Nearby, at the *Macano Inn* (413-274-6636; Rte. 183), a steady diet of driving rock keeps the blues away, with regular live bands Fridays and Saturdays such as Blue Highways and Pandoura. Over in Stockbridge, the *Lion's Den* under the Red Lion Inn (413-298-5545) presents almost nightly live entertainment of high quality, such as folksinger David Grover. On a hot night, the subterranean Lion's Den is thick with music, laughter, banter, and dish clatter, each apparently competing for center stage. Around the corner, at *Michael's* (413-298-3530; Elm St.) occasional live bands, like Wishful Thinnking, liven the otherwise staid Stockbridge soundscape. *Oak n' Spruce* (413-243-3500; South Lee) features DJ-spun music in their Bear Tree on Friday and Saturday nights. Also in East Lee, the *Belden Tavern* (413-243-4660; Rte. 20) features the Fabulous Hi Fi's, playing big band and swing.

In *Central County*, specifically Lenox, the *Roseborough Grill* (413-637-2700; 71 Church St.) offers music with dinner. *Lenox 218* restaurant (413-637-4218; 218 Main St., Lenox) offers music in its Fireplace Lounge. *Barkley's Pub* (413-637-4940; 36 Housatonic St.) presents bands on weekends. *Cranwell* (413-637-1364; Rt. 20), sometimes offers dinner music on weekend evenings.

In Pittsfield, *The Studio*, in the old England Brothers building, is the latest site for a Mort Cooperman extravaganza, its first, highly successful productions, Black 47 and Max Creek, in the fall of 1996. The *Park Square Grille* (413-499-2000) at the Berkshire Common presents karaoke Wednesday, Friday, and Saturday nights. Mellowest of the clubs is probably *La Cocina* (413-499-6363; 140 Wahconah St.). The crowd can occasionally eclipse the performers. Wednesday is open-mike night.

On the north side of Pittsfield, the *Itam Lodge* (413-443-7134; Waubeek Rd.) offers music, and farther north, in Lanesborough, The *Old Forge Restaurant* (413-442-6797) also jumps.

Up the mountain, in the town of Washington, *Bucksteep Manor* (413-623-5535; off Washington Mountain Rd.) has cut back on rock fare, heading for a softer, more country beat, with bands like Dooley Austin and Shake 'n' Bake.

Popular artist Annie Di Franco plays to a sellout crowd at the Night Shift Cafe in North Adams.

Judith Monachina

Out in Dalton, the *Hard Hat Bar and Grill* (413-684-9787; 26 Daly Ave.) books some wicked acts on weekends.

In *North County*, the *Blarney Room* at Brodie Mountain (413-443-4752; Rte. 7, New Ashford) and *Kelly's Irish Pub* both present occasional live music. *Founder's Grill* (413-738-5500) at Jiminy Peak in Hancock swings during ski season. *The Springs* (413-458-3465; Rte. 7, New Ashford) offers a pianist at the grand piano, on Saturdays. Up Williamstown way, *The Williams Inn* (413-458-9371; Main St., Williamstown) is still hosting the popular Walt Lehman and his band, playing jazz, and guitarist Jim Bayliss. And during the summer, the finest late evening entertainment in the county might be found at the 1896 House, with the *Williamstown Theatre Festival Cabaret* (413-597-3400), a combination of Cabaret troupe and current WTF stars. The '96 House hosts the Billsville Bailey's and Uncle Bob's Band at other times. *Wild Amber Grill* (413-458-4000) hosts Acoustic Brew — mostly mellow folk and blues — on Thursdays, the *Water Street Grill* (413-458-2175) has live music on Fridays and Saturdays, and *The Orchards* (413-458-9611) features Howie Levitz on piano Saturday evenings. In North Adams, *Due Baci* (413-664-6581) hosts a band on the deck summer weekends, *Gringos* (413-663-8552) has music Thursday nights and *Freight Yard Restaurant and Pub* (413-663-6547) features entertainment Friday and Saturday evenings. The funky *Chaise Lounge Gallery at Milltown Studios* (413-662-5770), presents live music with an edge. And Mort Cooperman's *Nightshift Cafe* (413-664-6228) at the Massachusetts Museum of Contemporary Art in North Adams promises a good time.

Just *Outside the County*, over in Northampton, the *Iron Horse Music Hall* (413-584-0610; 20 Center St.) presents the region's best and most regular folk and jazz, offering concerts with such greats as Aztec Two Step and Acoustic Junction. Nearby, *Pearl Street* (413-584-7771; 10 Pearl St.) presents the hot stuff, such as Johnny Winter, with the accent on dancing.

Folk Festivals in Hilltown Farms

Just over the border, where the Berkshire Hills still run tall and majestic, a couple of major folk festivals have been drawing thousands of fans from all over America. For over 20 years now, the Rothvoss Farm in Hillsdale, NY, has been hosting the *Winterhawk Bluegrass & Folk Festival*. This is a big, three-day-long music fest in the country, held mid-July, and that old tribal feeling is quickly established. Recent standout artists have included Alison Kraus and Union Station, Jimmy Martin, and Riders in the Sky.

Just a week later, at another Hillsdale farm, the Long Hill Farm, the *Falcon Ridge Folk Festival*: another three-day music fest, with music almost nonstop, day and night. Falcon Ridge covers its folk end of the deal quite well, but the festival goes way beyond in its musical offerings, most mixing in pop, blues, gospel, rock, funk, metal, jazz, reggae, New Age, and hip-hop. In between, musicians and ordinary folk were making up new forms of music, then improvising.

THEATER

Miriam Margolyes, Kandis Chappel, and Kate Burton in Molière's The Learned Ladies, on the Williamstown Theatre Festival's MainStage.

Richard Feldman, courtesy the Williamstown Theatre Festival

WILLIAMSTOWN THEATRE FESTIVAL
413-597-3400.
Box 517, Williamstown, MA 01267.
1000 Main St.
Season: Summer only.
Tickets: $14–$35.

"**M**iracles every summer since 1955," the *Boston Globe* once wrote. The miracles continue. On Berkshire summer nights, nowhere are the stars brighter than on stage at the Williamstown Theatre Festival. Here in a typical show you'll find the likes of Broadway and Hollywood luminaries Elaine May, Marsha Mason, Dick Cavett, Blythe Danner, Edward Herrmann, Richard Chamberlain, and Richard Thomas — all performing live in the region's most sophisticated summer theater. And Christopher Reeve, a regular until a riding accident put him in a wheelchair, hopes to come back as a director.

People Magazine once put it this way: "The showbiz capital of the U.S. may, for once, be on neither coast. The Williamstown Theatre Festival could boast the most powerful concentration of acting talent any place this summer."

Each summer, in addition to full-scale productions with first-rate sets and costumes on the Main Stage, WTF offers other more intimate theater experiences, including the four productions of works-in-progress mounted at the Other Stage. Most recently a stunning revival of Arthur Miller's *All My Sons* ran on the Other Stage with Miller's latest, *The Ride Down Mt. Morgan*, on the Main Stage, while Miller joined in a reading of his works at one of the regular events at the Clark. Late-night musical cabarets provide surprise cameo appearances by Main Stage celebrities like Dick Cavett, inveterate songster and raconteur. There are Staged Readings; Museum Pieces at the Williams College Museum of Art; Act I Performance Projects by the WTF young actor training ensemble, at work in Goodrich Hall on the Williams Campus; and a new Greylock Theatre Project, which will connect economically disadvantaged young people from North Adams with professional theater artists from WTF.

And playing to the pit, WTF offers the Free Theatre, in various venues. Shakespeare has been performed in woods and fields; recently an adaptation of *Hard Times* was presented at a former North Adams mill. Here's a rare opportunity for a picnic party, with complimentary first-rate theater.

It's no mistake, then, that *Newsweek* ranked WTF as "the best of all American summer theaters," with "the cream of America's acting crop."

**SHAKESPEARE &
COMPANY AT THE
MOUNT**
413-637-3353 box office;
 413-637-1197 off season.
The Mount, Plunkett St.
 Lenox, MA 01240.
On Plunket St. in Lenox,
 near southern jct. of Rtes.
 7 & 7A.
Season: Summer, fall.
Tickets: $13–$32.

Shakespeare is alive on stage in Lenox, at Edith Wharton's palatial estate, The Mount (described in this chapter under "Historic Houses"). Shakespeare & Company has made splendid use of The Mount's rolling lawn, performing most of their plays outdoors on a stage built in a glade, against the lovely stone wall of a rose garden. Seating is either on your own blanket or on the company's low-slung aluminum chairs.

Under the powerful artistic guidance of English actor-director Tina Packer and her artistic associate, Jonathan Epstein, Shakespeare & Company has brought new light, feeling, and clarity to Shakespeare's plays, making the works more accessible to many people. Shakespeare & Company works in area schools in the winter, spreading the wonder of the Bard even farther.

Part of the dramatic impact derives from the actors' ability to treat the audience as their alter ego, always privy to secrets of the drama. The plays are staged all around the seating area; intimacy with the action is inevitable, with stage and lighting design creating magical effects.

Shakespeare & Company's The Merry Wives of Windsor, directed by Tina Packer.

The company's inspired clowning is magical, too. Says Tina Packer, "The function of the clowns is of the utmost importance in Shakespeare's plays. The influence of comedia del arte on Elizabethan theater, with its knockabout and improvised humor, cannot be overemphasized. Because of the inordinate amount of 'seriousness' that has been attached to the 'Bard,' much of the sheer joy and fun of Shakespeare has been lost for modern audiences." Not so at The Mount, where you're in for a good time.

Wrote the *New York Times* critic Ben Brantley of the company's performance of *A Midsummer Night's Dream*: "The overall result is vulgar, overscaled and loud. And it works. . . . There are few productions of Shakespearean comedy in which the meaning of every joke (whether intended by Shakespeare or not) reads so clearly, and the audience was responsive to each one."

Having established a singularly rich tradition at The Mount, Shakespeare & Company has significantly enriched that, developing three new theaters — the 200-seat, outdoor Oxford Court; the 75-seat indoor Wharton theater, inside The Mount; and the 108-seat, indoor Stables Theatre. A recent summer saw five Shakespearean productions, four Wharton-oriented plays, and four or five modern plays. Recently the troupe brought Wharton's *Ethan Frome* to life in the fall.

Shakespeare & Company perform A Love Story, *directed by Dennis Krausnick, in the Wharton Theatre.*

Courtesy Shakespeare & Co.

The company has toured, for performances and workshops, to Denver, Toronto, and other cities and, under the aegis of Joe Papp's New York Shakespeare Festival, they have also taken productions from The Mount to Brooklyn's Prospect Park.

In our opinion, Shakespeare & Company is a "must see" for locals and visitors alike.

World premiere of L-Play by Beth Henley in the newly
renovated Unicorn Theatre of Berkshire Theatre Festival.
This was the first production in the new theatre, August 1996.

Neil Hammer, courtesy Berkshire Theatre Festival.

**BERKSHIRE THEATRE
FESTIVAL**
413-298-5576; 413-298-5536
off season.
Box 797, Stockbridge, MA
01262.
East Main St., Rte. 102,
Stockbridge.
Season: Summer.
Tickets: Main Stage,
$27–$36; Unicorn
Theatre, $15, Children's
Theatre, $4.
Gift shop.

In 1887, architect Stanford White completed his design for the Stockbridge Casino Company, created for the "establishment and maintenance of a place for a reading room, library and social meeting." Forty years later, when the structure had fallen into disuse, Mabel Choate, daughter of Ambassador Joseph H. Choate of Stockbridge, gave the building to the Three Arts Society, which in turn moved the Casino to its present site at the foot of Yale Hill and rented it to Alexander Kirkland and F. Cowles Strickland, who opened the Berkshire Playhouse in 1928.

Since that time, the playhouse, later renamed Berkshire Theatre Festival, has been at the forefront of American summer theater. Major works by nearly every American playwright of note have been performed here, including plays by Lillian Hellmann, Tennessee Williams, Eugene O'Neill and Thornton Wilder. The playhouse produced Wilder's *Our Town* and *The Skin of Our Teeth*, with Wilder himself in featured roles.

Leading lights of the theater appear regularly at the theater, from a young Katharine Hepburn in 1930 to Joanne Woodward in 1996.

The last two decades have been a period of growth and refocusing for BTF. In the spring of 1976, the building was entered on the National Register of Historic Places. Since then, gradual refurbishment has continued, with a new paint job, and most noticeably, all new seats, making the theater truly comfortable at last. The Theatre Festival has expanded its educational and rehearsal facilities, principally upon the gift of the Lavan Center (formerly Beaupre Art School), a few miles north of the playhouse. Interns and apprentices live at the center and rehearse there, while pursuing a program of classes in acting, voice, movement, and design.

BTF also features shows at the recently remodeled, 100-seat Unicorn Theatre, a showcase for younger artists. These are becoming increasingly substantial, recently being highlighted by the painterly Mississippi Nude, by John Reaves, one artist's life in living color. A Summer Readings Festival also sees staged readings of important new plays and musicals, again at the Unicorn. And for the local community, BTF has several outreach programs, offering discount tickets to the elderly and dramatization of prize-winning plays written by local grade schoolers.

Barrington Stage's Lady Day at Emerson's Bar & Grill., starring Gail Nelson.

Courtesy Barrington Stage.

BARRINGTON STAGE COMPANY
413-528-8888
Mail: Box 946, Gt.
  Barrington, MA 01230.
Consolati Performing Arts
  Center, Mount Everett
  Regional High School,
  Sheffield, MA 01230.
Season: Summer–fall.
Tickets: varies by theatre;
  main stage $10–30;
  second stage $12–15;
  students half price.

Julianne Boyd, late of the Berkshire Theater Festival and now artistic director of the Barrington Stage Company, knows a good thing when she hears it. Recently *Lady Day at Emerson's Bar & Grill*, starring Gail Nelson as blues singer Billie Holiday, returned for a sixth short run. It's the show that launched Barrington in 1995, playing to sell-outs at restaurants since. In fact, just about everything the new company has touched has turned to gold; witness *Magic Upclose*, a Stage II production in the music room at the high school, a two week run that was stretched to four. *Avenue X* brought out hoards of stomping kids when it moved from Sheffield to an underwritten performance in Pittsfield.

**MUSIC THEATRE
GROUP**
413-298-5504; 212-366-5260
off season.
During season: Box 42,
Glendale, MA 01229.
Off season: Suite 1001, 30
West 26th St., New York,
NY 10010-2011.
Season: Jun.–Sept.
Tickets: $15–$20.

For their innovative and penetrating explorations of music-theatre, the Music Theatre Group/Lenox Arts Center has won 20 Obie awards in New York, and they bring to the Berkshires a world-class adventure for all lovers of music and drama. Under the leadership of producing director Lyn Austin, the group has tackled difficult, esoteric works and created ones that are close to sublime.

"The Music-Theatre Group blazes trails. . . ." raved the *Boston Globe*. Theater here is minimally staged; the emphasis is more on script and musical development as many of these works prepare for a New York run.

Said the *New York Times*: "The Music-Theatre Group has produced one of the most innovative and original bodies of work in American theatre."

Locations vary.

OTHER THEATER

There are more than a dozen other theater companies in and about Berkshire.

In *South County*, the biggest little theater in the world is *Mixed Company* (413-528-2320; at the Granary, 37 Rosseter St., Great Barrington), where fall-off-your-seat comedy alternates with moving drama. Under the direction of Joan Ackermann and Gillian Seidl, Mixed Company has built a solid following, and there is often competition for the theater's few dozen seats. Ackermann's award-winning *Zara Spook and Other Lures* premiered here, as did her droll *Bed and Breakfast*, in which she played an addled Mrs. Digby.

The *Central County* theater scene has never been livelier. The *Berkshire Community College Players* regularly appear at the Robert Boland Theater at BCC (413-499-0886; West St., Pittsfield). *The Town Players* (413-443-9279) also occasionally perform at either BCC or the Berkshire Museum, in a recent season presenting *Into the Woods* by Stephen Sondheim. The *News in Revue* performs political satire summers at the Seven Hills Inn in Lenox.

North County is especially theatrical. Besides the Williamstown Theatre Festival, Williamstown has other theater companies. The *Starlight Stage Youth Theatre* (413-458-4246), a hands-on theater experience for youth from eight years to 18, performs at the First Congregational Church.

After such a busy summer season of theater, the fall-winter slack is picked up by *Williamstheatre*, the Williams College theater group (413-597-2342; Adams Memorial Theatre), producing impressive revivals of plays by the likes of Brecht and Beckett; and by the drama department at *North Adams State College* (413-662-5000).

Outside the County, in neighboring Chatham, New York, just west of Central Berkshire, the *Mac-Haydn Theatre* (518-392-9292; Rte. 203), has been offering 15-week-long summer seasons of robust Broadway musicals since 1969. Productions are staged in the round, and their high energy casts are guaranteed to deliver a supercharge of musical theater. Less than truly sophisticated, but usually a whole lot of fun. In New Lebanon, NY, at the *Theater Barn* (518-794-8989; Rte 20), producers Joan and Abe Phelps zero in on musical comedy, with an occasional murderous dose of Agatha Christie thrown in. *Proctor's* in Schenectady (518-382-1083) and the *Egg* in Albany (518-473-1061) both provide stages for national acts, shows and dramas. Up in Bennington, southern Vermont, the *Oldcastle Theater Company* (802-447-0564; at the Bennington Center for the Arts) can always be counted on for some fun, such as *Nunsense: The Second Coming*. Back in Massachusetts, *StageWest* in Springfield (413-781-2340) provides top quality theatrical experiences, and the tiny *miniature theatre of Chester* (413-354-6565; in the Town Hall), has hosted some large-as-life drama.

SEASONAL EVENTS

There are a number of special Berkshire events tuned to the weather, and somehow the Berkshire year wouldn't unfold properly without them. Leading the parade are Pittsfield's **4th of July Parade** and the North Adams **Fall Foliage Parade** the first Sunday in October.

SPRING

Riverfest is North County's favorite outdoor event every May, celebrating the revitalized Hoosac River, which threads through Adams, North Adams, and Williamstown. A highlight is a remarkable environmental art show in the woods and along the riverbanks, as well as raft and canoe rides, food, bluegrass music, and displays of artworks by North County schoolchildren studying the river.

La Festa explodes every June in celebration of North Adams's Italian heritage. A true community effort, La Festa features great food, top-name music, ethnic dance, a carnival, and children's activities, and the profits go to North County schools.

SUMMER

Summerfest in Great Barrington has become a highlight on South County's early summer schedule. Held on a Saturday evening in mid-June, the last edition was the most successful ever, raising thousands of dollars for Hospice of South Berkshire, and raising the spirits of thousands who attended. With the entire downtown closed off to motor traffic, locals and visitors have a grand old time — listening to music, watching dance or magic, or grazing on various snack foods. Dozens of performers from the Olga Dunn Dancers to the Bluestars contribute their time and talent, making this a community celebration of unqualified good cheer.

Big Apple Circus declares: forget the three rings; less is more! With one ring under a colorful big top, this international troupe has been making an annual summer landing. As we go to press, the word is that the circus may be at the Great Barrington Fair Grounds starting in 1997; check local newspapers for details. Each year, a totally new show is created around a specific theme — in recent seasons celebrating Coney Island and an adventure around the world. With acts from dozens of nations globally, this circus also brings the world right to you, highlighting performers of enormous strength, dexterity, and balance, accompanied by original live music. Modeled on the opulent spectacles of the Belle Epoque, when circus arts were on a par with opera and ballet, the Big Apple has an intimacy and a quaint elegance entirely absent in a larger circus. Great fun; highly recommended.

Berkshire Crafts Fair is a mid-August event, held at Monument Mountain Regional High School (413-528-3346; Rte. 7, between Stockbridge and Great Barrington). Top local and regional craftspeople offer their extraordinary creations, from handmade paper to handblown glass, from handwoven clothing to exotic woodenware.

The Best of the Berkshires Festival is Pittsfield's newest celebration of countywide talents, in many fields, from music to dance, from food to drink. Held in mid-August, the festival brings a jolt of life to North Street, luring thousands to the traffic-free party. The Berkshire Public Theatre Children's Ensemble has performed, as has acclaimed magician Timothy Wenk.

Fireworks over Stockbridge Bowl are spectacular because of echoes from the hills. The biggest bangs and most colorful starbursts come from Tanglewood, on the Fourth of July, and following *The 1812 Overture* at the end of "Tanglewood on Parade," a highlight of the BSO Berkshire season.

The Monument Mountain Author Climb is a literary event commemorating the August day in 1851 when Melville, Hawthorne, Holmes, and friends scaled the Great Barrington peak. They imbibed a good deal of champagne, weathered a thunderstorm, read William Cullen Bryant's poem about the Indian maiden who threw herself in sorrow from the top, and began a lasting friendship. Becoming a fixture is an annual recreation of Henry **David Thoreau's climb up Mount Greylock**, on or about July 20. Watch the *Berkshire Eagle* for announcements.

FALL

The Great Josh Billings RunAground is likely Berkshire's greatest one-day party, an athletic extravaganza that involves thousands of participants and many more admiring, supportive spectators. This late September biking-canoeing-running triathlon takes its name from Lanesborough's Henry Wheeler Shaw, an inveterate 19th-century prankster, who fashioned something of a career for himself as a humorist, under the penname of Josh Billings. "If a fellow gets to going down hill, it seems as if everything were greased for the occasion," wrote Billings (more or less); and every fall at the RunAground the bike racers, shooting down that last hill on Rte. 183 to Stockbridge Bowl, prove how right old Josh was. After the race, there's a huge party at Tanglewood with food, drink, dancing, and Berkshire camaraderie.

The Tub Parade is one of Berkshire's oldest annual events, dating back to the Gilded Age. The late September parade has been revived without a hitch. Actually, there were plenty of hitches, but they were supposed to be there, hitching show ponies to the ornate, flower-decked carts they pulled. Under the auspices of the Lenox Village Association and the Colonial Carriage and Driving Society, the Tub Parade gives a glimpse back into the fancy-free world of turn-of-the-century Berkshire, where dogs rode with ruffled collars right next to their masters. Brief but brilliant, the Tub Parade is a high note in the Berkshire fall calendar.

Greylock Ramble On Columbus Day the town of Adams sponsors an event, at the height of fall foliage, when 3,000 people of every dimension hike the big hill. Other hikes and climbs to and around the lofty top of Mount Greylock in North County are sponsored by the Appalachian Mountain Club, beginning at Greylock Glen in Adams, the Visitors Center in Lanesborough, the Sperry Road Campground, or Bascom Lodge, often narrated by well-informed guides.

Harvest Festival at the Berkshire Botanical Garden, Stockbridge (described under "Nature Preserves" in the *Recreation* chapter) is an early-October event packed with seasonal goodies such as cider and doughnuts, apples

Bicycle-powered cider mill, a highlight of the Harvest Festival at Berkshire Botanical Garden, Stockbridge.

Jonathan Sternfield

and pumpkins, haywagon and fire engine rides, plants and seeds, and mayhem of all sorts appealing to children and grownups of every persuasion. The event has recently been expanded to two days, with a live performance tent featuring the likes of the Bluestars. Besides a plant sale and flea market, a book sale and second-hand clothes mart, the festival has also attracted a greater number of craftspeople, selling an increasingly refined collection of crafts. A true highlight of the Berkshire calendar.

La Festa explodes every June in celebration of North Adams's Italian heritage. A true community effort, La Festa features great food, top-name music, ethnic dance, a carnival, and children's activities, and the profits go to North County schools.

Octoberzest is a new fall foliage festival of music and ballet, presented at Simon's Rock by the Barrington Performing Arts. Mixing and matching poets with musicians, dancers with actors into various ensemble pieces really does add a zesty melange to the southern Berkshire fall. We hope their sprout develops legs, showing up fall after fall.

WINTER

Naumkeag at Christmas is extra-special, because that's when the Choates' Christmas decorations are taken out and the house is made to look ever so festive. Look in on a quiet turn-of-the-century Christmas; it might make yours a bit merrier. The historic home in Stockbridge (described under "Historic Homes" in this chapter) offers this opportunity to the public on an irregular basis.

Celebrate Wassail! exuberantly brightens the darkest season of the year — the winter solstice in December — with a recreation of a medieval celebration. Sacred and traditional music, mummers' plays, dragons, costumed revelers, storytellers, swordplay . . . it's all here, presented annually by a multi-generational community group in Williamstown. Fun for the entire family.

First Night is Pittsfield's salute to the New Year, beginning around 7 p.m. on New Year's Eve. Wearing an inexpensive tag, revelers are able to drop in on dozens of performances ranging from hardest rock to young ballerinas, playing in assorted sites in downtown. The same tag entitles wearers to ride for free on the B Bus, in case the walk gets burdensome. Noticeably absent are drunks and other bores. Fireworks announce the actual calendar change.

The Tea Ceremony at Great Barrington Pottery is a moving meditation, a highly stylized form of social communion for both the Tea Mistress and those she serves. Enter the Chashitsu (Japanese Ceremonial Teahouse and Formal Garden) at Richard Bennett's Great Barrington Pottery (described in the *Shopping* chapter) and you'll be taken back in time to 14th-century Japan. Leading with the concept of *wabi* — quiet simplicity — both the building and the slow-moving ceremony gently harmonize you. Bow, as you must, to enter the ceremonial washing area, and follow the Tea Guide's instruction in the proper ritual cleansing. Then follow her, bowing, through the low door into the teahouse itself. In the *tokonoma*, or ceremonial alcove, observe the calligraphy, and below it, note the grace and appropriateness of the flower arrangement, a bouquet the Tea Mistress has made especially to meet the mood of this day. Then observe the silent power of the Tea Mistress, for whom serving tea is "The Way."

VIDEO RENTALS

The following video rental outlets stock the standard Hollywood movies and a smattering of foreign art titles.

South County

Alice in Videoland (413-528-4451; 301 Stockbridge Rd. [Rte. 7], Gt. Barrington).
Impoco's (413-528-9162; 54 State Rd. [Rte. 7], Gt. Barrington).
Lee Video (413-243-3636; 23 Park Plaza, Lee).
Patrick's Video (413-528-5575; 740 Main St., Gt. Barrington).
Shanahan's Elm St. Market (413-298-3634; Elm St., Stockbridge).
Video File (413-243-0468; 60 Main St., Lee).
West Stockbridge Video (413-232-7851; 18 Main St., West Stockbridge).

Central County

Action Video (413-499-4208; 44 S. Main St. [Rte. 7], Lanesborough).
Blockbuster (413-443-3323; 455 Dalton Ave., Pittsfield).
Dalton Video (413-684-4480; 69 Depot St., Dalton).
East Street Video (413-443-2000; 10 Lyman St., Pittsfield).
Master Darkroom and Video (413-443-9763; 758 Tyler St., Pittsfield).
Patrick's Video (413-442-6666; 200 West St., Pittsfield).
Plaza Video (413-443-0943; 452 West Housatonic St., Pittsfield).
Variety Video (413-637-2046; 26 Housatonic St., Lenox).
Video Studio 12 (413-447-7595; 180A Elm St., Pittsfield).

North County

Dox (413-458-4420; 320 Main St., Williamstown).
Video Studio (413-743-7007; 1 Myrtle St., Adams).
Video Studio of North Adams (413-664-7880; North Adams Plaza, off American Legion Dr., N. Adams).

CHAPTER FIVE
Pleasing the Palate
RESTAURANTS & FOOD PURVEYORS

Some of the county's best restaurants are found in the "cottages" of the Gilded Age: at Orleton, which is now called the Gateways, and at Blantyre and Wheatleigh. Yet a great table is still set in more humble Berkshire settings — there are old mills, pre-Revolutionary farmhouses, and inns.

The fare is no longer just American, with a dash of the continental, but is studded with many other cuisines including Vietnamese, Japanese, Chinese, Indian, even Finnish.

Judith Monachina

Getting ready for a lunch crowd at the Union Bar & Grill in Great Barrington. This new restaurant was designed by local sculptor Joe Wheaton.

"A Taste of the Berkshires" is an annual festival celebrating Berkshire foods. And five books of Berkshire recipes are also currently available. The Williamstown Theatre Festival's *As You Like It* is a prize-winning compilation of the favorite recipes of the festival's stars, directors, writers, and associates. For the Berkshire County Historical Society's *Berkshire Victuals*, editor Janet Cook researched all county cooks, both dead and alive, and came up with scores of delicious local recipes. Two other Berkshire-based books, *The Red Lion Inn Cookbook* by Suzi Forbes Chase and *Best Recipes of Berkshire Chefs* by Miriam Jacob, celebrate respectively the cuisine of the county's best-known inn and the culinary specialties of a range of fine contemporary county chefs. *The Kripalu Cookbook* by Atma Jo Ann Levitt features vegetarian recipes from the kitchen of the Kripalu Center in Lenox, in proportions suitable for home use.

The number of restaurants in the county is vast — more than 225 (36 in Williamstown alone!). To cover all of them would require a book twice this size. Diners should be guided by what we have here, but follow their own hunches, as well. We would be pleased to hear of discoveries for a future edition. Please note that we have grouped the best breakfast and lunch eateries into a special section of their own (pages 189–92). There are dozens of specialty food suppliers, too, engaging alternatives to supermarkets.

We have concentrated on the establishments we found most interesting and most successful, sometimes risking critical judgments. *De gustibus non est disputandum.* The food, of course, is primary, but we have also based our judgments on other factors: the range of the menu, the decor and ambience of the restaurant, the quality of service, and value for price.

We designate each restaurant with a price code, signifying the approximate cost of a meal, including appetizer, entrée, and dessert, but not cocktails, wine, tax, or tip. Restaurants with a prix-fixe menu are noted accordingly.

Reviews are organized first by section of the county, then alphabetically by town, then by restaurant name. Food purveyors are grouped alphabetically by type, then by name of establishment. Every entry appears in the general index, too. Nevertheless, it is always prudent to call ahead.

Dining Price Codes

Inexpensive	up to $10
Moderate	$10 to $20
Expensive	$20 to $35
Very Expensive	$35 or more

Credit Cards

AE — American Express
CB — Carte Blanche
DC — Diner's Club
MC — MasterCard
V — Visa

Meals:

B — Breakfast
L — Lunch
SB — Sunday Brunch
D — Dinner

RESTAURANTS SOUTH COUNTY

North Egremont

ELM COURT INN
413-528-0325.
Rte. 71, N. Egremont.
Closed: Mon. & Tues. in
　winter; Mon. Jul.–Aug.

The Elm Court's hosts, Glee and Urs Bieri, continue its excellent Swiss tradition. Glee handles the pleasantly decorated dining room, ensuring her guests' good time. Urs is Swiss and a former execu-

Price: Expensive.
Cuisine: Continental.
Serving: D.
Credit Cards: AE, MC, V.
Reservations:
   Recommended.
Special Features: Fireplaces.

tive chef at the United Nations. At the Elm Court, he's able to concentrate his substantial culinary talents on far fewer meals, and the results are extraordinary.

Among starters, both the lobster bisque and French onion soup are superior, the onion soup featuring a first-class Gruyère lid, the bisque delicate yet distinct.

The Elm Court's wine list offers a nice range of French, Swiss, German, Italian, and California bottles, at surprisingly affordable prices. Many good wines are priced around $15, with some of the best up around $100. Service is superior — and our waitress could confidently tell us just what was in the fillet of sole's sauce — a light hollandaise with diced tomatoes and herbs. Fillet goulash Forestière is another clear winner, the goulash made with the tenderest filet mignon.

Although the menu at Elm Court appears to be strictly for carnivores, a request from a vegetarian friend of ours brought out a vegetable plate that was both beautiful and delicious, with grilled golden bell pepper, zucchini, string beans, and shiitake mushrooms, along with pasta in tomato basil sauce.

Awesome desserts are standard fare here. The whipped cream served on most of these is about the finest we've tasted — stiff, rich, and only slightly sweetened. The pear tart is at once hearty and delicate with a thick, cakey crust. A recently sampled berries and cream in a cookie bowl was a true devastator: the berries ripe and sweet, the cream rich and mellow, the cookie bowl simply divine. The dessert menu also offers eight cognacs, two Armagnacs, two ports, and four cordials. Call the Elm Court for a reservation on weekend and holiday nights.

South Egremont

THE EGREMONT INN
413-528-2111.
Old Sheffield Rd., S.
   Egremont.
On side street off Rte. 23 in
   center of village.
Closed: Mon. & Tues.
Price: Moderate to
   expensive.
Cuisine: American.
Serving: D; SB summer
   only.
Credit Cards: MC, V.

Personable and committed innkeepers Karen and Steve Waller have restored the Egremont Inn to its natural position as a center of hospitality in South County. Dining is available in the friendly tavern room, or in one of the four dining rooms adjoining. On a cool night, you'll prefer a spot beside one of the inn's many crackling hearths. On your table will be fine linens, china, crystal, candlelight, and a seasonal bouquet. In warm weather, the inn serves a delightful Sunday brunch on its curved porch.

Steve Waller has an ear for music and an eye for talent. On Thursday evenings, diners can enjoy one of the area's talented folk singers (strictly acoustic guitar!). On Saturday evenings, dinner is accompanied by an excellent jazz combo ("The best mood music for dining," says Steve). In the Dining Room, we recently enjoyed crab cakes with Thai sauce, a delicious salad of greens, apples, cranberries, walnuts, and Maytag blue cheese (America's Roquefort) vinaigrette, excellent potato and-leek-encrusted fillet of salmon, and cappellini with artichokes, tomato, basil, and olive oil. The Thai sauce somewhat overwhelmed the tasty crab cakes; otherwise, we couldn't have asked for a better meal. Desserts are hearty, home cooked, and delicious. Have one even if you split it. The Tavern at the Egremont menu features many of the dining room's specialties along with steaks, InnBurger with fries, etc.

THE GASLIGHT CAFE
413-528-0870.
Rte. 23, S. Egremont.
Price: Inexpensive.
Cuisine: American.
Serving: B, L, SB.
Credit Cards: None;
  personal checks
  accepted.

In this popular little spot in the historic downtown of Egremont, owner Mike Layne knows many of his patrons. Serving breakfast and lunch daily, he chats with customers and refills their coffee cups. Plenty of choices among the omelettes and other breakfast items, and the food is good.

Layne, who bought the place six years ago, calls the restaurant "a work in progress." Every spring he decides what he would like to change. In 1997 he'll add some new booths, he says.

Breakfast or lunch on the patio, weather permitting, is made even more pleasant since the spot overlooks a sloping backyard leading to a brook below.

Completing a fine meal, at John Andrew's.

Jonathan Sternfield

JOHN ANDREW'S
413-528-3469.
Rte. 23, S. Egremont.
W. of village 2.5 mi.
Price: Expensive.
Closed: Rarely.
Cuisine: American.
Serving: D.

Can a great restaurant get better? In the hands of Susan and Danny Smith it can; John Andrew's pleases diners at every turn. First the warmth and sophistication of the dining rooms create a bit of Upper East Side, set in a gracious Berkshire manse. The service is superior, always attentive, never intrusive. Most significantly, chef Danny Smith's

Credit Cards: MC, V.
Reservations: Recommended.
Special Features: Glassed-in
    porch in back, fireplace,
    outdoor deck and terrace
    in season.

culinary creations are innovative, artful and, above all, delicious.

A trio of freshly baked, hot-from-the-oven breads begins the latest feasts. It takes discipline to keep the focaccia and Tuscan breads from becoming the meal. Panfried oysters with mesclun greens and anchovy mustard vinaigrette make a fabulous opening. The crisp duck confit, sautéed duck breast with roast garlic mashed potatoes, is no less than sublime. An array of pastas and pizzas augments the ample list of entrées. A thoughtful wine list, with some special California selections, assures an appropriately excellent bottle. Desserts such as plum crisp with homemade vanilla ice cream cap one of the most consistently satisfying dining experiences in Berkshire.

MOM'S
413-528-2414
Rte. 23, S. Egremont.
Price: Inexpensive.
Cuisine: American &
    Italian.
Serving: B, L, D.
Credit Cards: None.

Disregard novelist Nelson Algren's admonition: "Never eat in a place called Mom's." This one features a brookside dining room, serving breakfast and lunch all day long, and Mom's has one of the few open kitchens in the county, with chefs scurrying about and the pots and pans hanging from a wheel above. Omelettes such as the feta and tomato are excellent; sandwiches are meaty and flavorful, especially the enormous fresh turkey sandwich, along with daily specials, good pizza, and a fine array of burgers. The Veggie Melt, with its generous layerings of avocado, sprouts, and cheese, makes a substantial vegetarian meal for any diner.

Mom's service is pleasant and efficient, even in times of great demand, and the brookside deck behind the restaurant, perched 30 feet above Karner's Brook, is one of Berkshire's most tranquil and picturesque dining areas.

In the evening, Mom's turns a bit more formal, with delicious pasta dishes and meaty entrees.

THE OLD MILL
413-528-1421.
Rte. 23, S. Egremont.
Closed: Mon. in winter.
Price: Moderate to
    expensive.
Cuisine: American.
Serving: D.
Credit cards: AE, CB, DC,
    MC, V.
Reservations: Recommended
    for parties of 5 or more.
Special Features: Private
    dining room; fireplace.

With an ambience of sophisticated, understated elegance and a clientele to match, this 1797 grist mill continues to be one of south Berkshire's premier dining attractions. A rare rave review by the *New York Times* didn't hurt business, so the tables are in great demand. Should you fail to snag a table, the Old Mill can accommodate as well in a quaint and cozy bar that serves a bar menu and regular menu except on Saturdays.

Under the new culinary guidance of French chef Christian Urbain, the Mill's kitchen has smoothed, its consistency even more reliable. The food is not

Elegant simplicity at the Old Mill.

Jonathan Sternfield

overly fancy. Instead, the elements of a dish are clearly noted, likely fewer in number than other top-of-the-line restaurants. Black soy seared loin of tuna on a recent menu was terrific, as was a roast rack of lamb in pecan crust. Everything, in fact, is appetizing, from table setting and service to delicious rolls, butter, and chèvre, so you're likely to mellow out, eating everything in sight. But save room for dessert — at least a few of those creamy little profiteroles au chocolat.

Great Barrington

BARRINGTON BREWERY & RESTAURANT
415-528-8282.
420 Stockbridge Road (Jenifer House Commons), Gt. Barrington.
Price: Inexpensive to Moderate.
Cuisine: American & Miscellaneous International.
Serving: L, D.
Credit Cards: AE, MC, V.
Special Features: Own brewed beers.

The South County entry in the burgeoning category of micro-brewery *cum* restaurant, Barrington Brewery is a barnlike but cozy place with a genuine and complete brewery in the hayloft section of the Tavern. Taking the distinctive feature first, Brewer Andy Mankin's "Barn Brewed™" beer is darned good. "Mohican" Amber Ale, "Hopland" Pale Ale, "Barrington" Brown Ale, and "Black Bear" Stout, in increasing order of weight, are the regulars always on tap. They are always supplemented by one or two seasonal selections. Of those, the India Pale Ale is light and crisp, but still flavor-filled, while the Porter is dark, thick and rich — the best we have tasted since we outgrew McSorley's in NYC. There are at least six others. To assist your exploration, they offer a "sampler" of the five current offerings in 4-oz. glasses, which makes for good tasting fun in the taproom.

The luncheon menu is soups, salads, and "super" sandwiches, a plowman's lunch (sausage, cheese, chutney, and bread), or jacket potatoes with various cheese, chili, or steamed broccoli toppings. After 5 p.m., the luncheon menu is supplemented with such dinner offerings as the chef's pot pie (made fresh here, your choice of white, dark, or mixed meat), the traditional English pub favorite, shepherd's pie, a seasoned ground beef, lamb, and corn casserole covered with a mashed potato crust, or, for the vegetarian, delicious sautéed eggplant slices rolled with roasted sweet peppers and provolone, topped with marinara sauce and baked. The portions of both the sandwich plates and the main courses are quite ample. Desserts are rich and good. The apple crisp is fresh made, fruity, and good and crisp. All in all, Barrington Brewery offers good, hearty food, and the best beer you'll drink south of Pittsfield (where you will find The Brewery on North Street).

A Japanese greeting in the entryway at Bizen on Railroad Street in Great Barrington.

Judith Monachina

BIZEN
413-528-4343.
17 Railroad St., Gt.
 Barrington.
Price: Expensive.
Cuisine: Japanese.
Serving: L, D.
Credit Cards: AE, D, DC,
 MC, V.
Handicap Access: Yes.
Nonsmoking.
Reservations:
 Recommended.
Special Features: Sushi bar.

After four years of intensive apprenticeship in Bizen, a Japanese province where a 1,000-year-old pottery tradition continues to thrive, Michael Marcus returned to Berkshire to build a 45-foot-long kiln and to practice and perfect the ancient craft of 12-day-fired pottery. Now focusing on the art and craft of the Japanese restaurant and sushi bar, Michael and chef/associates Hideo Kikuchi and Hideo Furukawa have created a restaurant to delight both eye and palate, complete with huge rustic beams and Bizen pottery. It is the single most transporting restaurant in the county, appealing and authentic.

From fabulously fresh sushi, sashimi, hand rolls,

and nori maki such as giant clam, sea urchin, smelt roe, and sunshire bass, to incredibly plump rolls of shrimp tempura and soft shell crab tempura, Bizen is state-of-the-art sushi for Berkshire. Combined with flavorful soups, refreshing salads, deeply satisfying noodles, outrageous appetizers, and an entrée list as delicious as traditional, it creates a memorable Japanese dining experience.

A Taste of the Berkshires

Settling into a September Saturday on Berkshire's crowded social calendar, "A Taste of the Berkshires" gives new meaning to the concept of grazing. If you love the nibbler's lifestyle, sampling a bit of this and a bit of that, then this festival is the ideal spot for you, with its tents poised just behind the Great Barrington bandstand. Unforgettable treats in our last outing included grilled shiitake mushrooms from Delftree and Maryland crab cake from Thornewood Inn, among many others.

Other facets of the food fest, which is a fund-raiser for Southern Berkshire Community Services, include a Berkshire's Best Pie contest, sheepshearing, and music, so the whole family can enjoy. One recommendation for this extravaganza: an empty stomach; don't leave home without it.

CASTLE STREET CAFE
413-528-5244.
10 Castle St., Gt.
  Barrington.
Closed: Tues.
Price: Inexpensive to
  Moderate.
Cuisine: American, French,
  Italian.
Serving: D.
Credit Cards: AE, D, MC,
  V.
Special Features: Cruvinet
  wine bar.

Few things change at Castle Street except the excellent special offerings every night. Chef Michael Ballon continues to preside over one of the liveliest and most consistently satisfying eating establishments in Berkshire. The upscale bistro decor with exposed brick walls, white linen tablecloths, fresh flowers, and a handsome bar at the back of the dining room is attractive and inviting. One excellent new option: for a special event, plan ahead for a dinner for 4 to 12 in the downstairs wine cellar. The service is always attentive, professional, and prompt — from a waitstaff that changes less often than any other we can recollect. Michael prides himself on seeking out and highlighting on the menu the best of Berkshire's now dazzling array of locally produced fine foods, from goat cheese to French bread to fresh produce.

The eclectic menu combines French, Italian, and American influences. We recently enjoyed the zesty grilled Cornish game hen, a regular on the menu, and a delightful shellfish pasta that combined wonderfully fresh shrimp, scallops, and mussels in a garlic-basil sauce with al dente penne. Several vegetarian choices are hearty and tasty enough to please even a hardened carnivore: for instance, the eggplant roulade with three cheeses. The desserts are few, but absolutely first class, most notably a chocolate mousse which *Newsday* declared to be "the world's best." Or go for the bread pudding which is even better than Mom used to make.

Castle Street Cafe faces ever-stiffer competition among the fine dining options growing apace in chic downtown Great Barrington, but Michael Ballon and his team are up to the challenge.

DOS AMIGOS
413-528-0084.
250 Stockbridge Rd. (Rte. 7), Gt. Barrington.
Closed: Tues.
Price: Inexpensive.
Cuisine: Mexican.
Serving: L, D.
Credit Cards: AE, D, MC, V.
Reservations: Preferred for groups of six or more.
Special Features: Vegetarian dishes; Children's menu/ highchairs; Entertainment.

Under proprietor Ari Zorn, who took over in 1997, Dos Amigos continues to offer a pleasant, informal setting. It has always had a steady local and second-home clientele. The stiffening competition in Mexican restaurants in South County has led Dos Amigos to spiff up the menu and the preparation appreciably. Their margaritas have always been excellent. There are lots more fresh ingredients, vegetarian offerings, fruit salsas, marinated meat dishes, and quite special specials offered now. Try the portobello mushroom fajita or grilled Cajun catfish with passion salsa as specials when available, or the chicken and cheese chimichangas or quesadillas, typical of the new and tasty regular menu items. Some reviewers in our party thought them not hot enough, but if you ask earnestly, the heat will be turned on.

Dos Amigos brings in musicians like David Grover to attract kids and families on weekend afternoons and occasional winter evenings, and other jazz and folk artists at night for the music and dining crowd.

HELSINKI TEA ROOM
413-528-3394.
284 Main St., Gt. Barrington.
Prices: Moderate.
Cuisine: North.
Serving: L, D.
Credit Cards: MC, V.

Portugal and Provence may provide more popular dishes these days, but the "old country home recipes" of Finland and the Ukraine comprise a cuisine to be proud of. At the Helsinki Tea Room one sits in a cluttered room reminiscent of the eclectic decor of an emigrée aunt's apartment, while ordering a Mad Russian: potato latkes heaped with gravlax, sour cream, caviar, and appleberry compote. Or one might share a grilled portobello mushroom with goat cheese, roasted garlic, and sundried tomatoes. Or devour Ukrainian vegetable pirozhki, presented on a bed of lettuce and fresh tomatoes.

Teas and teapots reside prominently on shelves. A children's menu is available. The desserts are delicious. Live jazz on Thursday nights. Chefs are Damian Spurlock and Jenny Finkle.

Hickory Bill himself at Berkshire's best barbecue.

Jonathan Sternfield

HICKORY BILL'S BAR-B-QUE
413-528-1444.
405 Stockbridge Rd., Gt. Barrington.
Closed: Mon.
Price: Inexpensive.
Cuisine: American.
Serving: L, D.
Credit Cards: AE, MC, V.

Hickory Bill's barbecue is just *the best* you can find. This is no made-up name; Mr. William C. Ross is Hickory Bill. You'll find him presiding in the kitchen in his trademark ten-gallon straw Stetson most days. All Bill's meats are smoked and cooked at least six hours to his special specifications. The results are fantastic — smoky, juicy, tender beef and pork spare ribs, fancy brisket, and chicken. Add your choice of Bill's own regular or hot homemade barbecue sauce and tuck in! Bill's collard greens (with bits of brisket), barbecue baked beans, and Mexican corn bread (laced with jalapeño pepper) are done to the same world-class standard. Mrs. Evelyn's sweet potato pie for dessert makes a fitting finish, or try another helping of chopped brisket on a soft roll, our choice.

Hickory Bill's offers al fresco dining on the banks of the Housatonic behind the restaurant all summer. Better yet, he has become one of the region's favorite caterers.

JODI'S COUNTRY COOKERY
413-528-6064.
327 Stockbridge Rd., Gt. Barrington.
Price: Inexpensive to Moderate.
Cuisine: Italian.
Serving: B, L, D, SB.

Jodi's immediate locale (amid a shopping center, a car dealership, and a McDonald's) doesn't suggest country charm, but proprietors Steven and Jodi Amoruso and their partner, Carole Altman, have succeeded in establishing a rustic and welcoming ambience inside. Both dining rooms are pleasant, spacious, and "country" feeling, while the porch that wraps around the front of the old

Credit Cards: AE, D, MC, V.
Reservations: Recommended.

farmhouse is a very popular spot in warmer weather, despite the nearby traffic.

Although the dinner menu very much reflects the Amorusos' Italian restaurant roots, the luncheon offerings tend more toward American. At lunch, the food is good, solid, well prepared, and nicely served, though at times a bit bland. The dinner offerings are very good Italian — a somewhat rare commodity in Berkshire — though the decor and the cuisine aren't quite in synch. Dinner specials run more to International — grilled duck breast with figs & apples, tuna au poivre, etcetera, and are uniformly good.

KINTARO
413-528-6007.
Railroad Station, 48 Castle
    St., Gt. Barrington.
Closed: Mon., Tues.
Price: Moderate.
Cuisine: Japanese,
    American.
Serving: D.
Credit Cards: D, MC, V.
Reservations:
    Recommended.

Kintaro has moved into the Great Barrington Railroad Station, co-opting The Bronze Dog's space while incorporating a few of its favorite entrées. One of Berkshire's largest dining rooms, somehow each table nevertheless maintains an intimacy. The waitstaff are uniformly cheerful and pleasant, helpful in explaining the intricacies of the predominantly Japanese menu.

Kintaro sushi remains outstanding, deftly prepared at a bar that also seats a dozen diners. California rolls are available with crabmeat, eel, or salmon. Daily specials include catch of the day, prepared blackened, teriyaki, or misoyaki (with a sweet miso sauce). Left over from Dog days is a simple rosemary lemon roasted chicken with garlic mashed potatoes and vegetables, comforting and savory. Kintaro presents an eclectic beverage list: sakes; wines from Washington State, South Africa, Argentina, and Australia; beers; plum wine by the glass; Reed's Ginger Brew; juices; spritzers; and espressos. An outstanding tiramisu and organic sorbets complete one of Berkshire's most balanced dinners.

THE PAINTED LADY
413-528-1662.
785 S. Main St., Gt.
    Barrington.
Price: Moderate.
Cuisine: Northern Italian,
    Continental.
Serving: D.
Credit Cards: MC, V.
Reservations:
    Recommended.

Owners Julie and Dan Harris team up to present a comfortable atmosphere and good food. The old Victorian house that gives the place its name is colorful and lovingly decorated.

Much of the extensive menu depends on the mood of the chef; that is, there are several nightly specials. The regulars, such as a good variety of pasta dishes, are also worth trying. A salad comes with all the entrées.

An enticing feature is a snack of garbanzo bean salad to have with a basket of warm bread as soon as diners are seated. Pesto pasta and chicken with wild mushrooms were tasty and satisfying. Apple raspberry pie is an excellent way to end an evening.

PANDA WEST
413 528-5330.
300 State Rd., Gt.
  Barrington.
Price: Inexpensive to
  Moderate.
Cuisine: Hunan, Szechuan,
  Mandarin, Cantonese.
Serving: L, D.
Credit Cards: AE, MC, V.

This is one of three excellent Pandas in Berkshire (see also Lenox and Pittsfield), all serving Peking, Hunan, Szechuan, Shanghai, and Cantonese specialties. Although the menus of all three are nearly identical, the Great Barrington Panda is our favorite. The dining room is expansive, woody, and welcoming. In warmer weather, Panda's deck makes a fine outdoor dining spot. Even though you're right by Route 23, the traffic is rarely noisy and the atmosphere always invigorating. Or order out (you have to pick up) for the best Chinese take-out dinner you'll have this year.

Don't miss the steamed dumplings, either pork or vegetable, served in a woven bamboo steamer and with a special spicy dipping sauce, or their fried "potsticker" counterparts. Both superb! It's hard to miss on entrées. We particularly enjoy: General Tso's chicken, a crispy, spicy item; tangerine beef, tender sautéed filet strips both spicy and sweet; cold sesame noodles and eggplant with garlic sauce, two hearty vegetarian selections that will satisfy the omnivore as well; and moo shu pork, a roll-your-own crêpe filled with pork and sprouts stir-fry and a sweet brown sauce. Assembly required.

**SPENCER'S
  RESTAURANT**
at Thornewood Inn.
413-528-3828.
Stockbridge Rd., jct. Rtes. 7
  & 183, Gt. Barrington.
Closed: Mon. & Tues.
Price: Moderate to
  Expensive.
Cuisine: Country
  Continental.
Serving: D, SB.
Credit Cards: AE, D, MC,
  V.
Reservations: Preferred.
Special Features: vegetarian
  dishes.

Terry and David Thorne's remarkable restaurant-inn now offers a choice of four distinctive dining rooms: the library, the atrium, the porches, or the music room. With the feel of a well-decorated British B&B replete with tiny bar, the Thornewood is strong on charm. On Sundays at brunch and on some weekend nights, innkeeper David Thorne changes hats to lead his David Thorne Trio, a jazz ensemble whose mellowness can complement your meal.

We recently tried out their deck, overlooking Taft Farms and the Monument Valley, where we delighted in every instant of the evening sunset and our evening meal. Among the appetizers, mushroom charlotte with port and currant sauce was our favorite — a creamy mushroom pâté baked in a bread crust and set in an ambrosial sauce. Also offered were palate-pleasing eggplant rounds, slightly breaded and layered with goat cheese and served with a tomato-basil salsa.

For entrées, a vegetable pie with a French-bread crust and layered with roasted garlic and lemon pesto made vegetarian eating regal once more. Salmon stuffed with scallop mousse caught us by surprise — the counterpoint of subtle fish flavors and textures working rather well.

"Fresh homemade desserts prepared on the premises," says a Thornewood flyer, and their desserts deliver satisfactions aplenty. A simple lemon pound cake was light, delicate, and delicious. Death by Chocolate, Spencer's dessert of the season, was aptly named, delivering as it does a base layer of chocolate walnut torte topped by a tall wedge of double chocolate mousse.

20 RAILROAD STREET
413-528-9345.
20 Railroad St., Gt.
  Barrington.
Price: Inexpensive.
Cuisine: American.
Serving: SB, L, D.
Credit Cards: MC, V.
Special Features: Open late.
Handicap Access: Yes.

20 Railroad Street is the Granddaddy of the Railroad Street revival and practically an historical monument in chic new Great Barrington. And it's still good! It is popular with locals, the second-home crowd, and visitors; with families, couples, softball teams, and ski patrol squadrons. The warm, brick-walled dining room is dominated by a handsome, 28-foot-long mahogany bar and backbar which was built in New York City in 1883 and moved to Great Barrington in 1919. Informally named "Mahogany Ridge" by those who told their spouses they were hunting, the bar served as one of the area's speakeasies during Prohibition.

But good food is what makes 20 Railroad Street go. For lunch, dinner, or whenever, their starters, salads, sandwiches, and burgers are legendary. Unusual starters include the plowman's snack, a combination of Brie, soprassata sausage, and French bread. Pocket sandwiches are outstanding, with the vegetarian side pocket — lettuce, fresh veggies, and blue cheese in a pita all "smothered under melted swiss cheese" — being among our favorites. They are justly famous for their "family" of pastrami (Papa), ham (Mama), turkey (Rebecca), and roast beef (Roland) Reuben sandwiches. More than a dozen different burgers and an equal number of sandwiches fill out Railroad Street's printed menu. Chalkboard specials usually include soups, a variety of meaty entrées, and sometimes a vegetarian dish. Portions are generous, preparation always careful, and the service is efficient and always friendly.

UNION BAR & GRILL
413-528-6228.
293 Main St., Gt.
  Barrington.
Closed: Wed.
Price: Moderate.
Cuisine: New American.
Serving: L, D.
Credit Cards: MC, V.

Instantly popular, Union Bar & Grill has quickly settled in as Berkshire's hottest hangout, a place where you could comfortably lunch, share drinks, have dinner, and drop by for a later night snack. With its massive insets of brushed aluminum, high dark ceilings, and hard-edged sophistication, Union could easily pass for a SoHo bar and grill, attracting a similar upscale, hip crowd. Expect also

*Ordering at the Union Bar &
Grill in Great Burrington.*

Judith Monachina

Handicap Access: Yes.
Reservations: Not
Accepted.
Special Features: Smoking;
40-foot bar; Kids' menu;
Food served till 1 a.m.

to party with families and kids of all ages, because Union has a special kids' menu, and is just noisy enough — with the sound system wired to rock — to allow kids to be kids.

The second of Susan and Danny Smith's Berkshire restaurants, Union Bar & Grill carries the same panache as John Andrew's (Egremont) and some of the same quality fare, at a much reduced tab. Serving New American cuisine, the Grill's food will seem familiar, with unfamiliar overtones. It is framed American, with possibly Asian, Indian, Middle Eastern, or American Southwestern flavors and ingredients spiced in.

The appetizers are indeed appetizing. You might want to make a meal of two, with choices like barbecue duck with blue corn tortillas, or a wild rice and butternut squash fritter with cranberry jam. There are equally appealing sandwiches, including a Union burger, salads including a delicious chicken salad with chèvre, pastas, and small gourmet grilled pizzas. Fun side orders include fried zucchini with parmesan, the kids' menu, and a selection of modestly priced but outstanding entrées, our favorite of which is lacquered salmon with vegetable spring rolls.

Housatonic

JACK'S GRILL
413-274-1000.
Main St., Housatonic.
Open: Mid-May–late Oct.
Price: Moderate.
Cuisine: American.
Serving: D, SB.
Credit Cards: AE, MC, V.

The Jack of Jack's Grill is Jack Fitzpatrick, the patriarch of Berkshire's first family of hospitality (the Red Lion, Blantyre). The Fitzpatricks know how to make dining out an entertaining experience. Housed in a former hardware store, the shelves overflow with memorabilia: Hard Rock Cafe meets "Leave it to Beaver." The menu restates the theme: pot roast, pork chops, and roast chicken,

The first greeter at Jack's in Housatonic.

Judith Monachina

a.k.a. comfort food, filling and satisfying. Someone in the party should order the hot dog, just to see the little tube steak served in a cardboard convertible.

The staff is entirely accommodating, professional, and efficient. Guiness and Harp are on tap, and the brief wine list offers good values by the glass or bottle. Red Jello is on the dessert menu together with Toll House cookies (5 for $2.50). One of our party, getting into it, rated German chocolate cake with a glass of icy cold milk "the best thing on the menu."

Lee

CACTUS CAFE
413-243-4300.
54 Main St., Lee.
Price: Inexpensive to
   Moderate.
Cuisine: Mexican.
Serving: L, D.
Credit Cards: AE, D, MC,
   V.

The Cactus Cafe continues to epitomize and lead the dining revolution in downtown Lee. Co-Proprietors Joanne Wentholt and spouse/Chef Jim Conroy take an exciting, home-cooked approach to Mexican cuisine, with lots of their own creations plus many an innovative twist on the old standards. The result, the best Mexican food in Berkshire!

The atmosphere is quaint, tin-ceilinged, Mexican, as close to the Baja as you'll find in these parts. The selection of Mexican beers, plus a few top U.S. and German choices, or the frozen margarita or sangria go well with the excellent, complimentary house-made chips and salsa, or perhaps even better with creamy-spicy chili con queso. For a different appetizer, sopa de lima — scallops, swordfish, and shrimp in a lime bouillon — is sensational, an oceanic meal in itself. Or the ceviche, a mix of marinated shrimp, marlin, and scallops, is up to top seaside standards, and the quinoa salad is a vegetarian delight, large enough to do as a main course. Main courses are mighty ample — we sometimes even pass up a full appetizer. *Always* ask about the pescada del día (fish

Lunchtime at the Cactus Cafe.

Judith Monachina

of the day) served grilled, with a mango salsa. Or try the caldo quintanaro, "Yucatan bouillabaisse" in a rich, chili-charged fish broth. But this isn't a fish restaurant; all the classic Tex/Mex (actually Cal/Mex here) classics are on offer, too, and all very interestingly done. You're going to have to go here lots to enjoy it all — we do!

CORK 'N HEARTH
413-243-0535.
Rte. 20.
On Laurel Lake, N. of Lee.
Price: Moderate.
Cuisine: American/New
  England Contemporary.
Serving D.
Credit Cards: AE, MC, V.
Special Features: Rustic
  fireside ambience;
  panoramic views of
  Laurel Lake.

Nestled on the edge of Laurel Lake, the Cork 'n Hearth has offered friendly service and inventive takes on traditional New England fare for over four decades.

At press time, the Cork 'n Hearth was coming under the ownership of Chris Ryan, a Johnson and Wales-trained chef (previously a partner at Zampano's in Lenox), and his wife, Jasmine. Though relatively young, Chef Ryan is a culinary veteran, having already opened three restaurants in Charleston, South Carolina, and he has also worked extensively on the West Coast (most recently as executive chef at Scott's Seafood in Palo Alto).

An interview with Chef Ryan confirmed that he and his wife plan on maintaining the Cork 'n Hearth's distinctive rustic ambience, as well as its emphasis on American cooking. However, given his West Coast training, he expects to rethink many aspects of the menu, creating a selection of new dishes he calls "Contemporary New England Cuisine."

CYGNET'S AT THE
  BLACK SWAN INN
413-243-2700,
  800-876-SWAN.

In its airy dining room overlooking Laurel Lake, the Black Swan Inn (a Best Western property) provides a dining experience marked by unex-

Rte. 20, Lee.
At Laurel Lake, N. of Lee.
Price: Moderate.
Cuisine: Continental.
Serving: D.
Credit Cards: AE, CB, DC, MC, V.
Special Features: Atrium restaurant overlooking Laurel Lake.

pected pleasures. In addition to the lovely setting, the restaurant offers an inspired continental menu and a wine list to match — featuring bottles from France, the U.S., Germany, Italy, Australia, even Hungary, ranging in price from $15 to $225. Dessert wines and wines by the glass are also offered.

The menu is suberbly complemented by such a list. Chris Bonnivier, Cygnet's young executive chef, is a rare talent who has chosen to return to his native Berkshire County after culinary stints at the Phoenician in Scottsdale and in the south of France.

In the appetizer category, a portobello mushroom soup with endive and garlic was sensational, as were steamed mussels (flown in from New Zealand and remarkably plump) with tomatoes and leeks, swimming in a fragrant broth.

Standout entrées included the juicy grilled sirloin steak, crowned with a halo of delicate sweet potato fries and served with roasted artichokes and shallots. The fricassee of pousan (a European-bred bird, slightly larger than a Cornish game hen) was downright succulent, nestled between morels, goat cheese, apples, and a savory bread pudding studded with rosemary sprigs. As Chef Bonnivier prefers to incorporate vegetables and starches directly into his entrée creations, there are no side dishes. Two salad selections are available, both featuring locally grown organic ingredients.

Among desserts, the Belgian chocolate hazelnut terrine was a revelation — slightly denser than most chocolate confections and set off by luscious strawberries.

JOE'S DINER
413-243-9756.
85 Center St., Lee.
At corner of Center & Main Sts.
Closed: Sun.
Price: Inexpensive.
Cuisine: American.
Serving: B, L, D.

A politician wouldn't think of campaigning in Berkshire without a photo-op stop (and maybe a meatloaf platter, too) at Joe's Diner, a county institution. Joe's is in a wonderful time warp, full of mill workers just off or going onto shift and hunters early and late in every season, open 24 hours a day (except for late Saturday night — when Joe says the crowd tended to arrive a little too exuberant — and closed all day Sundays), still stocking packets of Red Man Chewing Tobacco right next to buckets of lifetime-guarantee combs, and posting prices that make a New Yorker think it's 1948 again. Prominently displayed is Norman Rockwell's famous "The Runaway," featuring a little boy running away from home at a lunch counter, with kindly cop and worldly-wise counterman assisting in the drama. Rockwell set it here with Joe himself as a model.

But the real secret of his long-running success: Joe Sorrentino and his family serve good food. Joe creates a tasty special every day. "We'll go through a whole hip of beef every Monday, 120 pounds of corned beef every Thursday,"

Joe Sorrontino, of Joe's Diner.

Courtesy of The Advocate Newsweeklies.

says Joe, and many regulars are attuned to his menu. If you're serious about taking in one of Joe's specials (like a roast beef dinner with vegetable, potato, and bread for under five bucks), you'd better arrive early. We came on corned beef night recently and watched the last of the 120 pounds disappear quickly, leaving latecomers disappointed. If it happens to you, don't despair! Have breakfast at 10 p.m., or delicious pot roast at 7 a.m.. All things are possible, and everything's tasty, at Joe's.

MORGAN HOUSE INN &
RESTAURANT
413-243-0181.
33 Main St., Lee.
Closed: Christmas Day.
Price: Moderate.
Cuisine: New England
 Contemporary.
Serving: L, D, SB.
Credit Cards: AE, D, DC,
 MC, V.
Reservations:
 Recommended.

The Morgan House is a sanctuary for the hungry tourist. It's good to know if we're in Lee on a Monday (when many restaurants are closed), we still have a really terrific restaurant to rely on. Built in 1817 as a private residence, it became an inn in 1855, when the lodging across the street burned to the ground. It retains that feel of a stagecoach stop. Comfortable, serviceable, the fireplace, paneling, booths, and woven placemats make it cozy.

Chef/owner Lenora Bowen takes a fresh approach to familiar dishes, however. By adding a pistachio crust to swordfish, she creates an entrée that is novel and exciting. The pot roast was accompanied by a wonderful cranberry relish and the pasta with sun-dried tomatoes. The popovers are simple yet sublime. The salad that comes with every entrée is a refreshing mix of mesclun greens. Fish, pasta, side vegetables all arrived cooked to perfection.

The Morgan House is a reliable spot to dine and a great find off-season. Those who aren't timely, however, will find that on slow nights they seriously close at 9 p.m. — and some visitors have found that service and quality decline as that hour approaches.

PARADISE OF INDIA
413-243-0500.
5 Railroad St., Lee.
Price: Inexpensive to
    Moderate.
Cuisine: Indian.
Serving: L, D.
Credit Cards: AE, D, MC,
    V.

Paradise of India, tucked just off Main St. in Lee, seems to have established a loyal clientele of Indian food lovers. Serving lunch and dinner without a break in between, the restaurant offers a treat for those in the Berkshires who have unusual schedules or want lunch in mid-afternoon. The menu offers a wide variety of curries, vegetarian and non-vegetarian, and a selection of specialities cooked in a tandoori clay oven. Breads are delicious. Desserts are mildly sweet and creamy, such as rasmalai (made from the essence of milk, garnished with nuts, and served chilled) or kulfi (sweetened cream frozen and flavored with cardamon and pistachio).

The masala tea is a treat not to be missed.

SULLIVAN STATION
413-243-2082.
Railroad St., Lee.
Price: Moderate.
Cuisine: New England.
Serving: L, D.
Credit Cards: AE, D, MC,
    V.
Reservations: Accepted.
Special Features: Summer
    dining on deck or in
    refurbished caboose.

Located in an old New York, New Haven & Hartford Railroad depot, Sullivan Station has a convivial mahogany bar with a brass footrail from a Methodist church. The wainscoted dining room walls are decorated with railroad memorabilia, and soft pop — The Beatles, Hall & Oates — plays over the stereo.

Chef Todd Ranolde specializes in hearty, home-style fare. For starters, a recent evening menu offered shrimp cocktail and a bean and barley soup. Entrées, accompanied by butternut squash and mashed potatoes, included baked scrod in lemon butter and charboiled sirloin steak served fresh off the cowcatcher. The waitstaff is good-natured and prompt. Complete dinner for two and tip runs about $55.

South Lee

FEDERAL HOUSE INN
413-243-1824.
Main St., Rte. 102, S. Lee.
1 1/2 mi. E. of Stockbridge.
Price: Expensive.
Cuisine: Continental.
Credit Cards: AE, D, MC,
    V.
Reservations:
    Recommended.
Special Features: Fireplaces.

The Federal House is a handsome, columned building, shaded by magnificent old trees and set in surprisingly charming downtown South Lee. Owners Robyn and Ken Almgren have created a rich and welcoming atmosphere, with white linens, silver, and fresh flowers adorning every candlelit table, and a fire crackling in the dining room hearth on fall and winter evenings.

The waitstaff are young, attentive, and well trained — a reflection of the owner/proprietors' training in top New York City restaurants. The reg-

Dinner by the flower-decked fireside, at the Federal House.

Jonathan Sternfield

ular menu is, of course, supplemented with changing specials, including a different pasta entrée each day. We recently began with broiled Malpeque oysters on spinach puree with béchamel sauce, a special, and crabmeat soufflé cakes with corn and red pepper relish, from the menu. The oysters were creamy and delicious, perfectly done, though they could have stood another dollop of béchamel for this gourmand's palate. The crab cakes were outstanding — light, flavorful, and with a lovely medley of tastes. For the main course, we had sautéed medallions of pork with wild mushrooms and watercress spaetzle and another special, lightly grilled fillets of sea bass in a cream sauce. Both were excellent, the sea bass especially tender and aromatic.

Chef Ken is a dessert master, notorious among dieters for his apple fritters — feathery fruity pancakes in a sauce of ice cream, stiff whipped cream, and kirsch — and his chocolate-bathed profiteroles. Relax, enjoy, diet tomorrow. A Federal House meal is worth the sacrifice.

New Marlborough

THE HILLSIDE
413-528-3123.
Rte. 57, New Marlborough.
Closed: Mon.; Mon. & Tues.
  in winter.
Price: Moderate.
Cuisine: Continental.
Credit Cards: AE, MC, V.
Serving: D; Sun. lunch 12–2.
Reservations:
  Recommended.
Special Features: Outdoor
  dining; Fireplace.

The Hillside dining room is sparkling clean and neat, as if a determined Swiss housewife were in charge. Simple elegance predominates, from the pale blue table linen to the fresh-cut flowers, from the rubbed honey-colored woodwork to the pleasant candlelight. Waitresses are friendly but formal (we like that), experienced, and absolutely first rate. The overall atmosphere is one of casual conviviality.

Chef/Proprietor Giuseppe Chigine presents classic continental dishes beautifully done. There are no surprises, unless meticulous appointments, excellent preparation, and faultless service throw you off. His onion soup is perhaps Berkshire's best. The salads are aways crackling fresh — and come with real Roquefort if you care for the granddaddy of blue cheeses. If veal Oscar, filet of sole meunière, or chicken cordon bleu sound a little dated or trite, try them here and learn again how great they can be in the hands of a master. Desserts are the same — classics well done. Flaky-crusted pecan pie with delicious whipped cream and a chocolate crêpe filled with chocolate ice cream and topped with semisweet chocolate sauce seduced us. For the less self-indulgent, there is a selection of special coffees (Irish, Calypso, Jamaican, etc.), and an excellent espresso served with its own espresso pot for a second cup.

OLD INN ON THE GREEN AND GEDNEY FARM

413-229-3131.
Rte. 57 (6 mi. E. of Rte. 23), New Marlborough.
Closed: Mon.–Wed.; July–Oct. closed Tues. only.
Price: Weekday & Sun.: Moderate to Expensive. Weekends: Very expensive, prix fixe.
Cuisine: French, American.
Serving: L at Gedney Farm; D at Old Inn.
Credit Cards: AE, MC, V.
Reservations: Appreciated.
Special Features: Intimate candlelit dining rooms; Fireplaces; Outdoor patio.

For those of us who have accepted the notion that we are what we eat, the Old Inn on the Green in New Marlborough will clearly make better men and women of us. Lighted entirely by candlelight, the inn makes guests immediately feel they are genuinely respected and they, in turn, respect the inn. The atmosphere is warm and comfortable. Food and service are excellent without a trace of stuffiness or pretension.

"Weekdays' Firesides à la carte" feature such appetizers as grilled scallops Provence, sautéed sweetbreads with pancetta and water cress, potato fritter with crème fraîche arugula, and American sturgeon caviar. All of those, and the vegetarian entrée of the evening, mixed wild mushrooms and pasta, are delicious, as was a shared tavern salad.

Desserts are also superbly presented. Crème brûlée was no doubt created by someone who loves what he or she is doing. Presentation, not pretense; ambience, not ambivalence. Executive chef: Christopher Capstick.

Sheffield

STAGECOACH HILL INN

413-229-8585.
Rte. 41, Sheffield.
On Rte. 41, several mi. N. of Lakeville, CT.
Closed: Wed.
Price: Moderate to Expensive.

The Stagecoach Hill is a bastion of good dining and drinking on the southern edge of Berkshire and an excellent waystation for the arriving New Yorker. A coach stop since the early 1800s, Stagecoach Hill Inn continues to offer "Fine Victuals and Ardent Spirits." The comfortable pub has an excellent selection of beers on tap and in

Cuisine: English, Italian.
Serving: D.
Credit Cards: AE, DC, MC, V.
Reservations: Recommended.
Special Features: Outdoor dining; Formal, candlelit dining rooms; Fireplace.

bottle along with the more ardent stuff, and a crackling fire in a double-sided hearth in the winter.

Ms. Sandy MacDougall, the proprietess for some two years now, has lured her son, Chef David Essenfeld, down from the Old Mill in South Egremont. The classic British flavor has been maintained, but updated with a rather lighter touch. Among appetizers, the smoked Gruyère and mushroom tart is commendable, and the homemade gravlax salmon with red onion relish and sour cream horseradish is exceptional. The Saturday dinner special now is prime rib of roast beef served with excellent mashed potatoes. A delicious steak and mushroom pie has replaced the traditional steak and kidney combination. Speaking of pie, try Chef David's delicious grilled chicken and portobello pie with mashed potato crust.

Stockbridge

THE RED LION INN
413-298-5545.
Main St., Stockbridge.
Price: Expensive.
Cuisine: Traditional American.
Serving: B, L, D.
Credit Cards: AE, D, DC, MC, V.
Reservations: Recommended.
Handicap Access: Yes.

The Red Lion epitomizes most people's idea of a New England country inn, and it ought to, because that's just what it has been since 1773. It was the site of some genuine pre-Revolutionary agitation in its earliest days. The present building exactly duplicates one burned to the ground in 1896, from which the endless collections of antiques and antique stuff were saved by a dedicated citizenry. Since 1968, the inn has been owned by the Fitzpatrick family and has served as headquarters for their Country Curtains mail-order business and as locus for countless events in support of practically every worthy cause in the Berkshires, all generously subsidized by the Fitzpatricks. Daughter Nancy now supervises the innkeeping business and is adding some more contemporary notes to the traditional New England cuisine.

Dining options abound. The inn's quaint 19th-century main dining room (jackets required at dinner, gents) is decorated with the antique teapot collection of former Innkeeper, Mrs. Plumb, one of the treasures saved from that long-ago fire. The Widow Bingham's Tavern, by contrast, permits casual attire, is dimly lit, rough-hewn and intimate, and includes a cozy alcove with beaded curtain you can reserve. The rear porch and adjoining shaded garden is one of the most pleasant outdoor restaurant settings in Berkshire. For an evening to late-night option, try the Lion's Den downstairs, with bar, live entertainment, and a menu running to soups and sandwiches and featuring one of the better hamburgers in Berkshire.

But before dinner, if time and weather allow, have a cocktail on the legendary front porch at the Red Lion and drink in some old-time feeling. This has seen more rocking and more rockers than all other porches in the Berkshires combined.

The menu (except in the Lion's Den) is traditional, solid New England fare updated now with some lighter and vegetarian offerings. The New England clam chowder wins awards every year, though a trifle thick for our taste. Other appetizers are traditional and excellent, more due to their fine ingredients and freshness than any inventiveness in their design. Entrée portions are quite ample. The broiled double thick lamb chops are an inch-and-a-half thick, succulent, cooked to order, and delicious. The crisp roasted duckling and the grilled venison and wild juniper sausage, served with corn cakes, appear regularly and are deservedly popular. But we try to steer visitors to the Red Lion/ New England classics: the creamed chicken and biscuit, just as old-fashioned and delicious as Grandma's; the New England lobster, shrimp, and scallop seafood pie (or sometimes traditional New England lobster pie); the baked meatloaf with mushroom gravy (don't chuckle until you've tried it); or fresh, delicious broiled Boston scrod with crumb topping for the lighter palate. For desserts likewise, we push the traditions; Red Lion Indian pudding with vanilla ice cream (or ask for it with maple syrup if you're a real classicist), apple brown betty with lemon sauce, or (our favorite) New England bread pudding with warm whiskey sauce. For the less historically minded, there are plenty of permutations of ice cream, chocolate-based concoctions, pies and sauces in various modes — all delicious. Save room if you can.

The Red Lion serves meals from breakfast (an elegant bargain) through to a most welcome light, late-night menu upstairs in the summer months and in the above-mentioned Lion's Den year-around. The inn is a mighty popular dining spot. In summer, breakfast may be restricted to lodgers; be sure to phone ahead. Special holiday and Sunday dinner menus are announced in the *Berkshire Eagle* and require reservations. But whatever the day, service is always exemplary throughout the Red Lion, a bright, attentive enthusiasm that never becomes intrusive.

West Stockbridge

LA BRUSCHETTA RISTORANTE
413-232-7141.
1 Harris St., W. Stockbridge.
Closed: Wed.; Mon.–Thurs. in winter.
Price: Expensive.
Cuisine: Italian.
Serving: D.
Credit Cards: AE, MC, V.

Each of the three small dining rooms in this well-established West Stockbridge restaurant offers a sense of intimacy and a degree of comfort that helps to define the experience of La Bruschetta. The varied menu changes with the seasons to feature as much local produce as possible. The accompanying wine, from the ever-growing list, juxtaposes the products of the best of American vineyards with Italian and French favorites.

While La Bruschetta's pastas have always been the best, the menu offers many fragrant and fabulous alternatives. For example, as an appetizer, the combination of mussels and clams, redolent of garlic and served steamed in a light, soupy gravy, excelled. The pearl barley, with seasonal mushrooms, was a bit dry to the tastebuds but nevertheless nicely prepared — moist in texture and aromatic.

Among their finest main courses (or "primo"), the lamb shank with white beans, olives, and sun-dried tomatoes was a delectable choice, the meat firm yet succulent, falling from the bone at the touch of a knife. The accompanying vegetables and sauce were flavorful and spiced to match the meat's intensity. At $17 not a bargain, but worth the money; while the veal ragout in a red wine sauce, at a dollar less, was as good as any we've had.

The feast fills, but those with room might wish to try the assortment of fresh fruit sorbets, such as lemon, white chocolate, and nectarine combined.

This shop is a recent addition to Truc Orient Express, a Vietnamese restaurant in West Stockbridge. It features many of the items, including food items and cooking gear, found in the restaurant.

Judith Monachina

TRUC ORIENT EXPRESS
413-232-4204.
Harris St., W. Stockbridge.
One block off Main St. (Rte. 102), over Williams River.
Price: Moderate.
Cuisine: Vietnamese.
Serving: L, D.
Credit Cards: AE, D, MC, V.

Truc, a beloved fixture of the Berkshires, offers a pleasant change of pace from pervasive New Englandiana. The decor is a tasteful exercise in bamboo furniture and fixtures, honeyed walls with softly colored hangings and greenery, visible evidence that owners Luy Nguyen and Trai Duong have dedicated themselves to quality and good taste. And now their small, attractive gift shop adjacent to the restaurant offers a tasteful selection of Oriental objects, as well.

Vietnamese cuisine is no longer the total mystery it was when Truc opened its doors almost two decades ago. It offers many of the subtle flavorings of Cantonese Chinese and fewer blazing risks to the

Reservations:
  Recommended.
Special Features: Vegetarian
  dishes; Outdoor dining.

adventurous "let me try *that*" (pointing) diner than others. So experiment here. Point blindly, or ask the waiter for his recommendations, or give the chef free rein.

From the appetizers, we enjoy sampling the Truc special shrimp roll, a triangular package of crabmeat, pork, vegetables, and shrimp, served with a garnish of ruby red lettuce and a spicy sweet-and-sour Vietnamese dipping sauce; and the beef on a bamboo stick, marinated in a sesame seed sauce and charcoal broiled. Among the very many entrées, the fried fish, a whole fresh flounder crisply fried in a hot and pungent sauce, and the Nhatrang pork barbecue, small grilled pork meatballs served with cucumber, lettuce and rice paper wrappers and a special sauce, are quite distinctively flavored. The barbecued pork is a good, hearty entrée with plenty of pork, enough to satisfy the lusty American appetite. "Lemon Grass" is a very thin and delicate rice noodle which underlies several of the entrées; definitely worth having. And "Happy Pancake," a rice batter crêpe stuffed with a choice of shrimp, pork, or chicken with fresh mushrooms, onions, and bean sprouts, served with Vietnamese sauce, covers a good-sized plate and is a medley of luscious flavors. Altogether, fine fresh ingredients and a deft touch with seasonings make Truc's offerings consistently tasty, pleasant, and easy on the digestion. A delicious way to enjoy a meal, and an excellent excuse to visit West Stockbridge.

THE WILLIAMSVILLE INN
413-274-6118.
Rte. 41, W. Stockbridge.
About 10 mi. N. of Gt.
  Barrington, in hamlet of
  Williamsville.
Closed: Mon.–Wed. in
  winter.
Price: Expensive.
Cuisine: American.
Serving: D.
Credit Cards: AE, MC, V.
Reservations: Requested.
Handicap Access: Partial.
Smoking in bar only.
Special Features: Fireplace.

The hamlet of Williamsville, of which this 18th-century inn is one of the last thriving remnants, offers an opportunity to step back into the Berkshire of yesteryear: a quieter time, a simpler time, when people knew your name and looked you in the eye. Those genuine qualities remain inside the Williamsville's venerable walls, inspired perhaps by the crackling hearths, antique furnishings, Colonial art and artifacts.

The service and food complement the traditional excellence, affording meals of classic New England. Outstanding popovers, piping hot from the oven, start the feast. The soups, salads, and appetizers that follow easily mix regional with Continental cuisine, delivering fresh ingredients in well-prepared, tasty combinations. We've always favored the Williamsville duck, succulent with gamy juices, sometimes served with an orange-fig sauce. Then again, we fondly remember a sole, a chicken. . . .

On Sundays November through April, the Williamsville offers an evening of storytelling, complete with a prix-fixe dinner.

RESTAURANTS CENTRAL COUNTY

Lenox

APPLE TREE INN
413-637-1477.
10 Richmond Mountain
Rd., Box 699, Lenox.
On Rte. 183, S. of
Tanglewood main gate.
Closed: Mon.–Wed. off
season.
Price: Moderate to
Expensive.
Cuisine: Continental.
Serving: SB, D.
Credit Cards: AE, D, DC,
MC, V.
Reservations:
Recommended.
Handicap Access: Yes.

Up above Tanglewood, looking over Lake Makeenac (Stockbridge Bowl) and all of southern Berkshire, the Apple Tree Inn's octagonal dining room and lovely daytime vistas provide an aura for food, friends, and conversation. By night, hundreds of tiny "starlights" glow from the ceiling. There is also a delightful deck with awning overlooking the lake, giving Apple Tree the best-dressed view in the Berkshires.

New innkeepers Sharon Walker and Joel Catalano have kept the eclectic menu of their predecessors. Start with the five-onion soup, a house specialty, combining Bermuda and Spanish onions with shallots, leeks, and scallions — served with seasoned croutons. Or try an eggplant dish, roasted pepper salad, or stuffed mushrooms for appetizers. Some of the pastas and meats are prepared with cream sauces, while others will appeal to those who follow a lowfat diet. The choice includes several veal offerings, marinated and grilled fish, at least two chickens. The night we dined the special was crispy duck with chutney sauce. Most of the creative pastas are vegetarian. For the less adventurous, grilled black angus steak is available.

Desserts are home baked and change daily.

BLANTYRE
413-637-3556
(Winter: 413-298-1661).
Off Rte. 20, several mi. NW
of Lee.
Closed: Nov. 1–early May.
Price: Very expensive, prix
fixe.
Cuisine: French.
Serving: D.
Credit Cards: AE, DC, MC,
V.
Reservations: Required.
Special Features: Fireplaces;
Private dining room.
Handicap Access: Yes.

The crown jewel of the Fitzpatrick family innkeeping empire and a member of the distinguished worldwide Relais & Châteaux association, Blantyre recalls the Berkshire life of the wealthy of the Gilded Age. A true "cottage" of the era, Blantyre almost alone has been restored to the *luxe* condition and appearance of its heyday. One cruises up the gently curving drive through neatly trimmed woods past acres of closely cropped lawn dotted with magnificent specimen trees and handsome pieces of sculpture to an impressive (it was meant to be!) red brick Tudor mansion. Inside the manor hall, the decor and appointments all bespeak luxury and taste, albeit not understated taste. A magnificent carved and painted rocking

Making dinner selections, in the baronial splendor of Blantyre.

Jonathan Sternfield

horse by Berkshire artist Tilo Kaufman and a sterling potpourri bowl the size of a birdbath convey an appropriate air of the flamboyance of the era.

Before dinner, the tuxedo-attired maître d' offers drinks from a serve-your-self rolling bar; champagne seems almost obligatory under the circumstances. Then to the menu. Chef de Cuisine G. Michael Roller offers six to eight appetizers and the same number of entrées on the prix-fixe menu. You simply can't go wrong, but for our first course, we swooned over sautéed foie gras with sweet corn crêpes and rhubarb compote. Buttery, light, smooth, and delicious! Our partner swore by Maine lobster cake with tomato, coriander, and chives. As entrées, we enjoyed respectively a tart/spicy seared pepper-crusted tuna with leeks, Chanterelles, and red wine jus, and a richly flavored roast saddle of rabbit and foie gras with basil and bell pepper confit. The wine list is excellent, suiting the food and the surroundings. Desserts are varied, tending toward rich.

The summer luncheon menu is a bit lighter, but still a full and elegant meal with dessert. You can skip the latter and save $7 a head, as if it made a difference. The breakfast menu, for inn stayers only, is likewise varied, imaginative and doubtless delicious. Under affable Manager Roderick Anderson, Blantyre has achieved the level of perfection the Fitzpatricks always envisioned for it.

CAFE LUCIA
413-637-2640.
90 Church St., Lenox.
Closed: Sun. & Mon.
Price: Expensive.
Cuisine: Italian.
Serving: D.
Credit Cards: AE, CB, DC, MC, V.
Reservations: Recommended.
Special Features: Outdoor dining.

Many Berkshire restaurants strive to get the little things right. Cafe Lucia owners Jim and Nadine Lucie accomplish that with ease. A remodeled house that was once an art gallery offers a cozy atmosphere combined with elegantly prepared house dishes that will cater to all except strict vegetarians.

Appetizers include a medley of grilled vegetables served with roasted garlic and peasant bread, and an antipasto made with prosciutto, mozzarella, house-roasted peppers, anchovies, and Calabrese olives. Salads are a must, from the traditional Caesar with a house dressing to a savory mixture of arugula and radicchio greens tossed with orange slices.

Several pasta dishes are offered, ranging from linguine con melanzante (thinly sliced eggplant in a zesty marinara sauce) to a ravioli filled with fresh spinach and cheese baked in tomato and fresh basil pesto sauces. Other entrées include the ever-popular ossobuco (veal shank sautéed, then braised in a sauce consisting of diced vegetables and fresh herbs, served with rice) and an Italian hot sausage specially prepared with new potatoes, escarole, and seedless grapes.

A tasty lemon torte and tiramisu are just two of the many desserts that top off a truly fine dining experience.

THE CANDLELIGHT INN
413-637-1555.
35 Walker St., Lenox.
Price: Moderate to
  Expensive.
Cuisine: Continental.
Serving: L (Fri.–Mon. in
  summer and fall); D.
Credit Cards: AE, MC, V.
Reservations:
  Recommended.
Special Features: Fireplaces.

With exposed wood beam ceiling, fireplace, lace-covered french doors, Victorian-styled windows, mirrored wall, flickering candles, dried flowers on every table, and soft background music, the Candlelight Inn provides an amiable atmosphere in which to enjoy its pleasing food. The greeting at the door was warm and sincere enough to offset a little something missing in the service. We had to ask for the proper spoons and fresh ground pepper for the pasta. They were then provided quickly enough.

The pasta puttanesca was spicy and satisfying, although a tomato/spinach pasta with garlic oil lacked flavor and substance. Desserts, however, were plentiful and uniformly wonderful. Among the offerings: chocolate truffle, chocolate chip pie with ice cream and hot fudge, cheesecake, spiced pear, cranberry and apple crisp, crème brûlée, and an especially flavorful lemon tart: sweet and crisp yet just the right amount of tartness.

In warmer weather, the Candlelight offers dining al fresco in their lovely backyard garden. This leaf-shaded glade is the catbird seat of Lenox. From this perch there, diners can watch passersby on Church Street and music pilgrims on their way to Tanglewood.

CHURCH STREET CAFE
413-637-2745.
65 Church St., Lenox.
Price: Moderate.
Cuisine: American.
Serving: L, D.
Credit Cards: MC, V.
Closed: Sun., Mon. until
  Memorial Day.

If the word *bistro* brings to mind a restaurant with a warm, friendly atmosphere where fine food and beverages are served, then an American bistro is an apt description of the Church Street Cafe. In mild weather, lunch is served on the spacious deck. Inside, each of the three, cozy dining rooms is simply and tastefully decorated.

Reservations:
  Recommended.
Special Features: Outdoor
  dining.

An outstanding offering on the autumn menu, one of the four pasta dishes, was a ragout of little-neck clams, roasted tomato and bacon, and garlic. One of eight entrées, the autumn vegetable platter consisted of a sumptuous roasted acorn squash, with five-grain pilaf, grilled endive, braised greens, and root vegetable puree. This was a delectable dish, with a green house salad and crusty, warm rolls perfectly complementing the presentation.

And all that was followed by a tantalizing dessert menu.

CRANWELL
413-637-1364.
Rte. 20, Lenox.
Price: Expensive.
Cuisine: Eclectic.
Serving: B, L, D.
Credit Cards: AE, CB, D,
  DC, MC, V.
Reservations:
  Recommended for SB, D.

Candlelight, soft background music, fresh flowers, and a fireplace create just the right atmosphere in which to enjoy the inspired culinary wonders waiting at this glorious restaurant inn. The main dining room, with its cream-colored oval relief ceiling and damask curtains, is the kind of artistic grandeur one might expect to find at the White House.

The staff was impeccably dressed and totally knowledgeable about every ingredient and cooking method for each item on the menu. They were equally informed and helpful about the wine selections, which are varied and interesting. The crab and salmon cake appetizer with braised greens, Tuscan bean salad, and sauce rémoulade was generous and delectable; as was the pistachio-crusted goat cheese salad with baby greens, the caramelized onions, and cracked peppercorn Dijon. The soup special of pureed carrot and red pepper had a smooth, velvet texture.

Executive Chef Carl DeLuce's entrées, all beautifully prepared and artfully presented, included breast of duckling, cappellini, and a blackened yellowfin tuna, pan-seared with New Orleans spice and fresh herb mayonnaise. The sesame chicken breast with figs, sour apple, cranberries, apricots, and a Drambuie demi-glace was an imaginative delight, as was the substantial and tender stuffed veal chop. The salmon fillet with quinoa and black sesame seed crust and saffron rice was simply superb. Specialty of the house is baby rack of lamb with maple syrup, mustard crust, roasted garlic, and rosemary.

Equally as unique and splendid were the array of desserts, such as a rich, four-chocolate-layer raspberry truffle cake with raspberry ganache, triple chocolate torte, crème brûlée with Frangelico and raspberry, and a mocha ice cream torte with Belgian chocolate sauce.

Cranwell was originally Wyndhurst, the "cottage" of John Sloane, a formal Tudor estate, with gardens by Frederick Law Olmsted.

**THE GATEWAYS INN &
RESTAURANT**
413-637-2532.
551 Walker St., Lenox.
Located in the heart of
Lenox.
Price: Moderate to
Expensive.
Cuisine: Continental.
Serving: D year-round, L
and SB during the high
season, B for inn guests
only.
Credit Cards: AE, CB, D,
DC, MC, V.
Reservations: Requested.
Special Features: Private
dining room with
fireplace; Terrace dining
in summer; Convenient
to Tanglewood.

Rich in history, the Gateways Inn and Restaurant is being ushered toward the millennium by owners Fabrizio and Rosemary Chiariello, who acquired the lovely Victorian property in June 1996. Once known as "the house that Ivory Soap built" (it was Harvey Proctor's summer cottage during the last turn-of-the-century), the Gateways is worth a visit for its winding mahogany staircase — designed by Stanford White — as well as the innkeepers' private collection of vintage prints of Italian peasant costumes hanging on its gorgeous terra-cotta-colored walls.

Moreover, the hungry reader may rest assured that the creations of the Gateways chef are as pleasing to the palate as the physical surroundings are to the eye. Chef Jan Wheeler offers a broad continental menu featuring many classic Italian dishes. For example, there is a daily risotto offering, as well as many wonderful and satisfying Italian-inspired soups.

The dining room's signature entrée is a rack of lamb Provinciale, but we opted to try some of the other stand-out dishes, including Salmon Continentale — sautéed or grilled by request — served in a fragrant dill champagne sauce dotted with lobster and shrimp. The sweet and savory pork chops featured two extremely generous chops, one stuffed with apples and raisins, the other with wild rice and mushrooms, both versions remarkably simple and remarkably flavorful. On a previous visit earlier in the week, one of our reviewing team had sampled the tournedos Gateways, two hand-cut filets mignon wrapped in bacon and topped with béarnaise sauce.

To accompany such heartily portioned, savory fare, Chef Wheeler offers a thoughtful presentation of vegetables in season. The wine list is restricted to vineyards in California and Italy, but the selection is broad enough to satisfy any connoisseur.

Although the dessert menu features a number of decadently rich treats — including a white chocolate mousse that nobody in the dining room seemed to be able to finish — we chose the slightly less sinful route: creamy lemon sorbet, cleverly presented in an empty lemon rind.

LENOX 218
413-637-4218.
218 Main St., on Rte. 7A,
Lenox.
Price: Moderate.
Cuisine: New American,
Continental.

From the crackling fire, sleek bar, and framed prints, to the spacious room, comfortable chairs, and art deco decor, Lenox 218 is a feast for the eyes as well as the palate. The breads and warm muffins were so irresistibly light and flavorful, they could

Serving: L, D, SB.
Credit Cards: AE, D, DC, MC, V.
Handicap Access: Yes.

have been meals in themselves. Wines are varied; service and presentation attentive and gracious.

Recent entrées by Chef Jimmy DeMayo, teamed with chefs Hugh Pecon Jr. and Christina Gonzalez, included delectable salmon fillets with red roasted pepper sauce; chicken parmesan with penne pasta; and an interesting assortment of veal, chicken, duck, and fish. Several vegetarian selections are available as well.

Desserts such as the toll house nut pie with chocolate sauce and ice cream and deep dish fruit pies are delectable. Lenox 218 meets expectations.

PANDA HOUSE
413-499-0660.
664 Pittsfield-Lenox Rd., Lenox.
Price: Moderate.
Cuisine: Szechuan, Mandarin, Hunan.
Serving: L, D.
Credit Cards: AE, MC, V.

Though not a chain, this Panda very much resembles the others in Berkshire (see Panda West, Gt. Barrington, for more details), except that it's on the strip just south of Pittsfield. As with the other local Pandas, the food is delicious, chock-full of good ingredients that have been well prepared. Threatened with extinction elsewhere, Pandas continue to thrive in Berkshire.

ROSEBOROUGH GRILL
413-637-2700.
71 Church St., Lenox.
Closed: Tues. & Wed. in winter.
Price: Moderate to Expensive.
Cuisine: American.
Serving: L, D.
Credit Cards: AE, D, DC, MC, V.
Reservations: Recommended.
Special Features: Old New England home, variety of dining nooks.

The Roseborough Grill looked great on paper when we sat down to order. Our attentive and friendly waitperson rattled off a number of sophisticated specialties in addition to the menu's varied array of grilled meats and fish, vegetable, risotto, and pasta entrées prepared New England bistro-style by chefs Laura Shack Willnauer and Will Metcalf. Unfortunately the execution was far from expectations. In our appetizer, roasted garlic plate with sun-dried tomato goat cheese, cider caramelized onions, and calamata olives, the cheese was gloppy and indistinct, the onions were lifeless, and the olives seemed canned. A house salad followed, featuring a few lettuce leaves topped with mealy, ice-cold cherry tomatoes and large chunks of inedibly harsh red onion.

Our choice for a main dish, the grilled swordfish, was undercooked, verging on raw. The olive pesto was a red glob, unmarried to the fish. The bed of rice underneath was bland, and an unappetizing, orangey pureed substance resembling squash completed the dish. Even the glass of stout we ordered from Roseborough's excellent imported and micro-brewed beer list was flat. We'll just have to take their word for the presence of four different berries in our dessert, the Roseberry Pie.

THE SWEET BASIL GRILLE

413-637-1270.
306 Pittsfield-Lenox Rd. at Brushwood Farm, Lenox.
Closed: Monday in winter.
Price: Moderate.
Cuisine: Italian.
Serving: D; L may be served in summer; call ahead.
Credit Cards: AE, MC, V.
Reservations: Recommended.
Special Features: 1700s house; 5 separate dining rooms.

Set in an 18th-century home, the downstairs speaks of warmth and congeniality. The upstairs rooms are bare, uncarpeted, and unfriendly. We headed for the main room, with the working fireplace, red brick design, and green curtains hung from brass rods. The restaurant is always busy because the service is good, the help familiar with the menu, the portions satisfying, the food tasty, and the price right.

Most of the main dishes are served with homemade pasta slightly on the soft side. The penne and fancy pastas are fine. The fresh, crisp salad was set on the table in a large bowl. (Memo to SBG: drop the little packages of crackers.) Appetizing appetizers include deep-fried, three-cheese and vegetable ravioli, hot antipasto, baked stuffed mushrooms, baked artichoke-broccoli, and sausage. The cream of roasted garlic soup is worth the trip on its own.

Entrées popular with us: chicken, the broccoli, pesto, and arrizzo versions, served with sun-dried tomatoes; veal with sausage or peppers or Veal SBG, with sautéd garlic, onion, and basil, simmered in white wine with fresh diced tomatoes; and frutti di mare with clams, shrimps, and calamari over linguini. Chicken penne in light garlic sauce was delicious and filling. The shrimp scampi was loaded with shrimp, served over linguini.

On weekends SBG makes its own desserts, including cheesecake. Even more tempting are Chocolate Raspberry Temptation and tiramisu.

TRATTORIA IL VESUVIO

413-637-4904
242 Pittsfield Road, Lenox.
Rte. 7, bet. Pittsfield & Lenox.
Closed: Closed Tues., open every day in summer.
Price: Moderate to Expensive.
Cuisine: Italian
Serving: D; L Wed.–Sat., possibly more often in summer.
Credit Cards: AE, D, MC, V.

Trattoria Il Vesuvio is a comparatively recent entry in the Berkshire restaurant sweepstakes, but has not lost a moment in establishing itself as one of the better places to dine in the county. Situated in a not terribly convenient spot on Rte. 7 between Lenox and Pittsfield, Vesuvio is figuratively and almost literally built around a monumental domed brick baking oven modeled on one found in the excavations of Pompeii (Vesuvio, get it?). This provides a perfect medium for every baking chore from producing their own delicious bread to turning out the finest baked stuffed breast of veal (arrosti di vitella) outside of Rome or New York. Following the classic Italian dictum that the bread only achieves perfection if the baker builds the oven himself, co-proprietor Davide Monzo built it while the building was being converted from its original use as a barn.

The menu offerings are the usual for a good Italian restaurant; the distinction comes in the preparation, the fine, helpful service, and the distinctive difference which that classic oven seems to lend to any number of the dishes. Among appetizers, the caprese, a classic salad of basil, tomato, and mozzarella with an herbed oil and balsamic vinegar dressing, features their own homemade mozzarella cheese. The frutti di mare, a large ramekin of fish and shellfish baked hot and quickly in that oven, is another excellent entrée, and the tiramisu dessert is homemade, too, and delicious. And as a delightful bonus for dining late, Signor Monza gives a mighty loaf of that delicious bread to each of the last few tables every evening, a lagniappe that may last you for a week of tasty breakfast toast. Trattoria Vesuvio may be a newcomer, but it is definitely a contestant for the best Italian dining in the Berkshires.

THE VILLAGE INN
413-637-0020; 800-253-0917.
16 Church St., Lenox.
Closed: Mon. for dinner.
Price: Moderate.
Cuisine: Regional
  American/New England.
Serving: B, Tea (weekends);
  D (mid-June–Oct).
Credit Cards: AE, CB, DC,
  MC, V.
Reservations:
  Recommended.
Special Features:
  Traditional English tea
  served on weekends.

The Village Inn serves dinner nightly except Monday during the summer and fall, specializing in regional American cuisine at moderate prices, with emphasis on New England dishes. Breakfast is served every day till 10:30 a.m., till noon Sunday.

The most distinctive dining opportunity is a proper English tea, which is served every afternoon from 2:30 to 4:30, featuring an assortment of homemade scones with strawberry preserves and clotted cream, as well as a dessert tray. A choice of select teas accompanies this delightfully light repast.

A considerably more elaborate high tea is offered on one Sunday afternoon each month from January through May. On those occasions (be sure to phone — reservations are required), the event begins with live chamber music, then proceeds into the dining room for traditional English high tea — a light supper in three courses. The first course includes finger sandwiches as well as the customary scones with clotted cream and strawberry preserves. The second course is a hot savory such as creamed mushrooms on toast, Welsh rarebit, or asparagus wrapped in ham with cheese sauce; and the finale is a traditional English trifle. The accompanying teas are an unusually large assortment from the John Harney Tea Company of Connecticut.

The Critics on Wheatleigh

"Sets a table fit for a prince." — Marion Burros, *New York Times.*

"One of the finest tables in the United States."— *Elle Magazine.*

*The ornate elegance of
Wheatleigh.*

Jonathan Sternfield

WHEATLEIGH
413-637-0610.
W. Hawthorne Rd., Lenox.
Price: Very Expensive, prix
fixe.
Cuisine: Contemporary
French.
Serving: B, L; D Fri. and
Sat. only in winter.
Credit Cards: AE, CB, DC,
MC, V.
Reservations: Required;
"seating" charge for no
shows.
Special Features. Fireplaces;
Private dining room.

The food is magnificent, the presentation artistic, the service faultless, the setting regal.

Executive Chef Peter Platt's menu changes nightly. On our visit four "tastings" were displayed, one lowfat that was mostly game, one vegetarian, one on the seafood side, and the "dinner," of which the meat course was a succulent lamb. Each tasting listed four courses, and guests were invited to substitute dishes from one tasting to another. A surprise pre-appetizer, based on a potato pancake, greeted us. Warm bread was always available — and replenished. Although the four-course dinner, no matter how pieced together, was ample, we were relieved that individual servings were modest in size. The browned portobello mushroom was exquisite, as was the eggplant. After the lamb came a wonderful palate cleanser of three varieties of sherbet. After that arrived a chocolate soufflé that surely was the envy of any other soufflé breathing that winter night.

In season, Wheatleigh opens a Grill Room, less expensive but still in the grand tradition.

Wheatleigh lists 200 wines, some of which are available in half bottles. A glass of very smooth Roger Brut champagne started the evening. The wine list earned the 1989 Spectator Award of Excellence as one of the outstanding restaurant wine lists in the world.

The building itself, with the shrubs along its circular drive illuminated by hundreds of miniature bulbs, is another of the South Berkshire "cottages," a

19th-century Palladian villa built for New York heiress Georgie Bruce Cook and her husband "Count" Carlos de Heredia.

Hancock

FOUNDERS' GRILLE
413-738-5500.
Corey Rd/Brodie
    Mountain Rd.
At the Inn, Jiminy Peak, the
    Mountain Resort.
Price: Moderate.
Cuisine: American.
Serving: B, L, D during ski
    season; D only in
    summer.
Credit Cards: AE, MC, V.

Founders' Grille at the Country Inn, Jiminy Peak, celebrates the three men who began the ski area in the late 1940s with a hearty menu in a rustic setting overlooking the ski slopes. The antique tools and sporting equipment adorning walls and ceiling create a warm, casual atmosphere in the large dining and bar space, but do not lower the noise level, which we found intrusive. There are quieter areas adjacent to the main room. A large fireplace harkens of a ski lodge and appeals to skiers and non-skiers alike. The service is friendly.

The menu offers three types of steaks and several types of seafood, pasta, and chicken. The large, fresh grilled shrimp from the appetizer menu were delicious, despite the uninspired peanut sauce. A tasty mountain bread appetizer, topped with sun-dried tomato pesto and melted mozzarella, could easily be a light meal. The grilled steak entrée was cooked appropriately and tasty. For variety, it is offered blackened or teriyaki style. A beautifully presented striped ravioli of broccoli and sausage with pine nuts and tomato basil cream sauce was delicate and divine. Fresh baked country bread and a fresh salad provided the balance to the meal.

Desserts included carrot cake, Key lime pie, a caramel apple dish, chocolate spoon, and a densely chocolate bash.

THE HANCOCK INN
413-738-5873.
On Rte. 43 from
    Williamstown or via Rte.
    22 N. of New Lebanon,
    NY.
Closed: Mon.–Thurs.; open
    weekends.
Price: Expensive.
Cuisine: Continental.
Serving: D.
Credit Cards: AE, D, MC, V.
Reservations: Required.

The Hancock Inn may well be the quintessential New England inn, offering warmth and charm alongside rustic elegance. The fare served by innkeepers Ellen and Chester Gorski is pricy by local standards, but worth every penny.

We began our meals with a scrumptious plate of fried goat cheese with garlic jam and grilled polenta points. Both appetizers were so awesomely delicious they could have satisfied as an entire meal. Fortunately we progressed to fresh Norwegian salmon with black sesame crust and veal medallions with smoked mozzarella cheese, prosciutto, and asiago cheese compote. Both dishes, like the dining room itself, were remarkably elegant in their simplicity — genuine works of art. From a dessert menu including Napoleons, frozen white chocolate mousse, and brownie sundae, we succumbed to a lethal black tie truffle.

Pittsfield

DAKOTA
413-499-7900.
1035 South St., Pittsfield.
Price: Moderate.
Cuisine: American.
Serving: D, SB.
Credit Cards: AE, D, DC,
   MC, V.
Reservations:
   Recommended.
Special Features: Fireplaces.

With its pine walls, raised fieldstone fireplaces, mounted deer and moose heads, and over-hanging birch-bark canoes, Dakota communicates the feeling of a grand hunting lodge. In addition, the restaurant fills its odd spaces and some of its walls with Native American artifacts, all of museum quality. Comfortable and well managed, Dakota is probably the county's single most popu-lar restaurant.

With good reason. The restaurant usually oper-ates with clockwork precision, serving an imagina-tive, well-prepared menu that features Texas mesquite broiling and easily the best salad bar in the region. You can choose from steak kebab and shrimp, salmon, swordfish, and chicken teriyaki, among others. A lobster pond up front offers lobster lovers their pick, with the day's price per pound clearly posted above.

All meals come with huge slabs of freshly baked whole-grain bread and an invitation to the salad bar. The wine list offers two dozen popular varieties. Desserts are dandy, portions are bountiful, and prices are moderate, making Tony Perry's Dakota a Berkshire roadside delight.

THE DRAGON
413-442-5594.
1231 W. Housatonic St.,
   Pittsfield.
Price: Inexpensive.
Cuisine: Vietnamese.
Serving: D.
Reservations: Not accepted.
Special Features:
   Vegetarian specialties.

Kim Van Huynh's Dragon, serving 48 entrées plus crispy spring roll appetizers, soups, and fruit desserts, can teach even those who can't maneuver the chopsticks about Vietnamese culture — in a digestible way. It makes no difference that the waitress is as American as anyone at the diner farther down Housatonic St. In fact, Kim wants Americans to understand: the menu is in English, with reassuring notes that "the chef will be glad to adjust the spices to your taste" and sage advice: "We ask that you allow at least an hour for dining."

His Vietnamese pancake, listed as a "chef's suggestion," is a rice batter crêpe filled with shrimp, pork, mushrooms, bean sprouts, and onion, and served with nuoc mam' sauce. This savory meal wraps up a variety of this world's pleasures — and a vegetarian version of this pancake is also available. The tofu and mushrooms succulently separates those who think they are vegetarians from those who truly are. Servings are generous. A squirm of squid dishes is offered, from squid curry and squid sauté to squid with black bean sauce, as are more familiar dishes based on chicken, pork, rice noodle, and beef. Dragon serves a thoughtful variety of beers.

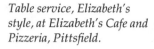

Table service, Elizabeth's style, at Elizabeth's Cafe and Pizzeria, Pittsfield.

Jonathan Sternfield

ELIZABETH'S CAFE PIZZERIA
413-448-8244.
1264 East St.
Across from "the G.E."
Price: Inexpensive to Moderate.
Credit Cards: None. Personal checks and "believe it or not, IOUs from all over the world."
Special Features: Specialty pizzas; No smoking

Right in the heart of Pittsfield's industrial history, Elizabeth's stands like a tiny beacon to homeyness. Its arty interior is a tip to the mix of the modern and traditional here. Elizabeth's attracts such a loyal following that those who want one of the few dozen seats better get there early.

Although Elizabeth's is known for having some of the best pizza in the region, many travel from all over the county to experience the fresh, varied, and thoroughly delicious pasta dishes, many if not most of which are vegetarian. The salads are superior, such as the insalata mista, chunked with delicious feta cheese, studded with Old World olives, stripped with roasted pepper, crowned with slices of kiwi, and supported by a bed of the freshest, youngest, tenderest baby salad greens from the heart of the lettuce. The bread is also among the best available hereabouts.

As good as the soups, salads, sandwiches, and entrées are at Elizabeth's, it is their pizza for which the place is justly renowned, especially the "white pie," called Rustica. "Imagine yourself a painter," the menu coyly beckons, "before you lies a canvas of silken dough. It beckons you in some primitive way. 'Come close,' it says. 'Caress me with oils, flavor me with herbs and cheeses, paint me with fresh vegetables. Use me, I am yours.'" Is this food . . . or what?

HOUSE OF INDIA
413-443-3262.
Galleria, 122 North St., Pittsfield.
Open: Daily 11:30 a.m.–10 p.m.; Sundays, 5 p.m.–9

Pittsfield's House of India, conveniently located on the city's main drag, boasts little atmosphere and less charm. To use the rest room, for example, one must ask for a key and descend two flights to the basement. Yet it has fast become one of our favorite dining-out places. The food is superb and,

Price: Inexpensive.
Cuisine: Indian.
Serving: L, D.
Credit Cards: AE, DC, MC, V.
Reservations: Recommended for weekends.

with a luncheon buffet for only $5.95, a great value. From authentic Indian appetizers like samosas — turnovers stuffed with meat or vegetables — to homemade Indian breads like nan and roti, to a variety of Indian soups, curries, kebabs, and vegetable dishes, diners in the heart of Berkshire can familiarize themselves with the exotic yet oddly comforting cuisine of the Asian subcontinent.

At dinner we had Raja Thaali, a combination plate with Tandoori chicken, Seekh kebab, lamb curry, chana masala (marinated chickpeas), saffron rice, papadum (crisp lentil bread), and galub jamun (cream balls dipped in syrup and rose water) for dessert. We washed it all down with genuine Indian Kingfisher beer. Simply marvelous.

PANDA INN
413-445-5580; 413-443-0819.
795 Dalton Ave., Pittsfield.
Price: Inexpensive to Moderate.
Cuisine: Chinese.
Serving: L, D.
Cards: AE, MC, V.

Newest Panda on the block, this Coltsville outpost is one of the best, with a huge glassed-in atrium that's daylight-filled every day, rain or shine.

Panda's all-you-can-eat "Most Valuable Buffet" is a Chinese-food lover's dream. Here are half-a-dozen of your favorite entrées, spread out before you with an open invitation to take whatever you want. There are also two soups, hot and sour and egg drop, spring rolls, and dozens of other offerings, from pork fried rice to Chinese dumplings.

Most Valuable Buffet is amazing, but Panda Inn does much else besides, and for your health's sake uses only vegetable oil and low-sodium ingredients during food preparation. Beyond their standard (but certainly excellent) Panda-style entrées, Panda Inn offers Neptune's Blessing, a Shanghai dish of shrimp, lobster, scallop, and crabmeat, sautéed with broccoli and snow peas in a traditional sauce.

TEO'S HOT DOGS
413-447-9592.
1410 East St., Pittsfield.
Price: Inexpensive.
Serving: L, D.
Cuisine: American.
Credit Cards: None.

An ordinary bar and grill on a dingy street, Teo's is justly famous for its zesty miniature hot dogs (about four inches long) that are best consumed covered with "the works," a chili-sauce/chopped-onions/mustard combo not designed to reduce gastric acidity. The preferred and perfect antidote to any heat-stoking tendency of the dogs *cum* sauce is, of course, a chilly brew. Their Genessee and Rolling Rock work best for us under these fiery conditions, but numerous selections are available.

Don't be intimidated. The regulars are quite accustomed to and entirely tolerant of strangers come to sample their urban/industrial ambrosia — downright friendly. Or if you're incurably shy or in a hurry or just passing through Pittsfield, try Teo's mini-equivalent of the traditional "family entrance," a tiny, screened take-out window (dogs only, no beer) on the front of the building. *Vaux le détour*, as another diners' guide puts it.

TRUFFLES & SUCH
413-442-0151.
Allendale Shopping Center
  (Rtes. 8 & 9), Pittsfield.
Closed: Sun.
Price: Moderate.
Cuisine: American.
Serving: L, D.
Credit Cards: AE, D, DC,
  MC, V.
Reservations:
  Recommended.

Truffles & Such is a first-class and creative dining room. The setting is modern, with sleek tables and chairs and a sophisticated buzz in the air. Owners Mike and Irene Maston have created one of the Berkshires' best restaurants.

To start with, there are typically two special soups, plus wild mushroom stew. Caribbean crab cake with avocado rémoulade and roast red pepper vinaigrette is both attractive and tasty. One of the gourmet quesadillas should satisfy a Tex-Mex craving. The salads are fresh and creative, although the Caesar may be too salty for some tastes. Any pasta dish can be ordered with Truffles & Such handmade linguini for an extra $2.50. Groups can order several of the creative pastas to share. Then menu includes beef, veal, pork, and some poultry selections; fish and vegetarian offerings including a risotto dish. The Oriental salmon provides an Asian flavor.

Lunch is a real pleasure, too. Many of the same dinner appetizers are offered, some hardy enough to fill any gaps. For dessert we chose from among such diverse items as kiwi tart, deep-dish sour-cream apple pie, rich carrot cake, fine Napoleons, chocolate hazelnut tortes, and chocolate . . . truffles & such.

RESTAURANTS NORTH COUNTY

Adams

MISS ADAMS DINER
413-743-5300.
53 Park St., Adams.
Price: Inexpensive.
Cuisine: Diner plus . . .
Serving: B, L.
Special Features: Authentic
  Lunch Car; Smoking
  prohibited.

Nancy Garton arrived in Adams eight years ago with her husband-to-be, Barry. She was immediately taken by the town, which was in a downtown restoration mode at the time. The Gartons purchased a 1937 business that received its present home in 1949, when the Worcester Lunch Car Co. deposited a replacement diner on Park St.

The diner is now an Adams institution — and people eat there, too. A Vermont couple comes down every weekend for the eggs Benedict. The home-baked breads go down just so smoothly; the pies have distinctively flaky crusts, and the cream pies come with flavor and portions to satisfy the truck driver the farthest from home. All of this might be expected at a top-notch diner; but Nancy adds to it an entire range of vegetarian dishes and forbids smoking. Ten-four, good buddy.

BASCOM LODGE

At the summit of Mt.
 Greylock.
413-743-1591
 (Winter: 413-443-0011).
On top of Mt. Greylock, off
 Rte. 7 to S. Main St.,
 Lanesborough, then 7 mi.
 up on Rockwell Rd. to
 the top. Accessible via
 Notch Road from N.
 Adams also.
Closed: Late Oct.– mid-May.
Price: Inexpensive.
Cuisine: American.
Serving: B, L (snack bar), D.
Credit Cards: MC, V.
Reservations: Required B, D.
Special Features: 70-mi.
 view.
Handicap Access: Yes.

Whether you've climbed on foot, on bike, or in your car, this mountaintop restaurant is worth the effort. Breakfasts and special dinners are the main events, served in the rustic stone and wood lodge. Berry-laden pancakes shine in the morning, the weekly barbecue buffets and New England dinners star Tuesday evenings, followed by informative programs. Whatever the hour, the views are breathtaking, the elevation heady. The "croo," mostly college age, some Appalachian Trail through-hikers working off their lodging, strives to please. Clearly, "the lowest price for the highest elevation in the state." No liquor license, but you can B.Y.O.

New Ashford

Jonathan Sternfield

Mastering the art of French cuisine — Chef Maurice Champagne.

MILL ON THE FLOSS
413-458-9123.

The atmosphere at Maurice Champagne's Mill on the Floss is informal and warm, with mas-

Rte. 7., New Ashford.
Closed: Mon.
Price: Expensive.
Cuisine: French.
Serving: D.
Credit Cards: AE, MC, V.
Reservations:
 Recommended.

sive rough-hewn beams overhead, candlelight, and firelight from the brick hearth in colder weather. The focus of the dining room is, however, its open kitchen, where, behind a Dutch tile counter and a gleaming array of hanging copper pots, chef Champagne in his tall white hat prepares meals before our very eyes.

We can begin with delicious crab cakes, also offered as an entrée; or try the onion soup, bold in broth with still-firm bread and perfectly browned Gruyère topping. Other offerings may include escargots in garlic butter or a pasta creation with a creamy garlic sauce.

Entrées are uniformly excellent. Although delicious fish and poultry dishes are always available, Chef Maurice does not apologize for offering several beef and veal selections. The veal marsala is an excellent choice. But those with dietary preferences should not be shy about asking to have a fish dish prepared in a lighter sauce.

Desserts range from a delicate crème caramel or chocolate mousse to the gâteau du jour. An evening we dined there was a lower calorie fruit crisp as well. All the baked goods, including the dinner rolls, are perfection.

THE SPRINGS
413-458-3465.
Rte. 7.
Closed: Christmas.
Price: Moderate.
Cuisine: Continental,
 American.
Serving: L, D.
Credit Cards: AE, CB, D,
 DC, MC, V.
Reservations:
 Recommended.
Handicap Access: Yes.

A large, popular restaurant, owned and operated by the Grosso family since the 1930s. The original building burned in the mid-1970s. Its replacement, in spite of a friendly fireplace, lacks charm, an impression amplified by the piped-in music. The food is good. The eclectic menu includes complimentary relishes, yummy cheese bread, baked stuffed clams, and a sherbet palate cleanser. An accent on veal, a variety of chicken, roasts, steaks and chops and lighter entrées are well prepared and presented. The Springs is an institution.

North Adams

DUE BACI
413-664-6581
40 Main St. (Holiday Inn),
 N. Adams.
Price: Moderate.
Cuisine: Italian.
Serving: B, L, D.
Credit cards: AE, MC, V.

The name means two kisses, one on each cheek, in the Italian way. It's owner John Moresi's nice idea. The Italian way has given a distinct flavor to this restaurant that, in favorable weather, overflows the first floor corner onto a terrace where, on summer evenings, the band plays on. To be sure, the room itself smacks of motel modern, but the food is savory. The veal, in wine sauce, was tender; the clams in the linguini succulent, the tomato sauce on the pasta very pleasant. We liked the family style serving of an attractive salad, enabling diners to indulge when and how much they wished.

The meal came to an elegant conclusion with tiramisu: Italian cottage cheese on top of ladyfingers soaked in rum and, from somewhere, a puddle of chocolate. The service was attentive and well trained. The luncheon buffets Monday–Friday are rumored to be a bargain.

THE FREIGHT YARD RESTAURANT AND PUB
413-663-6547.
Western Gateway Heritage State Park, N. Adams.
In Heritage State Park.
Price: Inexpensive to Moderate.
Cuisine: American.
Serving: SB, L, D.
Credit Cards: AE, MC, V.
Special Features: Fireplace; Patio

One of the few pubs in all of Berkshire (although the owners have recently opened Water Street Grill; see under Williamstown), the Freight Yard is in a two-story former railroad building in a historic district — with patio seating in the summer. For lunch, a generous, well-stocked salad bar is an alternative to menu selections and blackboard specials.

A wide variety of enticing foods includes generously portioned hamburgers and steaks, a daily pasta special (second helping gratis), grilled Cajun chicken, and the best and most filling Mexican "sizzlin' Fajita" in the area. Soups, salads, sandwiches (we like the grilled chicken breast with pub fries), desserts (from apple pie to "Death by Chocolate"), and popular appetizers (including spicy buffalo wings) go well with a good beer/drink selection.

Williamstown

COBBLE CAFE
413-458-5930.
27 Spring St., Williamstown.
Closed: Easter, Thanksgiving, Christmas, New Year's Day.
Price: Inexpensive.
Cuisine: American.
Serving: B, L, D.
Credit Cards: None.

The Cobble Cafe is a lively and attractive spot for breakfast and lunch. Chef Mark Hruska always produces a tasty vegetarian dish along with the interesting burgers, grilled steak sandwiches, and simple entrées. The trademark "Cobblewich" — grilled eggplant, basil, tomato, and goat cheese on grilled rye toast — is a delightful update of the traditional toasted cheese. The breakfast menu offers interesting omelettes and other egg dishes, such as a breakfast burrito. Fresh fruit is offered along with the usual breakfast accompaniments. Service is cheerful and prompt, even on busy football weekends. And as we go to press, the good news is that Cobble is opening for dinner, with a slightly different menu.

1896 HOUSE RESTAURANT
413-458-1896 (of course).

All of Williamstown roots for Denise Richer and Sue Morelle, PanAm flight attendant and

366 Cold Spring Rd.,
Williamstown
Price: Moderate.
Cuisine: American.
Serving: D, SB.
Credit Cards: AE, D, DC,
MC, Transmedia, V.

teacher, respectively, who first purchased the 1896 Motel (in 1985), then in 1993 the motel across the street (now 1896 Pondside), and then, fearing what would happen to the long-dormant barn-as-restaurant, purchased that as well, in 1994; opening it in 1996. They re-roofed and redecorated, including unusual but homey overstuffed dining chairs.

The '96 House aims to be straightforward and filling. One member of our group found the stuffed, baked potatoes disappointingly cold; another, the ale-steamed mussels "adequate"; a third really got into the split green pea soup. The roast turkey, a favorite there (second choice, shepherd's pie) contained tasty spiciness in the gravy and in the mashed potatoes; the House-made cranberry sauce was smooth. The apple pie should have stayed in the box, but the pumpkin cheese cake was a winner. A confusing party confused the service, which nevertheless was well-meaning.

In short it is a new restaurant, straightening out its miscues under the watchful eyes of its owners. We expect it to regain the traditional place the 1896 House of old held in the hearts of locals, travelers, and Williams College alumni. Williamstown Theatre Festival Cabarets hold forth in the function room in the summer.

HOBSON'S CHOICE
413-458-9101.
159 Water St.,
Williamstown.
Price: Moderate.
Serving: L (Tues.–Fri. only),
D.
Credit Cards: AE, MC, V.
Reservations:
Recommended.

Locals know that Hobson's Choice is a good one in Williamstown for lunch, a quiet drink, dinner, or a late evening's snack. Dark wooden booths line the walls of the restaurant's two rooms, creating a sense of privacy — even intimacy (except for a few seconds when the outside door opens). Hobson's is a comfortable place to linger.

With chef Dan Campbell playfully holding court from the open kitchen behind the salad bar, one of the tastiest in northern Berkshire, the customer is likely to get a custom-cooked meal, just the way she likes it.

Hobson's offers a wide variety of chicken (grilled, blackened, barbecued, teriyaki, and Santa Fe style), beef, fish, pasta, and vegetarian specialties, all flavorfully prepared. It makes its own soups; the onion soup gratinée is especially good. The desserts are also excellent, especially the mud pie.

A comfortable, well-stocked bar includes a nice selection of imported beers and ales, plus a modest wine list. Hot mulled cider, espresso, and cappuccino provide warmth and cheer for the abstemious.

LE JARDIN
413-458-8032.
777 Cold Spring Rd.
South of Williamstown.

High on a hill, Le Jardin appeals to the eye of those who stroll up its path. Inside, the mood is that of a country inn. Two chefs serve more of a

Closed: Tues. off season.
Price: Moderate to
  Expensive.
Cuisine: French.
Serving: D, SB.
Credit Cards: AE, D, MC,
  V.
Reservations:
  Recommended.
Special Features: Fireplace;
  vegetarian dishes; 3
  dining rooms.

continental menu than strictly a French one, with a greater emphasis on steaks and chops than on subtlety of sauces.

A favorite among Williams grads and parents, Le Jardin offers a pleasant evening without getting too fussy. We found the breads undistinguished, but were pleased that the tomatoes, in an appetizer with mozzarella cheese and in the salads, were fresh — even though the season had passed. We enjoyed the presentation of the salad and the main courses, well thought through and arranged in an attractive way. The tortellini retained a distinct feta cheese flavor with spinach and pasta; lamb chops and roast beef were cooked as directed, their servings more than ample. Vegetables were not inspired, but not overcooked either.

The service was pleasant and accommodating. A varied wine list included a fine Bordeaux. Save room for desserts, whether hot fudge sundae with real whipped cream, a tangy lemon mousse, or the mortifying "Death by Chocolate."

Judith Monachina

The newest restaurant on the Williamstown scene is Mezze. Owner Nancy Thomas consults with kitchen staff.

MEZZE
413-458-0123.
84 Water St., Williamstown.
Price: Inexpensive to
  Moderate.
Cuisine: Mediterranean.
Serving: D and light dishes.
Credit Cards: AE, MC, V.
Special Features: Specializes
  in appetizers; deck
  overlooking Green River.

Nancy Thomas presides over this friendly Mediterranean bistro and bar, a welcome addition to the North County restaurant scene. "Mezze" means middle: between a restaurant and a bar. Its creative menu changes frequently. Guests are equally welcome whether interested in a light pre-theater snack, a full meal, or dessert and coffee. Well-known theatrical figures are apt to be found at the bar après-theatre in the summer.

Meat, fish, poultry, and several vegetarian offerings tempt the palate. We recommend creating a meal by ordering several appetizers. Couscous, chickpeas, lentils, Greek feta, olives, fresh fruits, and vegetables are woven into the dishes. Among entrées, the seared tuna steak with ginger is exceptional. Desserts are made on the premises.

THE ORCHARDS
413-458-9611.
222 Adams Rd.,
  Williamstown.
Price: Expensive.
Cuisine: American, French.
Serving: B, SB, L, D.
Credit Cards: AE, CB, DC,
  MC, V.
Reservations:
  Recommended.
Special Features: Table
  settings and linens; All-
  day pub menu, lighter
  fare 12–9.

In its appointments and its fine meals, Sayed Saleh's Orchards gets high marks. The tables are set with real Irish linen, graceful stemware, and colorful, fresh bouquets. The service is knowledgeable, efficient, and friendly — in a discreet way. The restaurant feels like a club for people who live graciously.

Our goat's cheese salad was beautifully presented and tasty, the bread warm and crusty. Items on the brief menu of entrées included a pasta, two fish, and three or four meat offerings. We choose a roast rack of young lamb, which crowned a small dome of mashed potato, onions, and peppers — lovely to look at and delightful to down. The preparation of all of the food was exquisite. For dessert we chose the profiteroles, a delicate pastry with ice cream and chocolate sauce — and strawberries that suffered slightly for being out of season. The ample and imaginative wine list befits the club image.

The club atmosphere, impeccable service, smallish helpings, and pricy tab may not make everyone feel comfortable, but those whom that fits will much enjoy The Orchards.

**PAPPA CHARLIE'S DELI
  SANDWICH SHOP**
413-458-5969.
28 Spring St.
Price: Inexpensive.
Cuisine: American.
Serving: B, L, D.
Special Features: Open late.

Pappa Charlie's reigns supreme as a people's place and local hangout, convenient to Images Cinema and the Williams College gymnasium. It serves sandwiches, chili, and such. The overstuffed, delicious sandwiches and elaborately adorned, well-stuffed bagels are mostly named for actors at the Williamstown Theatre Festival, politicians, and local well-known. Anyone for a bite of a "Bo Derek"? Or an "Avocado Smoothie" — bagel of your choice, spread of cream cheese, slices of avocado: all zapped in the steamer? The philosophical issue is whether or not the names are a commentary on the named.

The fresh cider runs hot and cold; root beer that traces its roots to the A&W where Charlie Nikitas began; exotic fruit juice combos, like strawberry-banana-OJ. The cooler holds one of North County's better arrays of domestic

Pappa Charlie's is a popular spot for students and others in Williamstown.

Judith Monachina

and imported cheeses. The ambience is created by the friendly service and plain wooden booths. The benches in the small park to the north are a fine alternative; the basement is reminiscent of a school lunchroom.

ROBIN'S
413-458-4489.
Spring St., Williamstown.
Price: Moderate to
  Expensive.
Cuisine: American/French.
Serving: SB, L, D.
Credit Cards: AE, MC, V.
Reservations:
  Recommended in
  summer.
Special Features:
  Wraparound deck under
  pine trees; Take-out
  service.

At the foot of Spring Street, Robin's is a welcoming outpost for imaginatively prepared, thoroughly satisfying food. "A pleasure," said the *New York Times*, and we heartily concur. The menu changes daily, featuring organic local produce in season and influences from both California and the Mediterranean. And the expansive, tree-shaded deck has established Robin's as the primo warm-weather eatery in Williamstown. In the winter, Robin serves meals on fewer days but offers take-out up to the usual high standards.

The winter menu is equally satisfying as the summer's, with generous portions for a cold evening in the Berkshires. Enticing openers from a recent menu featured grilled eggplant with goat cheese and tomato terrine. Entrées included black lobster and shrimp ravioli in a pesto cream sauce, butternut sage ravioli, roasted vegetables with Robin's special polenta, and baby back ribs with black bean and garlic sauce. Extraordinary!

WATER STREET GRILL
413-458-2175.
123 Water St. (Rte. 43),
  Williamstown.
Price: Moderate (Grill
  inexpensive).

The owners of the Freight Yard Pub in North Adams took over the former Savories as an upscale outlet. The Grill is more like the FYP, open for lunch and dinner, with nachos, fajitas, burgers and seafood. In the Tavern (open dinner only)

Cuisine: Contemporary
    American.
Serving: L, D.
Credit Cards: AE, DC, MC, V.
Reservations: Recommended.
Special Features: Tavern;
    expanded menu in Grill,
    with fireplace.
Handicap Access: Yes.

recently we enjoyed Absolute chicken (with vodka) and the special, sirloin tips with mushrooms. The house chardonnay was above average. The house salad offered a great variety of dressings and the bread sticks received a bonus for being served warm. Our waitperson seemed interested without hovering. Overly live acoustics in this all-wood room can make innocent diners into eavesdroppers.

Judith Monachina

*Acoustic Brews: All around the county, restaurants —
    including the Wild Amber Grill in Williamstown and the
    Cactus Cafe in Lee — host acoustic brews, where musicians
    are invited to come in and play music together.*

WILD AMBER GRILL
413-458-4000
101 North St., Williamstown.
Price: Moderate.
Cuisine: Eclectic.
Serving: L, D.
Credit cards: AE, MC, V.
Special features: Smoking in
    lounge only; Terrace in
    summer.

A welcome addition to the Williamstown dining scene, owned by the three Smiths (brothers Alexander and Ned; unrelated Gerard), who also own the popular Cobble Cafe on Spring St. The gracious ambience of Wild Amber nicely complements the more casual Cobble.

The menu is creative and multicultural. The tasty Thai shrimp is the closest to a real Thai restaurant one can get in Berkshire. Because the menu is eclectic, something is sure to please everyone. Several specials are offered, including fresh fish and pasta creations. We recently enjoyed a wonderful lobster ravioli and a salmon fillet with special salsa that was as pretty as it was delicious.

The chefs have created a new and exciting dessert menu that includes favorites such as tiramisu and chocolate box. The chocolate chip rumcake is exceptional.

In season, the terrace grill opens, serving a separate menu featuring grilled foods. The terrace is also open for summer lunches.

RESTAURANTS OUTSIDE THE COUNTY

Hillsdale, New York

AUBERGINE
518-325-3412.
At junction of Rtes. 22 & 23,
　Hillsdale.
Closed: Mon., Tues.
Price: Very Expensive.
Cuisine: French inspired.
Serving: D.
Credit Cards: MC, V.
Reservations:
　Recommended.
Special features: Fireplace;
　Vegetarian dishes.

Renowned Chef Jean Morel has retired from his famed L'Hostellerie Bressane, passing the mantle to Chef David Lawson and his wife, Stacy, who now call the place Aubergine. By any name, it continues to be one of the region's treasures, an inspired country inn that serves fare fit for royalty. The menu retains a strong French accent, but is no longer bound by strict Gallic codes of cuisine. Instead, David brings in American, Asian, and other culinary influences that strike his fancy, as in his Maine scallop cakes with shiitakes, scallions, and bean sprouts, with a warm ponzu vinaigrette. American, Asian, and French, all in one mouthful.

Chef Lawson is not about to kill the goose that laid the golden oeuf, however, so many of Chef Morel's signature classic French dishes remain, served in good versions, most notably the spectacular dessert soufflés (which must be ordered at the start of the meal). Entrée offerings might include game, such as venison or rabbit, and a variety of ocean and freshwater fish. A tuna, roasted with a coating of peppercorns, was packed with succulent, spicy flavor, sushi in the center, well done outside.

The wine cellar here is a significant part of the legacy; the Lawsons can take you to rarified heights. In fact, everything at Aubergine elevates, leaving the diner satisfied in the grand style.

Hillsdale, New York

SWISS HUTTE
518-325-3333.
Rte. 23, Hillsdale.
Price: Expensive.
Cuisine: French, Swiss.
Serving: D.
Credit Cards: MC, V.
Reservations:
　Recommended.
Special Features: View of
　ski slopes; Outdoor
　dining.

The Swiss Hutte deserves its large and loyal following. Sited almost at the base of Catamount ski area, it nevertheless seems off in an Alpine space of its own while offering entertaining views of skiing — day and night — in winter and attractive wooded slopes in other seasons. The dining rooms are cozy and attractive, with fresh flowers and homespun linen on every table. They are frequently full. We ventured in one recent Wednesday in order to sample the regular musical offerings of The Organic Fruit Jam Band, a local piano and brass combo with an oompah air, along with the cuisine. Although we aren't always wild about music with dinner, TOFJB were not obtrusive, and they lent a festive air to a nice crowd that plainly enjoyed them. Thursday through Sunday, you have to hum.

The food is mighty good — International style, with not as many Swiss specialties as you might expect. Their onion soup is hearty, and though more than amply topped with melted Gruyère can hold its own with that of other Berkshire restaurants. Risotto Milanese was excellent, quite creamy, *al dente* and served with a nutty, grilled portabella mushroom. As a main course, the New England "bouillabaisse," a clear, saffron-flavored stew of salmon, mussels, clams, scallops, and shrimps, was delicious. While quite ample, it had a lighter effect than some of the other entrées. A special offering of beef goulash on noodles was quite spicy and piquant, well worth the venture off the menu. Swiss Hutte is also justly proud of its grilled meats, from herb crusted rack of lamb with a red wine glaze to their hearty, peppery, crunchy, and excellent 12-oz. steak au poivre, "certified black Angus." Desserts, in the Berkshire tradition, are rich and delicious. But as long as you're whooping it up, and especially if you mix in a few dances, why not?

New Lebanon, New York

SHUJI'S
518-794-8383.
At junction of Rtes. 20 & 22, New Lebanon.
Closed: Wed.; mid-Nov.–end of Mar.
Price: Moderate to Expensive.
Cuisine: Japanese.
Serving: D.
Credit Cards: MC, V.
Reservations: Recommended.
Special Features: Tatami rooms; Vegetarian dishes.

Alas, this edition of the Berkshire Book filled its covers after Shuji's had gone to bed for the winter. We were, therefore, unable to spend another pleasant evening there. We have not the slightest doubt that Shuji's will remain a unique dining experience and do not hesitate to recommend it, however. For more than 25 years now, Shuji's has delighted regional diners who've yearned for an elegant Japanese culinary experience.

The atmosphere at Shuji's combines the Victorian splendor of former Governor Tilden's mansion (he lost the U.S. presidency to Rutherford B. Hayes in 1876 by a single electoral vote) with the delicacy of Japanese domestic decor. In four of the mansion's upstairs rooms, you must remove your shoes to enjoy the cushioned realm of tatami. With authentic pillow chairs to recline upon, even diners unaccustomed to this type of sitting will be comfortable. Two of these tatami rooms are for private parties only. Downstairs there is Western-style seating.

Shuji's menu is authentic, comprehensive, and imaginative. You could start with some plum wine or hot saki, but you might also like a Samurai Lord (the Far Eastern sour made with Suntory whiskey) or a Black Belt (vodka, kahlua, and saki). Ashai and Kirin Japanese beers are also available.

For appetizers, Shuji offers sashimi (raw fish), sushi (raw fish with rice), tempura (batter-dipped, deep-fried vegetables and fish), and maki (raw tuna and rice wrapped in seaweed). Several elaborate dinners are offered regularly, among them "King of the Sea" and the "Japanese Gourmet Dinner." The "King" is a melange of lobster, crab, shrimp, scallops, clams, and vegetables, all lightly steamed in a seasoned broth. Shuji's Japanese vegetables are grown especially for the restaurant. The eight-course "Gourmet Dinner," delicious as it is, may be misnamed, being better suited to gourmands or possibly sumo wrestlers. When you have lost count and think you're home, Shuji hits you with course number eight, a huge, half-inch-thick porterhouse steak cooked teriyaki style.

Shuji's also features two delectable vegetarian dinners, one a tempura and the other a teriyaki. And from the ocean comes Shuji's seafood misonabe, a Japanese-style bouillabaisse with half a lobster, king crabmeat, shrimp, scallops, tofu, and vegetables, cooked with a soy-flavored sauce in an earthenware pot.

At dessert time, stick to Shuji's simpler fare, such as artfully served fresh fruit or sherbet.

BREAKFAST & LUNCH

O f the many Berkshire eateries designed to gladden the morning and/or early afternoon, we have selected a handful.

THE GASLIGHT CAFE (413-528-0872; Rte. 23, S. Egremont)

Yankee Magazine loves The Gaslight, and so do parents with kids and old-time sentimentalists of all ages. The food is always fun — well-prepared sandwiches, burgers, omelettes, and pancakes, and the ambience is straight out of Norman Rockwell.

MOM'S (413-528-2414; Rte. 23, S. Egremont)

Meeting someone from Connecticut halfway? Heading South and hungry? Choose Mom's for well-made soups, sandwiches, and salads in an attractive, sunny dining room, or dine on the open deck in back above the rushing Hubbard Brook in fine weather. One of Berkshire's best kept secrets.

THE DELI (413-528-1482; 343 Main St., Gt. Barrington)

The *best* sandwich menu in the Berkshires — try a "Jacques Cousteau" seafood-filled marvel, for instance — two great soups every day, plus gobs of local color and a loyal local following encompassing the whole social/commercial/artistic spectrum of Berkshire make The Deli a treat for the eye and ear as well as the tummy. Breakfast starts here at 5:30 a.m., with omelettes like the Cisco Kid, Eve Arden, and Miss Piggy rolling off Chef Frank's pan till 10. Go in hungry!

MARTIN'S (413-528-5455; 49 Railroad St., Gt. Barrington)

Martin's is bright and light, and a very popular spot for breakfast and lunch. Breakfast is served all day long. The omelettes are varied and outstanding. Pancakes come in standard form, plus a daily special, such as pumpkin. For lunch, there are burgers in many styles, including the Berkshire cheeseburger (mushrooms, onions, tomatoes, and peppers), sandwiches, salads, and soups, as well as daily specials such as beef bourguignon. Beer is available in addition to the usual beverages. Martin's supplies crayons at every table, so artists of all ages can illuminate their paper placemats. The more complimentary ones end up on the wall.

COPPER WILLIE'S DINER (413-528-8226; 282 Main Street, Gt. Barrington)

The decor is genuine diner — plate glass front, linoleum floor, Naugahyde booth upholstery, bentwood chairs, and wood wainscoting — with enough copper trim and decorative implements to justify the name. The menu is ditto. Breakfast offerings are quite comprehensive and straightforward: eggs/omelettes, sausage/ham/bacon, home fries/grits, pancakes/french toast/waffles, etc. You can order eggs Benedict, but it doesn't seem quite right. At lunch, the extensive sandwich menu is supplemented with daily special plates which always include a vegetarian and a seafood offering along with the meaty choices, and always two soups in addition to the regular chili. It is all good to very good. The service is prompt, and attentive far beyond diner standards. Not on the gourmet trail, but a fine spot to stop if you feel like tucking into a real breakfast or lunch.

JILL'S COUNTRY KITCHEN (413-298-0224; 3 Elm St., Stockbridge)

Simple and to the point, Jill's is an unpretentious luncheonette, delivering wholesome, fresh-made lunches and snacks at modest prices — sandwiches, soups, and Middle Eastern specialties. A Greek pita we recently enjoyed was chockablock full of fresh cut greens, olives, feta, and artichoke hearts. A wide range of herbal teas, sparkling waters, and sodas is offered to go with your meal. Ice creams and delicious desserts could top it all off. Nicely spaced, utilitarian tables give a bit more elbow room than in other local eateries.

MIDGE'S (413-298-3040; 4 Elm St., Stockbridge)

Sharing space with (husband Jim) Shanahan's Market, Midge's is a classic lunch counter diner, much favored by Stockbridge locals for breakfast and lunch. Midge offers a tasty chili and two good soups every day, sandwiches filled the way a hungry person likes to see them, and a hearty luncheon special, all at reasonable prices, along with very good ice cream cones for strolling on warm days. There are a few small tables for the formal set, and always plenty of cheery banter with the Prop.

THERESA'S STOCKBRIDGE CAFE (413-298-5465; 40 Main St., Stockbridge.)

Theresa is the latest restaurateur to take on the space that housed the original Alice's Restaurant, and is carrying on with much the same menu as her predecessor, Naji. Specialties run to Middle Eastern delicacies and other gourmet foods, with more staple sandwich and salad fare on the menu. The deli case features a changing selection of bowls of shrimp with pasta, stuffed grape leaves, egg rolls, artichoke hearts, hummus, falafel, and so on. Desserts include an authentic baklava and western cakes and pies. And she offers a very good selection of pizzas, there or to go.

CAFFE POMO D'ORO (413-232-4616; 6 Depot St., W. Stockbridge)

Very good things come in small packages, and Pomo D'Oro is the dining proof of the principle. About eight smallish tables in a portion of the former West Stockbridge train station comprise the restaurant. The very attractive decor consists largely of the tastefully displayed gourmet packaged food offerings which make up the balance of Pomo D'Oro's business — pastas, rather exotic (non-alcoholic) beverages, cheeses and sausages, etc. For breakfast, try the excellent French toast, a chèvre omelette, or perhaps the bagel with cream cheese and smoked salmon. The lunch menu always includes a soup and a pasta special, several salads, and about ten delicious sandwich offerings, a number of them vegetarian and largely of the Italian persuasion in ingredients. While simple, the food is excellent, making Pomo d'Oro the gourmet's choice in the Breakfast/Lunch Section.

CAROL'S (413-637-8948; 8 Franklin St., Lenox)

Serving in what was formerly an elder services center, Carol's offers scant ambience, but good and popular down-home food, including especially Carol's own homemade seven grain and sourdough breads baked daily and offered for breakfast toast and sandwich wrappers. Breakfast is served all day, highlighted by imaginative pancake and omelette options and justly famous home fries. Lunch features big and tasty sandwiches and a good number of hearty vegetarian selections.

JACK'S HOT DOGS (413-664-9006; 12 Eagle Street, N. Adams)

After a brief hiatus, Jack's Hot Dogs has resumed its historic position as *the* place to get hot dogs in North County. Continuing a 70-year family tradition, owner Jeff Levanos and manager Maria Carmain provide a continuous flow of hot dogs, plain and fancy, with rapid-fire conversation accompanying the bustle behind the counter. Whether pressed against the wall waiting for a "to go" or wedged into one of the 12 stools along the counter munching hot dogs and fries, customers are experiencing a very lively bit of history. Four of us ordered our dogs with "the works": sauerkraut, chili, and cheese, plus condiments. Together with French fries, fried onions, and beverages, the total tab was just under \$12!

Heather Austin steam-heating a fragrant coffee at her Berkshire Coffee Roasting Company.

Jonathan Sternfield

FOOD PURVEYORS

From the freshest sweet corn from the farm stand, raced from purchase to pot, to the latest imported gourmet specialty, appearing by candlelight on a Tanglewood picnic blanket, Berkshire supplies food that ranges from pure and simple to sophisticated and innovative. The food and beverage purveyors listed below are sources for baked goods, coffee and ice cream, produce and other farm products, picnic provisions, and health and gourmet food. The surprising array of unique food specialties created and produced in the Berkshires are listed at the end of the chapter.

BAKERIES

European pastries, New York bagels, French baguettes, and grandma's pies: breads and baked goods from Berkshire bakeries offer the staff of life and all its variations. Many of these bakeries also provide dining areas.

Bagels, Too (413-499-0119; 166 North St., Pittsfield) Several great flavors of New York-style bagels are made on the premises, accessorized by cream cheese spreads, lox, soup, and specialty coffees. Take them away or eat them on the spot.

The Baker's Wife (413-528-4623; 312 Main St., Great Barrington) Breads are baked on a weekly schedule, and include, among others, five-grain, honey-oat, Italian twist, corn rye, San Francisco sourdough, seedy oat, and wheat germ. Tasty muffins range from a honey-sweetened ginger-pumpkin to sour cherry-pecan, from cranberry-hazelnut to blue cornmeal-blueberry. There's a piano, too.

Christina's Just Desserts and Country Cafe (413-274-6521; 218 Pleasant St., Housatonic) The bakery offers chocolate truffles, cakes, pastries, and breads; enjoy a light lunch in the cafe

Clarksburg Bread Company in Williamstown.

Judith Monachina

Clarksburg Bread Co. (413-458-2251; 37 Spring St., Williamstown) Wholesome offerings baked "fresh from scratch daily": bread, muffins, scones, cookies, biscuits, coffee cakes, pies, and other assorted pastries. Juices, cheese, and yogurt are also available, as are tea, coffee, and gift items. Closed Mon.

Daily Bread (413-528-9610; 285 Railroad St., Great Barrington; *in Stockbridge,* 298-0272; Main St., Stockbridge) Give us our daily bread: real, crusty sourdough French baguettes fresh out of the oven, and almond crescent cookies, hazelnut torte, sticky buns, and other necessities of life. Closed Sun.

Suchèle Bakers (413-637-0939; 27 Housatonic St., Lenox) Geraniums in the window, Victorian accoutrements inside, and tarts and tortes, sticky buns, muffins, wholesome bread, pastries, cakes, fresh fruit pies, and more, baked daily. Closed Mon. off season; open 7 days July–August.

COFFEE SPECIALISTS

Berkshire Bistro (413-442-4226; 44 West St., Pittsfield) Just opening at press time, offering coffee (Seattle's Best) and light breakfast fare Mon.–Fri. from 7 a.m., Sat. from 9 a.m. Lunch is the main meal, served Mon.–Sat., but on those same days you can get specialty sandwiches and desserts till 9 p.m — or possibly later during high season. Takeout service, and gourmet coffees to roast at home.

Berkshire Coffee Roasting Company (413-528-5505; 286 Main St., Great Barrington. Also: 413-637-1606; 52 Main St., Lenox) A top choice for exceptional coffee in an unpretentiously funky setting, conducive to the related activities of conversation, relaxing, people-watching, reading, or admiring the latest art exhibit on the walls. The beans responsible for all this pleasure are imported green, then roasted here. Choose from a selection of coffee flavors, and cappuccino, espresso, hot chocolate, cookies, muffins, and biscotti (try the chocolate-covered variety). Bags of coffee beans are for sale, too. The popular coffee take-out set-up thoughtfully provides raised lids for preserving the foam on your cappuccino.

Conversations at the Cold Spring Coffee Roasters in Williamstown.

Judith Monachina

Cold Spring Coffee Roasters, Ltd. (413-458-5010; 47 Spring St., Williamstown) More than 60 varieties of specialty coffees are roasted on the premises here (and there are 25 varieties of loose teas). Order cappuccino, latte, or espresso, and treat yourself to ice cream and other goodies in a cafe atmosphere. Recently expanded. There's an array of tea- and coffee-making gear, too.

The Mystery Cafe (413-229-0075; 137 Main St., Sheffield) Gourmet coffee, lunch, desserts, and mystery books.

Sip of Seattle (413-445-5143; 216 Elm St., Pittsfield) Coffee, salads, soups, desserts, light breakfasts.

FARM, ORCHARD, AND PRODUCE MARKETS

Fresh tomatoes right off the vine, crisp and juicy apples, enormous heads of organically grown lettuce, bounty from Berkshire fields and hills is available at area produce markets, farm and orchard outlets, seasonal farm stands, and farmers' markets, where area growers truck in their harvests to a central outdoor location one or two days a week. The power of home-grown is potent: since a number of farmers formed the Berkshire Growers' Cooperative to specialize in squash, Berkshire butternuts have been in the supermarkets and on restaurant menus. (Sources of non-Berkshire produce throughout the county, for those occasions when only kiwifruit or bok choy will do, are listed as well.)

The Berkshire County Extension Service (413-448-8285; 44 Bank Row, Pittsfield) can provide up-to-date information on seasonal farm stands and farmers' markets.

Bartlett's Orchard (413-698-2559; 575 Swamp Rd., Richmond) "Buy 'em where they grow 'em." Apple varieties throughout the season include Empire, Macs, Delicious (red and gold), Cortland, Northern Spy, Macoun, Ida Red, Jonagold, and more. Each variety is labeled with a description of its distinct flavor and best use. Bartlett's own cider is all-natural and preservative-free. The shop also stocks an array of apple products and other country-gourmet condiments and preserves; the bakery offers doughnuts, turnovers, pies.

Burgner's Farm Products (413-445-4704; Dalton Division Rd., Pittsfield) The turkey farm is a neighborhood gathering place for fresh produce, including Burgner's own, especially their corn in season; plus other fruits and vegetables from local farms and farther afield. Eggs, chicken, and turkey products are a specialty.

Chenail's Farmstand (413-458-4910; Luce Rd., Williamstown) Not easy to find since cornhuskers must follow Luce Rd. a mile from Rte. 2 in Williamstown on a road that eventually goes to Mt. Greylock; but the corn and other vegetables Chenail's puts out are tastefully fresher than those at stands not on the farm.

The Corn Crib (413-528-4947; 1840 N. Main St., Rte. 7, Sheffield) Their own farm produce, plus that of other local farmers — fresh fruit, veggies, plants, perennials. Carol's Cookery has coffee and doughnuts; Dolls & Dwellings offers dolls, supplies, doll houses, miniatures, dried flowers.

Guido's Fresh Marketplace (413-442-9909; 1020 South St., Pittsfield. Also: 413-528-9255; 760 S. Main St., Gt. Barrington) A fine place to buy vegetables and fruit in the county, with local produce in season and a multi-cultural array of standards and exotics from all over the world year-round — baby carrots, cilantro, radicchio, endive, fresh herbs, oriental vegetables, tropical fruits, mushrooms. A true marketplace ambience, with distinct Guido touches: the signs posted at the carefully arranged but overflowing produce bins are polite and informative, and you can have help carrying bags out to the car. Also at Guido's (Pittsfield) are Berger's Bakery and Deli, Hillsdale Meat Market, Mountain Seafood, and Pasta Prima (described in the appropriate categories below), and all sorts of cooking supplies, health foods, earth-conscious cosmetics, gourmet items, candles, baskets, Guido's T-shirts. . . .

Farmers' Markets

Farmers' markets, where local growers set up temporarily to offer this week's freshest harvest, have sprung up throughout the county. They are held from June to the first frost. For the markets' days, times, and locations check a newspaper or the extension service (413-448-8285). In *Pittsfield*, the Allendale Shopping Center hosts a market on Wednesday & Saturday mornings, and downtown Pittsfield sets up an open-air market on Columbus Ave. on Friday. In *Great Barrington*, the Farmer's Market is on Saturdays from 8:30 a.m to 12:30 p.m. in the yard of the old train station, with vegetables plus local cheeses and hand-crafted products related to farming. In *Lee*, Fridays 12–6, next to the Post Office, find fresh seafood (Vic's), herbs, veggies, flowers, and more. In *Williamstown*, on Saturday mornings, July through September, local farmers set up in the parking lot at the foot of Spring St.

Jaeschke's Brothers Farms (413-743-3896; West Rd., Adams) The farm store is in Pittsfield, 736 Crane Ave. (Allendale area; 413-443-7180). You can also pick — or pick up — apples and pears at the orchard after the pro pickers have been through. Flowers at the farm in May and June.

Taft Farms (413-528-1515, 800-528-1015; Rte. 183 & Division St., Great Barrington) Taft Farms' own delicious produce in season, including potatoes, tomatoes, peppers, broccoli, cucumbers, and their famous just-picked sweet corn. It's all grown according to the "integrated pest management" system, which minimizes or eliminates the use of pesticides. Taft also offers fruit and vegetables from other climes, such as radicchio, kiwifruit, or pomegranates. Baked goods, jams and jellies, cider, and seafood from the fish market (Thursday through Saturday) will provision you healthfully, delectably, and completely. Flowers and plants from the greenhouse, too.

Picking Your Own Fruit

A berry or apple picking expedition is a great way to enjoy the Berkshire countryside, while gathering the makings for a special dessert, muffin, or pancake breakfast. Blueberries in particular are available wild throughout these hills, but few natives will reveal their special picking spots. Call ahead at the following farms and orchards for picking conditions.

Blueberries abound at Blueberry Hill Farm, which offers 320 acres for family picking from late July until frost (East St., 7 mi. up the Mount Washington ridge; call 413-528-1479 for a recorded message about the status of picking). At Strawberry Acres (413-655-2672; off Rte. 8, Hinsdale) there are blueberries and Christmas trees, too.

Three acres of *strawberries* are at Crooked Row Farm (413-698-2608; Dublin Road, Richmond). Strawberries can also be picked at *Ioka Valley Farm* (413-738-5915; 3475 Rte. 43, Hancock). *Apples* at Windy Hill Farm (413-298-3217; Rte. 7, Great Barrington) are waiting to be picked in season; there's also a garden shop and nursery. Open Apr.–Oct.

Maple Sugar and Syrup

Turner Farms Maple Syrup in Egremont.

Judith Monachina

Maple sugaring and syrup-making is a Berkshire tradition. Watch the process or participate at the following places during the season (usually March), or just pick up some of the final product at any time of year. Williams College's Hopkins Forest (413-458-3080; Northwest Hill Rd., Williamstown) usually demonstrates sugaring off.

At *Ioka Valley Farm* (413-738-5915; 3475 Rte. 43, Hancock) the sugar-maker will explain the process and teach the kids how to tap trees. *Sunset Farm Maple Products* (413-243-3229; Tyringham Rd., Tyringham) has an open sugar house. *Turner Farms Maple Syrup* (413-528-9956; Phillips Rd., S. Egremont): the sugar shack operation is open to the public; groups of 15 or more should make an appointment for a tour. Other sources of local maple products include *Gould Farm* (413-528-2633; Roadside Store, Rte. 23, Monterey); *Holiday Farm* (413-684-0444; Rte. 9, Windsor); *Mill Brook Sugar House* (413 637 0474; 409 New Lenox Rd., Lenox); and *Quimby's Farm* (413-458-5402; Rte. 43, Hancock).

GOURMET & DELI MARKETS, & CATERERS

The small grocery markets and specialty food shops and caterers of the Berkshires will please the palates of just about everyone, from the classicist to the experimenter. These markets and food specialists combine the latest culinary styles with ethnic traditions and personal service, and also magnificently maintain the celebrated Berkshire custom of the gourmet picnic. There's an old-time country store or two thrown in, too.

Berger's Specialty Foods (413-442-1898; 1020 South St., Pittsfield, at Guido's) Some assert that the best baguettes to be found in the Berkshires are here; others avoid the controversy by selecting from the abundant variety of cheeses, crackers, condiments, pasta and other salads, and gourmet items from far and wide. Berger's also caters and does gift baskets.

Berkshire Hills Market (413-458-3356; 60 Spring St., Williamstown) Relatively new, but old-fashioned in feeling, this market includes fresh meat and fish, plus smoked meat and sausage made on the premises. Gourmet items, including coffee and tea of the day, are to-go and by the pound. There's more: fresh produce, deli items, overstuffed sandwiches, gift baskets, and boxed meals. Call in orders or eat at the tables.

Caffe Pomo d'Oro (413-232-4616; 6 Depot St., West Stockbridge) Gourmet provisions and a cafe in a sunny room in West Stockbridge's small-scale downtown. Cheese and deli items, bread, imported gourmet foods, even their own gourmet vinegar. Catering.

Cheesecake Charlie's (271 Main St., Gt. Barrington) Toasted Almond, Creamsicle, Piña Colada, Peppermint Patty — these are only a few of the cheesecake flavors that you can get here. Available in different sizes, and they'll ship it too. Look for their re-opening in Gt. Barrington in mid-July 1997.

Chez Vous Catering (413-298-4278; Box 1162, Stockbridge) Elegant food, beautifully presented, including oriental roast beef, Madeira chicken, lentil salad plates, and desserts.

Country Glazed Hams (413-637-2288; Lenox House Country Shops, Rte. 7, Lenox) Honey-glazed hams, spiral-sliced, are the specialty here; plus smoked and deli meats, gourmet coffee, fresh baked goods, overstuffed sandwiches, and seemingly the world's record for the number of different gourmet mustards.

Picnic Provisions

The Berkshires are ideal picnic territory, whether the context for your al fresco dining is a hike, literary or otherwise, an all-day canoe trip, or the prelude to an outdoor performance at The Mount or Tanglewood. Your picnic may start with turkey and end with ice cream, but the picnic specialists listed here also offer many other options. And, of course, you can provision your picnic yourself, at any of the markets and gourmet shops described above.

Cheesecake Charlie's makes a special New England Clambake Picnic for Two, which includes lobster, mussels, clams, shrimp, corn on the cob, melon, and bread. *Cher's* in the Glendale section of Stockbridge on Rte. 183 has boxed picnic meals featuring sandwiches; no advance notice needed. The Great Barrington *Marketplace* will customize a gourmet picnic, with 24 hours' notice. *The Red Lion Inn* offers pick-up picnics, too. Robin's Restaurant in Williamstown will pack up entrées and side dishes. *Samel's Deli* has boxed meals ideal for portable dining. *The Store at Five Corners* will pack a picnic from their deli. *Truffles & Such* will also create gourmet picnics-to-go.

Gorham & Norton (413-528-0900; 278 Main St., Great Barrington) This authentically old-fashioned market has up-to-the-minute good things: groceries, gourmet items, imported cheese, an excellent wine selection. Real people work here, too; recently when they didn't happen to have a certain item, they immediately suggested other sources and offered to call them to make sure.

Helen Hayes Catering (413-243-2035; Lee) .

The Marketplace (413-528-5775; 760 Main St., Great Barrington) Take out a complete gourmet restaurant meal — lunch or dinner. A variety of salads, hot and cold, fish, cold cuts, and more are also take-out ready. All explained and served up with enthusiasm and panache.

Merrimac Smoked Fish, Inc. (413-528-2004; 955 S. Main St., Great Barrington) Their own fine smoked salmon, the equal of any produced in the U.S., smoked and peppered bluefish, and other gourmet and homemade seafood items.

Monterey General Store (413-528-4437; Rte. 23, Monterey) Not necessarily a gourmet shop, but an established oasis in southeastern Berkshire, this old-time general store stocks fresh vegetables, cold cuts, preserves, and locally made maple syrup. With a lunch room in the back and a front porch for people-watching, this spot is a perennial gathering place.

Samel's Deli and Catering (413-442-5927; 115 Elm St., Pittsfield) Bread, chicken, wine, cheese, pepperoni, legendary pickles, and much more in the deli and gourmet line. It delivers in the Pittsfield area.

The Store At Five Corners (413-458-3176; junction of Rtes. 7 & 43, South Williamstown) The upscale country store, with well-chosen wine and beer selections, juices and waters, imported and domestic cheeses, fresh-baked breads and treats, homemade fudge, picnic and gift baskets, gifts, fresh produce, deli items such as sandwiches and salads, fancy preserves, gourmet coffee and ice cream, and various international offerings. Enjoy breakfast and light fare here, too, in all this abundance. It will ship and cater. In a building that was a tavern in 1770; the Greek Revival façade was added in 1830.

Truffles & Such (413-442-0151; Allendale Shopping Center, Rtes. 8 & 9, Pittsfield) A restaurant with take-out and catering. The pasta or bean salads are highly recommended and the desserts are simultaneously heavenly and sinful. Try a "potato," a cake and marzipan concoction dusted with cocoa and studded with almond eyes.

Other area restaurants or markets with catering services include the *Castle Street Cafe, Harry's Supermarket, Hickory Bill's,* the *Silver Screen,* and the *Sweet Basil Grille.*

HEALTH/NATURAL FOOD STORES

Berkshire Co-op Market (413-528-9697; 37 Rosseter St., Great Barrington) Open to the public, but co-op members get a 2% discount. Ingredients for healthy eating and living, including organic produce, much of it grown

---

A Place for Pasta

Pasta Prima (413-499-7478; 1020 South St., Pittsfield, at Guido's. Also: 413-528-3755; 740 Main St., Gt. Barrington) Fresh pasta made on the premises, before your eyes. Have it cut to order or purchase in sheets for cutting at home. Selection of other pastas of the dried variety, sauces, and Parmesan and Romano cheese for grating.

---

locally; and baked goods, macrobiotic foods, bulk pasta, beans, grains, and herbal and homeopathic remedies.

Clearwater Natural Foods (413-637-2721; 11 Housatonic St., Lenox) Fresh bread, sandwiches, a wide range of groceries, including macrobiotic and allergy-free selections, organic produce, and nondairy and dairy ice cream. Look for monthly specials.

Locke, Stock and Barrel (413-528-0800; 265 Stockbridge Rd./Rte. 7, Great Barrington) Where health food meets gourmet food, artfully and abundantly arranged: a large selection of cheeses, and cold cuts, fish, honey, teas, yogurt, juices, fresh tofu, flours, grains, rices, and soy and tamari sauces. There's a wall-length case of frozen health foods, and vitamins, mineral supplements, and natural cosmetics.

Sprout House (413-528-5200; 284 Main St./PO Box 1100, Gt. Barrington) Steve Meyerowitz, the "Sproutman," has sprouting kits and books, indoor vegetable kits and organic seeds; via mail order and wholesale.

Sunflower Natural Foods (413-243-1775; 42 Park St., Lee) Organic and natural items include bread, coffee, fat-free snacks, and natural personal care items; products are available here that are wheat-free, gluten-free, sugar-free. Vitamins, books, even a health video club.

Wild Oats Community Market (413-458-8060; Rte. 2, Colonial Shopping Center, Williamstown) Organic and local produce, whole foods, gourmet and specialty items, vitamins, natural cosmetics, along with food and health books and magazines. Members get discounts but the public is welcome; the offerings have broadened to appeal to a wider audience.

ICE CREAM

Berkshire-made ice cream, plus that of those two guys from Vermont, can be found in strategic locations throughout the county. Reliably delicious *Friendly* ice cream, in cones, containers, and sundaes, is also available at one of the many Friendly restaurants near you.

Ben & Jerry's Ice Cream (413-448-2250; 179 South St., Pittsfield) Vermont's famous ice cream, in cones, cakes, sundaes, and containers; frozen yogurt. Worth standing in line for.

Berkshire Ice Cream (413-232-4111; 4 Albany Rd., W. Stockbridge) The county's own premium is sold in specialty shops. You can own part of the Jersey herd. Give 'em a call.

Bev's Homemade Ice Cream (413-637-0371; 38 Housatonic St., Lenox; 5 Railroad St., Gt. Barrington) Bev's is made daily on the premises, and comes in traditional to exotic flavors. You can also get ice cream sodas and sundaes, malteds, and egg creams, plus coffee and baked treats.

The Ice Cream Scene (282 Main St., Great Barrington) Gourmet to soft-serve to frozen yogurt and other goodies.

Lickety Split (413-458-1818; 69 Spring St., Williamstown) With Herrell's Famous Ice Cream from Northampton, Lickety Split is a great day or evening stop; hot soup in the winter.

MEAT, FISH, & POULTRY MARKETS

Burgner's Poultry Farm (413-445-4704; Dalton Division Rd., Pittsfield) Burgner's raises and sells turkeys and chickens; order them uncooked, roasted, or stuffed and roasted, in all sizes. Burgner's turkey pot pies are local favorites. The farm store also carries eggs, produce, their homemade bakery items, and fresh homemade potato salad and cole slaw.

Greilich's Meat Market (413-743-0012; 24 N. Summer St., Adams) A friendly family operation with German- and Polish-style sausage, kielbasa, bratwurst, and homemade bacon, in a no-frills, back-of-the-house shop with a view of Mount Greylock thrown in.

Masse's Seafood (413-499-3474; 1020 South St., Pittsfield, at Guido's) A variety of fresh and frozen former denizens of the sea.

Mazzeo's Meat Center Meat concessions at Guido's: Great Barrington (413-528-4488; 760 S. Main St.) and Pittsfield (413-442-2222; 1020 South St.).

Otis Poultry Farm (413-269-4438; Rte. 8, Otis) "Custom Laid Eggs" says the sign. You can get them and chickens, geese, ducks, and capons, too. Their excellent frozen chicken and turkey pies are a staple of well-stocked Berkshire refrigerators. Various homemade goodies join sheepskin gloves and slippers and so forth in the country store.

Additional options for meat and fish include *Harry's Supermarket* (413-442-9084; 290 Wahconah St., Pittsfield), *Swanson's Seafood & Deli* (413-743-9040; 87 Summer St., Adams), *Vic's Seafood* (at the Lee Farmers Market, Fridays 12–6), *The Other Brother Darryl's* (413-269-4235, 800-6FLOPIN; Rte. 8, Otis. Also: 413-528-8088; 760 S. Main St., Gt. Barrington). They offer wholesale seafood to retail customers, and promise "still-floppin'" freshness).

WINE & LIQUOR

Keep in mind that Massachusetts law prohibits the sale of alcoholic beverages on Sunday, except in stores within 10 miles of the Vermont or New Hampshire borders.

The Buttery (413-298-5533; Elm St., Stockbridge).

Domaney's (413-528-0024; 66 Main St., Gt. Barrington).

Gorham and Norton (413-528-0900; 278 Main St., Great Barrington).

Liquors Inc. (413-443-4466; 485 Dalton Ave., Pittsfield) The biggest and best for discount wine, beer, and spirits.

Liquor Mart (413-663-3910; 885 State Rd., Adams) Beer, liquor, and wine.

Nejaime's Wine & Liquor (413-448-2274; 444 Pittsfield-Lenox Rd., Lenox), **Nejaime's Stockbridge Wine Cellar** (413-298-3454; Elm St.), and **Lenox Wine Cellar and Cheese Shop** (413-637-2221; 27 Church St.) In addition to wines, beers, and spirits, they offer gourmet and deli items, helpful, knowledgeable assistance, and perhaps the best wine selections in the Berkshires.

Queensborough Spirits (413-232-8522; Main St., West Stockbridge). Beer, liquor, and wine.

South Egremont Spirit Shoppe (413-528-1490; Rte. 23) "The wine shop of the Berkshires." Also a good selection of cigars.

Pizza

Pizza cravings will be easily satisfied anywhere throughout Berkshire County, but all pizzas are not created equal. Top choices include the following:

Babalouie's Sour Dough Pizza Company (413-528-8100; 286 S. Main St., Great Barrington) offers Italian-style pizzas (thin-crust organic sourdough pizza bread or wheat-free crusts), cooked in a wood-fired oven. *Manhattan Pizza Company* (413-528-2550; 490 S. Main St., Great Barrington) Pizzas here are big, flat, oozing, and delicious. They reheat well, and are available by the slice. *The East Side Cafe* (413-447-9405; 378 Newell St., Pittsfield) is essentially a bar, and they make pizza only on Thurs.–Sun. evenings from 5:00 p.m. on; it's small, thin, crisp, and tasty. *Elizabeth's Cafe Pizzeria* on East St. in Pittsfield (reviewed in *Restaurants*, above) offers signature "white pies" with abundant toppings, and fresh, innovative ingredients. The unbeatable taste of a wood-fired brick-oven pizza is somewhere *Over The Rainbow* (413-445-6836; 109 First St., Pittsfield). Generous toppings and imaginative combinations include chicken pesto, spinach and broccoli, or the "primavera" — eggplant, black olives, broccoli, and more. Take-out or eat in and watch the flames in the oven. *Hot Tomatoes* (413-458-2722; 100 Water St., Williamstown) may be the best in town for those who prefer the thinner crust; while *Michael's Restaurant and Pizzeria* (413-458-2114; 460 Main St., Williamstown) is the dependable traditional; Michael's also has a heated truck for large orders.

Spirit Shop (413-458-3704; 280 Cole Ave., Williamstown) Beer, liquor, and wine.

Stockbridge Wine Cellar (413-298-3454; Elm St., Stockbridge) (see Nejaime's above).

Trotta's Discount Liquors (413-528-3490; 490 S. Main St., jct. of Rtes. 7 & 23, Great Barrington) Beer, liquor, wine, plus fine cigars

Val's Pipe & Package Store (413-743-0962; 7 Columbia St., Adams) Beer, liquor, wine; also groceries, milk, and lottery tickets.

Berkshire Food and Beverage Specialties

Nurtured by Berkshire soil, or created by Berkshire entrepreneurs, this select group of food and beverage specialties includes condiments and sauces; breads and other baked goods; sweets and sweeteners; and dairy products, spring water, and soft drinks. Some are world famous; all are locally treasured. There's no individual retail outlet for many of these products, but look for them at Guido's, Bartlett's, the Store at Five Corners, Berkshire Cupboard, and most other gourmet shops, farm and produce markets, and many supermarkets. In some cases, you can also contact the food entrepreneur for more information. Or consider giving — or receiving — a gift basket or box with a selection of these unique items, cleverly packaged by Gifts of the Berkshires (800-BERKCTG) through Berkshire Cottage, the kitchen and gourmet store.

Beverages

Berkshire Spring Water (413-229-2086, 800-244-3212; Norfolk Rd., Southfield) Bottled daily at the spring, it's sodium-, bacteria-, and additive-free. Or try *Sand Springs* Spring Water Co. (413-458-8281; 160 Sand Springs Rd., Williamstown). Have either delivered, or buy it in 1-gallon jugs in supermarkets. *Gilly's Hot Vanilla* (413-637-1515) was created by Lenox resident Joanne Deutch as a hot-chocolate alternative; just add hot water to the caffeine-free vanilla-flavored powder. Buy it by the bag locally, or have a cup at many local eateries. *Squeeze Beverages* (413-743-1410; 190 Howland Ave., Adams) are soda drinks with fabulous flavors: sarsaparilla, cream, birch beer, gentian root, cranberry, and "half and half" — half grapefruit, half lemon-lime. Cola and root beer for traditionalists, too, and some sugar-free choices .

Bread & Baked Goods

Look for some local goods made locally but not sold retail, such as *Berkshire Mountain Bakery*. Their traditional sourdough breads should be sought out at area natural food stores. The peasant bread and the raisin bread are particular favorites; try their crisp biscotti, too. *Cedars of Lebanon* makes pita bread that's in area

Continued on next page

supermarkets and groceries and is pure, simple, and delicious. *Nejaime's Lavasch* is deliciously addictive: a Mideast specialty, lavasch is a crusty cracker-like bread. Nejaime's is made with a variety of flavorings, all good.

Condiments & Sauces

Bear Meadow Farm (413-663-9241) products from Florida include preserves, mustards, vinegars, chutneys, apple ketchup. *Hickory Bill's Barbecue Sauce* from his Great Barrington restaurant (see the review above) comes in a variety of moods, from mild to hot, including "medium," "mad," and "mean."

Dairy Products

Afternoon milking time for High Lawn's Jersey Cows

Jonathan Sternfield

Monterey Chèvre is made from the milk of goats at **Rawson Brook Farm** (413-528-2138; New Marlboro Rd., Monterey) and from acid starter from France. It's sold deliciously plain, or flavored with chives and garlic, or with a particularly tasty combination of wild thyme and olive oil. It is sold younger than imported chèvre and has a milder, more delicate flavor. Milk (with the cream on top) and light or heavy cream from **High Lawn Farm** (413-243-0672) is available at many grocery stores or can still be delivered to your door. Admire the Jersey cows as you drive by the farm on Lenox Road in Lee.

Desserts, Sweets, and Sweeteners

Baldwin's Extracts (413-232-7785; Depot St., West Stockbridge) offers "since 1888, the best in vanilla." This manufacturer of flavoring extracts and maple table syrup uses only the best — the Bourbon Vanilla Bean from Madagascar - for their Pure Vanilla Extract. It's made in a copper percolator (the "still") and aged in 100-year-old oak barrels, which you can see in their small and fascinating retail outlet in a former carriage shop. Inhale essence of vanilla and admire the ranks of extract bottles — including lemon, orange, mint, and more — on the old-fashioned counter. Also available is *Baldwin's Table Syrup,* a blend of maple and cane sugar syrup from a recipe created in the 1920s.

Catherine's Chocolates (413-528-2510; Stockbridge Rd., Great Barrington) are made on the premises from a century-old family recipe. These smooth and flavorful concoctions include chocolate truffles, a variety of hand-dipped candies, and fudges and brittles and barks. The nonpareils are, in fact, unequaled. By the piece, the pound, or in a boxed gift assortment. *David Rawson's honey* from Richmond is pretty close to nectar for the gods, who get it in 1-lb. jars at Bartlett's.

And . . .

The Delftree Corporation (234 Union St. North Adams, 413-664-4907) grows shiitake mushrooms on hardwood logs in a 19th-century textile mill building in North Adams. They're shipped all over the place, but available here.

CHAPTER SIX
For the Fun of It
RECREATION

Berkshire beckons bikers, boaters, hikers, horseback riders, runners, skaters, skiers, swimmers, and nearly every other variety of sportsperson to come outside. And although nature gave the area few large bodies of water, the 19th-century industrialists dammed well, to some degree making up the deficiency. Mountains and trails, lakes and rivers, and Berkshire valley air — which thankfully can

Lauren R. Stevens

be breathed without seeing — are all invigorating. The ski areas assure groomed winter sport with extensive snowmaking and, in warmer weather, Berkshire's golf courses and tennis courts draw sportspeople from all quarters.

Berkshire offers unusual sports, from croquet to soaring. There is a luxury spa with a multi-million-dollar state-of-the-art fitness center and over 50 classes a day to choose from (Canyon Ranch), and two YMCAs offer programs from camping and tennis to aerobics and sailing.

For the spectators among us, high school and college sports are competitive and fun in fall, spring, and winter, including downhill and nordic skiing. The hills are alive with bouncing balls, from youth programs to secondary school teams to adult leagues. Three of the four Berkshire colleges — **Berkshire Community** in Pittsfield, **North Adams State** in North Adams, and **Williams** in Williamstown — field men's and women's teams in soccer, basketball, and baseball hard and soft. Williams perennially ranks among the best in the nation in Division III soccer, field hockey, football, cross country, basketball, ice hockey, track, tennis, squash, volleyball, swimming, lacrosse, and crew. In the fall of 1996, Williams won the Sears Cup as the winningest small college in the nation. The athletic departments of the colleges can provide schedules.

SPORTING GOODS STORES

The following stores provide sporting goods for a range of activities. Additional listings are provided under individual sports (e.g. bicycling, skiing).

South County

Appalachian Mountain Gear 413-528-8811; 777 S. Main St., Gt. Barrington.
Gerry Cosby & Co. 413-229-6600; 103 S. Under Mountain Rd., Sheffield.
Rick Moon's Outdoors 413-528-4666; 107 Stockbridge Rd., Gt. Barrington.

Central County

Arcadian Shop 413-637-3010; 91 Pittsfield-Lenox Rd. (Rte. 7), Lenox.
Champ Sports 413-448-2123; Berkshire Mall, Lanesborough.
Dave's Sporting Goods 413-442-2960; 1164 North St., Pittsfield.
Dick Moon Sporting Goods 413-442-8281; 114 Fenn St., Pittsfield.
Marshall Sporting Goods, Inc. 413-443-4595; 207 Elm St., Pittsfield.
Main Street Sports and Leisure 413-637-4407, 800-952-9197; 48 Main St., Lenox.

North County

Berkshire Outfitters 413-743-5900; Route 8, Adams.
Goff's Sports 413-458-3605; 15 Spring St., Williamstown.
The Mountain Goat 413-458-8445; 130 Water St., Williamstown.
Points North Outfitters 413-743-4030, Rt. 8, on Adams/Cheshire line.
The Sports Corner 413-664-8654; 61 Main St., North Adams.

BASEBALL (& SOFTBALL)

The first collegiate baseball game ever was played in Pittsfield, July 1, 1859, Amherst defeating Williams 73-32 in a 26-inning game (the rules have changed since). Williams triumphed in a companion chess match.

Professional baseball in the Berkshires began later in the 19th century, but it wasn't till the Roaring Twenties that the hardball action was continuous. The Pittsfield Hillies played some admirable ball in the A-level Eastern League and won a couple of pennants. When the Depression came, baseball went. Through some of the 1940s, the Pittsfield Electrics played to large home crowds, but were finally short-circuited by the advent of televised baseball. Then in 1965 a Red Sox farm club came to play at Pittsfield's Wahconah Park. The Pittsfield-Berkshire Red Sox played in the AA Class of the Eastern League. Starring George "Boomer" Scott and Reggie Smith (both of whom went on to shine with the Sox), the club drew nearly 80,000 fans for the season. The Red Sox farm club moved from the Berkshires in 1976.

Jonathan Sternfield

Grounding out, at the Pittsfield Met's Wahconah Park.

Now the **Pittsfield Mets** play in Wahconah. Once again there's an opportunity to watch budding big leaguers. The fastballs are wicked, homers are truly belted, and the playing field is real dirt (and grass). A moment straight out of Norman Rockwell happens when the setting sun shines directly in the batter's eyes, causing a brief game delay due to sunshine. (We hope rumors of a new park are just that — rumors.)

The Pittsfield Mets 413-499-METS (6387); Wahconah Park, 105 Wahconah St., Pittsfield.

Women's softball is a feature of Berkshire colleges and secondary schools in the spring, and the sport is played with a passion. Nowhere is the action thicker, however, than at the Berkshire County Softball Complex, a three-field park that sees at least six games a night during the summer. The complex is home to the Berkshire County Slow Pitch Softball League, a 30-team men's league sponsored by local businesses. To facilitate matters, the complex has a two-story clubhouse with bar and restaurant.

Berkshire County Softball Complex 413-499-1491; 1789 East St., Pittsfield.

BICYCLING

How sweet the cycling! While dedicated bikeways in the county are still in the planning stage, for the views, the rolling terrain, and the variety of roadways, Berkshire is made for rider and derailleur. For racers, there's the *Josh Billings RunAground* in September and an annual July race around Brodie Mountain. The *Greylock Cycling Club* sponsors an annual Greylock Hill Climb, a 9.2-mile, decidedly uphill race.

For those who are touring, the back roads are tranquil, and some main roads have wide shoulders. The varied terrain intrigues cyclists: stunning views are followed by exhilarating descents that call for wel-l-l-l-tuned equipment.

Mountain bikers thrive in these hills, rolling on 18-speeders through the picturesque landscape, leaving the blacktop behind to ride up into the mountains. Not too steep, not too torturous, the Berkshire hills beckon those who have enough brawn, coupled with the right machine. Mountain bikers frequently gather at the *Mountain Goat*, 130 Water St., Williamstown, taking to the hills en masse for some "undulating all-terraining." Mountain bikers should remember that some hiking trails are not open to bikers.

Similarly, cyclists out on the roadways should remember that, until The Revolution, motorists in their quaint way still claim the right-of-way. It seems wise to oblige. So: right-hand riding, single file. After dark: a headlight, a red rear reflector, as well as side and pedal reflectors. In traffic, turns require hand signals with the left hand: extended for left turn, raised for right turn, held low for stopping. Helmets help, in a crisis, to keep us from losing our heads. Bicycles should be registered at local P.D.s, so they can help you locate a lost one. The fee: 25 cents.

Pittsfield resident Lewis Cuyler, writer and avid bike rider, sums it all up in *Bike Rides in the Berkshire Hills,* available at book and sports stores.

BICYCLE DEALERS

South County

Berkshire Bike and Blade 413-528-5555; 326 Stockbridge Rd., Gt. Barrington.
Harland B. Foster, Inc. 413-528-2100; 15 Bridge St., Gt. Barrington.

Central County

Arcadian Shop 413-637-3010; 91 Pittsfield-Lenox Rd. (Rte. 7), Lenox.
Main Street Sports & Leisure 413-637-4407, 800-952-9197; 48 Main St., Lenox.
Mean Wheels 413-637-0644; 57A Housatonic St., Lenox.
Ordinary Cycles 413-442-7225; 247 North St., Pittsfield.
Plaine's Bike Golf Ski 413-499-0294; 55 W. Housatonic St., Pittsfield.

Cycling to the finish, at the annual Josh Billings RunAground.

Jonathan Sternfield

North County

The Mountain Goat 413-458-8445; 130 Water St., Williamstown.
The Spoke 413-458-3456; 620 Main St., Williamstown.
The Sports Corner 413-664-8654; 61 Main St., N. Adams

BOATING

Henry Ward Beecher called Berkshire the "American Lake District," referring not to the number of lakes here but to the number of writers and poets, similar to those in England's home of the Romantic poets. While we have nothing the size of Lake Windermere, we have nearly 100 ponds, a few lakes, and at least one "bowl." Otis Reservoir, at 1,056 acres, is the largest recreational freshwater body in the state. Mainly we have water bodies for small craft, right down to inner tubes. Even shells: spring and fall we can watch the Williams College crew on Onota Lake.

Main St. Sports & Leisure (413-637-4407, 800-952-9197; 48 Main St., Lenox) offers canoe rental with delivery service. *Berkshire Outfitters* (413-743-5900; just north of Cheshire on Rte. 8) rents canoes and kayaks. Or we can row. Lew Cuyler has founded *Berkshire Sculling Association* (413-496-9160), which provides rentals, lessons, or even purchase. Lew says: "It takes but an hour to learn the fundamentals. The rest is practice."

South County

Benedict Pond, Beartown State Forest, 413-528-0904; Blue Hill Rd., Monterey. Sylvan pond suitable for canoe or rowboat only.

Lake Buel, Rte. 57, Monterey.

Goose Pond, Tyringham Rd., Lee. Boat rentals.

Laurel Lake, Rte. 20, Lee. Boat rentals.

Lake Garfield, Kinne's Grove, Rte. 23, Monterey. Boat rentals.

Otis Reservoir, Tolland State Forest, 413-528-0904; Reservoir Rd., off Rte. 8, Otis. Small powerboats, sunfish, and sailboats for rent at the largest of Berkshire's lakes. J&D Marina (413-269-4839) rents small boats; Miller Marine (413-269-6358) provides mooring, sales and service, but no renting. Summer weekends the water is crowded.

Prospect Lake, 413-528-4158; Prospect Lake Rd., N. Egremont. Canoe, paddle-boat, rowboat, and sailboard rental and instruction at a private-access family campground and lake.

York Pond, West Lake, Abbey Lake, Sandisfield State Forest, 413-258-4774; New Marlborough and Sandisfield.

Stockbridge Bowl Rte. 183, Stockbridge. Public launching site on one of the county's prettiest lakes, just below Tanglewood.

Central County

Buckley-Dunton Pond, October Mountain State Forest, Yokum Road, Becket. An intriguingly remote spot.

Greenwater Pond, Pleasant Point, Becket. Boat rentals.

Onota Lake, Onota Blvd., Pittsfield. Free launching area for motorboats. Good windsurfing. Onota Boat Livery (413-442-1724; 463 Pecks Rd.) rents small powerboats.

Pontoosuc Lake, Rte. 7, Pittsfield. The YMCA's Ponterrril (413-499-0640) offers

Lew Cuyler sculls on Onota Lake.

Lauren R. Stevens

John Hitchcock

Sailing on Pontoosuc Lake.

sailboat and canoe rentals. U-Drive Boat Rentals (413-442-7020; Rte. 7, Pittsfield) features ski boats and jet skis.

Richmond Pond, Swamp Rd., Richmond. Boat rentals.

North County

Mausert's Pond, Clarksburg State Forest, 413-664-8345; Middle Rd., Clarksburg.

Cheshire Reservoir (Hoosac Lake), Rte. 8, Cheshire. Launching site.

North Pond, Savoy Mountain State Forest, 413-663-8469 (summer only); for camping area call 413-664-9567; Off Rte. 2 in Florida, in Savoy. North Pond and South Pond are two jewels in the hills, quite remote, rarely busy.

BOWLING

Strike after strike is being bowled in Berkshire. For those eager to get in on the action, there are locales throughout the county. In *South County*, try *Cove Lanes* (413-528-1220; 109 Stockbridge Rd., Gt. Barrington) or *Lee Bowling Lanes* (413-243-0095; Rte. 102, Lee). *Central County* offers *Candle Lanes* (413-447-9640; 255 North St., Pittsfield); *Imperial Bowl* (413-443-4453; 555 Dalton Ave., Pittsfield); and *Ken's Bowl* (413-499-0733; 495 Dalton Ave., Pittsfield). In *North County*, bowling's best at *Mt. Greylock Bowl* (413-663-3761; Roberts Dr., off Rte. 2, N. Adams) and *Valley Park Inc.* (413-664-9715; Curran Hwy., Rte. 8, N. Adams).

CAMPING

It's easy to get back to nature in the Berkshires. A dozen private areas and nine of the county's state parks offer camping, facilities ranging from showers and flush toilets to campsites that are little more than terraces hewn out of the mountainside. The private campgrounds usually offer more amenities, but state-run ones frequently have more privacy. Many Tanglewood fans camp out.

Campsites in *state parks* are available on an unreserved basis. Due to state budgetary restraints, it is a good idea to obtain complete information in advance from *Massachusetts Environmental Management Department*, Region Five Headquarters, Box 1433, Pittsfield, MA 01201; telephone 413-442-8928.

Fees are as follows at all state parks and forests: Season pass $15. Camping, per night: wilderness, free; unimproved toilets $4; flush toilets $5; flush toilets with showers $6; water utility fee $1; sewer utility fee $1; group camping $8. Log cabins: one-room $8; three rooms $10. Day use, per car, $2 per day.

State campgrounds, noted below with an asterisk (*), are of two kinds: "Type-1" denotes facilities with showers and flush toilets; "Type-2" denotes those with outhouses.

Before planning your trip, be sure to double-check on facilities, fees, restrictions, and recreational activities available; these are subject to change from year to year.

South County

* **Beartown State Forest** (413-528-0904; Blue Hill Rd., Monterey, MA 01245; Mailing Address: Box 97, Monterey, MA 01245; N. from Rte. 23 in Monterey) Includes Benedict Pond; 10,555 acres, 12 Type-1 campsites, bicycling, boating (nonmotorized), boat ramp, fishing, hiking, hunting, horseback riding trails, picnicking, xc skiing, snowmobiling, swimming.

Camp Overflow (413-269-4036; Box 645, Otis, MA 01253; 5 mi. from Rte. 8) 100 sites, electric hookups, dumping station, camp store, fishing, swimming, boating, seasonal rates, on Otis Reservoir.

Laurel Ridge Camping Area (413-269-4804; Old Blandford Rd., E. Otis, MA 01029) Electric and water sites.

Maple Glade Campground (Managers: Thomas & Karen Shaffer; 413-243-1548; 339 Woodland Rd., Lee, MA 01238; across from October Mtn. State Forest) 70 sites; hook-ups available. $15 for tents, $17 with water. Electric and sewer. Swimming pool.

* **Mount Washington State Forest and Bash Bish Falls State Park** (413-528-0330; East St., Mt. Washington, MA 01258; From S. Egremont, take Rte. 41 S., then next right onto Mt. Washington Rd. and follow signs) 3,289 acres, including spectacular Bash Bish Falls, bicycling, canoeing, 15 Type-2 wilder-

ness campsites, fishing, hiking, horseback riding trails, hunting, boating (nonmotorized), boat ramp, snowmobiling, xc skiing. Nearby Mt. Everett State Forest offers three-state views from a road that approaches the summit.

* **October Mountain State Forest** (413-243-1778 or 413-243-9735; Woodland Rd., Lee, MA 01238; Mailing Address: R.R. 2, Box 193, Lee, MA 01238) Follow signs from Rte. 20 in Lee. 16,021 acres, 50 Type-1 campsites, bicycling, fishing, hiking, boating (nonmotorized), Appalachian Trail, horseback riding, hunting, xc skiing. Some campsites wheelchair accessible.

Prospect Lake Park (413-528-4158; Prospect Lake Rd., N. Egremont, MA 01252) 130 sites, tennis, swimming, boat rentals, basketball court, volleyball, snack bar, playground.

* **Tolland State Forest** (413-269-6002 or -7268; Rte. 8, East Otis, MA 01029; 5 mi. from Rte. 8; Mailing Address: Box 342, East Otis, MA 01029) 90 Type-1 campsites, on 8,000 acres, including lovely Otis Reservoir. Private, secluded campsites, some on the lake or overlooking lake. Bicycling, boating, fishing, hunting, hiking, horseback riding trails, picnicking, xc skiing, snowmobiling, swimming.

Central County

Bissellville Estate & Campground (Owners: Lorraine Brunet; 413-655-8396; Washington Rd. [Rte. 8], Hinsdale, MA 01235) 13 campsites with sewer hookups; 18 with water & electricity; 13 with all three. Closed winter.

Bonnie Brae Cabins and Campsites (Manager: Richard Halkowicz; 413-442-3754, 108 Broadway St., Pittsfield, MA 01201; 3 mi. N. of downtown Pittsfield, off Rte. 7 at Pontoosuc Lake) Full hookups, free showers, trailer rentals, new pool, cabin rentals May 1–Oct. 31. Closed Nov.–Apr. 30.

Bonnie Rigg Campground (413-623-5366; P.O. Box 14, Chester, MA 01011-0014; corner of Rtes. 8 & 20 in Becket) 200 campsites, but by owner/membership only. Call for information. Adult lounge, playground, swimming pool, sauna, Jacuzzi.

Bucksteep Manor (413-623-5535; 885 Washington Mtn. Rd., Becket, MA 01223; 10 mi. E. of Pittsfield, across from October Mtn. State Forest) 15 sites, 9 cabins; showers, swimming pool, tennis, hiking, xc skiing.

Fernwood Forest Campground (413-655-2292; 41 Plunkett Reservoir Rd., Hinsdale.) 30 campsites with water, toilets, showers, electricity. Recreation field; about 1 mi. from the Appalachian Trail. Closed mid-Oct.–May 1.

* **Mount Greylock State Reservation** (413-499-4262; Rockwell Rd., Lanesborough, MA 01237; from Rte. 7 in Lanesborough, take N. Main St. to Rockwell Rd.; access as well from Notch Road, N. Adams; Mailing Address: Box 128, Lanesborough, MA 01237) 12,000 acres which includes the state's highest peak (see Chapter Three, *Lodging*, for historic Bascom Lodge). 100-mi. view from War Veterans Memorial Tower, 35 wilderness campsites, 45

mi. of trails including the Appalachian Trail, xc skiing, hunting, snowmobiling, picnicking, interpretive programs.

* **Pittsfield State Forest** (413-442-8992; Cascade St., Pittsfield, MA 01201; From Rte 7 take West St. to Cascade St.) 9,695 acres with streams, waterfalls, wildflowers, panoramic views, and famous Balance Rock. Two camping areas offer 31 Type-1 and Type-2 campsites, plus boating (electric motors only), canoeing, xc skiing, ski lodge, bicycling, fishing, hiking, picnicking, hunting, interpretive programs, snowmobiling, swimming, and wheelchair-accessible picnic areas and trails.

Ponterril (Manager: Kevin Fitzpatrick, Pittsfield YMCA; 413-499-0640; North St., Pittsfield, MA 01201; off E. Acres Rd. at Pontoosuc Lake N. of Pittsfield via Rte. 7) 12 campsites, swimming pool, tennis, sailing and sailing instructions.

Summit Hill Campground (Manager: Vicki Roberts, 413-623-5761; Summit Hill Rd., Washington, MA 01235) 110 campsites for tents and trailers, 83 sites with electricity and water, adult lounge, swimming pool and recreation hall. Closed in winter.

* **Windsor State Forest** (413-698-0948; in winter 413-442-8928; River Rd., Windsor, MA 01270; Off Rte. 9 just E. of Windsor town line; off Rte. 116 in Savoy) 1,626 acres with spectacular cascade at Windsor Jambs. 24 Type-2 campsites, bicycling, fishing, hiking, hunting, picnicking, swimming, xc skiing, snowmobiling.

North County

Brodie Campgrounds (Managers: Brodie Mtn; 413-443-4754; Brodie Mtn. Ski Resort, New Ashford, MA 01237; off Rte. 7, just N. of Lanesborough town line) 120 campsites for tents and trailers, rented by the day or seasonally. Heated swimming pool, tennis, recreation hall.

* **Clarksburg State Park** (413-664-8345, in winter 413-442-8928; Middle Rd., Clarksburg, MA 01247; From Rte. 8 N. take Middle Rd. in Clarksburg) 3,250 acres of unspoiled forestland with panoramic views; Mauserts Pond offers landscaped day-use area; 47 Type-2 campsites; boating (electric motors only), canoeing, xc skiing, fishing, hiking, hunting, snowmobiling, picnicking, bicycling, swimming.

Historic Valley Park Campground (Manager: Les Griffin; (413-662-3198; Box 751, N. Adams, MA 01247) 100 campsites with electric and water hookups, laundry, camp store, recreation hall, hiking trails, on beautiful Windsor Lake, public and private beaches with lifeguards.

Privacy Campground (413-458-3125; Hancock Rd., Hancock, MA 01267; on Rte. 43, 5 mi. S. of Rte. 7) 475 acres, 35 sites, waterfall, pond, 10 mi. of hiking trails, paddle boats, volleyball, badminton, horseshoes, tetherball, basketball, campfires, waterwheel, windmill and own hydroelectric, trolley car, playground, sauna. 4 small cabins.

* **Savoy Mountain State Forest** (413-663-8469 summer only; 413-664-9567 for camping area; Central Shaft Rd., Florida, MA 01256) 11,000 acres, including Bog Pond and Tannery Falls; 45 Type-1 campsites in old apple orchard, 3 log cabins with stone chimneys overlook South Pond and are available for rental year-round by writing RFD 2, N. Adams, MA 01247; picnicking, boating, bicycling, canoeing, xc skiing, fishing, hiking, interpretive programs, snow-mobiling, swimming.

CAMPS

There's a colorful list of overnight summer camps in the Berkshires — some specializing in sports, some tuned to the arts, some with other enthusiasms. If you or your youngsters are interested in dance or the theater, hiking or canoeing, tennis or gymnastics, dressmaking or computers, Berkshire has a camp for you. Most camps take advantage of the beauty of their natural settings, which for many of them that includes lakes and mountains. Warm days and cool nights make for season-long aquatics and sound sleeping. Berkshire cultural life also enriches campers' time here, with Tanglewood and Jacob's Pillow being two of the more popular side trips.

The Indians were the first campers in the Berkshires, and many camps still bear Indian names. Following is a list of addresses and telephone numbers. "Full program" indicates availability of both arts and sports activities.

Skateboarding in the park at Stockbridge.

Judith Monachina

South County

Camp Half Moon Directors: Edward Til & Gretchen Mann; 413-528-0940; 400 Main St., Gt. Barrington, MA 01230; Day & resident camp; Coed; Full program.

Camp High Rock Director: Chris Coker; 413-528-1227; Mt. Washington, MA 01258; Sessions for coed groups and adults; Full program; Day and summer camp (children).

Camp Kingsmont Director: Keith Zucker; 413-232-8518; RFD #2, W. Stockbridge, MA 01266; Coed; Nutrition and dietary education program, physical fitness.

Camp Lenox Directors: Monty and Richard Moss; 413-243-2223, summer; 954-340-6634, winter; Rte. 8, Lee, MA 01238; Coed; Sports.

Crane Lake Camp Directors: Barbara and Ed Ulanoff; 413-232-4257, summer; 212-362-1462, winter; State Line, W. Stockbridge, MA 01266; Coed; Full program.

Eisner Camp Institute Director: Dave Friedman; 413-528-1652, summer; 212-650-4130, winter; 53 Brookside Rd., Gt. Barrington, MA 01230; Coed children's and adult retreats; Full program and Jewish education.

Central County

Belvoir Terrace Directors: Nancy Goldberg and Diane Goldberg; summer, 413-637-0555, Belvoir Terrace, Lenox, MA 01240; winter, 212-580-3398, 145 Central Park West, N.Y., N.Y. 10023; Girls; Fine and Performing Arts.

Camp Becket Director: David DeLuca; 413-623-8972; 748 Hamilton Rd., Becket, MA 01223; Boys; Full program; Operated by Becket–Chimney Corners YMCA.

Camp Emerson Directors: Addie and Marvin Lein, Susan Lein and Kevin McDonough; 413-655-8123, summer; 617-784-0448, winter; 212 Long View Ave., Hinsdale, MA 01235; Coed 7-15, Full program.

Camp Greylock Directors: Michael Marcus and Lukas Horn; summer, 413-623-8921, Rte. 8, Becket, MA 01233; winter, 212-582-1042, 200 W. 57th St., Suite 307, N.Y., N.Y. 10019; Boys; Full program.

Camp Mah-Kee-Nac Directors: Danny and Nancy Metzger; 413-637-0781, summer; 201-429-8522, winter; 6 Hawthorne Rd., Lenox, MA 01240; Boys; Sports.

Camp Mohawk Directors: Ralph and Sue Schulman; 413-443-5091; P. O. Box 624, Lanesborough, MA 01237; Coed; Full program.

Camp Romaca Directors: Jennine and Jeff Saltz; 413-655-2715, summer; 800-779-2070, winter; P.O. Box 402, Long View Ave., Hinsdale, MA 01235; Girls; Full program.

Camp Taconic Directors: Robert and Barbara Ezrol; 413-655-2717, summer; 914-762-2820, winter; Hinsdale, MA 01235; Coed; Full program.

Camp Watitoh Directors: Sandy, William & Suzanne Hoch; 413-623-8951, summer; 914-428-1894, winter; Center Lake, Becket, MA 01223; Coed; Full program.

Camp Winadu Directors: Arleen and Shelley Weiner; 413-447-8900, summer; 561-994-5500, winter; Churchill St., Pittsfield, MA 01201; Boys; Full program.

Chimney Corners Camp Director: Shannon Donovan-Monti; 413-623-8991; Becket, MA 01223; Girls; Full program; Operated by Becket–Chimney Corners YMCA.

CANOEING AND KAYAKING

Besides all of Berkshire's lovely lakes to canoe and kayak, the paddler has four rivers to choose from, with stretches varying from lazy flatwater to rushing rapids. The Housatonic River rises in Washington and the lakes near Pittsfield, flowing southward between the Taconic Range and the Berkshire Plateau, heading for Long Island Sound near Stratford, Connecticut. Four Berkshire trips down the Housatonic are recommended by the Appalachian Mountain Club: Dalton to Lenox (19 mi.); Lenox to Stockbridge (12 mi.); Stockbridge to Gt. Barrington (13 mi.); and Gt. Barrington to Falls Village, Connecticut (25 mi.). Send for *The AMC River Guide to Massachusetts, Connecticut and Rhode Island* ($9.95, from AMC, 5 Joy St., Boston, MA 02108) or ask local booksellers.

A Canoe Guide to the Housatonic River: Berkshire County, a nifty little booklet published jointly by the Housatonic River Watershed Association and the

William Tague

Berkshire whitewater has challenged generations of canoeists.

Berkshire County Regional Planning Commission, contains line drawings, a history of the river and its flora and fauna, as well as dozens of access points with river descriptions. Highly recommended for any Housatonic paddling; see local booksellers.

In *South County*, the stretch on the Housatonic from Gt. Barrington to Bartholomew's Cobble in Ashley Falls is classic, lazy river paddling. Canoes can be purchased and rented in Sheffield at *Gaffer's Canoe Service* (413-229-0063; Rte. 7).

In the fall, when the dam on Otis Reservoir is opened, the West Branch of the Farmington River swells. The stretch south of Rte. 23, along Rte. 8 in Otis and Sandisfield, is the site of an annual Olympic kayak racing event. In early spring, this stretch is a Class Three rapids, making for exciting white-water paddling and great viewing. The Westfield offers whitewater racing in the spring.

For lovely lake paddling, canoes can be rented at *Prospect Lake* (413-528-4158; Prospect Lake Rd., N. Egremont) and *Lake Garfield* (413-528-5417; Rte. 23, Monterey).

Up in *North County* the Hoosic River flows northwards, and in those parts *Berkshire Outfitters* (413-743-5900; Rte. 8, Adams), canoe and kayak specialists, rent craft and offer sound advice on the best in area boating. The Hoosic River Watershed Association has put out a recreational map of the river all the way to the Hudson, available at sports stores.

CROQUET

In the Berkshires, croquet has a small but tenacious group of followers. Many heated battles have been fought on the lawns of the Lenox Club in Lenox, and the town of Lenox has the largest collection of courts in Massachusetts. There are private courts elsewhere in the county, too.

Blantyre, also in Lenox, offer resident guests the use of imported equipment — and lessons by a certified professional — during the season from July to September. See Chapter Three, *Lodging,* for more information on Blantyre.

The Lenox Club and Blantyre each host a tournament in this wicket sport once a year. Watch the newspapers for announcements.

FITNESS FACILITIES

Getting in shape was never so organized. Now that most jobs age us before our time, Berkshire has joined the growing revolution to reverse that trend. Residential fitness facilities are listed later in this chapter, including Canyon Ranch as a "Luxury Spa." Here are some other exercise and recreation centers around the county.

Berkshire Mountain Yoga (413-528-5333; 30 Elm Ct., Great Barrington) Yoga (including Ashtanga, Hatha, Kali Tri-Yoga), Tai Chi, Chi Kung, and meditation. Performing arts classes for children, Sept.–May.

Berkshire Nautilus (413-499-1217; 205 West St., Pittsfield) Nautilus, stationary bikes, rowing machines, treadmill, StairMaster, whirlpool, sauna, steam, and certified instruction.

Berkshire West (413-499-4600; Dan Fox Dr.; Pittsfield) Nautilus, stationary bikes, free weights, tennis, racquetball, aerobics, treadmills, saunas, steam room, hot tub, and certified instruction. Also has a nursery.

Fitness Express (413-528-5600; 42 Bridge St., Gt. Barrington) Aerobics, ballet, karate, myotherapy, massage, weight room, rowing machines, stationary bikes, treadmills, pro shop.

The Health Club (413-243-3500; Oak n' Spruce, Meadow St., S. Lee) Universal equipment, Nautilus, StairMaster, stationery bicycles, free weights, 2 indoor pools and 1 outdoor pool, water-aerobics classes, hot tub, saunas, tennis, basketball, treadmills, rowing machine, plus tanning beds.

Lenox Fitness Center (413-637-9893; 68 Main St., Lenox) Nautilus, stationary bikes, rowing machines, StairMasters, aerobics, steam rooms, tanning booth, free weight rooms, yoga, and certified instruction.

YMCAs in North Adams and Pittsfield (see under separate heading, this chapter).

FOOTBALL

There are high school games and pick-up touch football games throughout the county, but only in Williamstown will you see spirited collegiate gridiron action, as presented by the Williams College Ephmen (named after their school founder, Ephraim Williams). This is "football at its sweetest": no athletic scholarships, studies really do come first, and competition with Amherst and others is even and spirited.

Williams College Football, Weston Field, Williamstown: 413-597-2344.

The Berkshire Mountaineers, a professional team in the Empire League, can be located through the sports pages in season.

GOLF

In 1895, Joseph Choate, Jr., son of the prominent Stockbridge lawyer, returned from a Canadian trip with three rudimentary golf clubs. Using tomato cans for holes, he made a course in his backyard at Naumkeag and thus brought golf to the Berkshires. Three years later, having perfected his swing, Joseph Choate, Jr. won the National Championships with a record low score. (A variation on the tomato can tale cites the Taconic as the first course in the county.)

Golf has grown in the Berkshires, and there are now more than a dozen courses county-wide, with hardy sportsfolk teeing up from March through November. Every course and club runs tournaments, and a call or visit will provide exact dates. Long-distance driving options have expanded, too. First there were wood woods, then metal woods, and now, new for the nineties — developed from Pittsfield-GE engineered resins — Lexan woods, by Thermo Par. And for those who just have to hit some in the dark of night, *Baker's Family Golf Center* (413-443-6102: Rte. 7, Lanesborough) keeps its driving range open from 10 a.m. till 10:30 p.m. Possibilities in the miniature division: *Par 4 Family Fun Center* (413-499-0051; Rte. 7, Lanesborough); *Jiminy Peak* (413-738-5500; Hancock); the *Diversions Restaurant and Fun Center* in N. Adams (413-662-2688; N. Adams Plaza); and in South County there's *Rainbow's End Miniature Golf* (413-528-1220; Rte. 7, Gt. Barrington) inside Cove Bowling Lanes.

GOLF CLUBS

Price Code — Greens Fees
Inexpensive — Under $17
Moderate — $17 to $30
Expensive — Over $30

South County

Egremont Country Club Pro: Bob Dastoli; 413-528-4222; Rte. 23, S. Egremont; 18 holes; Par 71; 5,900 yards; Price: Moderate.

Greenock Country Club Pro: Michael Bechard; 413-243-3323; W. Park St., Lee; 9 holes; Par 70; 5,990 yards; Price: Moderate.

Stockbridge Golf Club Pro: Jim Walker; 413-298-3423; Main St., Stockbridge; 18 holes; Par 71; 6,294 yards; Price: Expensive; Must be introduced by a member.

Wyantenuck Country Club Pro: Dennis Perrone; 413-528-3229; W. Sheffield Rd., Gt. Barrington; 18 holes; Par 70; 6,137 yards; Price: Expensive.

Central County

Bass-Ridge Golf Course 413-655-2605; Plunkett Ave., Hinsdale; 9 holes; Par 70; 5,164 yards; Price: Inexpensive.

Berkshire Hills Country Club Pro: Jim Turbeville; 413-442-1451; 350 Benedict Rd., Pittsfield; 18 holes; Par 72; 6,606 yards; Price: Moderate; Must be introduced by a member.

Country Club of Pittsfield Pro: Brad Benson; 413-447-8504; 639 South St., Pittsfield; 18 holes; Par 71; 6,100 yards; Price: Expensive; Must be introduced by a member.

Cranwell Golf Course Pro: Bran Meekins; 413-637-1216 or 413-637-0441; 55 Lee Rd. (Rte. 20), Lenox; 18 holes; Par 70; 6,387 yards; Price: Moderate.

General Electric Athletic Association Pro: Ed Rossi, PGA pro; 413-443-5746; 303 Crane Ave., Pittsfield; 9 holes; Par 72; 6,205 yards. Lessons available; call for information. Price: Inexpensive.

Pontoosuc Lake Country Club 413-445-4217; Ridge Ave., Pittsfield; 18 holes; Par 70; 6,305 yards; Price: Inexpensive.

Skyline Country Club Pro: Jim Mitus; 413-445-5584; 405 S. Main St., Lanesborough; 9 holes; Par 72; 6,200 yards; Price: Inexpensive.

Wahconah Country Club Pro: Paul Daniels; 413-684-1333; Orchard Rd., Dalton; 18 holes; Par 71; 6,541 yards; Price: Expensive.

North County

Forest Park Country Club Mgr.: Bruce Cardin; 413-743-3311; Country Club Ave., Adams; 9 holes; Par 68; 5,100 yards; Price: Inexpensive.

North Adams Country Club 413-664-9011; 641 River Rd., Clarksburg; 9 holes; Par 72; 5,600 yards; Price: Inexpensive.

Taconic Golf Club Pro: Rick Pohle; 413-458-3997; Meacham St., Williamstown; 18 holes; Par 71; 6,614 yards; Price: Expensive.

Waubeeka Springs Golf Links Pro: Jack Kelly; 413-458-8355; 137 New Ashford Rd. (Rte. 7), Williamstown; 18 holes; Par 72; 6,296 yards; Price: Moderate.

Keep your eyes open for the reopening of an 18- or 27-hole course at Greylock Glen, judged one of the most lovely and challenging around during a brief, earlier incarnation.

HIKING

Massachusetts may be the sixth smallest state in the union, but its forest and park system is the sixth largest. And of the state's quarter-million protected acres, nearly three-fifths are in Berkshire County. Of the 606,000 total county acres, those owned publicly include 97,000 managed by the state Forests and Parks and 12,500 by Fisheries and Wildlife. There are 21 state parks in the county, all of which have interesting tales and trails. Berkshire nature centers each have scenic paths. In addition, 86 miles of the Appalachian Trail run up Berkshire County, entering near Bartholomew's Cobble in Ashley Falls and exiting from Clarksburg.

The real pleasures are qualitative, however. With trails along lakes and rivers, up hills and steep mountains, the Berkshires offer all types of terrain for "anyfling" from an afternoon's jaunt to a full-fledged pack trip.

With enthusiasm we assert that no other place has Berkshire's variety of trails, from light walks to heavy hikes, suiting any available amount of time, convenient from anywhere in the county, and open to the public. These trails are marked and maintained by volunteers, who give of their time because they love this remarkable place and want visitors to like it, too.

Although a compass and maps are advisable for any deep-woods hiking, it's comforting to note that in Berkshire County, no matter how wild the surroundings, hikers are never more than five miles from the nearest paved road. Nevertheless, for hikes of any length, and especially for those taken alone, you should notify a friend of plans, including estimated hour of return. Carry water.

STATE PARKS WITH MAINTAINED TRAILS

South County

Beartown and East Mtn. State Forest 413-528-0904; Blue Hill Rd., Monterey; 10,500 acres.

Mt. Everett State Reservation, Mt. Washington State Forest, Bash Bish Falls 413-528-0330; East St., Mt. Washington; 3,289 acres.

October Mtn. State Forest 413-243-1778, 413-243-9735; Woodland Rd., Lee; 15,710 acres.

Otis State Forest 413-528-0904; Rte. 23, Otis.

Sandisfield and Cookson State Forest 413-258-4774; West St., Sandisfield (New Marlboro); 4,378 acres.

Tolland State Forest 413-269-6002, 413-269-7268; Rte. 8, Otis; 8,000 acres.

Central County

Mt. Greylock State Reservation 413-499-4263, 413-499-4262; Visitors Center, Rockwell Rd., Lanesborough; also accessible from Notch Road, N. Adams; 12,000 acres. La creme de la creme of Berkshire hiking.

Pittsfield State Forest 413-442-8992; Cascade St., Pittsfield; 9,695 acres.

Windsor State Forest 413-684-0948; River Rd., Windsor; 1,626 acres.

North County

Clarksburg State Park 413-664-8345; Middle Rd., Clarksburg; 346 acres.

Savoy Mtn. State Forest 413-663-8469; Rte 2, Florida and Rte. 116, Savoy; 10,500 acres.

Taconic Trail State Forest 413-499-4263, Williamstown.

For more detailed information on the county's state parks, write: *Massachusetts Department of Environmental Management*, Division of Forests and Parks (617-727-9800; 100 Cambridge St., Boston, MA 02202), or its Region V office (413-442-8928; Box 1433, Pittsfield, MA 01202).

History of the Trustees of Reservations

In 1890, before the present national interest in the environment, a young landscape architect returned from study in Europe with a deepening concern for the need to preserve the natural beauty and historic sites of his community.

Charles Eliot (1859-1897), just 31 years old and son of Charles W. Eliot, then president of Harvard University, proposed the establishment of an organization "empowered to hold small and well distributed parcels of land . . . just as the Public Library holds books and the Art Museum pictures for the use and enjoyment of the public."

Incorporated by the Massachusetts General Court a year later, in 1891, the Trustees of Reservations was the first independent organization in the United States established for the purpose of preserving land.

The Trustees of Reservations 413-298-3239; P.O. Box 792, 19 Main St., Stockbridge 01262.

Excellent hiking opportunities await you at the following properties of The Trustees of Reservations:

Bartholomew's Cobble 413-229-8600; Weatogue Rd., (Rte. 7A), Ashley Falls (Sheffield).

Field Farm 413-458-3135 or -3144; Sloan Rd., off Rte. 7 at the Five Corners in Williamstown.

Monument Mtn. Stockbridge Rd. (Rte. 7), Gt. Barrington.

Notchview Reservation 413-684-0148; Rte. 9, Windsor.

Tyringham Cobble 413-298-3239; Jerusalem Rd., Tyringham.

There are several hiking clubs in the Berkshires. Among them, the *Appalachian Mountain Club* (413-443-0011), *Taconic Hiking Club* (Troy, New York), and the *Williams (College) Outing Club* (413-597-2317) are the most active. Each organizes hikes through the county. The map on page 234 shows the entire length of the Appalachian Trail in Berkshire County.

Greylock Discovery Tours will guide group tours along the Appalachian and Taconic Range trails in half- or whole-day hikes, while arranging tickets to a

Tanglewood concert, perhaps, and a sumptuous dinner and comfortable lodging to follow. From a long, vigorous hike up a mountain to a slow meander through a birch-shaded path, Berkshire Hiking will help the urbanite back to nature. Trail snacks and lunches are included, as are stopovers at scenic vistas and cascading waterfalls. Packages vary from a weekend to 10 days in length. This is for those who like to meet nature while maintaining their comfort. *Greylock Discovery Tours* (413-637-4442; 800-877-9656; P.O. Box 2231, Lenox, MA 01240).

Berkshire County Land Trust

The Berkshire County Land Trust and Conservation Fund is an offshoot of Berkshire Natural Resources Council, a private, not-for-profit environmental advocacy group, established in 1967. Led by President George S. Wislocki and Director Tad Ames, this group believes that the wealth of Berkshire lies in its quality of life, in its natural environment and cultural heritage. The council works with state and local agencies to ensure that those lands are protected from abuse.

There are about 200 land trusts in America, many of them in New England. By all counts, BNRC and its offspring in several Berkshire towns are some of the more successful. In Pittsfield, the Trust was responsible for increasing the Pittsfield State Forest by 1,800 acres. Along the Housatonic, south of Pittsfield, the Resources Council is coordinating the creation of a 12-mile-long river park, reaching to Woods Pond in Lenox. The Land Trust facilitated the preservation of Gould Meadows, that gorgeous 95-acre pasture reaching from Tanglewood to Stockbridge Bowl. The Stockbridge-Yokun Ridge Reserve is another land corridor the Trust is assembling to remain forever wild, an eight-mile-long, 6,300-acre spread of Berkshire park.

Berkshire County Land Trust and **Berkshire Natural Resources Council, Inc.** President: George Wislocki; 413-499-0596; 20 Bank Row, Pittsfield, MA 01201.

Two excellent books on Berkshire hiking are available: *Hikes & Walks in the Berkshire Hills* by Lauren R. Stevens; and for the Williamstown environs, *The Williams College Outing Club Trail Guide*, first published in 1927 and now in its seventh edition. Stevens' book covers not only a wide variety of challenging hikes for the energetic and ambitious, but also a large number of easy strolls for those with less time or gumption. A section outlines walks for the blind and physically handicapped. There is also the *Appalachian Mountain Club Trail Guide*, extremely detailed but limited in number of trails.

HORSEBACK RIDING

O ver meade and under mountain, there's a slew of riding academies and stables in and around Berkshire County. A quick look in the Yellow Pages opens the barn door to information on horse breeders, dealers, trainers, farriers, and saddle shops. The following is a partial list.

Aspinwall Riding School 413-637-0245; 293 Main St. (Rte. 7), Lenox; English lessons, indoor and outdoor rings; year-round.

Bonnie Lea Farm 413-458-3149; 511 North St. (Rte. 7), Williamstown; private and group lessons; English, Western; indoor and outdoor rings. Year-round; guided trail rides summer only. Summer horse program for children 6 and up (9 a.m.–12 p.m.); call for information.

Eastover 413-637-0625; 430 East St., Lenox; trail rides for guests only at Eastover resort; year-round.

Oakhollow 413-458-9278; 651 Henderson Rd., Williamstown; English lessons, trails, indoor and outdoor rings; special therapeutic riding program; year-round.

Overmeade School of Horsemanship 413-499-2850; 940 East St., Lenox; English private and group lessons; year-round.

RCR Stables 413-637-0613; 430 East St., Lenox; guided trail rides at Eastover Resort; guests have priority; year-round.

Stepping Stone Stable 413-684-3200; 619 East St., Dalton; summer riding program, year-round lessons.

Undermountain Farm 413-637-3365; Undermountain Rd., Lenox; English lessons, trail rides; indoor and outdoor rings; year-round.

HUNTING AND FISHING

Fly fishing the Green River.

Jonathan Sternfield

The first settlers found Berkshire teeming with fish and game; now the wildlife is more plentiful than it has been in 150 years. Deer visit town to devour ornamental shrubbery; wild turkey and beaver have been successfully reintroduced; bear, pheasant, quail, rabbit, raccoon, fox, coyote, and gray squirrel are sufficient to satisfy nearly every hunter's aim. In Berkshire's waters, large and small mouth bass, northern pike, white and yellow perch, horned pout, and trout of all varieties still swim in abundance. Numerous brooks, rivers, ponds, and lakes are stocked with trout each year.

Essential equipment for any hunting or fishing is a free pamphlet containing abstracts of the *Massachusetts Fish and Wildlife Laws*, available at local sporting goods shops; from the **Division of Fisheries and Wildlife** (617-727-3151; 100 Cambridge St., Boston 02202); or from the **Western Wildlife District Manager**, Tom Keefe (413-447-9789; 400 Hubbard Ave., Pittsfield, 01201). This pamphlet carefully outlines the rules and regulations of Massachusetts fishing and hunting. Also essential is a license, which can be obtained through either city or town clerks, through the Division of Fisheries and Wildlife at the Boston address above, or through many local sporting goods stores (see the list at the beginning of this chapter).

A license permits hunting, fishing, or trapping on property that is not posted, although some towns also require owner permission. State lands are open with a few exceptions, such as a three-quarter-mile radius around the tower on Mount Greylock. No hunting is allowed on Greylock during the summer and early fall. Deer season varies by a few weeks between Massachusetts and neighboring states, and hunters are responsible to know what state they are in.

A LIST OF TROUT-STOCKED BERKSHIRE WATERS

South County

Alford Seekonk Brook, Green River.

Egremont Green River, Hubbard Brook.

Great Barrington Green River, West Brook, Thomas & Palmer Brook, Williams River, Lake Mansfield.

Lee Beartown Brook (west branch), Hop Brook, Goose Pond, Greenwater Brook, Laurel Lake, Washington Mountain Brook.

Monterey Lake Buel, Lake Garfield, Rawson Brook, Konkapot River.

New Marlborough Konkapot River, Umpachene Brook, York Pond.

Otis Farmington River, Otis Reservoir, Dimock Brook, Little Benton Pond, Big Benton Pond.

Sandisfield Buck River, Clam River, Farmington River.

Sheffield Hubbard Brook, Konkapot River.

Stockbridge Marsh Brook, Stockbridge Bowl.

Tyringham Hop Brook, Goose Pond Brook, Goose Pond.

FISH, EXCLUSIVE OF TROUT, IN BERSKHIRE WATERS

TOWN	WATER	NP	LMB	SMB	CP	WP	YP	BB
South County								
Egremont	Prospect lake				✔		✔	✔
Lee	Goose Pond		✔	✔	✔		✔	✔
Lee	Laurel Lake		✔		✔	✔	✔	✔
Monterey	Benedict Pond		✔				✔	✔
New Marlborough	Thousand Acre Swamp			✔	✔		✔	✔
Otis	Benton Pond			✔	✔	✔	✔	✔
Otis	East Otis Reservoir	✔	✔	✔	✔	✔	✔	✔
Stockbridge	Stockbridge Bowl		✔	✔	✔		✔	✔
Central County								
Becket	Center Pond		✔	✔	✔	✔	✔	✔
Becket	Yokum Pond		✔				✔	✔
Hinsdale	Ashmere Lake		✔	✔			✔	
Pittsfield	Onota Lake	✔	✔		✔		✔	✔
Pittsfield	Pontoosuc Lake		✔		✔		✔	✔
Pittsfield	Richmond Pond		✔	✔	✔		✔	✔
Windsor	Windsor Pond		✔		✔		✔	✔
North County								
Cheshire	Cheshire Reservoir	✔	✔		✔		✔	✔
Clarksburg	Mauserts Pond					✔		✔

Symbols
NP— Northern Pike
LMB— Largemouth Bass
SMB— Smallmouth Bass
CP— Chain Pickerel
WP— White Perch
YP— Yellow Perch
BB— Brown Bullhealds
(Horn Pout)

West Stockbridge Williams River, Cone Brook, Flat Brook.

Central County

Becket Shaker Mill Brook, Greenwater Pond, Yokum Brook, Westfield River (west branch), Walker Brook, Shaw Pond.

Dalton Sackett Brook, Housatonic River (east branch), Wahconah Falls Brook.

Hancock Kinderhook Creek, Berry Pond.

Hinsdale Bennet Brook, Housatonic River (east branch), Plunket Reservoir.

Lanesborough Town Brook, Sachem Brook, Pontoosuc Lake.

Lenox Sawmill Brook, Marsh Brook, Yokum Brook, Laurel Lake.

Peru Trout Brook.

Pittsfield Daniel Brook, Housatonic River (southwest branch), Lulu Cascade Brook, Sackett Brook, Smith Brook, Onota Lake, Lake Pontoosuc, Jacoby Brook.

Richmond Cone Brook, Furnace Brook, Richmond Pond, Mt. Lebanon Brook.

Washington Depot Brook.

Windsor Westfield River (east branch), Windsor Jambs Brook, Windsor Pond, Windsor Brook, Westfield Brook.

North County

Adams Anthony Brook, Hoosic River (south branch), Tophet Brook, Southwick Brook.

Cheshire Hoosac Lake, Hoosic River (south branch), Dry Brook, Kitchen Brook, South Brook, Thunder Brook, Penniman Brook.

Clarksburg Hoosic River (north branch), Hudson Brook.

Florida Deerfield River, North Pond.

North Adams Notch Brook, Windsor Lake.

Savoy Chickley River, Cold River, Westfield River (east branch), Center Brook.

Williamstown Broad Brook, Hemlock Brook, Green River (west branch), Green River, Roaring Brook.

OUTDOOR SITES

In addition to its vast forests, Berkshire is blessed with many other interesting outdoor sites, each of which shows off natural features, such as waterfalls, unusual geology, or plant life. For a listing of Natural Places in the county, see *A Guide to Natual Places in the Berkshire Hills* by René Laubach.

South County

Bartholomew's Cobble 413-229-8600; Weatogue Rd. (Rte. 7A), Ashley Falls (Sheffield). This National Natural Landmark is a 277-acre sanctuary with limestone outcroppings about 500 million years old. The terrain supports wildflowers, trees, and ferns in great variety and number. It's a fine place to view the Housatonic River and its surrounding valley. On the site is the Bailey Museum of Natural History (Closed: Mon., Tues.). Group tours on request; picnic privileges available. Season: Apr. 15–Oct. 15; Fee.

Bash Bish Falls 413-528-0330; Bash Bish Falls Rd. in Mount Washington. The falls are .5 miles from the lower parking lot. Celebrated by painters of the Hudson River School and poets, these falls say their name to those who listen carefully.

Berkshire Botanical Garden 413-298-3926; Junction of Rte. 102 & Rte. 183, Stockbridge. The foremost botanical complex in the county for more than 50 years spreads over 15 acres of gently rolling land. The magnificent plantings include primroses, conifers, day lilies, perennials, and shrubs. A terraced herb garden, a rose garden, raised-bed vegetable gardens, and exotic flowers abound. The greenhouses (one of them a passive solar model) grow seedlings, cuttings, and plants of all sorts. Visitor Center, Garden Gift Shop, and Herb Products Shop offer information, practical garden items, and invigorating odors. Fee.

The Botanical Garden runs a full schedule of activities, May through October, ranging from flower shows and herb symposiums to lectures on flower arranging and on English country gardens. Its fine reference library offers books, magazines, and the latest seed catalogs.

The Garden calendar culminates with a Harvest Festival in early October, offering fun and food for children and adults — and bargains on used clothes.

Campbell Falls State Park Campbell Falls Road leaves Norfolk Rd. at the Connecticut line in New Marlborough. A lovely little falls in a park.

Ice Glen Ice Glen Rd., Stockbridge. Cross the footbridge over the Housatonic River, follow the trail southward to walk a primeval path of glacial boulders — not recommended for the weak-kneed.

Sages Ravine Rte. 41 in Sheffield. The pullover at the side of the road is marked and usually full of cars. A couple miles of hiking leads to the cascades or, farther on, the Appalachian Trail.

Central County

Balance Rock, Balance Rock Rd., Pittsfield State Forest, Pittsfield. Of the county's glacial erratics, apparently about to tip off their small bases, this is the most dramatic.

Canoe Meadows Wildlife Sanctuary 413-637-0320; Holmes Rd., Pittsfield; 262-acre preserve of forest, ponds, streams, the Housatonic River banks, and flood plain; owned and managed by the Massachusetts Audubon Society. Fee.

Dorothy Francis Rice Sanctuary South Rd. (off Rte. 143), Peru; 300-acre preserve of woodland trails, owned and managed by the New England Forestry Foundation.

Notchview Reservation 413-684-0148; Rte. 9, Windsor; 3,000 acres of forest, crossed by miles of trails; owned and managed by The Trustees of Reservations. Fee.

Pittsfield State Forest 413-442-8992; Cascade St., Pittsfield. 10,000 acres of forest, fields, ponds, streams; trails for walks, hikes, x-c skiing, horseback riding.

Pleasant Valley Wildlife Sanctuary 413-637-0320; 472 West Mountain Rd. (off Rte. 7, opposite the Quality Inn), Lenox; 700 acres of forest, field, ponds (beaver dams with real beaver), and streams with miles of trails; educational programs; owned and managed by the Massachusetts Audubon Society. Fee.

Wahconah Falls Rte. 9, Dalton. One of the county's largest cascades.

Windsor Jambs 413-684-0948; On River Rd. between rtes. 8 and 9 in Windsor. A 0.5 mile trail leads to gorge.

North County

Bear Swamp hydroelectric project 413-424-5213; River Road, Florida. A stop at the visitors center reveals how pumped storage works; a call ahead can result in a tour of the works deep in the mountain.

Duvall Nature Trail Rte. 116 (at Hoosac Valley High School), Adams; two miles of nature trails overlooking the Greylock Range.

Hopkins Memorial Forest 413-597-2346; Bulkley St. (off Rte. 7), Williamstown; 3,000 woodland acres on the slopes of the Taconic Range with miles of hiking trails.

Natural Bridge State Park 413-663-6392; Natural Bridge Road, N. Adams (just north of downtown on Rte. 8). Waters tumble over a marble dam and then course beneath a natural marble bridge.

RACQUET SPORTS

RACQUETBALL

There's a lively racquetball scene in Berkshire, with courts in Lenox, Pittsfield, New Ashford, and North Adams and at Williams College. The *North Adams YMCA* (413-663-6529; 22 Brickyard Court) has two nice courts.

At the **Brodie Mtn. Racquet Club** (413-458-4677; Rte. 7) in New Ashford, there are five courts, open from 8:30 a.m. to 10 p.m. **Pittsfield YMCA** (413-499-7650; 292 North St.) has four; and **Berkshire West** (413-499-4600; Dan Fox Dr., Pittsfield) has four. Both Pittsfield facilities offer top-flight teaching programs.

SQUASH

Squash in Berkshire? Yes, but it's mostly the garden variety. As for the sporting type, many squash courts do exist, but, alas, most are open only to people associated with the private schools maintaining them. Memberships are available at Williams College, which is remodeling its courts. For travelers: the court at the **Pittsfield YMCA** (413-499-7650; 292 North St.) is well built and lively.

TENNIS

In the Berkshires' Gilded Age, at the close of the 19th century, tennis was played on lawns, close-cropped and lined with lime. Wheatleigh was an especially favored site, and the lawn tennis parties there featured men in long white linen trousers and ladies in ankle-length tennis dresses. Most of the grass courts are front lawns now, and though a few Berkshire connoisseurs still play on turf, tennis — here as elsewhere — is now played principally on clay, composites, and hard courts.

Several tournaments are annual events and can be counted on to test the best skills or provide exciting viewing. Starting in late summer, tournaments are run by the **YMCA's Ponterril** (413-499-0687 or 413-499-0640 Rte. 7, Pontoosuc Lake, Pittsfield).

Southern Berkshire has traditionally been lacking in public tennis courts, the Simon's Rock courts having to meet the needs. But now *Monument Mountain High School* and the Berkshire Hills Tennis Association have created seven new hard courts at the school, for both for school and community play. The courts are open to the public, with priority given to the school tennis teams' needs.

TENNIS FACILITIES

South County

Egremont Country Club; 413-528-4222; Rte. 23, S. Egremont; 4 hard-surface courts. Fee.

Monument Mtn. Regional High School Rte. 7, Gt. Barrington; 7 hard courts, used by school students on weekdays from 3 p.m.

Monument Mtn. Motel 413-528-3272; Rte. 7, Gt. Barrington (opposite Friendly's); 1 lighted all-weather court. Fee. Call for reservation.

Greenock Country Club 413-243-3323; W. Park St., Lee; 2 clay courts. Fee.

Oak n' Spruce Resort 413-243-3500; Off Rte. 102, S. Lee; 2 clay courts. Fee.

Prospect Lake Park 413-528-4158; Prospect Lake Rd., N. Egremont; 2 courts. Fee.

Simon's Rock College of Bard 413-528-0771; Alford Rd., Gt. Barrington; 4 hard courts plus backboard; Summer memberships available.

Stockbridge Golf Club Pro: James Walker; 413-298-3838; Main St., Stockbridge (behind Town Hall); 3 clay, 2 hard-surface courts; non-members may arrange for lessons only.

Stockbridge Public Courts Pine St., 2 hard courts; The Plain School, Main St. (Rte. 7); 2 hard courts; For town residents and registered hotel guests.

Central County

Berkshire West Pro: Dave Bell; 449-4600; Dan Fox Dr., Pittsfield; 7 outdoor courts and 5 indoor hard courts; Memberships available.

Cranwell Resort 413-637-0441; Rte. 20, Lenox; 2 Har-Tru courts. Fee.

Jiminy Peak 413-738-5500; Hancock; 7 outdoor courts; instruction, tournaments. Fee.

Pittsfield Public Courts free to the public when school is not in session; all are asphalt courts.

    Herberg Middle School Pomeroy Ave.; 4 courts.

    Lakewood Park Newell St.; 2 courts.

    Pittsfield High School East St.; 4 courts.

    Taconic High School Valentine Rd.; 4 courts.

Ponterril/YMCA Pro: Sherry Scheer; 413-447-7405 or 413-499-0640; Rte. 7, Pontoosuc Lake, Pittsfield; 6 outdoor clay courts. Members only, but when courts are free, nonmembers may use them for a fee, and summer member ships are available.

North County

Brodie Mountain Tennis & Racquetball Club Pro: Mark Upright; 413-458-4677; Rte. 7, New Ashford; 5 indoor courts. Memberships available.

North Adams Public Courts free to the public; all courts are asphalt.

Greylock Recreation Field Protection Ave. (off Rte. 2), 2 courts.

Noel Field (in back of Child Care of the Berkshires); State St. (Rte. 8A); 2 courts.

Williams College 413-597-3131; Main St. (Rte. 2), Williamstown; 24 clay and hard-surface courts. Summer memberships available; apply to Buildings and Grounds Department. The town maintains a court off Main St., first come, first serve (ah!).

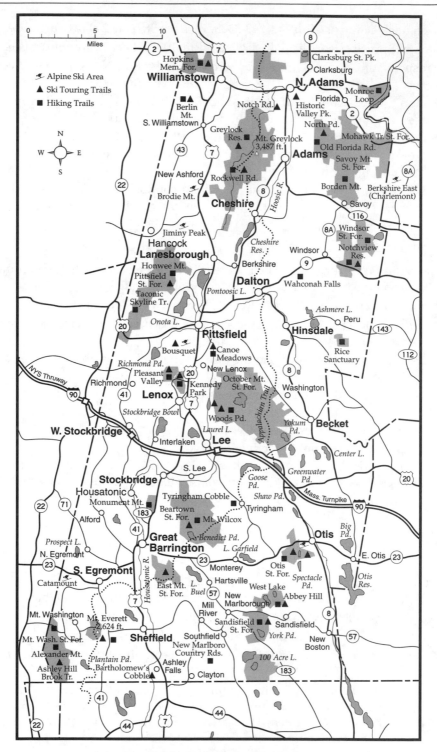

Berkshire Recreational Sites

RUNNING

R unners have run into the right neck of the woods in the Berkshires. With terrain and roadways of all types, clean mountain air, and inspiring vistas, Berkshire draws out the relaxed runner, that meditative runner who can run almost forever. Most back roads and byways have little traffic. Running may be even more pleasant on trails. For the rugged cross-country runner, some of the trails outlined in the "Hiking" section are suitable. For racers or wannabes, many towns and organizations across the county run road races; exact dates and entry information for these can be obtained from local Chambers of Commerce.

SKATING

F or ice skaters, there are many smooth and slippery possibilities in the Berkshires, most of them framed by the hills. There are three rinks open to the public: one at the *Pittsfield Boys Club* (448-8258; 16 Melville St.); another at *Lansing Chapman Rink* (413-597-2433) in Williamstown (*Williams College*); and the third in North Adams at the *Vietnam Veterans Memorial Skating Rink* (413-664-9474; S. Church St.). All the rinks offer low-priced children's programs. Outdoor skating on flooded fields is a Berkshire tradition, and during the colder months, you can do that both day and night on the Common in Pittsfield, at the Dalton Community House, and on the Stockbridge Town Field. Lake and pond skating is exquisite in Berkshire, and many of the "Swimming" sites noted later in this chapter are partially cleared after the snow flies.

For those who prefer their skating on wheels, many of the county's smoother back roads make for ideal blacktop cruising. Rollerblading, or in-line roller skating, has taken off of late, and bladers can now be seen skating the hills three seasons a year. Some prefer using poles, some blade without. The best introductory package is offered by the versatile folks over at Lenox's *Main St. Sports & Leisure* (413-637-4407, 800-592-9197; 48 Main St.), where for about $10, you can rent rollerblade skates, wrist guards, and knee pads, and view an instructional video.

SKIING — DOWNHILL

B erkshire downhill ski areas date back to the 1930s, and there's some evidence that three significant advances in modern skiing had their origins in the Berkshires: the surface ski lift, snowmaking, and the ski bar. Berkshire ski areas continue to be innovative, always questing for better, more consistent conditions over a longer season.

But it's not the technology that makes Berkshire skiing so appealing, so increasingly popular. The Berkshire hills are challenging yet picturesque, without being imposing. From the summits of the area's ski mountains, the vistas are splendid — mountains on the horizon (like the Catskills, seen from atop Butternut) and skinny bands of civilization below. With seven major ski areas in the region to choose from, skiers in the Berkshires can pick their mountain for a week or tour the hills and ski a different area on different days. Each ski mountain has its own character, each caters to a slightly different skier yet always welcomes all. Jiminy Peak and Berkshire East have the highest proportion of trails suited to advanced skiers only; but Butternut, Catamount, and even Bousquet have dicey runs, demanding enough for many experts. And for the best deal for the dollar, the Mt. Greylock Ski Club shines. Every Berkshire

Up Mt. Greylock.

John Hitchcock

ski area offers instruction; Bousquet with its ski school and Otis Ridge with its ski camp emphasize youth instruction.

BERKSHIRE SKI INFORMATION

From *Outside* Massachusetts: 800-237-5747.

Berkshire Ski Conditions: 413-499-7669. New England Ski Council reports are broadcast twice daily from radio station *WBEC-AM* and *FM*, **1420** and **105.5**, respectively, Pittsfield.

WHERE TO BUY AND RENT SKI EQUIPMENT

Besides the ski areas themselves, all of which have fully stocked ski shops, renting and selling equipment, the following specialty shops sell skis and related paraphernalia.

Arcadian Shop 413-637-3010; 91 Pittsfield-Lenox Rd. (Rte. 7), Lenox.

Berkshire Outfitters 413-743-5900; Rte. 8, Adams.

Main Street Sports & Leisure 413-637-4407, 800-952-9197; 48 Main St., Lenox.

Kenver Ltd. 413-528-2330; Rte. 23, S. Egremont.

The Mountain Goat 413-458-8445; 130 Water St., Williamstown.

Plaine's Bike Golf Ski 413-499-0294; 55 W. Housatonic St., Pittsfield.

The Sports Corner 413-664-8654; 61 Main St., Adams.

Bearing in mind that Berkshire areas are less expensive than those in northern Vermont, New Hampshire, and Maine, we call our highest price category — $30 to $40 for an adult, weekend and holiday pass — in 1996, "Moderate." Below $30 we call "Inexpensive." Skiers should contact ski areas for a more elaborate breakdown, which often includes lower rates for weekdays, for night skiing, for juniors and seniors. Bousquet's offers free skiing to those 65 years and older.

South County

BUTTERNUT BASIN
413-528-2000.
Rte. 23, Gt. Barrington, MA 01230.
2 mi. E. of town, toward Monterey.
Trails: 22 Downhill (20% Beginner, 60% Intermediate, 20% Expert). XC trails (7 km).
Lifts: 6 Chairlifts (1 quad; 1 triple, 4 doubles); 1 Poma; 1 Rope Tow.

Ski-resort developer Channing Murdoch, injured recently in an accident, is still a lucky man. Few entrepreneurs can realize their business dreams in their own backyards, as he did. His son, Jeff, now carries on the business.

Murdoch designed and built Butternut Basin Ski Area right there on a site that has become one of the Berkshires' premier winter recreation meccas. At Butternut challenging downhill runs, a separate beginner's slope, and extensive cross-country ski

Vertical drop: 1,000 ft.
Snowmaking: 100% of area.
Tickets: Moderate
Open: Wkdays 9–4;
   Wkends 8:15–4.
Ski school pro: Einar Aas.

trails offer ideal options for every kind of skier — from first-timer to serious racer.

But Butternut is more than terrific trails and the welcoming charm of its two lovely lodges. From the top of Warner Mountain there are extraordinary views of the distant Catskills in the west and Mt. Greylock at the northern end of Berkshire County. The mountain's timed slalom course is open to everyone, making a potential Olympic-class racer — at least in fantasy — out of even a beginner. Butternut's personable ski pro, Einar Aas, and his team of expert ski instructors can aide advanced skiers or those on the slopes for their debuts. Two snowboard parks have been opened. And should they want the latest in ski-wear and equipment, Butternut's ski shop is one of the most extensive and stylish at any Berkshire mountain.

Butternut's quadruple, fixed-grip lift replaces their base-to-summit double chairlift. New food facilities at the base include an area exclusively devoted to their Ski Wee kid's program, and their outside "Cruiser" barbecue deck.

From the mogul fields of the expert run, Downspout, to the meandering path of the novice Pied Piper's Trail, Butternut is a delight to the eye as well as a refreshing test of athletic skill.

CATAMOUNT
413-528-1262, 518-325-3200.
Rte. 23, S. Egremont, MA
   01258.
On New York State border.
Trails: 25 Downhill (Novice
   to Expert).
Lifts: 4 Chairlifts; 1 J-Bar; 1
   Rope Tow.
Vertical drop: 1,152 ft.
Snowmaking: 95% of area.
Tickets: Moderate
Open: 8:30–4 Wkends/
   Holidays; Midwk./Non-
   holidays, 9–4; Night
   Skiing, Wed.–Sat., 5–10.
Ski school pro: Bill
   Schmick.

"**O**n the cutting edge of Berkshire ski country," as *Skiing Magazine* put it, Catamount straddles two states and offers magnificent views of four: Massachusetts, New York, Connecticut, and Vermont. The slopes are primarily novice and intermediate, but seasoned skiers can find quite a bit of challenge through the glades near the summit, and down on through the Flipper and Dipper trails.

Called by some a vest-pocket Killington, Catamount is convenient, especially to New Yorkers. Not your trendiest, most competition-minded ski resort, but there's a pleasant quaintness here, right down to the Swiss Hutte restaurant at the mountain's base. Snowmaking equipment at Catamount has just been overhauled and expanded, and they're now firing state-of-the-art equipment at virtually all trails and slopes. Catamount has installed an additional 22 airless snow makers mounted on towers. Night skiing is also an attraction at Catamount. A new area for kids has opened.

A 1,200-foot extension of Ridge Run, one of the region's more splendid trails, now connects Esplanade to Promenade. For borderline skiing in the Berkshires, there's no better.

Central County

OTIS RIDGE
413-269-4444.
Rte. 23, Otis, MA 01253.
Trails: 11 (3 Novice, 5
  Intermediate, 3 Expert).
Lifts: Double chair; T-Bar; J-
  Bar; Pony-Bar; 2 Rope
  Tows.
Vertical drop: 400 ft.
Snowmaking: 90 % of area.
Tickets: Inexpensive.

Otis Ridge is the molehill among the mountains, but few slopes do so much to cater to beginners and youngsters, with Bob Demairio head of the ski school. Famous for its winter ski camp, the area takes on a special character on frosty weekends and holiday periods when camp's in session, starting the day after Christmas.

BOUSQUET
413-442-8316.
Dan Fox Dr., Pittsfield, MA
  01201.
Access off South St. (Rte. 7).
Trails: 21 Downhill (Novice
  to Expert).
Lifts: 2 Chairlifts; 1 Rope
  Tow; Snowboarding
  Half-Pipe.
Vertical drop: 750 ft.
Snowmaking: 98% of area.
Tickets: Inexpensive.
Open: 10–10 Wkdays; 9–10
  Wkends; 9–4 Sun.; Night
  Skiing, Mon.–Sat. 4–10.
Ski school pro: Court
  McDermott.

In 1932 a group of winter enthusiasts approached Clarence Bousquet about using the slopes of Bousquet Farm for some skiing. Three years later, the fledgling Bousquet Ski Area put together one of the Berkshires' great travel promotions: ski trains from New York to Pittsfield (with bus connector to Bousquet) for $2 round trip.

Now, over 50 years later, the Berkshires' oldest ski area continues to provide friendly slopes, primarily for novice and intermediate skiers. There are, however, several very demanding runs, and from the summit of Bousquet, there's a fine view of Mt. Greylock's whalelike profile (nearly the same view that so inspired Melville; see "Arrowhead" in Chapter Four, Culture). Bousquet is well known for its effective ski school, a corps of some 50 teachers under the direction of Court McDermott.

EASTOVER
413-637-0625.
430 East St., Lenox, MA
  01240.

For its guests only, Eastover, a resort hotel in a converted mansion, offers alpine ski runs suitable for beginners and intermediates. Because of the convenience of Eastover's lodging-dining-recreation facilities, learning to ski can be a pleasure at this Lenox resort. The vertical drop is gentle; the longest run about 0.75 mi. Besides skiing, Eastover offers the longest toboggan run in New England and, on a warmer note, indoor swimming and sauna.

JIMINY PEAK
413-738-5500.

Jiminy is committed to long seasons of well-groomed slopes. To that end, it goes to extraordi-

Corey Rd., Hancock, MA 01237.
Access from Rte. 7, Lanesborough, or Rte. 43, Hancock, via Brodie Mt. Rd.
Trails: 30 Downhill (Novice to Expert).
Lifts: 6 Chairlifts; 2 Mighty-Mite Tows.
Vertical drop: 1,140 ft.
Snowmaking: 95% of area.
Tickets: Moderate.
Open: Wkdays, 9–10:30; Wkends, 8:30–10:30.
Ski school pro: Jay Barranger.

nary lengths, frequently opening early in November and staying open well into March or April, utilizing advanced snowmaking equipment. It is also in the first stage of an $8 million to $109 million expansion program, opening up a new mountain, East Peak, and a cluster of five new buildings, called Bentley Brook. The build-out should be complete by the year 2000.

This is one of the area's most demanding mountains, with 40% of its trails being suitable for advanced skiers only. Those with such talents will greatly enjoy the North Glade, Upper Lift Line, and Whirlaway. For intermediates, there's the 360, the WestWay and the Ace of Spades. These last two trails reveal a magnificent vista of the Jericho Valley, northwards toward Vermont. New are two expert glades, an expanded beginners' area with a triple-chair; a mid-mountain rope tow to service a snowboard park; and improved snowmaking.

In addition to a full calendar of ski events (races, clinics, and demonstrations), Jiminy also runs a race team just for children, a more serious tri-state race team, a freestyle team, a night adult program, and a ski school. Those who ski at Jiminy spend most of their time skiing: lift lines are carefully monitored so that they rarely have to wait more than 12 minutes. Jiminy closes the parking lots when the area nears its capacity of 3,500 skiers.

Jiminy will undoubtedly soon offer facilities and activities to compete with any resort in Vermont. When the new condominiums are completed, it will have 500 beds, all ski-in, ski-out accessible. Added will be new lifts and snowmaking improved to operate at higher temperatures.

North County

BERKSHIRE EAST
413-339-6617.
Rte. 2 (near Savoy town line), Charlemont, Franklin County, MA 01339.
Trails: 25 (7 Novice, 9 Intermediate, 7 Expert).
Lifts: 4 Double Chairs; J-Bar; T-Bar.
Vertical drop: 1,180 ft.
Snowmaking: 75% of area.
Tickets: Moderate.

Billing itself as "Southern New England's most challenging ski area," Berkshire East's steep terrain lives up to that claim. With only 20% of its trails suited to novice skiers, this mountain is demanding, especially the steep Flying Cloud and Lift Line trails, both of which are over 4,000 feet long. For beginners, three separate open slopes around the west lodge provide plenty of room to learn the basics.

From the summit of Berkshire East, amid the pines, you can get a fine view of the Deerfield River valley (to the east) with mountains all around it. The area offers day and night skiing, and it has a rustic lodge with a bar upstairs.

The thrill of downhill.

Jonathan Sternfield

BRODIE MOUNTAIN
413-443-4752.
Rte. 7, New Ashford, MA
   01237.
Trails: 28 Downhill (Novice
   to Expert); XC (25 km).
Lifts: 4 Chairlifts; 2 Rope
   Tows.
Vertical drop: 1,250 ft.
Snowmaking: 98% of area.
Tickets: Moderate.
Open: 9–11; Twilight
   Skiing, 3–11; Night
   Skiing, 7–11.
Ski school pro: John Koch.

One of the oldest ski areas in the Berkshires, Brodie Mountain started out under the direction of Gregory Makeroff, acquiring a different flavor under the guidance of the Kelly clan. "Kelly's Irish Alps," they call Brodie, right down to the occasional staff leprechaun dressed in green and schussing downhill. Brodie is a fun area, and it has always had tremendous appeal to singles and younger skiers.

Three-quarters of Brodie's 20-odd trails and slopes are geared to novice and intermediate skiers, and one slope (Tipperary) offers a not-too-demanding 2.25-mi. glide. For experts, there's Mickie's Chute, Gilhooley's Glade, Danny Boy's Trail, and three new glade trails. Brodie is committed to its snowmaking, pioneering large-scale snowmaking in 1965 and now covering more than 95% of its slopes. They utilize state-of-the-art equipment, employing various systems and a super arsenal of Hedco Snow Cannons. In addition, Brodie invented its own "Master Blaster" snowgun. At sundown especially, the views from Brodie across the Rte. 7 valley are stunning. Of particular note is the view northward to Mt. Greylock. But the skiing doesn't stop at sundown at Brodie; for Kelly's Irish Alps is one of the largest night skiing areas anywhere, with over 17 mi. of trails and four chairlifts fully illuminated.

And after skiing, off the slopes, Brodie keeps the fun going, with five indoor tennis courts, five racquetball courts (racquets and sneakers can be rented for both), and a sauna. After sports, there's the Blarney Room and Kelly's Irish Pub.

MOUNT GREYLOCK SKI
   CLUB
413-458-3060.
Roaring Brook Road,
   Williamstown, MA 01267.

Mount Greylock Ski Club is a cooperative, which means that in exchange for low rates (family membership at about $100 for a season, including all children up to 18 years), everyone

In south Williamstown, turn east on Roaring Brook Road, beside the Rte. 7 state DPW garage. Continue up gravel road which, in season, is one way up until 2:30 p.m.
Trails: 4 novice, 9 intermediate, 3 expert. Groomed XC.
Lifts: two rope tows.
Vertical drop: 500 ft.
Tickets: By very inexpensive membership.
Open: No snow making, so wknds and holidays when snow permits.
Lodge, outhouses, ski school.

works. Jobs range from helping take care of the wood-heated lodge to cutting brush on the trail to running the antique Ford and GMC engines that power the lifts. It is a fine place for a family, because the adults look out for all the kids. The very young amuse themselves by the hour sliding near the lodge while parents ski. Members ski patrol and members teach.

The area, which has a base altitude of 1,200 ft, faces north and holds snow well, but if the snow doesn't fall . . . well then, members get to enjoy the social events and work parties the club sponsors. If the one-way traffic is daunting, the alternative is a pleasant 0.5 mile walk. MGSC sponsors a youth racing team.

Snowboarders on Berkshire Slopes

By now, snowboarders are a familiar and permanent fixture on Berkshire slopes. Popular especially among the younger set, snowboards offer both thrilling sport and a challenge to one's skills and coordination.

Most Berkshire ski areas can rent or sell you a board and follow up with instruction. Some areas offer special slopes for snowboarders; all urge caution and courtesy for snowboarders and skiers alike, for easier coexistence.

SKIING — CROSS-COUNTRY

Berkshire is made for cross-country skiers — from flat runs along the Housatonic to steep trails up Mt. Greylock, from tours in town, such as Kennedy Park in Lenox and Historic Valley Campground in North Adams, to wilderness paths like the one around North Pond in Savoy Mountain State Forest.

With no lines, no chair lifts, and no fees, generally, Berkshire x-c depends only on the whims of the weather. Since Nordic skiing has gained in popularity, private touring centers have multiplied in the Berkshires. For a small fee, trails are groomed, waxing huts warm, at a half dozen such places to cross-country ski.

It's best to ski accompanied, especially in a wilderness area. Those skiing in a state forest should check in at forest headquarters first. There maps and helpful hints are available; besides, it's a good precaution for staff to know a skier's out there. Skiers should carry a compass and extra clothes. Snacks and drinks

John MacGruer

are well-advised equipment on the trail, and the really well-prepared also carry a first-aid kit, knife, whistle, flashlight, and space blanket. Hypothermia is the greatest danger; if 20 minutes of exercise doesn't warm the blood, its time to head home.

Although many x-c skiers profess to dislike snowmobiles because of their growl and their tendency to prowl in packs, the going is easier if those creatures have packed the trail. And sometime an x-c skier in trouble might appreciate a snowmobiler's assistance. We recommend friendly relations with snowmobilers and, on their part, courtesy to skiers.

Dozens of public trails are described below, most with sufficient directions for a short tour. More detailed descriptions for some of these tours, including maps, can be found in the excellent and compact *Skiing in the Berkshire Hills* by Lauren R. Stevens. Skiers should know that if snow is not good in Berkshire, just over the line in Vermont a natural snowbelt provides some of the best cover in the east. **Prospect Mountain** (802-442-2575; Rte. 9, 8 mi. east of Bennington) benefits from nature's largess. Trails are groomed. A fee is charged.

South County

Southern Berkshire ski touring is more benign than in the other parts. The wilderness down south is a trifle less rugged, the variety of groomed trails much higher. Yet there's plenty of challenge, exciting views, and several long downhill runs that are pure pleasure.

PUBLIC SKI-TOURING

Many trails in the *Mt. Washington State Forest* offer quintessential Berkshire ski touring. No snowmobiles are allowed, so the whistle of the wind will be the loudest noise you hear all day. From the forest headquarters (East St.), the Ashley Hill Brook Trail runs south along the brook towards New York State, a four-mile, slightly uphill trip suitable for intermediate skiers. Nearby, from the parking lot just outside the Mt. Everett Reservation, you can ski up the 2,600-foot Dome of the Taconics. The climb up the mountain is gentle, passing Guilder Pond; the run down, long and exhilarating with plenty of room to maneuver.

Bartholomew's Cobble in Ashley Falls (Sheffield) has an interesting system of trails, with the runs on the far side of Weatogue Rd. being the best. Some spots wet in marginal weather. A map is posted in the parking lot. Donation box: $3 per person.

Beartown State Forest in Monterey has some lovely trails, starting at Benedict Pond and circling through the 14,000 acres of forest preserve. Maps are available at the *State Forest Headquarters* (413-528-0904; Blue Hill Rd., off Rte. 23). Triangular red blazes or wooden markers designate the ski-touring trail in Beartown, with a blue-blazed trail circling Benedict Pond, the white-blazed Appalachian Trail passing through, and the orange-blazed trails for snowmobilers.

The West Lake area of the *Sandisfield State Forest* is a fine site for Nordic skiing. No snowmobiles are allowed on the Abbey Hill Foot Trail (marked with blue blazes), and from the state forest headquarters and parking area, just off West St., a beautiful tour of about two hours will circle you around Abbey Lake, up Abbey Hill (1,810 ft.) and then down past West Lake. The area around York Lake in the forest also has some good trails.

You can ski the Knox Trail in the *Otis State Forest* if you take Rte. 23 to Nash Rd. in Otis. Where Nash joins Webb Rd. is a good place to wax up, and as you ski, watch for red K's and red blazes marking the trail.

PRIVATE TOURING CENTERS

In Gt. Barrington, *Butternut Basin* (413-528-2000; Rte. 23) has seven km of groomed novice and intermediate trails. In addition to their lovely lodges, to comfort you they also offer a pondside warming hut. *Otis Ridge* (413-269-4444; Rte. 23, Otis) has over six km of packed, but not tracked, trails. And *Oak n' Spruce Resort* (413-243-3500; off Rte. 102, South Lee) has six km of Nordic trails.

Central County

Central Berkshire ski trails are generally gentle with moderate slopes and climbs. Several "Nature Preserves" (see that section) maintain trails, and these are excellent and beautiful places to gain Nordic experience. Bucksteep Manor maintains private groomed trails.

PUBLIC SKI-TOURING

Lenox is graced with beautiful ski-touring areas, the most popular of which is *Kennedy Park*. Its 500 acres were once the site of the grand old Aspinwall Hotel (which burned to the ground in 1931). Now its long, rising driveway and its bridle paths are used for ski-touring. The Main Trail (white blazes) is the widest and simplest, with Lookout Trail (red blazes) being more of a challenge. Stately oaks dot this pretty highland, with access either at the Church on the Hill (Main St., Rte. 7A) or behind the Lenox House Restaurant (north of town on Rte. 7). Equipment available from the Arcadian Shop.

Pleasant Valley Wildlife Sanctuary (see "Nature Preserves"), also in Lenox, has a trail system laid out by the Massachusetts Audubon Society. For $3 ($2 for kids; members less), skiers go out on the trail marked with blue blazes and back on the one marked in yellow. There's also Yokun Brook Trail, Nature Trail, and others. Maps are free at the office next to the parking area (Closed: Mon.). The *Woods Pond* area in Lee and Lenox has a pretty, mostly flat trail running along the southern shore of Woods Pond, then north along the eastern bank of the Housatonic River for just over two mi. Plans call for reconstructing a foot bridge across the river. Enter via Woodland St. in Lee. The trail is best skied on weekdays due to weekend snowmobile traffic. *Canoe Meadows* (see "Nature Preserves") is another Massachusetts Audubon Society area, and it too has some lovely trails, open on weekends only. There is a $2 fee, which includes a map.

For more advanced Nordic skiers, the *Honwee Mtn.-Turner Trail* circuit is a challenge. Park just off Cascade Rd. in Pittsfield State Forest. Check in at forest headquarters, get oriented, then start up the Mountain Trail, initially marked in orange, then in white. This trail has some great views, tough climbs, and steep descents. Closer to the center of the city, in *Sackett Brook Park* (Williams St.), there are four mi. of marked trails.

Northeast of Pittsfield on Rte. 9 is the *Notchview Reservation*, in the town of Windsor. Generally here can be found the best snow in Berkshire. Trails are well marked and maintained, and there is a modest charge for touring. Maps are available for 50 cents. The Budd Visitor Center is open daily as a warming and waxing shelter. Notchview is owned by The Trustees of Reservations.

PRIVATE TOURING CENTERS

South of Lenox on Rte. 20, *Cranwell* (413-637-1364; 55 Lee Rd.) has a network of trails, crisscrossing their golf course. It ventured into snowmaking in the winter of 1996-97, an investment that will be watched as closely as the temperature. Opened to the public; fee charged. At *Canyon Ranch* (413-637-4100;

Kemble St.) closer to town, ski touring and instruction is available for spa guests, the trails sweeping across the majesty of the Bellefontaine estate.

In the hilltown of Washington, east of Pittsfield, **Bucksteep Manor** (413-623-5535; Washington Mt. Rd.) operates a long ski-touring season. Set on over 250 acres, at 1,900 ft., Bucksteep has 25 km of looped, interconnecting trails. There's a waxing room, a ski shop that sells and rents, as well as on-site lodging and dining. Nearby in Becket, **Canterbury Farm** (413-623-8765; Fred Snow Rd.) grooms 11 mi. of trails for its inn guests and daily cross-country ski guests. There is a ski shop for rentals, lessons are available, and the ski fee is $7.

North County

PUBLIC SKI-TOURING

Up at 2,000 ft., where the snows come early and stay late, **Savoy State Forest** has miles of cross-country trails, best navigated with a map obtainable at **State Forest Headquarters** (413-663-8469). Enter the forest from Rte. 2 (Florida) or Rte. 116 (Savoy). A 2.5-mi.-long trail (blue blazes) makes a challenging circuit around North Pond and then South Pond. In North Adams, **Historic Valley Park** offers ski touring quite close to downtown. The trail starts at the parking area next to Windsor Lake and is well marked by blue blazes and signs which even describe the degree of difficulty of the next stretch of trail. *The Greylock Glen*, a public-private development, proposes to offer cross-country skiing on its golf course in Adams. It will have snowmaking and a fee will undoubtedly be charged.

On *Mt. Greylock*, many opportunities for fine ski touring exist. Here again though, it's best to ski during the week, because weekends tend to draw much snowmobile traffic. (The snowmobiles are supposed to stick to the roads.) Check in at the Visitor Center on Rockwell Rd., off Rte. 7, Lanesborough. Depending on skills and fitness, there's an 8-mi. round trip up Rockwell Rd. to Jones Nose and back, 15-mi. round trip to Stony Ledge, or 17-mi. round trip to the summit. The views are breathtaking, the skiing sometimes testing, and the weather more dramatic than expected from below. Take extra warm clothing and some snacks.

The area in and around *Williamstown* is striped with trails, ranging from novice or intermediate, to demanding, like the **RRR Brooks Trail**. For Brooks, and the Taconic Crest Trail attached to it, begin either at the bottom of Bee Hill Rd., west of Rte. 2, or Petersburgh Pass, at the top of Rte. 2 west of town. The *Taconic Golf Club* course, which Williams College grooms, and the 4-mi. *Stone Hill* Loop in Williamstown are the area's most popular: relatively easy while offering all the splendor of the best ski touring. The golf course trail begins at the Clubhouse on Meacham St. Stone Hill starts and finishes in the Clark Art Museum parking lot (South St.), circling the 1,100-ft. Stone Hill, with its wonderful views. At *Hopkins Forest*, Williams College maintains a network of trails just off Northwest Hill Rd. The trails are sometimes groomed and maps are available at the forest "Carriage House." Many other trails exist, the best of which are described in the *Williams Outing Club's Trail Guide*.

PRIVATE TOURING CENTERS

In New Ashford, **Brodie Mountain Ski Area** (Rte. 7) maintains a 25-km. trail network, of which 10 km are groomed daily. The warming hut was recently expanded into a ski center with equipment rental. Training site of the Williams College cross-country ski team, Brodie's trails were laid out by ski coach Bud Fisher. Many of the trails are double-tracked and wind through field and wood. For those adventurous enough for a guided ski tour to the summit of Mt. Greylock, Brodie can arrange it (413-443-4752; call well in advance). See also the **Mount Greylock Ski Club**, under downhill skiing.

SOARING

Soaring skyhigh over Great Barrington.

Jonathan Sternfield

Altitude controls speed, which is ideally 51 mph. In this unearthly quiet, half a mile high, the Berkshires seem like a Swiss landscape, all rolling patterns of farm and woodland.

The **Berkshire Soaring Society** operates out of the Pittsfield Municipal Airport (413-443-6700; Tamarack Rd.); the **Mohawk Soaring Club** out of Harriman West Airport, North Adams (413-458-8650). Those wishing to soar should hang out with the glider pilots at the far edge of the airstrip on weekends. Those who watch and ask a few questions could end up floating on air.

Should an aircraft be an awful encumbrance to soaring, people are regularly jumping off the top of Mt. Greylock in Adams, and just as often off a steep slope of the Taconic Range, on Rte. 2, west of Williamstown, or at the Western Summit of the Mohawk Trail, in Florida — with only lightweight *hang gliders* to support their flight. We take no position on Icarian activity.

A LUXURY SPA

Toning up at Canyon Ranch.

Jonathan Sternfield

CANYON RANCH AT BELLEFONTAINE 413-637-4100; 91 Kemble St., Lenox.

Several years ago, health entrepreneurs Mel and Enid Zuckerman took their highly successful Tucson, Arizona, Canyon Ranch formula and transferred it to the sculpted hills of Lenox. There they transformed and built upon Giraud Foster's splendid "cottage," Bellefontaine — itself an exact replica of the French Le Petit Trianon — to create a world-class spa.

This is a spectacular facility, smoothly run by a group of skilled and friendly professionals. Whether for a short cool-out, a vacation, a chance to drop a few pounds and tone up, or an invigorating change of pace, Canyon Ranch lives up to its self-proclaimed billing as "The Spa that never leaves you." With over 50 fitness classes to choose from daily, swimming, racquet sports of all kinds, and a state-of-the-art gymnasium, the three-level spa complex offers a physical workout customized. Added to that, hiking, mountain biking, and cross-country skiing provide indoor/outdoor fitness possibilities unimaginable in the average spa.

Besides sumptuous Jacuzzis, steam rooms, and saunas, Canyon Ranch offers inhalation rooms (combining steam and eucalyptus) and a range of personal services to pamper you as never before. Massages include Swedish, shiatsu, Reflexology, cranial, Jin Shin Jyutsu, Trager, and Reiki, to which can be added an herbal wrap, an aroma wrap, clay or salt treatment, or hydrotherapy. Each of these ancient, exotic treatments is performed by experts, revitalizing inside and out. The healthful opportunities go on and on, from skin and beauty treatments to dietary education and stop-smoking hypnosis. Canyon Ranch visitors are automatically on a low-fat, low-cholesterol regime that's as delicious as it is healthy.

Prices vary seasonally but are always substantial. Access to the facility is limited to guests. Says *Vogue* magazine: "Not a fitness factory or fat farm . . . you go to Canyon Ranch anticipating short-term results . . . and return with a long-term resolve." "A cross between boot camp and heaven," says *Self*. Said Berkshire humorist Roy Blount, in a report to *Gentlemen's Quarterly*: "Made me feel like a jackrabbit!"

SPELUNKING

For you cave men and women out there, the hills are riddled with caves, each of which has a colorful name and legend to go with it. *French's Cave*, west of Williamsville in West Stockbridge, is 450 ft. deep, the longest cave in the whole of Massachusetts. Other Berkshire caves of note include *Radium Springs Cave* in Pittsfield; *Bat's Den Cave* in Egremont; *Cat Hole Caves* in New Marlborough; *Pittibone Falls* Cave in Cheshire; *Belcher's Cave* in Gt. Barrington; *Tory Cave* in Lenox; *Peter's Cave* in Lee; and the caves of western Lanesborough.

The *Williams College Outing Club*, Williamstown (413-597-2317), occasionally goes a-caving. These caves are on the small side, requiring wriggle, and not large underground caverns. Caving is great adventure, but it is also dangerous and should not be attempted alone or without an experienced guide.

SPORTS CAR RACING

Drivers, start your engines!

On the edge of Berkshire is the renowned *Lime Rock Race Track*, and an outfit even closer, the *Skip Barber Racing School* based in Canaan, CT, can teach how to drive safely at very high speeds. Barber operates two schools, the

BMW Advanced Driving School as well as the Skip Barber Racing School, both of which utilize the Lime Rock, CT, track as their training course. The Advanced Driving School uses BMWs to take students through accident evasion, performance braking, controlled slides, and the limits of lateral acceleration. The Racing School seats students in specially prepared, low-slung Formula I cars, teaching how to drive at speeds not suitable on the highway. With either course, driving skills are greatly enhanced, making for safer and more effective drivers on the road.

Those yearning to put the pedal to the metal should get on over to *Skip Barber Racing School* (860-824-0771; Rte 7, Canaan, CT).

SWIMMING

Berkshire swimming in full swing.

Paul Rocheleau, courtesy
the Berkshire Hills Conference

Berkshire is blessed with countless magical swimming spots, some secluded and known only to the likes of otter, and some quite public. There are sizable lakes and ponds, rushing green rivers, and deep, chilly quarries. For wintertime, and for those who prefer their water sport in a more controlled setting, there are numerous swimming pools, both indoor and out.

South County

Benedict Pond, Beartown State Forest, 413-528-0904; Gt. Barrington; Follow signs from Rte. 23 or from Rte. 102 in South Lee.

Berkshire Motor Inn 413-528-3150; Main St., Gt. Barrington; Indoor pool and sauna (being redone in 1997).

Egremont Country Club 413-528-4222; Rte. 23, S. Egremont; Outdoor pool.

Green River Off Rte. 23, 1 mi. west of Gt. Barrington; and off Hurlburt Rd., between Alford Rd. and Rte. 71; just look for the cars parked by the bridge. Clearest of the clear, greenest of the green, purest of the pure — a summer treat not to be missed.

Lake Garfield, Kinne's Grove, Rte. 23, Monterey.

Lake Mansfield 413-528-6080; off Christian Hill Rd., Gt. Barrington.

Oak n' Spruce Resort 413-243-3500; Off Rte. 102, S. Lee; Heated outdoor and indoor pools, saunas, whirlpool bath, physical fitness room; memberships available.

Otis Reservoir, Tolland State Forest, 413-269-6002 or 413-269-7268; Off Rte. 23, Otis; camping, fishing, picnicking, boating.

Prospect Lake 413-528-4158; Prospect Lake Rd. (3/4 mi. west, off Rte. 71), N. Egremont; Camping, day picnics, adult lounge; open to 6 p.m. daily.

Spectacle Pond Cold Spring Rd., Sandisfield.

York Lake, Sandisfield State Forest, 413-258-4774 or 413-229-8212; Off Rte. 57, New Marlborough; Picnicking, fishing, hiking.

Central County

Ashmere Lake Ashmere Beach, Rte. 143, Hinsdale.

Berkshire West 413-499-4600; Dan Fox Drive, Pittsfield; Outdoor pool open June–Sept. Bath house, snack bar, showers; Memberships available.

Boy's Club 413-448-8258; 16 Melville St., Pittsfield. (Under 18) Indoor pool open to members only; memberships available. Free swimming early eves. wkdays; Sat. 1–3 p.m..

Onota Lake Onota Blvd., Pittsfield; Free municipal beaches, supervised, 12–8 p.m. daily.

Pontoosuc Lake Rte. 7, Pittsfield; Free municipal beach.

Pittsfield Girls' Club 413-442-5174; 165 East St., Pittsfield; Indoor pool open for recreational swimming eves., Mon.–Fri.; Sat. 1–2:15.

Pittsfield State Forest 413-442-8992; Cascade St., Pittsfield; Swimming (lifeguards on duty 10 a.m. to 6 p.m.), picnicking, hiking and nature trails.

Pittsfield YMCA 413-499-7650; 292 North St., Pittsfield.

Plunkett Lake Lion's Club Beach, Church St., Hinsdale.

Ponterril 413-499-0647; Pontoosuc Lake, Rte. 7, north of Pittsfield; Operated by the Pittsfield YMCA (pool open to members only); Season memberships available.

Windsor State Forest 413-684-0948; Windsor; Follow signs from Rte. 9 in West Cummington or Rte. 116 in Savoy.

North County

Cheshire Reservoir, Horn's Beach, Farnam's Road, Cheshire.

Clarksburg State Park Rte. 8, Clarksburg, near Vermont line; Camping, picnicking.

Hoosic Valley High School 413-743-5200; Rte 116, Cheshire; Indoor pool open Sept. through June.

Jiminy Peak 413-738-5500; Corey Rd., off Rte. 7, Hancock; Outdoor pool.

Margaret Lindley Park Rte. 2, Williamstown; swimming pond. $10 season pass.

North Pond, Savoy Mountain State Forest, Florida; Follow signs from Rte. 2 (in Florida) or Rte. 116 (in Savoy); $5 day-use, $30 season pass.

Northern Berkshire YMCA 413-663-6529; Brickyard Ct., N. Adams.

Sand Springs Pool and Spa 413-458-5205; off Rte. 7, near Vermont line, Williamstown; 50x75-ft. mineral pool (year-round temperature of the spring, 74); 2 mineral whirlpools (temperature of 102), mineral showers, sauna, shuffleboard, picnic area, beach. Pavilion for private party use.

Windsor Lake 413-662-3047; North Adams. Access via Bradley St. from North Adams State College or via Kemp Ave. from E. Main St.; Municipal swimming area; Supervised daily; Residents, $3 with car sticker, non-residents, $15 with car sticker; One-time use, $2.00.

YMCAS

PITTSFIELD YMCA 413-499-7650; 292 North St., Pittsfield.

With its North St. facility and Ponterril Outdoor Recreation Center (see below), Pittsfield's YMCA undoubtedly serves more public recreational needs than any other complex in the county. At the *North St. Y*, the range of fitness and sports programs is formidable. Here clients can enjoy aerobics, Aeoreflex (musical aerobics with hand-held weights); here, too, they can swim and scuba dive, both with instruction if desired, and play racquetball, handball, and squash. The racquetball program is particularly fine, being led by top teaching-pro Mary McGinnis, who even offers a videotaped analysis. There are Nautilus machines and programs; special classes for kids, in basketball, gymnastics, swimming, and Indian lore. To smooth things out, the Y has a sauna, a steam room, sunlamps, and a lounge with color TV.

From Memorial Day through Labor Day, the Pittsfield Y's *Ponterril Outdoor Recreation Center* (413-499-0640; Rte. 7 at Pontoosuc Lake) comes to life, the facilities inviting, the programs enriching. There's an Olympic-sized pool, a wading pool, and a tot's spray pool; swim lessons are also offered. Down at the lake, the Y has a marina with moorings for 50 boats; it offers canoe, rowboat, and sailboat rentals; also sailing lessons; tennis camp and a soccer camp, a day camp, and a preschool camp. And up at Ponterril's six fast-dry clay courts, some of the best tennis in the county is played. Other Y memberships are honored (with a slight surcharge), and special short-term guest passes can be arranged.

NORTHERN BERKSHIRE YMCA 413-663-6529; 22 Brickyard Ct., North Adams.

North County's Y is another center of vitality in Berkshire, a facility that has continued to improve and upgrade its sports complex. There's a six-lane pool, a full gymnasium, a weight room and Nautilus, a new gymnastics room for children, and two new handball/racquetball courts, all with programs to match. As with the Pittsfield Y, other Y memberships are honored (with a slight surcharge), and special short-term guest passes can be arranged.

A YOGA RETREAT

Practicing the postures, at Kripalu.

Jonathan Sternfield

KRIPALU CENTER FOR YOGA AND HEATLH 413-448-3400; Rt. 183 (just south of Tanglewood and actually in Stockbridge); Mailing address: Lenox, MA 01240.

One of the grandest of Berkshire's summer "cottages" was Shadowbrook, a 100-room Tudor house built by Anson Phelps Stokes. Though the building burned to the ground in 1956, the view from its grounds was, and is, most inspiring: a panorama of Stockbridge Bowl and the mountains behind. The red-brick structure built to replace Shadowbrook is modern and functional, but the estate nevertheless continues to have a deeply moving effect on many who visit. It was a Jesuit monastery for several years.

How appropriate, then, that such a facility be used now as a center for yoga and health, offering a program of physically and spiritually rejuvenating practices. Facilities include aerobic dance and yoga studios; saunas and whirlpools; 300 acres of forests, meadows, meditation gardens, and miles of woodland trails; private beach on the Bowl; bookstore and gift shop; special health services; and a natural foods kitchen serving tasty, well-balanced vegetarian meals.

Kripalu's environment is nurturing, and people who come here sign on for short-term room and board combined with the programs. Local day-visitors are welcome, too; call for further information.

FOR KIDS ONLY

A pumpkin face in progress, at the Berkshire Harvest Festival, Berkshire Botanical Garden.

Jonathan Sternfield

As far as most kids are concerned, Berkshire is cool. Besides the dozens of children's camps here (see "Camps" in this chapter), there are horse programs for kids (see in particular Bonnie Lea Farm under "Horseback Riding"). In winter, most of the ski slopes operate children's ski schools. In between the summer camping and winter skiing, dozens of little events are happening on a small scale all over the county. Most local libraries have story hours, most of the museums and playgrounds have kids' programs, and many of the local theaters have innovative children's productions.

South County

In Great Barrington, the **Barrington Ballet** (413-528-4963) runs ballet classes for children Tues. and Thurs. **Dos Amigos** Mexican Restaurant (413-528-0084;

Stockbridge Rd.) often hosts David Grover, who sings and invites you to sing along, captivating kids of all ages. Across the way, at the Cove Bowling Lanes on Rte. 7, is the *Rainbow's End Miniature Golf Course* (413-528-1220), an indoor extravaganza to test even the deftest little putter. In West Stockbridge, *Clay Forms Studio* (413-232-4349; Austerlitz Rd., Rtes. 102W & 41) offers classes, workshops and other activities for kids eight and up who like to work in clay.

The *Stockbridge Library* (413-298-5501; Main St., Stockbridge) has a large and cozy children's section, and story hours are a regular event. During the summer, the *Berkshire Theatre Festival* (413-298-5536; Rte. 102, just east of the junction of Rte. 7, Stockbridge) gives Children's Theatre performances of plays written by local kids. They also offer an acting class for students, twelve to fourteen. The *Norman Rockwell Museum* (413-298-4100) offers a variety of activities geared to kids, one the best being their Family Day on the last Sunday of every month. Admission prices are lowered and special guides are provided to inform both parents and kids. The *Berkshire Botanical Garden* (413-298-3926) holds a wonder-filled day camp for kids in summer, offering children in grades one through six the opportunity to explore the world of nature. Their early October Harvest Festival has lots of kids' activities, too. Art classes are a part of the *Interlaken School of Arts* (413-298-5252) program, with special courses for kids eight through seventeen.

Central County

The *Lenox Library* (413-637-0197; 18 Main St.) has a terrific children's room, which always seems to be brimming with kid energy. *Pleasant Valley Wildlife Sanctuary* (413-637-0320; 472 W. Mountain Rd.) runs a Day Camp, one- and two-week sessions, featuring exciting educational outdoor activities for boys and girls, Grades 1 through 12.

Central County's other Massachusetts Audubon Society property, *Canoe Meadows Wildlife Sanctuary* (413-637-0320; Holmes Rd., Pittsfield), in conjunction with the Berkshire Museum, runs a one-week Native American camp for boys and girls, grades three, four and five. During the summer, *Hancock Shaker Village* (413-443-0188; Rte. 20, Hancock) offers a hands-on experience in its "Discovery Room," where children may try on Shaker-style clothes and participate in such facets of 19th-century life as spinning wool, weaving, or writing with a quill pen at a Shaker desk. Outside, children can see the farm animals and demonstrations of sheepshearing or sheep-herding trials. Hancock Shaker Village also conducts "School Vacation Crafts Workshops" in basketmaking, cooking, and textiles in February and April. *Jacob's Pillow* (413-243-0745) offers programs for children out in the New Studio Theater, Becket.

The *Robbins-Zust Family Marionettes* often perform a full range of "classic tales for children of all ages." Bringing out the heavyweight dramas such as

"Jack and the Beanstalk," "Beauty and the Beast," and "Winnie the Pooh" (original), the Robbins-Zust troupe often performs in Lenox and Pittsfield. For more information, call the Marionettes themselves (413-698-2591) or check out their info at www.Berkshireweb.com\Zust. They are "the smallest, established, permanent, floating repertory company in America."

In downtown Pittsfield, the *Berkshire Athenaeum*'s (413-499-9483; Wendell Ave. at East St.) children's library has a wide range of programs, from story hours to films. The *Berkshire Museum* (413-443-7171; South St.) also has an extensive series of educational children's events — theater, dance, and storytelling for the whole family. Call for information.

At *Dalton Community House* (413-684-0260; 400 Main St., Dalton) kids will find a positive plethora of fun activities. There's miniature golf in Lanesborough to keep little hands busy at *Baker's Family Golf Center* (413-442-6102; Rte. 7) and the *Par 4 Family Fun Center* (413-499-0051; Rte. 7). Upcounty a ways at *Jiminy Peak* (413-738-5500; Rte. 43, Hancock), the fun goes right into summer with the *Alpine Slide*, a scenic 15-minute ride up, and an exhilarating 5-minute slide down. Jiminy also has a miniature golf course, trout fishing, and a separate tennis program.

North County

Over in North Adams at the *Western Gateway Heritage State Park* (413-663-6312; 9 Furnace St. Bypass), a recent feature was a "Kid's Korner" craft workshop. In Williamstown, there's an extensive summer playground program at the public schools, along with swimming lessons and a Nature Program at *Margaret Lindley Park*. Information can be had by calling the *Youth Center* (413-458-5925; Cole Ave.). A score of winter recreational programs are also offered through the Youth Center. And treasure hunts, along with children's workshops on various artists, are a few of the *Clark Art Institute*'s (413-458-8109; South St.) offerings for kids. The *Williams College Museum of Art* frequently has imaginative children's programs; the *Williamstown Public Library* offers read-a-louds and a summer reading program. Children's tennis and soccer camps are available on the *Williams College* campus in the summer; call the Conference Office 413-458-2229. The *Williamstown Theatre Festival* (413-458-3200 has received a grant to run a program for youth.

CHAPTER SEVEN
Fancy Goods
SHOPPING

Even the shops that were closed offered, through wide expanses of plate-glass, hints of hidden riches. In some, waves of silk and ribbon broke over shores of imitation moss from which ravishing hats rose like tropical orchids. In others, the pink throats of gramophones opened their giant convolutions in a soundless chorus; or bicycles shining in neat ranks seemed to await the signal of an invisible starter; or tiers of fancy-goods in leatherette and paste dangled their insidious graces; and, in one vast bay that seemed to project them into exciting contact with the public, wax ladies in daring dresses chatted elegantly, or, with gestures intimate yet blameless, pointed to their pink corsets and transparent hosiery.

A description of shop windows on the main street of "Nettleton," the fictional name for Pittsfield in *Summer*, by Edith Wharton, 1917.

Judith Monachina

Strolling along North Street in Pittsfield can be as pleasant as it was in Edith Wharton's day.

Antiques, books, clothing, handcrafts, home furnishings — shoppers for the necessities and the accessories of life will find ample scope in the Berkshires, on still-vital downtown streets and at a variety of retail destinations. They'll find an ever-changing mix of the latest trends and styles, the genuinely old, and the timeless — sometimes all in one shop. They'll also find imaginative wares designed and made in the Berkshires, as well as goods from the farthest corners of the world. There are some chain stores, and outlets and discount centers, too. Note: Many Berkshire shops have been in place for generations; others sprang up last week and will have moved on by next Monday; it's helpful to call ahead before making a special trip.

Finally, owing to a fire early in 1997 that badly damaged the red barn at *Jenifer House Commons*, the dealers doing business there suffered serious losses. Many have reopened or have plans to do so, either here, nearby, or elsewhere (see, for example, **Olde — An Antiques Market**, listed below).

ANTIQUES

From formal 18th-century furniture to bold Art Deco tableware, with country primitive carvings and High Victorian accessories in between, antiques in the Berkshires are varied and abundant. Whether you hanker after museum-quality pieces of a specific style and period or whether you simply enjoy exploring for unique home furnishings, you'll find plenty to choose from. The antiques scene here includes furniture large and small; vintage clothing, textiles, and jewelry; prints, paper, and other ephemera; trunks and lamps, kitchenalia and militaria, clocks and rugs, baskets and wicker. European and Asian antiques specialists have also found their way to the Berkshires. And a number of antiques shops also include new furnishings and accent pieces that complement their antiques, a custom decorating services, too.

Recordings, Classical and Jazz

Compact discs, cassette tapes, and even those dinosaurs, records, are available throughout the county, in various chain stores and other retail outlets. Most places here with CDs and tapes have a small classical music selection, but if you're looking for more than the Three Tenors or the Four Seasons, visit the *Tanglewood Music* Store, at Tanglewood in Lenox, open for Tanglewood audiences, and featuring the music and performing artists of that week, plus much more. The *Berkshire Record Outlet* (413-243-4080; Rte. 102, Lee) has classical remainders listed in a catalog — send for one for $2 — from which you can select from thousands of classical CDs, tapes, and LPs, at closeout prices. On Saturdays, you can also browse through an eclectic selection of recordings in the small retail room, and you will be sure to turn up something you always wanted.

A well-chosen selection of classical, jazz, and blues is available at *Tune Street* (413-528-4999; 294 Main St., Gt. Barrington), along with pop, folk, New Age, and world music recordings. They also sell electronic gear (stereo equipment, TVs, VCRs, satellite dishes) and do custom home installations.

Jazz enthusiasts in particular will enjoy *Toonerville Trolley Records* (413-458-5229; 131 Water St., Williamstown) and its array of CDs, tapes, and LPs, out of print and current. In addition to jazz, there's rock, folk, and reggae.

South County in particular is an antiques center, with Rte. 7 the main artery for an array of multidealer shops, specialists, and generalists. They know their merchandise, and their prices reflect their knowledge. In Central and North County, prices are more flexible, but finding a bargain takes some looking.

Those who extend antiques hunting to auctions — or the sign of the true diehard — to yard sales and flea markets, should check listings in the helpful free weekly shoppers' guides (such as the *Berkshire Penny Saver*), which are stacked up at supermarket entrances and newstands around the county. The *Berkshire Eagle*, the largest daily paper in the county, also carries classified listings for antiques, tag sales, and auctions. A list of auctioneers is also given below. The annual brochure of the *Berkshire County Antique Dealer's* Association lists dealers and locations, with business hours, telephone numbers, and a brief description of what they offer. Members of this association "take pride in their merchandise and guarantee its authenticity." Their brochure is available in member shops or by mail (send a SASE to BCADA Directory, PO Box 594, Great Barrington MA 01230).

Several rare book specialists also make their home here; they're listed in the following section, "Books."

South County

GREAT BARRINGTON

Asian Antiques (413-528-5091; 199 Stockbridge Rd., Rte. 7) High quality Asian art, antiques, furniture for home, garden, and temple. If you've always wanted an opium bed or a temple gong, this is the place to find it.

Bygone Days (413-528-1870; 969 S. Main St., Rte. 7.) Country and formal furniture, large and small; tables and chairs, armoires, night stands, hutches, china closets.

Carriage House Antiques (413-528-6045; 389 Stockbridge Rd., Rte. 7) Tables, chairs, furniture, even a set of doors. Antique furniture restoration, repair, stripping, refinishing.

Coffmans' Country Antiques Market (413-528-9282; Jenifer House Commons, Stockbridge Rd., Rte. 7) Three floors of high-quality wares, pre-1949, from 100 New England and regional dealers, in the yellow house with two green doors. The large assortment is appealingly arranged in cases and room settings, and includes ephemera and prints, kitchenware, primitives, wood, pottery, furniture, tools, quilts, rugs, baskets, folk art, stoneware, glassware, and tin, brass, and copper. Books on antiques and collectibles are also sold here, and there's a lounge with coffee, tea, hot chocolate for customers and dealers.

Corashire Antiques (413-528-0014; Rte. 7 & 23, at Belcher Square) In the red barn: American country furniture and accessories.

Country Dining Room Antiques (413-528-5050; 178 Main St., Rte. 7) Complete accouterments for dining in style, formal or country. In lavishly coordinated rooms, dining tables boast elaborate place settings of china, silver, glass, crystal, porcelain — down to the matching damask napkins with silk rose napkin rings. Chairs, rugs, paintings, and other furnishings and accessories complete the look. For a less formal but still elegant approach, **Tea Garden Antiques**, upstairs, offers more place settings, linens, and other accents. Country Dining Room's own Sheila Chefetz wrote the stunning book that shows you how to put it all together, *Antiques for the Table.*

Elise Abrams Antiques (413-528-3201; 11 Stockbridge Rd., Rte. 7) Large selection of antique china and stemware, plus decorative accessories and fine linens, silver, art, and dining-room furniture.

Emporium Antique Center (413-528-1660; 319 Main St.) A variety of dealers here offer estate and costume jewelry, crystal, silver, accessories, furniture, furnishings, linens. June–Dec., open daily; Jan.–May, closed Tues. & Weds.

The Kahns' Antique and Estate Jewelers (413-528-9550; 38 Railroad St.) Antique jewelry is their specialty; appraisals, diamond grading, gem identification, repairs, and custom work.

Le Périgord (413-528-6777; 964 S. Main St., Rte. 7) A great source for French furniture, pottery, garden, and architectural accents from the 18th century to Art Deco. If you want to create a Gallic ambiance in your home, this is the place to shop.

Donald McGrory Oriental Rugs (413-528-9594; 12 Castle St.) Antique and decorative Oriental rugs. Tues.–Sat.

Jonathan Sternfield

Artifacts from a slower time, at Memories, Great Barrington.

Memories (413-528-6380; 306 Main St.) A well-chosen and decidedly eclectic array of antiques, collectibles, primitives, old cameras, furniture, lighting, nostalgia, old toys, musical instruments, and more. Many of these items —

such as lamps and radios — have been carefully restored and are in working order. Their collection is "ideal for authentic theatrical props and restaurant decorations," the owners suggest, although most of us will just want to take it all home.

Mullin-Jones Antiquities (413-528-4871; 525 S. Main St., Rte. 7) The fragrance of lavender pervades this importer of 18th- and 19th-century country French furniture and accessories, including large-scale farmhouse pieces and garden accents. Closed Tues.; call ahead in winter.

Olde — An Antiques Market (413-528-1840; Jenifer House Commons, Stockbridge Rd., Rte. 7) Jam-packed with potential treasures. Over 75 dealers temporarily housed in the green building (the red barn burned in a spectacular and disastrous fire), offering collectibles, dishes, china, glass, porcelain, silver, games, books, jewelry, decorative items.

Red Horse Antiques (413-528-2637; 117 State Rd.) "Whatever I like, I buy; and, like the peddlers of old, I sell," says owner April. That includes furniture, paper, glass, and catch-as-catch-can.

Reeves Antiques (413-528-5877; Jenifer House Commons, Stockbridge Rd., Rte. 7) Old trunks and blanket boxes, restored shoe racks and old workbenches are their specialty. They fit in both traditional and contemporary decors.

Reuss Audubon Galleries (413-528-8484; Jenifer House Commons, Stockbridge Rd., Rte. 7) Specializing in Audubon prints and artful adornments for the home.

Susan and Paul Kleinwald, Inc. (413-528-4252; 578 S. Main St., Rte. 7) 18th- and 19th-century American and English antique furniture, fine art, accessories; appraisals. Closed Tues.

Snyder's Store (413-528-1441; 945 S. Main St., Rte. 7) The pink flamingos in the flower gardens by the door are a clue to what's inside: funky furniture and accessories, with rustic pieces, wicker, tramp art, jewelry, linens, garden accents, and architectural elements. Open most days 12–5.

LEE

Aardenburg Antiques (413-243-0001; 144 W. Park St.) Early 19th-century furniture and accessories; restoration and refinishing. Weekends by chance; any time by appointment.

Henry B. Holt (413-243-3184; PO Box 699) Specialist in 19th- and early 20th-century American paintings. Call for appointment regarding appraisal, purchase, sale, or restoration.

SHEFFIELD/ASHLEY FALLS

Note: The following antique shops are in the township of Sheffield where there are two villages — Ashley Falls and Sheffield proper.

Ashley Falls

Don Abarbanel (413-229-3330; E. Main St., at the Lewis & Wilson shop) Formal furniture of the 17th through 19th centuries, and needlework, brass and other metalwork, English pottery, English and Dutch delft, Chinese export porcelain. In winter call ahead.

Ashley Falls Antiques (413-229-8759; Rte. 7A) American country and formal furniture, accessories, antique buttons, and authenticated antique jewelry.

Circa (413-229-2990; Rte. 7A) Good collections of Majolica and Canton; 18th- and 19th-century furniture, accessories, and "sophisticated oddments."

Lewis & Wilson (413-229-3330; E. Main St.) English, American, and Continental 18th- and 19th-century furniture and accessories; Oriental porcelains. Call ahead in winter.

The Vollmers (413-229-3463; Rte. 7A) 18th- and 19th-century furniture, formal and country, wine-related antiques, firearms and militaria, accessories, and tools. Open Fri.–Sun.

Sheffield

Anthony's Antiques (413-229-8208; 102 S. Main St., Rte. 7) English furniture from the 18th and 19th centuries, accessorized by ceramics, paintings and fine arts, and Chinese porcelain and furniture.

Berkshire Gilders Antiques (413-229-0113; 15 Main St., Rte. 7) Period French, English, and American gold-leaf mirrors. Upholstered furniture, dining tables, decorative pieces, and tableware. Closed Tues.

Carriage Trade Antiques (413-229-2870; 276 S. Undermountain Rd.) Country looks in a country setting, including furniture, blanket chests, kitchen items, jewelry, out-of-the-ordinary collectibles.

Centuryhurst Antiques Gallery (413-229-8131, 173 Main St., Rte. 7) Scores of ticking clocks sound like rainfall at this shop that also specializes in Wedgwood; with country and formal furniture, glass, paintings, prints, and accessories.

Classic Images Art & Antiques (413-229-0033; 527 Sheffield Plain, Rte. 7) Antique prints and reprints concentrating on natural and sporting subjects. Some Southwestern country furniture, fine arts photography, and 19th- and 20th-century color plate books. Call ahead.

Corner House Antiques (413-229-6627; corner of Rte. 7 & Old Mill Pond Rd.) Specialists in antique wicker furniture, including whole sets; with a variety of styles and finishes. A well-chosen selection of American country furnishings and accessories as well.

Cupboards & Roses Antiques (413-229-3070; 296 S. Main St., Rte. 7) Beautifully displayed antique 18th- and 19th-century paint-decorated fine furniture, featuring capacious armoires and chests. Closed Tues.

Darr Antiques and Interiors (413-229-7773; 28 S. Main St., Rte. 7) Two buildings of elegant room settings displaying formal 18th- and 19th-century American, English, Continental, and Oriental furniture and accessories, with a focus on dining room furnishings. June–Oct., closed Tues.; Nov.–May, closed Tues. and Weds.

Dovetail Antiques (413-229-2628; 440 Sheffield Plain, Rte. 7) A select collection of American clocks, country furniture, including pieces with original paint or finish, and appropriate accessories, plus spongeware, stoneware, and redware. Open daily; Tues. by chance.

Falcon Antiques (413-229-7745; 1985 S. Undermountain Rd., Rte. 41) Woodworking tools, plus a good selection of brass, copper, pewter, and treen (small wooden pieces).

Frederick Hatfield Antiques (413-229-7986; 99 S. Main St., Rte. 7) Antiques and collectibles from the 18th through 20th centuries, with country and formal furniture, paintings, silver, paper items, jewelry, architectural elements, and other treasures from New England homes.

Good & Hutchinson Associates, Inc. (413-229-8832; Main St., Rte. 7, on the Green) Specialists in fine antiques and decorative arts from the 18th and 19th century, with American, English, and Continental furniture, Chinese export porcelain, paintings, brass, lamps; for collectors and antiquarians. Summer: Mon.–Sat. 10–5, Sun. 1–5. Open Oct.–May by chance.

Kuttner Antiques (413-229-2955; S. Main St., Rte. 7) Formal and country American and English furniture and decorative accessories from the 18th and 19th centuries. Closed Tues.

Le Trianon (413-528-0775; 1854 N. Main St., Rte. 7) 17th-, 18th-, and 19th-century French and Continental furniture and accessories, country and formal.

Lois W. Spring Antiques (413-229-2542; Ashley Falls Rd., Rte. 7A) 18th- and 19th-century American furniture and accessories, country and formal. By appointment.

Ole T.J.'s Antique Barn (413-229-8382; Rte. 7) Antiques and collectibles on two floors from all over, some of it gathered by the owners on their travels in the Far East and Africa, and some of it early American and European furniture, jewelry, paintings, rugs, lamps, and other accessories. Thurs.–Mon. or by chance or appointment.

Robert Thayer American Antiques (413-229-2965; 197 Main St., Rte. 7) 18th- and early 19th-century country antique furniture and decorative arts, and folk art. By chance or appointment.

1750 House Antiques (413-229-6635; 414 S. Main St., Rte. 7) Specialists in the sale and repair of American, French, and European clocks. Also offering music boxes, phonographs, glass, china, and other accessories, and furniture.

665 North Main Street (413-229-9029; 665 N. Main St., Rte. 7) Group shop with eclectic mix of antiques and collectibles at good prices. On one visit, a step-

Cultural Shopping

Many Berkshire museums, and other institutions devoted to the arts and culture or to historical preservation, fund and publicize their operations with their own gift and book shops. They are excellent sources for unique Berkshire gifts, books about a wide range of historical subjects and the visual and performing arts, and fun and educational items for children. Institution members often get discounts at the shop.

Berkshire Museum Shop (413-443-7469; 39 South St., Pittsfield) An excellent array of items reflecting the scope of the museum's collections: books, prints, cards, plates and other home accessories, international crafts, and jewelry; and a treasure-trove of small and creative items for children, from the artistic to the scientific. Shop staff, mostly volunteers, are helpful and personable.

The Museum Store at the Clark Art Institute (413-458-2302; 225 South St., Williamstown) features items based on the Clark's collection and those of museums and art galleries around the world: cards, posters, and prints, matted and framed; fine art books; jewelry; and great toys from basic to upscale. The selection of books has been greatly enlarged, to include a more extensive collection of art books and regional titles.

Ex Libris: The Lenox Library Shop (413-637-0197; 18 Main St., Lenox) This pocket-sized shop offers cards, postcards, toys, T-shirts, bookplates, bookmarks, games, tote bags, sealing wax, and various Berkshire-related items.

Hancock Shaker Village Shop (413-443-0188; Rte. 20, Pittsfield) The spacious gift shop offers books, clocks, Shaker reproduction furniture, and other items, in kits or assembled — even the Shaker clock. Prints of drawings of the Hancock Shaker community and of Shaker "spirit drawings," too. Wonderful children's toys and kits. Open April through Nov., and for school vacation week in Feb.

The Norman Rockwell Museum (413-298-4100, Rte. 183, Stockbridge) A well-designed center for books, prints, and cards; the children's section has books and toys and art-related things to do. There are limited-edition artist's proofs signed by Rockwell; and there are even mugs and T-shirts.

Additional cultural shopping options include the shop at Massachusetts Audubon Sanctuary, *Pleasant Valley*; *Chesterwood*, particularly for their selection of National Trust publications; *Tanglewood*'s gift shop, with lots of Tanglewood-logo wearables and other items; the *Arrowhead Museum* shop, with books about Melville and county history, and cards, gifts; the *Garden Gift Shop* at the *Berkshire Botanical Garden*; *The Mount* (former home of Edith Wharton and current home of Shakespeare & Co.); *Williams College Museum of Art*; the *Berkshire Theatre Festival*; and the *Berkshire Scenic Railway Museum* (books, toys, T-shirts).

back cupboard and a pair of large cannisters that could almost be used as end tables seemed affordable and intriguing.

Saturday Sweets Antiques and Design (413-229-0026; 755A N. Main St., Rte. 7) 20th century decorative arts, including furniture, accessories, fashion prints, and vintage costume jewelry. Closed Tues.; in winter call ahead.

Susan Silver Antiques (413-229-8169; N. Main St., Rte. 7) English and Continental furnishings from the 18th and 19th centuries. Closed Tues.

Twin Fires Antiques (413-229-8307; Berkshire School Rd. & Rte. 41) Handmade imported country pine furniture, stained and painted, antique and reproduction. Armoires, cupboards, dressers, tables, beds from the British Isles and Europe — all attractively and abundantly displayed, along with other furniture and home accessories. Closed Tues.

David M. Weiss Antiques (413-229-2716; 604 Sheffield Plain, Rte. 7) 18th- and 19th-century American furniture, art, and decorative accessories. Open by chance or by appointment.

NORTH EGREMONT

Blackbird Antiques and Collectibles (413-528-5862; 60 Boyce Rd.) American collectibles, 1850-1950; the nostalgia accessories here include tins, dishware, medicine bottles, rugs, quilts, lighting, and furniture, recently featuring two charming small-scale Adirondack chairs. Fri.–Mon. or by chance.

John Sideli Art and Antiques (413-528-2789; Egremont Plain Rd., Rte. 71) Stylish objects from 18th, 19th, and 20th centuries. A gallery specializing in American folk art, including weathervanes, trade signs, painted furniture, etc. in a spectacular setting.

SOUTH EGREMONT

Bird Cage Antiques (413-528-3556; 47 Main St., Rte. 23, next to post office) An unusual variety of smalls and collectibles, including toys, dolls, fountain pens, silver, and jewelry; also clothes, linens, paintings. By appointment.

Douglas Antiques (413-528-1810; Rte. 23 at the Weathervane Inn, PO Box 571) Victorian and turn-of-the-century furniture in oak and walnut, with tables, chairs, desks, bookcases, dressers, and chests, and accessories, including lamps and quilts. By appointment only.

Geffner/Schatzky Antiques and Varieties (413-528-0057; Rte. 23, at the sign of the Juggler) 19th century to '50s furniture and accessories, jewelry, architectural elements. Open May–Aug., daily 10:30–5; Sept.–Apr., Fri.–Sun. 10:30–5, during the week by chance or appointment.

Howard's Antiques (413-528-1232; Rte. 23/PO Box 472) Specialists in American country lighting and furniture. Antique lighting fixtures from the late 1890s to the 1930s have been wired for the 1990s. 19th-century dining room tables and chairs are also offered, as well as other country-style antique furniture. Closed Tues.

Barbara Moran Fine Arts (413-528-0749; Main St., Rte. 23) Mostly contemporary artwork, but also offers antique country-style furnishings and accent pieces.

Red Barn Antiques (413-528-3230; 72 Main St., Rte. 23) Restored antique lighting from the early 19th century and onward, including kerosene, gas, and early electric fixtures. Repair and restoration of antique lamps on site; refinished furniture.

Elliott and Grace Snyder (413-528-3581; Undermountain Rd., Rte. 41, 0.5 mi. south of Rte. 23) By appointment. 18th- and 19th-century American furniture and accessories, with an emphasis on textiles; also textiles and folk art. By chance or by appointment.

The Splendid Peasant (413-528-5755; Rte. 23 and Sheffield Rd.) 18th- and 19th-century country furniture and accessories, and museum-quality American folk art, all stunningly displayed in a fascinating series of galleries and niches. Original paint a specialty.

SOUTHFIELD

The Buggy Whip Factory Antique Market Place (413-229-3576; Main St.) An antiques market of 85 dealers, featuring country to formal furniture, architectural pieces, kitchenware, tools, china. sterling, glassware, jewelry, and books. Cafe on premises. Closed Tues. & Weds. Jan.–Apr.

Kettering Antiques (413-229-2859; Main St.) Formal English and American 18th and 19th century furniture and decorative porcelain and brass. Cabinet restoration and polishing available.

WEST STOCKBRIDGE

Sawyer Antiques (413-232-7062; Depot St.) In a Shaker-built grist mill, early American furniture and accessories, in a variety of styles: formal, Shaker, country. Open Fri.–Sun; otherwise call ahead.

Central County

LANESBOROUGH

Amber Springs Antiques (413-442-1237; 29 S. Main St., Rte. 7) Country American furnishings "from as early as we can find to as late as we can stand." That description includes tools, pottery, country store items, trivia. The alternate motto, according to owner Gae Elfenbein, is "we have it but we can't find it." Open daily; weekends in winter, or call ahead.

LENOX

Charles L. Flint Antiques Inc. (413-637-1634; 56 Housatonic St.) Furniture, painting, accessories, folk art, Shaker items. The owner is a noted local historian with a scholar's knowledge of and enthusiasm for his wares.

La Vie en Rose (413-637-3662; 67 Church St.) Painted furniture (French Canadian), vintage jewelry, and gifts in a cottage-like setting.

Past and Future (413-637-2225; 38 Church St.) 19th- and 20th-century silver and small antiques and collectibles; including scales, inkwells, perfumes, sewing items, and sporting antiques.

Stone's Throw Antiques (413-637-2733; 51 Church St.) 18th-, 19th-, and early 20th-century china, glass, silver, furniture, and decorative accessories.

PITTSFIELD

Berkshire Hills Coins and Antiques (413-499-1400; 111 South St.) Specializing in collectible coins, estate gold and costume jewelry, sterling items, pocket watches, oak furniture, and a variety of antique decorative accessories.

Bargain Shop (413-499-0927; 1 Reed St., off South St.) Unprepossessing though it may seem, there are treasures here: recent finds include a pair of wire chairs, old shutters, and even a dolphin pedestal fountain. Also used Levis and vintage fabrics. Closed Tues. & Sun.

A Blue Moon (413-499-2219; 146 South St.) Furniture, kitchenware, china — used items along with some antiques. The owners have a great display sense. Recent finds include some Victorian papers, Czech china, and a sterling commemorative spoon from Colorado.

Memory Lane Antiques (413-499-2718; 446 Tyler St.) A recommended source for useful and decorative pieces: furniture, rugs, mirrors, lamps, accessories, china and glass, ephemera, other collectibles. Owner Bev Martin is helpful, friendly, and enthusiastic about her merchandise. Look for the mannequin in a vintage dress on the sidewalk outside. Closed Tues. & Sun.

Somewhere In Time (413-445-7176; 453 North St.) The emphasis here is on restored furniture. The owners do their own refinishing on the premises. There is a smattering of china and glass.

RICHMOND

Wynn A. Sayman (413-698-2272; Old Fields) A by-appointment-only specialist in English pottery and porcelain of the 18th and early 19th centuries, for collectors and museums; including saltglaze, redware, tortoiseshell ware, cream ware, pearl ware, and Staffordshire bocage figures, as well as Chelsea, Bow, Worcester, and Derby.

North County

CHESHIRE

Cheshire Antiques (413-743-7703; 80 Willow Cove Rd.) An eclectic offering of china, glassware, and furniture.

Winterbrook Farm Antiques (413-743-2177; Rte. 8) Late 19th- and 20th-century restored and refinished furniture and accessories. Howard's refinishing products and replacement hardware in stock. Closed on Sun.

WILLIAMSTOWN

Collector's Warehouse (413-458-9686; 105 North St., Rte. 7) Antiques; collectibles, including glassware, jewelry, frames, dolls, linen, furniture. Weds.–Sat. 12:30–5, or call ahead. In the McClelland Press Building.

The Library Antiques (413-458-3436; 70 Spring St.) Old and new items in a series of rooms, artfully displayed, including jewelry, furniture, writing supplies, housewares, pillows, prints, books, international decor pieces, silver, dishes, pottery, fabrics and textiles. They say they welcome browsers. A great place for gifts or for yourself.

Saddleback Antiques (413-458-5852; 1395 Cold Spring Rd., Rte. 7) Furniture, glass, pottery, prints, posters. A group shop in an old schoolhouse with a bell tower. The inventory changes weekly and includes a fine selection of pieces at realistic prices. Mon.–Sat. 10–5, Sun. 12–5.

Auctioneers

Berkshire Auction Gallery (413-528-4307; Rte 7, Jenifer House Commons, Stockbridge Rd., Rte. 7, Gt. Barrington)
Bradford Auction Galleries (413-229-6667; Rte. 7, Sheffield)
Roy C. Burdick (413-664-6055; 24 S. County Rd., Florida)
John and Dina Fontaine (413-448-8922; 1485 West Housatonic St., Pittsfield)
Ralph Fontaine & Heritage Auctions (413-442-2537; 348 Cloverdale St., Pittsfield)
T. A. Gage (413-528-0076; Rte. 23, South Egremont)
Lujohns Auctioneers (800-243-4420; Rte. 20, Lee)

BOOKS

The Berkshires' literary traditions are upheld by several excellent book stores, new and used, each with its own distinct character. Specialists, rare-book, and antique-book dealers are also listed.

South County

GREAT BARRINGTON

The Bookloft (413-528-1521; Barrington Plaza, Stockbridge Rd., Rte. 7) A thoughtfully chosen selection of books, mostly new and some used, and tapes, both music and books. It's also a good source for Berkshire-related titles. With its wooden bookcases and pleasant atmosphere, one of the nicest places in South County for browsing and consulting with fellow book-lovers, particularly owner Eric Wilska and assistant Debby Reed.

The window at Farshaw's Books.

Judith Monachina

Farshaw's Books (413-528-1890; 13 Railroad St.) A select offering of antique and used or out-of-print titles, for the reader, collector, and bibliophile, in a well-organized, browser-friendly shop. The owners, Helen and Michael Selzer, recently established Bibliofind, the largest inventory of old, used, and rare books. from an international list of booksellers, on the Internet: http://www.bibliofind.com.

Yellow House Books (413-528-8227; 252 Main St.) Bob and Bonnie Benson offer a fine selection of used and rare books in three rooms of a house that is more than 100 years old. Specialities include photography, Native American literature, art, music, children's illustrated books, cooking, metaphysical, and folklore. An unusual feature of the store is the fine Steinway piano once owned by Nat King Cole, on which Bob Benson can be heard performing classic standards by Gershwin and others.

LEE

Apple Tree Books (413-243-2012; 87 Main St.) Books, magazines, Berkshire cards, stationery, gifts, audio, puzzles.

SHEFFIELD

Berkshire Book Company (413-229-0122, 800-828-5565; 510 S. Main St., Rte. 7) The ideal used-book store for the reader, with an extensive and well-organized collection. Co-proprietor Esther Kininmonth truly knows and loves her stock and its authors, and it's a pleasure to consult with her about various writers and editions. Categories include literature, travel, biography, children's, art, and antiques.

SOUTH EGREMONT

B&S Gventer Books (413-528-2327; One Tyrrell Rd. & Rte. 23/PO Box 298) "Tons of books" from the 15th century to the 19th. Medieval manuscript pages on vellum, and various pages from books published from 1300 to 1600; 19th-century hand-colored engravings. Knowledgeable owner Bruce Gventer can tell you their stories. June–Oct., Weds.–Sun.; Nov.–May, Sat. & Sun.

Central County

LANESBOROUGH

Waldenbooks (413-499-0115; Berkshire Mall) Berkshire County's entry for this well-known chain, stocking current hardcover and softcover best-sellers, as well as representative collections in various categories, including children's books and books of local interest. Book tapes; magazine section.

LENOX

The Book Maze and Audio (413-637-1701; Lenox House Country Shops, Pittsfield-Lenox Rd., Rte. 7) Cards, puzzles, rubber stamps, tapes, CDs, gemstones, T-shirts, craft supplies, gift wrapping paper, fax service — and even books.

The Bookstore (413-637-3390; 9 Housatonic St.) A literate and imaginative selection of new fiction, old fiction, and nonfiction. There are collections of small-press titles and books by local and regional authors, and well-chosen children's and young-adult titles. The Bookstore is a community center, too, presided over by owner Matt Tannenbaum with grace and humor. Matt and his assistants know their books and are happy to converse with you about them; they organize book-signing parties and special events, too. "The world's oldest, permanent literary establishment, serving the community since last Tuesday."

PITTSFIELD

Berkshire Book Shop (413-442-0165; 164 North St.) Headquarters for best-sellers and paperback fiction; stock up here for backyard and beach reading. How-to and self-help titles, too, and lots of magazines.

Barnes & Noble (413-496-9051; Berkshire Crossing Mall, Rte. 9) This chain "superstore" has a large selection of the most popular titles, along with book tapes and some musical scores. The in-store cafe features Starbucks coffee and other goodies.

North County

NORTH ADAMS

Crystal Unicorn Bookstore (413-664-7377; 59 Main St.) New and used paperbacks and hardcovers; gifts, handmade jewelry, and a small selection of old and rare books.

WILLIAMSTOWN

Water Street Books (413-458-8071; 26 Water St.) A large selection in just about every category displayed on classy architectural shelving. The help is hip and friendly. There are sale books, children's books, and the Williams College bookstore is in the back. A booklover's paradise.

Farther afield, but a destination for a good browse: *Librarium* (518-392-5209; off Rte. 295, 1 mi. E. of East Chatham) More than 35,000 second-hand, out-of-print books "for all interests and ages." Apr.–Oct., Fri.–Mon. 10–6; Nov.–Mar., Sat & Sun. 10–5; by chance or appointment otherwise.

Book Dealers

These specialist book dealers do business by catalog or appointment.

J&J Lubrano (413-528-5799; 8 George St., Gt. Barrington) Specialist in old and rare music books and autographs.

Howard S. Mott (413-229-2019; 170 S. Main St., Rte. 7, Sheffield) Rare books from the 16th to the 20th centuries, autographs and manuscripts. Now under management of Donald Mott.

John R. Sanderson Antiquarian Bookseller (413-298-5322; W. Main St./Box 844, Stockbridge) Rare and fine books.

Adler Children's Books (413-298-3559; Stockbridge) Out of print, old and rare children's books; search services.

CLOTHING & ACCESSORIES

Visitors can outfit themselves in just about any style of their choice in the Berkshires: classic, traditional, designer, funky, all-natural, English country squire, buckaroo — it's all here. Some boutiques also feature designs and concepts created in the Berkshires, too. For clothing factory outlets, and there are a number of them, check the listings below plus the "Shopping Streets, Mews, & Malls" section.

Be sure, too, to check the list of sporting goods stores near the beginning of Chapter 7, *Recreation*. Many of these shops carry some very smart and practical lines suitable for all buyers, regardless of their level of activity or interest in sports.

South County

GREAT BARRINGTON

Barrington Outfitters (413-528-0021; 289 Main St.) A good selection of discounted shoes and sneakers for men, women, and kids, along with casual clothes for men and women.

Byzantium (413-528-9496; 32 Railroad St.) The sweaters in chenille, wool, and cotton will catch your eye first, but don't stop there. Stylish and easy women's dresses, blouses, skirts, and ensembles, casual to dressy; lots of lovely lingerie and sleepwear; jewelry, throws, and other accessories.

Diva (413-528-1754; 179 Main St.) Women's large-size clothier, contemporary looks, moderate prices.

Drygoods (413-528-2950; 42 Railroad St.) Contemporary women's clothes, hats, jewelry, accessories, and home decor items. **Body and Soul** is now sharing space in this cheerful shop, offering a wide variety of body care products.

Gatsby's (413-528-9455; 25 Railroad St.) Useful and funky stuff, including cotton nightgowns, Doc Martins, Teva sandals, Birkenstocks, denim, socks and turtlenecks, and housewares. Gatsby's covers the territory with shops also in Williamstown (413-458-5407; 31 Spring St.) and Lee (413-243-3412; 62 Main St.).

Hildi B (413-528-0331; 15 Railroad St.) Natural fiber clothes, including batik sweaters, skirts, blouses, dresses; handcrafted jewelry and other crafts, leather items, oils and soaps. A friendly atmosphere created by helpful sales people.

Jack's Country Squire (413-528-1390; 316 Main St., Gt. Barrington) *See description under Jack's Dept. Store, Lee.*

Especially for Children

Berkshire Child (413-528-6430; 30 Stockbridge Rd., Rte. 7, Gt. Barrington) Clothing and accessories from infant to size 14. The labels you love for kids: Oshkosh, Spumoni, etc.

kids and kin . . . (413-528-1188; Rte. 23, South Egremont) Bright unusual children's clothing and accessories, along with gifts for adults. Closed Tues. & Weds in winter.

M. Lacey (413-528-5991; 12 Railroad St., Gt. Barrington) A beautiful selection of clothing for infants and children, much of it imported. The whimsical designs are sure to delight both wearer and buyer.

Mary Stuart (413-637-0340; 69 Church St.) Toys, and gifts for children, as well as exquisite clothes for infants and toddlers, just right for grandmothers to give.

Matruska (413-528-6911; 252 Main St., Gt. Barrington) Toys and books chosen to enhance a child's imagination and sense of beauty. Wonderful dolls from Holland that do nothing but absorb a child's love.

The Gifted Child (413-637-1191; 72 Church St., Lenox) Children's clothing, newborns to pre-teens, with a contemporary flair; high-quality toys and gifts. Camp care packages — what a great idea. And don't miss the sale barn. Also in Gt. Barrington at 28 Railroad St.; 413-528-1395. featuring clothes from newborn to size 8.

Tom's Toys (413-528-3330; 307 Main St., Gt. Barrington) A happening place for kids that carries all the most popular toys and a great selection of inexpensive trinkets to amuse the most bored young traveler.

What Kids Want (413-743-7842; 31 Park St., Adams) Children's clothing, sizes newborn to 14, at less than retail prices.

In addition, several area museums and galleries, particularly the *Berkshire Museum* in Pittsfield, have gift shops with sections devoted to educational items disguised as toys.

Main Street (413-528-1923; 280 Main St.) "City styles, country prices," it says, with women's designer items at discount prices. Clothes include dresses, separates, sportswear, suits; accessorized with jewelry, belts.

Steilman European Fashion Outlet (413-528-8233; Jenifer House Commons, Stockbridge Rd., Rte. 7; planning to move to the Berkshire Outlet Village, Lee) Sportswear, dresses, jackets, and coats imported from Europe, including one-of-a-kind showroom samples. All at discounted prices.

LEE

Ben's (413-243-0242; 68 Main St.) A friendly store packed with clothing and footwear for the whole family.

A Change of Art (413-243-4800; 61 Center St.) 100 percent cotton separates for women, many hand-painted.

Jack's Dept. Store (413-243-0999; 53 Main St.) Family clothing and shoes, including Nike, Woolrich, Reebok, Levi. Also **Jack's Country Squire** (413-528-1390; 316 Main St., Gt. Barrington).

STOCKBRIDGE

Greystone Gardens (413-298-0113; The Mews, Main. St.) Antique clothing for men and women. *See the description under Pittsfield.*

Katherine Meagher (413-298-3329; 10 Elm St.) Women's clothing, casual and dressy, classically fashionable; sportswear, separates, dresses, accessories, jewelry.

Sweaters Etc. (413-298-4287; South St., Rte. 7) At the third house behind the Red Lion Inn is an outlet for South Wool, which designs and distributes women's handknit sweaters to stores and boutiques. Wool and cotton sweaters are discounted.

Vlada Boutique (413-298-3656; Elm St.) Retail therapy for sure. Sophisticated women's clothing with an emphasis on comfort. Witty gifts and accessories, lovely and outrageous cards and clever, contemporary jewelry.

Central County

LANESBOROUGH

The Berkshire Mall (413-445-4400; Old State Rd./Rte. 8; also accessible from Rte. 7) comprises many and varied clothes-shopping options for men, women, teens, and children: the Gap, American Eagle Outfitters, Weathervane, Limited, Casual Corner, Eddie Bauer, and Filene's.

Berkshire Pendleton (413-443-6822; Rte. 7 between Pittsfield and Williamstown) Classic wool clothes and accessories for the complete look. Men's sports shirts and sweaters, too, and a large selection of Indian trade blankets and robes.

Camellia's (413-442-9233; 5 Main St.) Shopping for women's clothes the way it used to be: a big mirror at one end of the store, fancy shoes to put on while modeling a potential outfit, and saleswomen who enjoy helping. Party, prom, and evening wear, mother-of-the-bride selections, and casual wear, too. Gifts and accessories. Look for the pink building.

LENOX

Berkshire Leather & Silver Outlet (413-637-4363; 98 Main St.) Native American-style jewelry, leather clothes, sandals, shoes, and accessories, especially some stylish bags.

Casablanca (413-637-2680; 27 Housatonic St.) Men's and women's contemporary clothes, stylishly displayed.

Chase Ballou (413-637-2133; 25 Pittsfield-Lenox Rd., Rte. 7) Women's clothing, dressy to casual with a large selection of bridal and special occasion dresses; and shoes, lingerie, sleepwear, and accessories. A large selection, frequent sales, and personable salespeople, too.

Clothes Works (413-637-0220; Lenox House Country Shops, Pittsield-Lenox Rd., Rte. 7) Discounted name brands like BD Baggies, casual clothing; also some gift items.

Cotton Connection (413-637-8181; Lenox House Country Shops, Pittsfield-Lenox Rd., Rte. 7) Cotton separates, casual wear, pajamas, lounge wear, and underclothes at discounted prices. Open seasonally.

Evviva! (413-637-9875; 22 Walker St.) Sophisticated dresses, separates, and accessories by designers "well known and undiscovered."

Glad Rags (413-637-0088; 66 Church St.) Clothes with an emphasis on easy fit and easy care in a variety of fabulous fabrics. Wonderful hats, scarves, other accessories, and jewelry. Also a source for Berkshire Humane Society T-shirts and sweatshirts.

K's Coats (413-443-5358; 450 Pittsfield-Lenox Rd., Rte. 7) Ladies' coats, dress and casual, in a variety of styles, with designer labels like Forcaster, Bromley, and Jones–New York. Across the hall from **Michael's Shoes** (413-443-3464), with footwear for men and women, handbags.

Leather Loft (413-637-1108; Lenox House Country Shops, Pittsfield-Lenox Rd., Rte. 7) Fine leather at discount prices, with briefcases, handbags, coats, luggage.

London Fog Factory Store (413-499-2779; 439 Pittsfield-Lenox Rd., Rte. 7; moving to Berkshire Outlet Village, Lee) Raincoats and accessories, with some leather items.

Purple Plume (413-637-3442; 35 Church St.) A large selection of fun and unusual clothing, some batiked or hand-painted, featuring the latest looks and natural fibers. The amazing array of accessories includes jewelry, headbands, and scarves. Gifts and cards, too.

Steven Valenti (413-637-0674; 4 Housatonic St.) Sophisticated men's clothing . . . *see description under Pittsfield.*

Talbot's (413-637-3576; 46 Walker St.) Classic women's clothing and accessories, and a special Petites section.

Tanglewool, Inc. (413-637-0900; 28 Walker St.) Sophisticated clothing, shoes, gorgeous sweaters (from Patricia Roberts and other well-known designers), for the fashion-conscious.

Weaver's Fancy (413-637-2013; 65 Church St.) One-of-a-kind clothing and hats in hand-created fabrics. Beautiful hand-painted silks and luscious rayon chenille. Don't miss the whimsical hats that provide both warmth and wit.

PITTSFIELD

Champion Factory Outlet (413-442-1332; 456 W. Housatonic St./Pittsfield Plaza) Sweatshirts and turtlenecks at discount prices, and other athletic apparel.

Cosmetic Design & Color Accents (413-443-0872, 137 North St., Crawford Square) Designer scarves, hats, belts, jewelry, lingerie, and various accessories for the boudoir, including English toiletries and other cosmetics. Instruction in make-up; color analysis; wardrobe planning.

The Cottage (413-447-9643; 31 South St.) A popular shop where women's clothing shares space with home and gift items (see below, under "Gift & Specialty Shops"). Styles range from Liz Claiborne to Putumayo.

Greystone Gardens (413-442-9291; 436 North St.) Victorian and vintage clothing, accessories, jewelry, and linens, for men and women. The long, high-ceilinged shop has floral carpeting, curtained dressing rooms with antique mirrors, stacks of hat boxes, swanky fashion prints, and vintage songs being crooned in the background — the perfect setting for '40s evening gowns, sporty rayon dresses, lacy camisoles, vintage tuxedos, top hats, tweed jackets and coats, bowling shirts, fringed scarves, and more, all eminently wearable. Owner Carla Lund, creator of this outpost of nostalgia, is a genius at putting it all together. Cards, soaps, and other niceties, too. Don't miss it or the shop in the Mews, Stockbridge.

Richard's Menswear (413-445-7704; Allendale Shopping Center) Woolrich items; a good selection of casual shirts and sports coats.

The Stock Room (413-445-5500; 456 W. Housatonic St.) Liquidators offer clothing from upscale department stores at a discount, from blue jeans to party dresses. You never know what you might find. For the whole family; some non-clothing items, too. A source for discounted Crane products.

Steven Valenti (413-443-2569; 157 North St.) Menswear for the '90s in a well-appointed store, with up-to-date styles by Perry Ellis, Jhane Barnes, and other contemporary designers. Shirts, sweaters, suits, jackets, and coats here feature fine fabrics and colors ranging from traditional to fashion forward styles. An outstanding collection of silk ties. Also in Lenox at 4 Housatonic St.

North County

WILLIAMSTOWN

The Cottage (413-458-4304; 24 Water St.) Specialty fabrics and apparel from designers like April Cornell, Vera Bradley, Putumayo, and Crabtree & Evelyn (nightware),

Fabrics and Weavers

For your home or for yourself, three sources of special textiles and fabrics:

Maplewood Fabrics (413-229-8767; Rte. 7A, Ashley Falls) Liberty of London, Scalamandre, Schumacher and other fine fabrics in a low-key setting.

Sam Kasten Handweaver (413-298-5502; Rte 183 at Interlaken Crossroad, Interlaken) A charming small red brick building, once Interlaken's general store, houses the looms of Sam Kasten's nationally renowned architectural fabrics firm. Fine wall coverings, upholstery fabrics and carpeting almost too fine to tread upon are the mainstay of his business, but shawls and wraps in exotic and unusual yarns are available, too. Call to arrange a visit.

Skilled hands and tools of the trade, at Undermountain Weavers, Housatonic.

Jonathan Sternfield

Undermountain Weavers (413-274-6565; 311 Gt. Barrington Rd., Housatonic / Rte. 41, just N. of W. Stockbridge–Gt. Barrington town line) In a restored barn, on century-old hand looms, traditional Shetland Island patterns are taking shape. Purchase by the yard, or tailoring can be arranged.

House of Walsh (413-458-8088; 39 Spring St.) Classic clothes for men and women in a classic setting, with sportswear, accessories, gifts, and Williams College items, too.

Williams Shop (413-458-3605; 15 Spring St.) A large selection of items bearing the Williams College logo, as well as athletic and sporting goods.

Zanna (413-458-9858, 800-773-9858; 41 Spring St.) Contemporary women's clothes and accessories, featuring natural fibers and up-to-the-minute looks — and a selection of sophisticated but comfortable shoes from Arche and Aerosoles.

GIFT & SPECIALTY SHOPS

South County

ASHLEY FALLS

Primrose Cottage (413-229-8401; Rte. 7A) In a cottage setting with soft lighting are lovely dried flowers, hanging in bunches from the beams overhead, spilling forth from baskets, artfully arranged in swags, topiaries, and other imaginative forms. They're from local gardens and from the wild. Primrose has its own signature potpourri, Berkshire Woods, and is also the source for Berkshire Twig furniture. Well worth a trip; call ahead for information about classes or to order special arrangements.

GREAT BARRINGTON

Church Street Trading Company (413-528-6120; 4 Railroad St.) A trendy mix of antiques, natural-fiber clothes, nature-oriented cosmetics, pottery, crafts, and various lifestyle accessories, attractively arranged.

Crystal Essence (413-528-0048; 39 Railroad St.) Geodes, jewelry, gemstones, ceramics, clothes, books, and other items for enhancing a New Age lifestyle.

The Gingham Rabbit (413-528-0048; 389 Stockbridge Rd., Rte. 7) A pastel palate predominates in this two-story shop that sells wonderful cards, pillows, gift items, infant clothing, lingerie, and bath products. The rabbit delivers to local hospitals for congratulating a new mother or cheering up a sick friend.

Mistral's (413-528-1618; 7 Railroad St.) "Provence in the Berkshires" is the way the owners describe their shop. French wire baskets, lamps, and vases; jacquard pattered napkins, Provençal olive oil, faience plates, cutlery, and serving pieces — all guaranteed to win a Francophile's heart. Upstairs are bath and bedroom products.

The Red Door (413-528-1899; 3 Railroad St.) Behind the red door is a tiny shop carrying a variety of gift items old and new.

Talavera (413-528-2423; 9 Railroad St.) Handcrafted gifts from around the world, in ceramics, wood, glass, plus unique handmade clothing, rugs — the creations of the globe.

T.P. Saddle Blanket & Trading Co. (413-528-6500; 304 Main St.) An outpost for the Southwest look, from cowboy-motif pajamas to saddleblankets for your living room, with a colorful abundance of boots, belts, pillows, books, candles, bedding, dishware, shirts, vests, and furniture accents.

LEE

Pamela Loring Gifts and Interiors (413-243-2689; 40 Main St.) Tastefully decorated shop, with carefully chosen merchandise. An emphasis on seasonal gifts and decorations. Candles, bath oils, soaps, and potpourri, along with charming gifts for children.

STOCKBRIDGE

Pink Kitty (413-298-1623; at the Red Lion Inn) A lovely shop with gifts, cards, and accessories, featuring Berkshire items.

Seven Arts (413-298-5101; Main St.) A concentration of items with Rockwell motifs, also T-shirts, jewelry, and gifts.

Williams & Sons Country Store (413-298-3016; Main St.) A Stockbridge institution, with jams and jellies, candy, soaps, gourmet foods, glassware, gifts, cards, and various nostalgia items. You'll enjoy the old tins displayed behind the counter.

Yankee Candle (413-298-3004; 34 Main St.) A huge variety of candles in a variety of shapes, colors, and scents.

WEST STOCKBRIDGE

Hotchkiss Mobiles Gallery (413-232-0200; 8 Center St.) Open Sat. & Sun. in summer; or call for an appointment. Contemporary mobiles for your home or office.

Central County

LENOX

B. Mango & Bird (413-637-2611; 48 Main St.) An eclectic mix of home furnishings and accessories in a bright, new location.

Colorful Stitches (413-637-8207; 48 Main St.) A rainbow of yarns in wools, silks, cottons, and blends would tempt even the novice knitter. Wonderful patterns, buttons, and all the necessary needles, etc. — even regular weekend instruction sessions.

Irish Missed (413-637-3111; Lenox House Country Shops, Pittsfield-Lenox Rd., Rte. 7) Celtic imports from Ireland, Scotland, Wales, and England, along with equestrian merchandise.

Mary Stuart (413-637-0340; 69 Church St.) Accessories for gracious country living, including china, glassware, linen, needlepoint, antiques, and toiletries; lingerie and sleepwear; books and cards. Beautiful clothing for infants and toddlers.

Naomi's Herbs (413-637-0616; 11 Housatonic St.) Dried herbs and flowers fill the rafters of this charming shop. There's an assortment of potpourri fragrances and ingredients to make your own. Teas, bath blends, massage oil, and floral arrangements are also offered here as "resources for a healthy and beautiful life."

The Silver Sleigh (413-637-3522; Lenox House Country Shops, Pittsfield-Lenox Rd., Rte. 7) Complete and imaginative Christmas accessorizing, plus gifts for all seasons.

Ville D'Eau (413-637-2906; 63 Church St.) Bath and beauty products from Aveda, Dr. Hauschka, Caswell Massey, and other well-known names.

Villager Gifts (413-637-9866; 68 Main St.) An engaging variety of gifts and collectibles, featuring jewelry, pottery, stationery, candles, cards. It is the largest area dealer for the Cat's Meow Village houses and custom pieces.

Yankee Candle (413-499-3626; 639 Pittsfield-Lenox Rd., Rte. 7) Candles, gifts, bath accessories. Also on Main St. in Stockbridge.

PITTSFIELD

The Cottage (413-447-9643; 31 South St./Downtown Pittsfield) Attractive tableware, including glasses, vases, dinnerware, table linens, baskets, frames, soaps, and soaps and jewelry. A deservedly popular shop.

Pasko Frame & Gift Center (413-442-2680; 243 North St.) Berkshire landscapes by Walter Pasko, the Berkshire map, superb custom framing, prints, and posters. Largest area dealer of P. Buckley Moss prints.

North County

WILLIAMSTOWN

The Cottage (413-458-4305; 24 Water St.) An eclectic mix of gift items including tableware and table linens, cards, toiletries from Crabtree & Evelyn, and women's clothes from designers like Putumayo.

Where'd You Get That? (413-458-2206; 20A Spring St.) This is a fun store that aims to provide gifts and toys to tickle your fancy, your brain, and your funnybone — and succeeds.

HANDICRAFTS

See Chaper Four, *Culture*, for additional listings of galleries with handcrafted art.

South County

GREAT BARRINGTON

Evergreen (413-528-0511; 291 Main St.) These contemporary American crafts include vases, tableware, floral-papered accessories, clocks, and handcrafted jewelry.

October Mountain Stained Glass (413-528-6681; 343 Main St.) A vivid array of lampshades, window panels, and glass accessories. Custom design work is a specialty, including commissions for home owners, builders, architects. Beveling, sandblasting, repairs, and supplies are also offered. Closed Mon.

Wonderful Things (413-528-2473; 232 Stockbridge Rd., Rte. 7) Handcrafted gifts, or make your own with yarn, needlework accessories, beads, feathers, stencils, paint, other craft supplies. Largest needlework store in the county.

HOUSATONIC

Richard Bennett, master potter, working the clay at his Great Barrington Pottery.

Jonathan Sternfield

The Great Barrington Pottery (413-274-6259; Rte. 41) Potter Richard Bennett uses a Japanese woodburning kiln for firing pottery designs that combine East and West. Visit the pottery showroom in a beautiful garden setting or participate in an ancient tea ceremony (See pages 138–39 for a description of the tea ceremony).

MONTEREY

Joyous Spring Pottery (413-528-4115; Art School Rd.) Potter Michael Marcus fires his climbing kiln once a year for a 10-day period for his Japanese-inspired unglazed ceramics.

SHEFFIELD

Fellerman & Raabe Glass Works (413-229-8533; 534 S. Main St., Rte 7) Glass art here includes perfume bottles, jewelry, vases, and paperweights — try one of these on a small light-box for a glowing miniature universe. Large glass bowls in organic shapes and glass sculpture, too. Call to find out when you can watch glass artists at work. Closed Mon.

Sheffield Pottery (413-229-7700; Rte. 7) New England potters' ware, including mugs, tea pots, platters, tureens; terra cotta items. Supplies and equipment.

WEST STOCKBRIDGE

Berkshire Center for Contemporary Glass (413-232-4666; 6 Harris St.) Iridescent bowls, glassware, and gifts; clever Christmas tree ornaments. Public viewing area.

Hoffman Pottery (413-232-4646; #103 Rte. 41/Gt. Barrington Rd.) Hand-thrown, hand-painted functional works that dance with energy.

New England Stained Glass Studios (413-232-7181; 5 Center St./PO Box 381) A specialist in Tiffany-style lamps. Admire the giant mushrooms and flowers in the windows next to the showroom, and a lion set in a door, on the way to the main entrance. Hundreds of lampshades; windows and other items, too. Custom work on a limited basis.

Central County

LENOX

Inspired Planet (413-637-2836; Brushwood Farm Shops, Pittsfield-Lenox Rd., Rte. 7) This abundant collection of distinctive "cross-cultural art" includes high-quality paintings, jewelry, primitives, rugs, icons, textiles, masks, pottery, carved wooden animals, and other sculpture. These are handcrafted items with symbolic meaning. Call ahead for hours.

Concepts of Art (413-637-4845; 65 Church St.) Fine crafts and local artisans, with lamps and other glass, wood sculpture, jewelry, throws.

Stevens & Conron Gallery (413-637-0739; Curtis Shops, 5 Walker St.) Fine art and rugs, handhooked and handwoven.

Wall Quilts (413-637-2286; 30 Cliffwood St.) Contemporary and imaginative wall hangings, in a variety of techniques: quilted, appliqued, embroidered. Daily 1–5 in July, Aug.; closed Weds.; Sunday 10–2, and by appointment. Call to confirm hours.

PITTSFIELD

Indonesian wooden cat watches a man pass Potala on North Street in Pittsfield.

Judith Monachina

Potala (413-443-5568; 148 North St.) Asian arts and crafts, including rugs of all sizes, baskets, carvings large and small, clothes made from antique textiles, silk scarves, jewelry, lacquerware — arrayed bazaar-style on the hardwood floor and brick walls.

North County

NORTH ADAMS

Milltown Studios (413-662-2725; 51 Main St.) An art, live music, film, and performance cafe and gift store.

WILLIAMSTOWN

Adelaide's Designs (413-458-3285; 96 Water St.) Formerly the Potter's Wheel, this shop offers designs of handcrafted jewelry — special bracelets, necklaces, and earrings, with semiprecious stones.

The Amber Fox (413-458-8519; 622A Main St., Rte. 2) Antiques and collectibles, unusual gifts and special treasures. Open Thurs.–Sat. 10–5, Sun. 12–5.; Mon.–Wed. by appointment only.

HOME & KITCHEN

South County

GREAT BARRINGTON

Berkshire Cottage Kitchen (413-528-0135; 290 Main St.) A hardware store for serious cooks, featuring innovative kitchen equipment including top-of-the-line cookware and knives. From garlic peelers to pasta pots, Kitchen has it all. Also pottery serving pieces and cookbooks.

Gatsby's (413-528-9455; 25 Railroad St.) In addition to wearables, you'll find futons, wicker and other furniture, bedclothes, and housewares.

Out Of Hand (413-528-3791; 81 Main St.) Every size, shape, and color of basket you could ever need or imagine — one upstairs room is full of them — plus rugs, throws, pillows, glassware in a rainbow of colors, toys, candlesticks, clothing. A great place for accessorizing your kitchen or sun porch. Or dining room or bedroom. Or . . .

The Lamplighter (413-528-3448; 162 Main St.) An exceptional lighting store with a wide selection and knowledgeable staff. Chandeliers, floor and table lamps, and outdoor lighting in all shapes, sizes, and styles, from Colonial to Art Deco to contemporary. Shades and other accessories.

STOCKBRIDGE

Country Curtains (413-298-5565; at the Red Lion Inn) Curtains and matching bedding are displayed in a series of bountifully accessorized room settings. You can select from a variety of styles and fabrics.

WEST STOCKBRIDGE

Anderson & Sons' Shaker Tree (413-232-7072; Main St.) Exquisite Shaker reproduction furniture, with quilts, herbs, and other wares. The craftsmanship is so highly regarded that the Andersons were entrusted with permission to measure the Shaker pieces in the noted Andrews' collection at the Metropolitan Museum of Art. The showroom is not always open; call ahead. All work is on commission.

Central County

HANCOCK

Hancock Union Store (413-738-5072; Main St./Box 1009) Fine reproductions of American cabinet furniture; tables, chairs, sofas, beds, in Queen Anne,

Shaker, Federal, and Chippendale styles. Michael Boulay, cabinetmaker. Call for an appointment.

LENOX

Different Drummer's Kitchen (413-637-0606; 374 Pittsfield-Lenox Rd., Rte. 7) All manner of equipment and accessories for kitchen and table, from pasta pots to measuring spoons.

Kaoud Oriental Rugs (413-499-5405; 444 Pittsfield-Lenox Rd., Rte. 7) Rugs from the Orient, plus dhurries and kilims, and "semi-antique" rugs.

Michael Charles Cabinetmakers (413-637-3483; 53 Church St.) Fine handcrafted furniture in a variety of finishes, all beautiful in their stylish simplicity.

Tassels (413-637-2400; Brushwood Farm Shops, Pittsfield-Lenox Rd., Rte. 7) Fine furniture and accessories in room settings in a variety of styles. A division of Designers Furniture Showcase, Ltd.

PITTSFIELD

Haddad's Rug Company (413-443-4747; 32 Bank Row/Park Square) Specialists in Oriental and Oriental-style rugs, new and antique, plus carpeting and other types of rugs.

Paul Rich & Sons Home Furnishings (413-443-6467, 800-723-7424; 242 North St.) A large and well-chosen selection of traditional, contemporary, and country furniture and accent pieces.

North County

ADAMS

Interior Alternative (413-743-1986; 5 Hoosac St.) A home furnishings center with seconds and discontinued famous-brand upholstery and curtain fabric, wallpaper, Oriental carpets, hooked rugs, area rugs, bedspreads, comforters, pillows. Two huge floors in this old mill.

Old Stone Mill (413-743-1042; Rte. 8) Factory outlet for famous brands of wallpaper; fabric for upholstery and drapes. Wallpaper is hand-printed and machine printed. Over-runs, seconds, close-outs up to 50% off.

NORTH ADAMS

International Outlet (413-664-4580; 192 State St./Rte 8) Despite the small warehouse ambiance, a good source for crystal, glassware, dinnerware, kitchen utensils, wicker furniture, rugs, brass, table and kitchen linen, candles, pottery, cookware. Terra cotta pots.

JEWELRY

For additional jewelry options, check the listings in "Antiques" and "Gift & Specialty Stores."

Heirlooms Classic Jewelry (413-298-4436; The Mews, Stockbridge) A glittering treasure-box of a shop, offering affordable, elegant antique and estate jewelry, plus one-of-a-kind creations. Truly an international selection. Closed Tues. & Weds.

Waterside Gallery (413-232-7187; 32 Main St., W. Stockbridge) "Art to wear"; handcrafted jewelry, mostly made on the premises. Other gifts, too.

L&R Wise Goldsmiths (413-637-1589; 81 Church St., Lenox) Richard Wise finds gemstones from all over the world and offers them superbly crafted in contemporary fine art jewelry. Imaginative and unique combinations of gems and precious metals. Custom design service. Closed Sun. & Mon. in winter.

SHOPPING STREETS, MEWS & MALLS

Many of the shops described in this chapter are, happily, on Berkshire downtown Main Streets, where real people actually walk along the sidewalks, go to the hardware store and post office, get books at the library, pick

Shopping in style at the Mews, Stockbridge.

Jonathan Sternfield

up a few groceries, run into friends, and stop for lunch or coffee or ice cream, against a backdrop of mostly 19th-century civic architecture, highlighted by a few notable historic buildings. For beyond-the-downtown shopping experiences, a short and usually scenic drive will take you to clusters of destination shops, some in genuinely venerable buildings, others where the quaintness is of more recent vintage. And, yes, there are even some malls. Following is a roundup of where to find favorite shops and shopping settings. More detailed listings of many of the establishments in these centers may be found in relevant sections of Chapters 4–7, *Culture, Restaurants & Food Purveyors, Recreation,* and *Shopping*.

South County

Southfield's Buggy Whip Factory (Main St./Rte. 272) The drive there takes you through classic New England scenery. The huge, two-century-old building houses a large antiques center and a cafe.

Downtown Great Barrington is a happening place, with a true Main Street atmosphere created by a combination of several shops and boutiques, antiques stores, bookstores, an outstanding selection of eateries, a first-rate coffee place, the grand old Mahaiwe Theatre and the new Mahaiwe Triplex, for current movies and special live performances. The action centers around Railroad St. and Main St., and takes in other side streets, too. Great Barrington hosts downtown food and music events throughout the year.

Jenifer House Commons (Stockbridge Rd., Rte. 7, Gt. Barrington) is just north of Great Barrington's center. This cluster of multilevel barns and buildings — some old and some new — houses an extensive group of antiques dealers' wares, fine linen and bedding, some art galleries, a women's clothing store, and a restaurant/brewery. Lunch is available there or nearby. (Unfortunately, some businesses here suffered losses when one building, the red barn, burned in a fire early in 1997; many of the affected businesses have either reopened or have plans to do so, either at the Commons or elsewhere; call ahead to verify the current location and hours of your favorite stores and dealers.)

Main St., Stockbridge still looks like — and is — Norman Rockwell territory, even though the Rockwell Museum has moved (but not far; see *Culture*). The welcoming expanse of the Red Lion Inn shares the scene with the gracious library, an excellent market, and several stores. Connected to Main St. is **The Mews**, a cozy cul-de-sac of shops offering clothes, jewelry, and gifts. Many Stockbridge shops offer Rockwelliana in one form or another, from T-shirts to signed prints. Also around the corner from Main St. is Elm St., with more shops, eateries, and the post office. Note: Main St. and The Mews can seem overrun on high season weekends, but less stressing during the week.

A side trip to the small downtown of **West Stockbridge** will reward with several galleries, good restaurants and cafes, and antiques — not to mention a hardware store and a shop devoted to flavoring extracts. The gallery scene offers outdoor sculptures on display, handcrafted jewelry, mobiles, stained glass, and reproduction Shaker furniture, and many other options for contemporary art and craft work. A vintage depot houses a cafe and studios; a Shaker mill building is home to antiques. A small concentration of excellent restaurants will please everybody from the hamburger-and-pizza crowd to the international gourmet.

A new offering on the Berkshire shopping scene is the *Berkshire Outlet Village*. These shops are all stocked with discounted (and some say, last year's) merchandise. Shoes, clothing, leather goods, cards, gourmet food, and watches are all available from top-of-the-line manufacturers to those more trendy and inexpensive. Conveniently located near Exit 2 of the MassPike in *Lee*, the Village's visibility is likely to attract out-of-town shoppers, but locals seem eager to give it a chance, as well. Local controversy over the design notwithstanding, it is an attractive, well-landscaped area.

Central County

Downtown Lenox still maintains a "real" downtown flavor, though the boutique and gallery contingent ascends. The appealing variety of architecture neoclassic and Victorian-cottage predominate — is home to inns and taverns, several dining options, an exceptional library and bookstore, and those shops and galleries: a number of clothing shops, mostly for women, covers the style territory from fine to funky, from classic to casual; art and handcraft galleries offer Berkshire scenes, world-renowned jewelry, and other creations. The *Curtis Shops* — in an imposing hotel building, the place to stay in the 19th century — is now home to a mix of fine shops and galleries, as well as housing for the elderly.

Just north of Lenox, on Pittsfield-Lenox Rd., Rte. 7, are the *Brushwood Farm Shops* and the *Lenox House Country Shops*. Brushwood Farm is a complex of barnlike buildings of specialty shops, with antiques, interior decorating and design, a hair salon, places to eat, and a craft gallery featuring Asian pieces. Lenox House Country Shops (413-637-1341) mix specialty shops and factory outlets; the latter include Bass, Corning/Revere, Harvé Benard, Izod, Van Heusen, and more. Specialty shops offer leather items, jewelry, books, kids clothing, and Christmas accessories. A big destination for many visitors.

Downtown Pittsfield was once the commercial and civic hub of the Berkshires and, although the glory of its main thoroughfare, North Street, has somewhat faded, it still hosts a number of services and shops. The downtown area includes several large churches and buildings that will interest the architecture buff, plus the Berkshire Museum and the Berkshire Athenaeum (the public library). Free concerts downtown are offered in the summer and on First Night.

Allendale Shopping Center offers an interesting mix of shops. Stores include Richard's Men Store, a photo store, Truffles & Such, a pet store, and T.J. Maxx (for more on T.J. Maxx, see *If Time Is Short* at the back of this book).

Local designer Crispina ffrench turned an old Housatonic paper mill into her studio and a production facility for her unusual designs, which are sold throughout the area and elsewhere in the country.

Judith Monachina

Berkshire Crossing Mall is one of the newer additions to the mall scene in Berkshire. Located on Rte. 9 in Pittsfield, it has a Barnes & Noble store, Pier One, and the ubiquitous Wal-Mart, along with craft, grocery, and clothing stores.

Lanesborough's Berkshire Mall, Rte. 8, can supply basic mall needs, with a multiscreen cinema complex, clothing and shoe stores, dozens of places to eat, two bookstores, and so forth. The Mall can be accessed from Rte. 7 as well.

North County

Spring Street and **Water Street** in **Williamstown** roughly parallel each other and are across from the main Williams College campus. Both easily walkable, they offer handcrafts, clothing, books, tapes and CDs, places to eat, antiques and accessories, sports gear, and all the Williams College memorabilia anyone would ever need.

Near Berkshire County

A recommended destination just outside the county is **Chatham, New York**. **Main Street** shops include the **Dakota** for clothes; the **Chatham Bookstore**; **Pavanne** jewelry and gifts; the **Handcrafters** for fine crafts; and the fantastico **Italian Accent** for paper, glass, jewelry, pottery, dishware.

CHAPTER EIGHT
Practical Matters
INFORMATION

Window shopping for a dream house in the Berkshires.

Jonathan Sternfield

W e offer here a small encyclopedia of useful information to help facilitate everyday life for residents and visitors in the Berkshires. This chapter provides information on the following topics.

Road Service   307
Schools   308

AMBULANCE, FIRE, POLICE

The general emergency number for Pittsfield and most Berkshire communities is **911**. This "enhanced-911" service is part of a state-wide system. Consult an up-to-date phone book for details.

In an emergency situation anywhere in the county, dial "O" and the operator will connect you directly to the correct agency.

Another county-wide set of emergency numbers is:

Fire	413-445-4559
Poison Control	800-682-9211
Police	413-442-0512
Rape Crisis Hotline	413-528-9434 (South County)
	413-443-0089 (Central County)
	413-664-6610 (North County)

AREA CODES, TELEPHONE EXCHANGES, ZIP CODES, TOWN HALLS/LOCAL GOVERNMENT

AREA CODES

The Area Code for all of Berkshire County is **413**. Area codes for adjacent counties are as follows:

Massachusetts
Franklin (most towns), Hampshire, and Hampden counties — **413**.

Connecticut
Litchfield County — **860**.

New York
Columbia and Rensselaer Counties — **518**.

Vermont
Bennington County — **802**.

TOWN HALLS

A ll Berkshire communities have town or city halls as the seats of local government. Most townships are governed by Boards of Selectmen; several
also have town managers. For general information,call the town offices at the
following numbers or write to the Town Clerk, c/o Town Hall in the village in
question.

Town	Telephone Exchange	Zip Code	Town Hall Office
Adams	743	01220	413-743-8310
Alford	528	01230	413-528-4536
Ashley Falls	229	01222	413-229-8752 (Sheffield)
Becket	623	01223	413-623-8934
Berkshire County Commissioners	Pittsfield	01201	413-448-8424
Cheshire	743	01225	413-743-1690
Clarksburg	663	01247	413-663-7940
Dalton	684	01226	413-684-6103
Egremont	528	01258	413-528-0182
Florida	662	01247	413-662-2448
Glendale	298	01229	413-298-4714 (Stockbridge)
Gt. Barrington	528	01230	413-528-3140
Hancock	738	01237	413-738-5225
Hinsdale	655	01235	413-655-2301
Housatonic	274	01236	413-528-3140 (Gt. Barrington)
Lanesborough	442, 443, 447, 499	01237	413-442-1167
Lee	243	01238	413-243-5505
Lenox	637	01240	413-637-5506
Lenoxdale	637	01242	413-637-5506 (Lenox)
Middlefield	623	01243	413-623-8966
Mill River	229	01244	413-229-8116 (NewMarlborough)
Monterey	528	01245	413-528-1443
Mt. Washington	528	01258	413-528-2839
New Ashford	458	01267	413-458-9096
New Marlborough	229	01244	413-229-8116
N. Adams	662, 663, 664	01247	413-662-3015
N. Egremont	528	01252	413-528-0182 (Egremont)

Otis	269	01253	413-269-0100
Peru	655	01235	413-655-8312
Pittsfield	442, 443, 445	01201	413-499-9361
	446, 447, 448	01202	
	494, 499	(Post Office)	
Richmond	698	01254	413-698-3882
Sandisfield	258	01255	413-258-4506
Savoy	743	01256	413-743-4290
Sheffield	229	01257	413-229-8752
S. Egremont	528	01258	413-528-0182
			(Egremont)
S. Lee	243	01260	413-243-5505
			(Lee)
Southfield	229	01259	413-229-8116
			(New Marlborough)
Stockbridge	298	01262	413-298-4714
Tyringham	243	01264	413-243-1749
Washington	623	01223	413-623-8878
W. Stockbridge	232, 274	01266	413-232-0301
Williamstown	458, 597	01267	413-458-9341
Windsor	684	01270	413-684-3878

BANKS AND CREDIT UNIONS

Several Berkshire County banks are linked electronically to banking systems elsewhere in the United States. If you are visiting here, you may find these options quite helpful, especially if you need extra cash or traveler's checks. It's best to inquire with your home bank to see which system you can use and which Berkshire bank can serve you.

As we go to press, banking in Berkshire County is changing through mergers. **Berkshire County Savings Bank** and **Great Barrington Savings Bank** have merged to create **The Berkshire Bank**; **City Savings Bank** and the **First National Bank of the Berkshires** intend to merge (once approval is obtained) to operate as the **City Savings Bank**.

Phone numbers below connect you to the main office, or — in the case of some 800 numbers — to all offices or to special services.

Adams Co-operative Bank
   93 Park St., Adams; 413-743-0001. Branch: N. Adams.
BankBoston (formerly Bank of Boston)
   Main Office: 99 West St., Pittsfield; also 1 Dan Fox Dr., 200 Elm St., 100 North St., and 600 Merrill Rd. 413-499-3000 (all Pittsfield branches); 800-252-6000

(banking services). Other branches in Adams, Dalton, Gt. Barrington, Sheffield, N. Adams, Williamstown.

The Berkshire Bank

Formed by merger May 1, 1997.

Former **Berkshire County Savings Bank** offices: Main office at 24 North St. (Cor. Park Square and North St.), Pittsfield; 413-443-5601; also Allendale Shopping Ctr., 165 Elm St., and Old Town Hall (Park Square). Other branches in Gt. Barrington and N. Adams. 800-773-5601 to all branches in 413 area.

Former **Great Barrington Savings Bank** offices: 244 Main St., Gt. Barrington; 413-528-1190. Branches: Lee, Sheffield, Stockbridge, W. Stockbridge.

Berkshire County Savings Bank *See The Berkshire Bank, above.*

City Savings Bank

116 North St., Pittsfield; 413-443-4421; 800-292-6634. Branch: Gt. Barrington.

First National Bank of the Berkshires

76 Park St., Lee; 413-243-0115. Branches: Gt. Barrington, Otis, N. Adams.

Fleet Bank

66 West St. and Allendale Shopping Ctr., Pittsfield. Branch: N. Adams. 800-841-4000 to all branches.

Great Barrington Savings Bank *See The Berkshire Bank, above.*

Greylock Federal Credit Union

75 Kellogg, Pittsfield, 413-443-5114; 660 Merrill Rd.; Pittsfield, 413-445-5555. Other branches in Adams, Gt. Barrington.

Lee Bank

75 Park St., Lee; 413-243-0117. Branches: Gt. Barrington, Stockbridge.

Lenox National Bank

7 Main St., Lenox; 413-637-0017. Branch: Pittsfield-Lenox Rd., Lenox.

Lenox Savings Bank

25 Main St., Lenox; 413-637-0147. Branch: Holmes Rd.-Rte. 7, Lenox

North Adams Hoosac Savings Bank

93 Main St., N. Adams; 413-663-5353.

Pittsfield Co-operative Bank

70 South St., Pittsfield; 413-447-7304. Branches: Dalton, Gt. Barrington.

Pittsfield Municipal Federal Credit Union

70 Allen St., Pittsfield; 413-499-9454.

South Adams Savings Bank

2 Center St., Adams; 413-743-0040. Branches: Williamstown, Cheshire.

Williamstown Savings Bank

795 Main St., Williamstown; 413-458-8191.

BIBLIOGRAPHY

Here are two lists of books about the Berkshires, many of which we used in researching this book.

"Books You Can Buy" shows titles available either through Berkshire bookshops, bookstores elsewhere or from the publishers. For information on Berkshire booksellers, see "Bookstores" in Chapter Seven, *Shopping*.

"Books You Can Borrow" suggests a wealth of other reading in earlier publications now no longer for sale. Some of the more rarefied material on this list does not circulate outside the libraries, and its use may be restricted to those with professional credentials. Several popular items here will especially interest history buffs. The best sources for book borrowing are described under "Libraries" in Chapter Four, *Culture*.

Books You Can Buy

COOKBOOKS

Chase, Suzi Forbes. *The Red Lion Inn Cookbook.* Lee: Berkshire House Publishers. 224 pp., photos, $29.95; pap., $16.95.

Conway, Linda Glick. *Country Inns and Back Roads Cookbook.* Lee: Berkshire House Publishers, 1995. 256 pp., illus., $29.95. Collection of recipes from inns around the nation, including Blantyre (Lenox), the Red Lion Inn (Stockbridge), and the Village Inn (Lenox).

Cook, Janet, ed. *Berkshire Victuals.* Stockbridge, MA: Berkshire County Historical Society, 1993. 208 pages, illus., $19.95. Historical and contemporary recipes.

Jacobs, Miriam. *Best Recipes of Berkshire Chefs.* Lee: Berkshire House Publishers. 208 pp., illus., $12.95.

Levitt, Atma Jo Ann. *The Kripalu Cookbook.* Lee: Berkshire House Publishers. 1995. 448 pp., $16.95. Recipes featured at the Kripalu Center in Lenox, tailored for home use.

Shortt, C. Vincent. *The Innkeepers Collection Cookbook.* Lee: Berkshire House Publishers, 1993. 272 pp., illus., $16.95. Collection of recipes from inns around the nation, including the Inn at Stockbridge and the Red Lion Inn.

Williamstown Theatre Festival. *As You Like It.* Williamstown, MA: Williamstown Theatre Festival Guild, 1993. 222 pp., illus, $15.00. Recipes from the festival's stars, directors, writers, and associates.

LITERARY WORKS

Howard, Walter. *Sisyphus in the Hayfield: Views of A Berkshire Farmer.* Cobble Press, 1988. 128 pp., photos, $14.

Melville, Herman. *Great Short Works of Herman Melville.* NY: Harper & Row, 1969. 507 pp., bibliog. $18.50.

Metcalf, Paul, ed. *October Mountain: An Anthology of Berkshire Writers.* Williamstown, MA: Mountain Press, 1992. 163 pp., $11.95, pap.

Nunley, Richard, ed. *The Berkshire Reader.* Lee: Berkshire House, Publishers, 1992. 544 pp., illus., $29.95.

Wharton, Edith. *A Backward Glance.* NY: Charles Scribner's Sons, 1985 reprint. 379 pp., index, $13.95, pap.

Wharton, Edith. *Ethan Frome.* NY: Scribner's, 1988 reprint. $5.95.

LOCAL HISTORIES

Burns, Deborah E. and Lauren R. Stevens. *Most Excellent Majesty: A History of Mount Greylock.* Lee: Berkshire House Publishers, 128 pp., photos, $8.95.

Chapman, Gerard. *Eminent Berkshire Women.* Gt. Barrington:Attic Revivals Press, 1988. 32 pp., $5.00.

_____. *A History of the Red Lion Inn in Stockbridge, Massachusetts.* Stockbridge: Red Lion Inn, 1987. 54 pp., illus., $12.00.

Drew, Bernard A. *A Berkshire Further Off the Trail.* Attic Revivals Press, 1992. 56 pp., illus., pap. $7.50.

_____. *A History of Notchview Reservation: The Arthur D. Budd Estate in Windsor, Massachusetts.* Gt. Barrington: Attic Revivals Press, 1986, 48 pp., illus., maps, $5.00.

_____. *History of The Mahaiwe Theatre in Great Barrington, Massachusetts.* Gt. Barrington: Attic Revivals Press, 1989, 48 pp., illus., $5.00.

_____. *Spanning Berkshire Waterways.* Gt. Barrington: Attic Revivals Press, 1990. 32 pp., photos, maps, $5.00.

_____. *William Cullen Bryant's "A Border Tradition."* Gt. Barrington: Attic Revivals Press, 1988, 32 pp., bibliog., $6.50.

Drew, Bernard A. and Donna M. *Mapping the Berkshires.* Gt. Barrington: Attic Revivals Press, 1985. 48 pp., illus. maps, $5.00.

Miller, Amy Bess. *Hancock Shaker Village/The City of Peace: An Effort to Restore a Vision 1960-1985.* Hancock: Hancock Shaker Village, 1984. 170 pp., illus., photos, appendices, bibliog., index, $19.95; pap., $12.00.

Murray, Stuart and James McCabe. *Norman Rockwell's Four Freedoms.* Lee: Berkshire House, Publishers, 1993. 176 pp., illus., $24.95; pap. $14.95.

Owens, Carole. *The Berkshire Cottages: A Vanishing Era.* Englewood, Stockbridge: Cottage Press, 1984. 240 pp., photos, illus., index, $29.95, pap.

Pincus, Andrew L. *Scenes from Tanglewood.* Boston: Northeastern University Press, 1989. 287 pp., photos, $14.95, pap.

The Stockbridge Story: 1739-1989. Stockbridge: Town of Stockbridge, 1989. 209 pp., illus., photos, index, $25.00.

PHOTOGRAPHIC STUDIES

Bazan, John. *Rails Across the Berkshire Hills. Railroad Photography, 1890-1984.* Pittsfield: The Author, 1984. Photos, $9.95, pap.

Binzen, Bill. *The Berkshires.* Lee: Berkshire House Publishers, 1995. 90 color photos, $24.95.

Chefetz, Sheila *Antiques for the Table.* New York: Viking Penguin, 1993. 232 pp., 275 color photos, bibliog., Berkshire resource directory, index. Many photographs of Berkshire summer cottages.

Gilder, Cornelia Brooke. *Views of the Valley: Tyringham 1739-1989.* Tyringham: the Hopbrook Community Club, 1989. 142 pp., photos, $15, pap.

Resch, Tyler, ed. *Images of America: Bill Tague's Berkshires.* Intr. by George A. Wislocki. Dover, NH: Arcadia Publishing, 1996. 128 pp., map., photos, $16.99. Berkshire landscapes and people from the 1950s to the 1980s, as seen in 178 black-and-white photos by a noted *Berkshire Eagle* photographer, editor, and reporter.

Scott, Walter. *The Norman Rockwell Bicycle Tours of Stockbridge.* Stockbridge: SnO Publications, 1980. 32 post cards, $10.95.

RECREATION AND NATURE

A Canoe Guide to the Housatonic River, Berkshire County. Pittsfield: Berkshire County Regional Planning Commission. Illus., maps. Updated in 1994.

Appalachian Trail Guide to Massachusetts-Connecticut. Harpers Ferry, WV: Appalachian Trail Conference, 1990. 189 pp., maps, $18.95.

Cuyler, Lewis C. *Bike Rides in the Berkshire Hills,* revised and updated edition. Lee: Berkshire House Publishers, 1995. 200 pp., illus., maps, $9.95, pap.

Laubach, René. *A Guide to Natural Places in the Berkshire Hills,* 2nd. ed. Lee: Berkshire House Publishers, 1997. 288 pp., illus., maps, $12.95, pap.

Lyon, Steve. *Bicyclist's Guide to the Southern Berkshires.* Lenox: MA: Freewheel Publications, 1993. 256 pp., $16.95., pap.

Stevens, Lauren R. *Hikes & Walks in the Berkshire Hills.* Lee: Berkshire House Publishers, 1990. 224 pp., maps, $9.95, pap.

_____. *Skiing in the Berkshire Hills.* Lee: Berkshire House Publishers, 1991. 232 pp., maps, $8.95, pap.

Strauch, Joseph G., Jr., *Wildflowers of the Berkshire & Taconic Hills.* Lee: Berkshire House Publishers, 1995. 160 pp., maps, illus. $12.95., pap.

TRAVEL

The Berkshire Hills: *A WPA Guide, with a new foreword by Roger Linscott.* Boston: Northeastern University Press, 1987. 390 pp., illus., photos, maps, lore, history, $14.95, pap.

Bryan, Clark, W. *The Book of Berkshire*. N. Egremont: Past Perfect Books, 1993 reprint. 304 pp., engravings, index, large color map of county, $24.95. A splendid reprint of the first guide to the Berkshires.

Davenport, John. *Berkshire-Bennington Locator*. Madison, WI: First Impressions, 1988. 112 pp., maps, $10.95, pap.

Whitman, Herbert S. *Exploring the Berkshires*. NY: Hippocrene, 1991. 240 pp., illus., $9.95, pap.

Books You Can Borrow

Annin, Katherine Huntington. *Richmond, Massachusetts: The Story of a Berkshire Town and Its People, 1765-1965*. Richmond: Richmond Civic Association, 1964. 214 pp., photos, illus., index. Only complete readable history of town.

Birdsall, Richard. *Berkshire County, A Cultural History*. NY: Greenwood Press, 1978 reprint. 401 pp., notes, bibliog., index. Only cultural study of region; emphasis on first half of the 19th century. Chapters cover development of law, newspapers, education, religion. Special attention to the literary heritage.

Bittman, Sam, and Steven A. Satullo, eds. *Berkshire: Seasons of Celebration*. Pittsfield: Either/Or Press, 1982. 112 pp., photos.

Boltwood, Edward. *The History of Pittsfield, Massachusetts from the Year 1876 to the Year 1916*. Pittsfield: The City, 1916. Covers history of most important county communities to early 20th century.

Brook, Robert R.R., ed. Williamstown: *The First Two Hundred Years Williamstown, 1953*. 458 pp., 69 illus.

Bulkeley, Morgan. *Mountain Farm: Poems From the Berkshire Hills*. Chester: Hollow Springs Press, 1984. 95 pp., illus.

Collections of the Berkshire Historical and Scientific Society. Pittsfield: Sun Printing Co., 1892-1899. Papers on historical topics read at Society meetings. Often composed by local authorities, subjects range from Berkshire geology to glass manufacture in Berkshire. Often unique and usually reliable.

Consolati, Florence. *See All the People: Or, Life in Lee*. Lee: The Author, 1978. Colorful, quaint history of the town and its citizens. 442 pp., photos, bibliog., index.

Coxey, Willard D. *Ghosts of Old Berkshire*. Gt. Barrington: The Berkshire Courier, 1934. Legends and folktales of Berkshire people and places.

Drew, Bernard A. *Berkshire Between Covers: A Literary History*. Gt. Barrington: Attic Revivals Press, 1985. 32 pp., illus., bibliog. Brief biographical sketches of deceased fiction writers with significant connections to the Berkshires.

_____. *Berkshire Off the Trail*. Gt. Barrington: Attic Revival Press, 1982. 96 pp., illus., index. Informal history of less traditional subjects.

Emblidge, David, ed. *The Third Berkshire Anthology: A Collection of Literature and Art*. Lenox: Berkshire Writers, Inc., 1982. 185 pp., illus.

Field, Stephen, ed. *A History of the County of Berkshire, Massachusetts*. Pittsfield:

Samuel W. Bush, 1829. Perhaps the first history of the Berkshires, sponsored by the Berkshire Association of Congregational Ministers. A general history of the county, followed by accounts of individual towns, each written by its minister.

Jones, Electa F. Stockbridge, *Past and Present: Or, Records of an Old Mission Station.* Springfield: Samuel Bowles & Co., 1854. History of Indian mission and Stockbridge Indians.

Kupferberg, Herbert. *Tanglewood.* NY: McGraw-Hill, 1976. 280 pp., photos, bibliog., index. Most thorough history of the Berkshire Music Festival.

Lewis, Joseph W. *Berkshire Men of Worth.* 4 Vols. Scrapbook of newspaper articles. From 1933 until well after Lewis' death in 1938, over 300 columns on Berkshire notables were published in the Berkshire Evening Eagle. Series featured penetrating biographical sketches of men whom Lewis regarded as important historical figures. Perhaps the most comprehensive biographical treatment of historical Berkshire figures.

Oakes, Donald, ed. *A Pride of Palaces: Lenox Summer Cottages, 1883-1933.* Lenox: Lenox Library, 1981. 83 pp., illus., photos.

Perry, Arthur L. *Origins in Williamstown.* NY: Charles Scribner's Sons, 1896. Detailed, well-researched history of early Williamstown and other segments of northern Berkshire.

Preiss, Lillian E. Sheffield, *Frontier Town.* Sheffield: Sheffield Bicentennial Comm., 1976. 188 pp., photos, illus., bibliog., index. Good, traditional town history.

Resch, Tyler, ed. *Berkshire, The First Three Hundred Years 1676-1976.* Pittsfield: Eagle Pub. Co., 1976. 163 pp., photos, illus., maps, bibliog., index. Photographs and illustrations of significant and interesting historical events and people, with concise captions.

Sedgwick, Sarah Cabot & Christina Sedgwick Marquand. *Stockbridge, 1739 1939: A Chronicle.* Stockbridge: The Authors, 1939. 306 pp., photos, illus., bibliog. Popular, readable history.

Smith, J.E.A., ed. *History of Berkshire County, Massachusetts, With Biographical Sketches of Its Prominent Men.* 2 Vols. NY: J.B. Beers & Co., 1885. Wide-ranging history covering every aspect of Berkshire life. Nine chapters on individual towns. Most comprehensive, reliable history of the first 200 years of Berkshire development.

Smith, J.E.A. *The History of Pittsfield (Berkshire County), Massachusetts, From the Year 1734 to the Year 1800.* Boston: Lee, Shepard, 1869. The History of Pittsfield (Berkshire County), Massachusetts, From the Year 1800 to the Year 1876. Springfield: C.W. Bryan & Co., 1876. The most detailed, thorough town histories for the county. Smith had access to much material since lost; covers surrounding communities as well.

Taylor, Charles J. *History of Great Barrington (Berkshire), Massachusetts 1676-*

1882. Part II, Extension 1882-1922 by George Edwin MacLean. Gt. Barrington: 1928. Detailed, accurate history of town, particularly the Taylor segment.

Wood, David H. Lenox, *Massachusetts Shire Town*. Lenox: 1968. Similar to Sedgwick history of Stockbridge but more detailed.

CLIMATE AND WEATHER REPORTS

CLIMATE

How the Berkshire climate strikes you depends on what you're used to. People visiting from outside the region may be helped by the following information.

In general, while summers are blessedly mild due to the elevation of the Berkshire hills, winters can be cold and snowy with tricky driving conditions. Of course, what a fellow who doesn't ski finds annoying in a New England winter, greases the skids for another who does ski. Summer visitors should remember that nights can be cool; bring sweaters and even light coats or jackets. And those in search of great snow should note that spring comes to South County well before it does up north and up higher. One day, we cross-country skied in the morning on good snow at Notchview in Windsor and then rototilled the garden in Great Barrington that afternoon.

TEMPERATURE AND PRECIPITATION

Average Temperature	October	F 48.4°
	January	20.4°
	April	43.4°
	July	68.3°
Average Annual Total Precipitation		
Rainfall plus water content of snow		44.15"
	Snow	75.7"

For people who are really into statistics or are interested for business or investment purposes, the source for this information and a great deal more, *The Berkshire County Data Book*, is available (for $100) from the Berkshire County Regional Planning Commission (413-442-1521; 10 Fenn St., Pittsfield, MA 01201).

WEATHER REPORTS

Great Barrington	413-528-1118
Pittsfield	413-499-2627
North Adams	413-663-6264
Williamstown	413-458-2222

GUIDED TOURS

If you want to be bused directly to Berkshire's high spots by an informed guide, there are hosts of possibilities, some based here in the hills, some coming from New York and Boston. From the big cities, there are fall-foliage tours, Tanglewood tours, and ski tours, all of which provide transport, tickets, meals, and lodging plus background on the sites. For an individual, these tours offer a taste of the area's delights in a perfectly packaged form. For groups, the tours turn a possible logistical nightmare into a fun-filled holiday.

Should you be coming from New York or Boston, a travel agent may be helpful in choosing the right tour. The best of the commercial tour companies belong to the National Tour Association. The best of the charter bus companies belong to the American Bus Association. Here are a few of the most experienced Berkshire guided-tour companies operating from New York and Boston.

NEW YORK

Parker Tours 516-349-0575, 800-833-9600; 255 Executive Dr., Plainview, NY 11803.

Tauck Tours 203-226-6911, 800-468-2825; 276 Post Rd. W., Westport, CT 06880.

BOSTON

Collette Tours 401-728-3805, 800-752-2655 (in New England except Maine), 800-832-4656; 162 Middle St., Pawtucket, RI 02860.

WITHIN THE BERKSHIRES

Within Berkshire, there are also a number of guided tour options. For something relatively brief and informal, a local cab driver can usually be persuaded to drive you around, adding colorful histories that only a cabbie might know. For more organized, detailed tours, consider the following.

Berkshire Cottages Tours 413-637-1899; The Mount, Plunkett St., Lenox. Tours of The Mount (Edith Wharton's home), a Women of Achievement Lecture Series (Mon., July–Aug.), plus several packages that include a tour of The Mount, slide talk about Berkshire cottages, and lunch. Call for more detailed information. Advance reservations required for bus groups.

Berkshire Tour Company (413-738-5224; Box 383, Pittsfield, 01202) Berkshire native Nancy C. Henriques provides a wide range of tour services, including group tours of Berkshire County sites (a favorite is the Berkshire Cottages tour), plus walking tours of the Main Streets of Stockbridge, Lenox, and Williamstown. She also provides customized tours including lunch or dinner at local restaurants, excursions to Tanglewood and other music and theater festivals, and combinations of tours for any size group. Phone for prices and schedules.

Greylock Discovery Tours — See the description under "Hiking" in Chapter Seven, *Recreation.*

HANDICAPPED SERVICES

A lthough Berkshire is a region with lots of rough terrain, handicapped people will find access quite easy to most cultural sites and events, to many lodgings and restaurants, and to most shops. In Chapter Three, *Lodging*, we specify those places where we know handicapped access is either feasible or not. Elsewhere, to confirm the situation, use the phone numbers we provide to get information.

The Berkshire Visitors Bureau (413-443-9186; Berkshire Common, Pittsfield, MA 01201) publishes an annual guide listing many Berkshire services and attractions, in many cases, specifying access to handicapped people. The *AAA Tour Guide*, available through the Auto Club of Berkshire County (413-445-5635; 196 South St., Pittsfield) also designates restaurants, lodging, etc. with handicapped access.

Centrally located, a phone booth just outside the Berkshire Center for Contemporary Glass and several restaurants in West Stockbridge.

Judith Monachina

As for transportation, the **Berkshire Regional Transit Authority** (413-499-2782 or in county 800-292-2782) runs the public bus system throughout the major towns in the county and has buses equipped with wheelchair lifts. See Chapter Two, *Transportation*, "Getting Around the Berkshires" for more information.

HOSPITALS

GREAT BARRINGTON
Fairview Hospital 413-528-0790; 29 Lewis Ave.

PITTSFIELD
Berkshire Medical Center 413-447-2000; 725 North St.
Hillcrest Hospital 413-443-4761; 165 Tor Court.

NORTH ADAMS
North Adams Regional Hospital 413-663-3701; Hospital Ave.

LATE NIGHT FOOD AND FUEL

Berkshire Truck Plaza (food and fuel); open all night: Rte. 102, W. Stockbridge, 413-232-4233.

Christy's (food and fuel); open all night: 223 Columbia St., N. Adams, 413-743-0322; 41 Housatonic St., Lee, 413-243-2088.

Convenience Plus (food and fuel); open all night: 90 Tyler St., Pittsfield, 413-499-1741; 241 Main St., Lee, 413-243-2399. Open till 11 p.m.: South St., Stockbridge. 413-298-4036.

Cumberland Farms (food and fuel); open all night: 140 Main St., Gt. Barrington, 413-528-9852; 594 Mohawk Trail, North Adams, 413-662-2721 and 413-664-9150; 446 Main St., Williamstown, 413-458-9170. Open till midnight: 70 Ashland St., N. Adams.

Dakota Restaurant (food); open till 11 p.m. Fri.–Sat.: Pittsfield-Lenox Rd./Rte. 7, Pittsfield, 413-499-7900.

Diesel Dan's (food and fuel); restaurant open all night Mon.–Thurs., Fri. till 11 p.m.; pumps open all night, exc. Fri. till midnight: Rte. 102, Lee, 413-243-1756.

Dunkin' Donuts (food); open all night: 5 Union St., N. Adams, 413-662-2274; 18 First St., Pittsfield, 413-499-0371; Main St, Lee, 413-243-1676.

Jimmy's (food); open Fri. till 11 p.m., Sat. till 10 p.m.: 114 W. Housatonic, Pittsfield, 413-499-1288.

Joe's Diner (food); open till midnight; closed Sat. from 6:30 p.m. and all day Sun.: Main St., Lee, 413-243-9756.

Luau Hale (food); open Fri.–Sat. till 11 p.m.: Pittsfield-Lenox Rd./Rte. 7, Lenox, 413-443-4745.

P.J.'s Convenience Store (food); open Mon.–Sat. till 11:30 p.m., Sun. till 10 p.m.: S. Main, Sheffield, 413-229-6610

Papa Joe's (food); open Fri.–Sat. till 11 p.m.: 107 Newell St., Pittsfield, 413-499-2151.

Price Chopper Supermarkets (food); open till midnight: Stockbridge Rd., Rte. 7, Gt. Barrington, 413-528-8415; Park St., Lee, 413-243-2238; Pittsfield-Lenox Rd./ Rte. 7, Lenox, 413-443-5449. Open Mon.–Sat. till 11 p.m., Sun. till 9 p.m.: Rte. 2, N. Adams, 413-663-9415; Curran Hwy./Rte. 8, N. Adams, 413-663-6252.

Salt & Pepper North (food); open Sat. & Sun. all night from 11:30 p.m. till 3 p.m. the next day: 641 North St., Pittsfield, 413-499-3306.

Stop & Shop Supermarket (food); open all night Mon.–Fri., Sat. & Sun. till midnight: Merrill Rd., Pittsfield, 413-499-0745; Dan Fox Dr. (off Pittsfield-Lenox Rd./Rte. 7), Pittsfield, 413-442-7600. Open all night Mon.–Fri., Sat. till midnight, Sun. till 9 p.m.: Rte. 2, N. Adams, 413-664-8100.

MEDIA: MAGAZINES AND NEWSPAPERS; RADIO STATIONS

MAGAZINES AND NEWSPAPERS

The Advocate (413-458-9000; 38 Spring St., Williamstown; Wednesdays) Highly readable freebie, well-researched articles, mostly on community-related topics, for northern Berkshire and southern Vermont.

The Berkshire Eagle (413-447-7311; 75 S. Church St., Pittsfield; morning daily) The county's newspaper of record, a Pulitzer Prize–winning publication with extensive world, national, state, and local news, plus features and comics ("Doonesbury"!). The Sunday edition is chockful of interesting features. The *Eagle* also publishes *Berkshires Week*, a supplementary magazine-in-newsprint containing colorful articles, a calendar of events, and lots of ads from local dining and entertainment places.

Berkshire Penny Saver (413-243-2341; 14 Park Pl., Box 300, Lee; Tuesday) Central County's free shopping guide, including classifieds, TV listings, nightlife, comprehensive business service listings.

The Berkshire Record (413-528-5380; 271 Main St., Gt. Barrington; weekly) This Southern Berkshire weekly features current affairs and articles of historic note.

Berkshire Trace & Commerce (413-447-7700; 137 North St., Pittsfield; monthly freebie) Berkshire's answer to *The Wall Street Journal*. Lively up-to-date news of Berkshire business doings.

Country Journal (413-667-3211; 25 Main St., Huntington, Hampshire County; Thursdays) Covers 16 of the central hill towns.

The Paper (518-392-2674; P.O.Box 336, Chatham, NY; monthly freebie, first Thursday).

The Pittsfield Gazette (413-443-2010; 141 North St., Pittsfield; Thursday) Lively, even acerbic local Pittsfield news. Distributed free.

Shopper's Guide (413-528-0095; 35 Bridge St., Box 89, Gt. Barrington; weekly) Southern Berkshire's free shoppers' guide, including enticing sections on real estate and automobiles.

The South Advocate (413-243-0380; 14 Park St., Lee; Wednesdays). *The Advocate* replated for Lee, Lenox. Distributed free.

The Transcript (413-663-3741; American Legion Dr., N. Adams; weekday noons, Saturday morning) Local, some state and national news; covers northern Berkshire County and southern Vermont.

The Women's Times (413-528-5303; 323 Main St., Box 390, Gt. Barrington; free monthly) A classy, well-written magazine-style paper, with articles by, for, and about Berkshire women. Good reading for men, too.

Yankee Shopper (413-684-1373; 839 Main St., Box 96, Dalton; weekly) Central and Northern Berkshire's free shopping guide, including scads of used cars, rototillers, computers, vacuum cleaners, baby bunnies as well as a business/professional services directory.

RADIO STATIONS

National Public Radio. There are four stations receivable in the Berkshires:
   WAMC-FM, 90.3; 800-323-9262; Albany, NY.
   WAMQ-FM, 105.1; 800-323-9262; Albany, NY
   WFCR-FM, 88.5; 413-545-0100; Amherst, MA.
   WMHT-FM, 89.1; 518-357-1700; Schenectady, NY.

Other Local Radio Stations:
   WBEC-AM, 1420; 413-499-3333; Pittsfield. General.
   WBEC-FM, 105.5; 413-499-3333; Pittsfield. Rock music.
   WBRK-AM, 101; 413-442-1553; Pittsfield. General.
   WBSL-FM, 91.7; 413-229-6683; Berkshire School.
   WCFM-FM, 91.9; 413-597-2197; Williams College.

WJJW-FM, 91.1; 413-662-5405; North Adams State College.
WMNB-FM, 100.1; 413-663-6567; N. Adams. General.
WNAW-AM, 1230; 413-663-6567; N. Adams. General
WNAW-FM, 100.0; 413-663-6567; N. Adams. General.
WSBS-AM, 860; 413-528-0860; Gt. Barrington. General.
WUHN-AM, 1110; 413-499-1100; Pittsfield. General.
WUPE-FM, 96; 413-499-1100; Pittsfield. Rock and other music.

TELEVISION

L ocal public access televison, run mostly by community volunteers, brings important meetings, events and opinion to listeners who subscribe to cable television. In addition to live broadcast of town meetings, city council meetings, and other events of civil and local interest, the locally run stations in each region generate such programs as "Adopt-a-Pet," live viewer call-ins, self-help and religious programs, along with musical and dramatic entertainments by local performers.

Community-based television channels:

Community Television for the Southern Berkshires (CTSB): Century Berkshire Cable Channel 11 (413-243-8211).

Pittsfield Community Television: Warner Cable Channel 3 (413-445-4234).

North Berkshire Community Television: Adelphia Channels 15, 16, and 17 (413-664-4408).

WilliNet (Williamstown): Adelphia Channels 15, 16, and 17 (413-458-0900)

Consult the *Berkshire Eagle* for schedules.

REAL ESTATE

W hat's your dream house? An isolated cabin, deep in the woods? A late 20th-century split-level, suburban tract house? A lakeside condo for time-sharing? Or a 40-room Gilded Age mansion that just needs a couple-of-hundred grand in handyman repairs? Berkshire County has them all.

If you are shopping for Berkshire real estate, you can obtain information as follows.

Lists of realtors: Consult the Yellow Pages of the telephone book or, if you're far away, contact any of the three Chambers of Commerce: *Southern Berkshire Chamber of Commerce* (413-528-1510; 362 Main St., Gt. Barrington, MA 01230); *Central Berkshire Chamber of Commerce* (413-499-4000; 66 West St., Pittsfield, MA 01201); *Northern Berkshire Chamber of Commerce* (413-663-3735; 140 Main St., N. Adams, MA 01247). All three organizations will send lists of their realtor members. The seasonal tourist information brochures from the

Berkshire Hills Conference (413-443-9186; 50 South St., Pittsfield, MA 01201) also list numerous realtors.

Once you're into the process of buying land or a house, it is essential to check with the local town government about zoning laws, building permits, etc. Such regulations vary widely from town to town. See: "Area Codes," in this chapter, for town hall telephone numbers.

You can also follow the real estate market in the newspapers; see "Media," in this chapter. *The Berkshire Home Buyers Guide* is a free monthly publication, distributed in local shops or available from 413-243-2500; 80 Runway, Windsock Industrial Park, Rte. 102; P.O. Box 280, Lee MA 01238.

RELIGIOUS SERVICES AND ORGANIZATIONS

B erkshire County has an active and unusually diverse religious community. The best source for information about church and synagogue services is the Saturday edition of the Berkshire Eagle. The Berkshire County Telephone Directory has a comprehensive list of all mainstream religious organizations, under the headings "Churches" and "Synagogues." For nontraditional groups, a helpful publication to consult is New Visions, published seasonally and distributed through various shops. Also, keep an eye on community bulletin boards at the area's colleges and in towns such as Great Barrington, Stockbridge, Lenox, Pittsfield, and Williamstown.

ROAD SERVICE

E mergency road service from AAA, anywhere in the county, can be obtained by calling 413-443-5635, Pittsfield. For non-AAA drivers, the following is a listing of emergency towing services.

South County

Decker's Auto Body, Gt. Barrington	413-528-1432
Mac's Garage, Gt. Barrington	413-528-1234
R W's Inc., Lee	413-243-0946
Stockbridge Motors, Stockbridge	413-298-4780

Central County

All Hours Towing & Repairs, Pittsfield	413-442-8765
Berkshire County Towing, Pittsfield	413-443-0881

County Auto Wrecking, Pittsfield	413-443-6665;
	800-232-5205
Sayers' Auto, Pittsfield	413-443-1635
Scratch-A-Ticket Towing, Pittsfield	413-443-1754
Southgate Motors, Pittsfield	413-445-5971

North County

Al's Service Center, Adams	413-743-9755
Bator's Service & Sales, Cheshire	413-743-3578
Carpinello's Service Center, Williamstown	413-458-2528
Dean's Quality Auto & Truck Repair, North Adams	413-664-6378
Ernies's Auto Sales, North Adams	413-663-3503
Mohawk Auto Wrecking, North Adams	413-663-6835
Ron's Getty, Williamstown	413-458-2238
T&M Auto Sales, North Adams	413-664-6697
Village Truck Sales, Lanesborough	413-442-0407
West End Auto Body & Glass, North Adams	413-664-6708

SCHOOLS

PUBLIC SCHOOL DISTRICTS

South County

Berkshire Hills Regional School District, Stockbridge; 413-298-3711
Farmington River Regional, Otis; 413-269-7105
Lee Public Schools; 413-243-0276
Southern Berkshire Regional School District, Sheffield; 413-229-8778

Central County

Central Berkshire Regional School District, Dalton; 413-684-0320
Lenox Public Schools; 413-637-5550
Richmond Consolidated Schools; 413-698-2207
Pittsfield Public Schools; 413-499-9512

North County

Adams-Cheshire Regional School District; 413-743-2939
Clarksburg School Department; 413-664-8735
Florida School Department; 413-663-6023

Lanesborough Schools; 413-442-2229
Mount Greylock Regional School District; 413-458-9582
New Ashford School Department; 413-458-5461
North Adams Public Schools; 413-662-3225
Northern Berkshire Vocational; 413-663-5383
Savoy School Department; 413-743-1992
Williamstown Public Schools; 413-458-5707

PRIVATE AND RELIGIOUS SCHOOLS

South County

Berkshire School, Sheffield; 413-229-8511.
De Sisto School, Stockbridge; 413-298-3776.
The Kolburne School, New Marlborough; 413-229-8787.
Rudolf Steiner School, Gt. Barrington; 413-528-4015.
St. Mary's School, Lee; 413-243-1079.

Central County

Berkshire Country Day School, Lenox; 413-637-0755
Berkshire County Christian School, Pittsfield; 413-442-4014
Hillcrest Educational Centers; 413-499-7924. Schools in Lenox (2),
     Gt. Barrington, Pittsfield (2), and Hancock.
Miss Hall's School, Pittsfield; 413-443-6401
Sacred Heart School, Pittsfield; 413-443-6379
St. Agnes School, Dalton; 413-684-3143
St. Joseph's High School, Pittsfield; 413-447-9121

North County

Buxton School, Williamstown; 413-458-3919
Notre Dame School, Adams; 413-743-1767
Pine Cobble School, Williamstown; 413-458-4680
St. Stanislaus, Adams; 413-743-1091

COLLEGES

Berkshire Community College, Pittsfield; 413-499-4660. In Gt. Barrington:
     413-528-4521.
North Adams State College, N. Adams; 413-662-5000
Simon's Rock College of Bard, Gt. Barrington; 413-528-0771
Williams College, Williamstown; 413-597-3131

IF TIME IS SHORT

Berkshire offers so much to the visitor that longer sojourns here are most rewarding, but sometimes that isn't possible. Here are some recommendations from the author, the publisher, and the editor from their personal favorites among the multitude of attractions which best exemplify the spirit of the place and might perfectly suit the visitor with only a weekend or a few days available for a first visit.

LODGING

The Red Lion Inn (413-298-5545, Main Street, Stockbridge) Satisfying meals, an excellent range of lodging options, and endless collections of fine furniture and antiques in a rambling, century-old inn in the old style, pleasing visitors and locals since 1793.

The Orchards (413-458-9611; 222 Adams Rd., off Rte. 2, Williamstown) A superb small luxury hotel offering a formal, clublike atmosphere. Huge rooms, many with bay windows and fireplaces; an award-winning restaurant. The service throughout is honed to a fine edge.

RESTAURANTS

Castle Street Cafe (413 528-5255, 10 Castle St., Gt. Barrington) The best *bistro* French cuisine in South County in a charming, brick-walled cafe.

Elm Court Inn (413-528-0325; Rte. 71, N. Egremont) Pleasant inn in South County serving continental cuisine in a cozy traditional setting.

The Hancock Inn (413-738-5873; Rte. 43, Hancock) A comfortable, unpretentious, and rustic inn serving excellent continental cuisine.

The Mill on the Floss (413-458-9123; Rte. 7, New Ashford) One of the greater gourmet experiences in North County, offering excellent French cuisine in an informal setting.

FOOD PURVEYORS

The Store At Five Corners (413-458-3176; junction of Rtes. 7 & 43, South Williamstown) A wonderful assortment of gourmet foods, wines, oils, jellies for gift baskets, prepared food for picnics, delicious ice creams and yogurt in a renovated Victorian building. Creative cooks will delight in the myriad of offerings and novice cooks will be inspired to experiment. They can even buy the newest cookbooks to assure culinary success. Devoted non-cooks should just stock up on the delicious ready-made salads, casseroles, and baked goods.

CULTURE

MUSEUMS

The Sterling & Francine Clark Art Institute (413-458-2305; 225 South St., Williamstown) Among the museums in the county, the one with the longest-standing national reputation; renowned for its collection of Impressionists, especially Renoir.

Williams College Museum of Art (413-597-2429; Main St., Rte. 2, Williamstown) One of the finest college museums in the country and a leading research center. Emphasis on early art and 20th-century American art, to complement the 19th-century collection at the Clark.

Norman Rockwell Museum (413-298-4100; Rte. 183, Stockbridge) Even connoisseurs of fine art find themselves captivated by Rockwell's evocations of America as we always wanted it to be. A guaranteed hit with every member of the family.

Hancock Shaker Village (413-443-0188; Rte. 20, near Pittsfield / Hancock line) Beautifully restored Shaker village, with numerous exhibits, Shaker buildings, and events for all the family.

SUMMER MUSIC

Tanglewood (413-637-1666 or 413-637-1940; West St., Rte. 183, Lenox) The obvious choice for the visitor with but one evening or day. Shed concerts Friday and Saturday evenings and Sunday afternoons from early July through late August; Wednesday or Thursday evening recitals in Seiji Ozawa Hall; operas in the newly refitted Concert Hall. In addition to world-class concerts by the Boston Symphony Orchestra and visiting soloists, the students of Tanglewood's summer program for aspiring professionals give numerous concerts in all venues seven days a week. Popular or Jazz artists often take the stage at the end of August. The grounds, justly famous for their cultivated beauty, are great for a stroll or a picnic.

South Mountain Concerts (413-442-2106; Rtes. 7 & 20, Pittsfield) Chamber music for the serious listener, primarily string quartets but other combinations, too (the annual appearance of the Beaux Arts Trio is a highlight of the season). Concerts are in a historic building built expressly for small ensembles, in a wooded setting above Pittsfield. Five Sunday afternoon concerts during September and early October.

Tannery Pond Concerts (518-794-7887, or for reservations & tickets call 888-846-5848; Rte. 20, New Lebanon, NY) Five chamber concerts, about one a month between late May and early October. Superb rising stars along with internationally renowned performers, in a former Shaker tannery now converted to a rustic and acoustically excellent hall situated in a beautiful meadow on the grounds of Darrow School.

SUMMER THEATER

Berkshire Theatre Festival (413-298-5576, 413-298-5536 off season; E. Main St., Rte. 102, Stockbridge) and **Williamstown Theatre Festival** (413-458-3400; Main St., Williamstown) The two granddaddies of American summer stock theater vie with each other to present superior theater in charming settings. Both offer main stage and studio presentations, traditional and new works from mid-June through Labor Day. Call ahead for schedules and reservations.

Shakespeare & Company at The Mount (413-637-3353 box office, 413-637-1197 off season; Plunkett St., near jct. of Rtes 7 & 7A, Lenox) Shakespeare's classics presented in both conventional and outdoor stagings at Edith Wharton's summer estate, plus a rich array of large- and small-scale works by other writers, including many stage adaptations of Wharton's short works.

RECREATION

Monument Mountain Reservation (413-298-3239; Stockbridge Rd., Rte. 7, Gt. Barrington) 503 acres. A short but rugged climb up Squaw Peak, the reservation's most prominent feature, offers excellent views of three states from a summit 1,642 feet above sea level.

Mount Greylock State Reservation (413-499-4262; Rockwell Rd., off Rte. 7, Lanesborough; also accessible from Notch Road, N. Adams) 12,000 acres, including the state's highest peak, along with 45 miles of trails.

SHOPPING

CLOTHING

Evviva! (413-637-9875; 22 Walker St., Lenox) A recent expansion has increased the offerings of this clothing store for women. Dresses for special events, romantic hats, unique jewelry, casual country clothes, and hand-painted silks combine to create a feast for the eye. The windows (which change monthly) are fascinating in and of themselves.

Steven Valenti (413-637-0674; 4 Housatonic St., Lenox; also in Pittsfield: 413-443-2569; 157 North St.) A men's store with an emphasis on customer satisfaction and stylish yet comfortable clothes for all occasions.

BOOKS

The Bookstore (413-637-3390; 9 Housatonic St., Lenox) A most knowledgeable owner and a slightly '70s air makes this a great place to browse and chat about books.

Barnes & Noble (413-496-9051; Berkshire Crossing Mall, Rte. 9, Pittsfield) Say what you will about chains . . this one offers plenty of parking and is fully stocked with books, related activities, and that great Starbucks coffee, so one is definitely tempted to indulge. Most book lovers try to spread the wealth: they support the independents feeling righteous and indulge in the chains feeling guilty!

GIFTS

The Gingham Rabbit (413-528-0048; 389 Stockbridge Rd., Rte. 7, Gt. Barrington) A large shop with an eclectic mix of giftware, infant ware, indulgent bath and boudoir items just for a treat or to indulge a shut-in. Many of the clothing and gift items can be monogrammed. They also wrap and will delivery locally to hospitals, etc.

Mistral's (413-528-1618; 7 Railroad St., Gt. Barrington) A most elegant, sophisticated collection of tableware, linens, and home furnishings from France. The upstairs houses a collection of items for the bed and bath. A beautiful shop to visit for an infusion of French chic.

Pamela Loring Gifts and Interiors (413-243-2689; 40 Main St., Lee) Very attractive shop on Main St. with excellent service, they will wrap packages and provide gift cards. Mostly giftware with an emphasis on floral, pretty gifts for women, and seasonal merchandise.

B. Mango & Bird (413-637-2611; 48 Main St., Lenox) A new location on Main St., with walls painted a deep, luscious red will bring this shop to the attention of many newcomers, but those who visited it in its previous location will be pleased to find the same interesting accessories for the home and table. Browsing in this store will give you lots of ideas for creating more visually appealing rooms.

GREAT BARGAINS

T.J. Maxx (413-443-9644, Allendale Shopping Center., Jct. Rtes. 8 & 9, Pittsfield) One of the best of the chain, according to those who have scouted these stores in other locations. In a shopping center that has Farmer's Markets on Weds. & Sat., May–Oct. Next to a bagel store serving great sandwiches and soups. Note the whimsical sinking ship in the middle of the parking lot — sometimes taken to be a metaphor for the city of Pittsfield.

Index

RESTAURANTS BY PRICE CODE

RESTAURANTS BY CUISINE

LODGING BY PRICE CODE

SHOPPING BY AREA

GREAT BARRINGTON

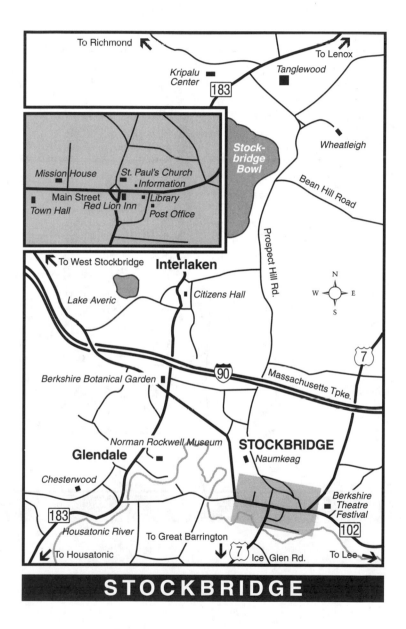

To Richmond

To Lenox

Kripalu
Center

Tanglewood

183

Stock-
bridge
Bowl

Wheatleigh

Bean Hill Road

Mission House

St. Paul's Church
Information

Main Street

Library

Town Hall

Red Lion Inn

Post Office

To West Stockbridge

Interlaken

Prospect Hill Rd.

Lake Averic

Citizens Hall

N

W E

S

7

90

Berkshire Botanical Garden

Massachusetts Tpke.

Norman Rockwell Museum

STOCKBRIDGE

Glendale

Naumkeag

Chesterwood

Berkshire
Theatre
Festival

183

102

Housatonic River

To Great Barrington

To Housatonic

7

Ice Glen Rd.

To Lee

STOCKBRIDGE

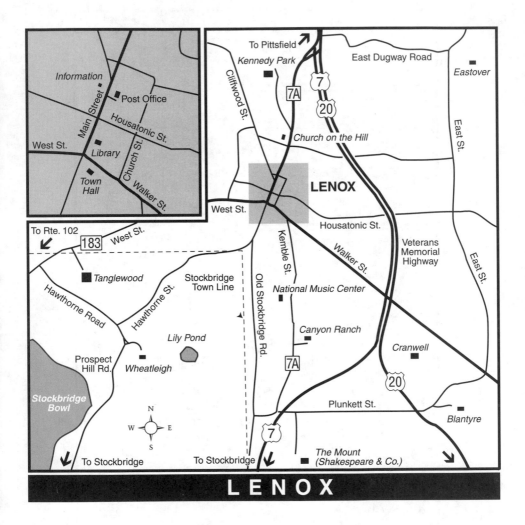

LENOX

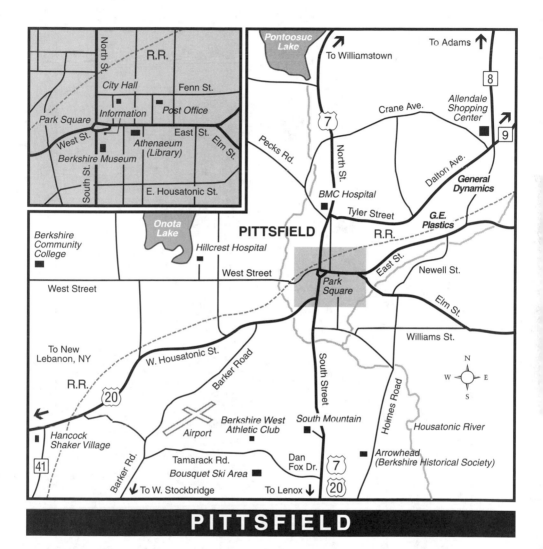

PITTSFIELD

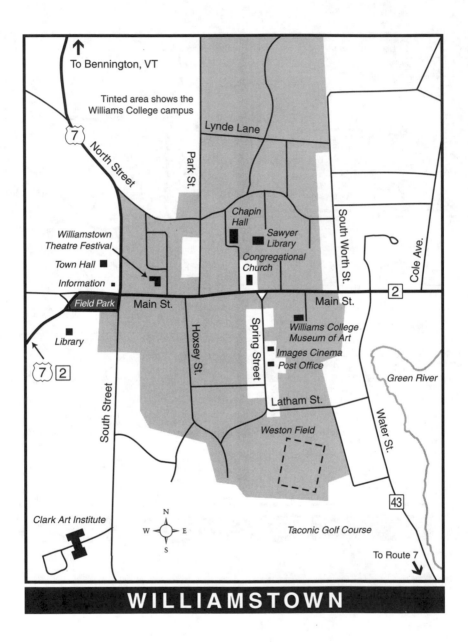

To Bennington, VT

Tinted area shows the
Williams College campus

Lynde Lane

North Street

7

Park St.

Chapin
Hall

Sawyer
Library

Congregational
Church

Williamstown
Theatre Festival

Town Hall ■

Information ■

Field Park

Main St.

Main St.

2

South Worth St.

Cole Ave.

Library

7 2

South Street

Hoxsey St.

Spring Street

Williams College
Museum of Art

Images Cinema
Post Office

Green River

Latham St.

Weston Field

Water St.

43

Clark Art Institute

N
W ● E
S

Taconic Golf Course

To Route 7

WILLIAMSTOWN

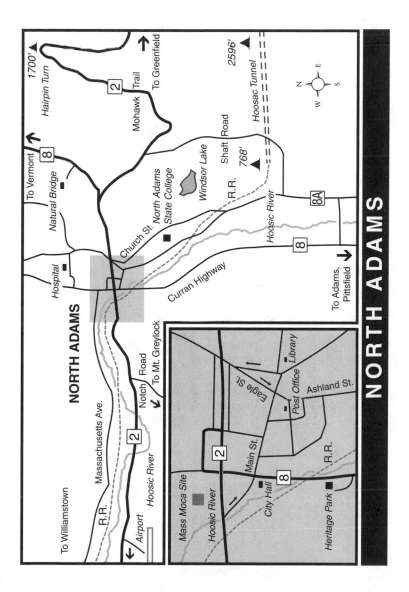

NORTH ADAMS

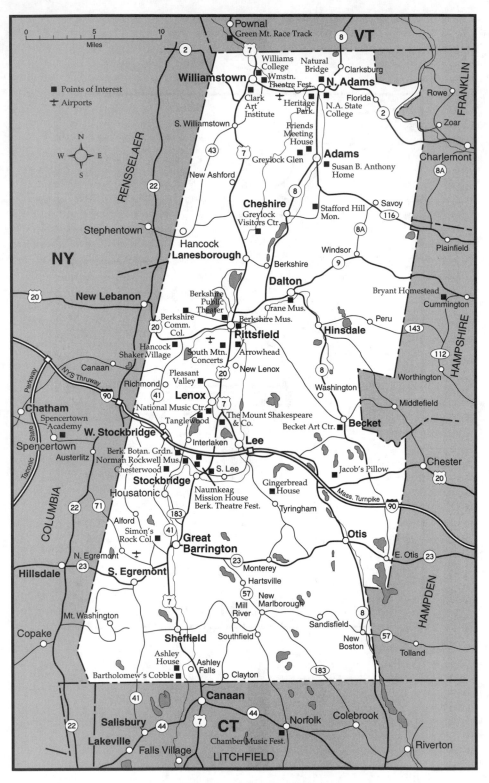

BERKSHIRE COUNTY

About Jonathan Sternfield

Mark Sternfield

Jonathan Sternfield, born in New York City, has lived in the Berkshires since shortly after graduating from the University of Pennsylvania in 1969. His publishing credits include *The Complete Book of Mopeds* (Funk and Wagnalls), *Starring Your Love Life* (Lynx), *The Look of Horror* (Running Press), and numerous articles for *Berkshire Magazine* as well as pieces on electric cars and solar energy for other publications. His book *Firewalk* was published by Berkshire House in 1992. As a photographer, he has created images for advertising, for actors, for book illustration, and for rock videos. When he's not writing or photographing, Jonathan Sternfield is a tennis pro at Canyon Ranch in Lenox.

About Lauren R. Stevens

Judith Monachina

Lauren R. Stevens is the author, with Richard W. Babcock, of *Old Barns in the New World* and, with Deborah E. Burns, of *Most Excellent Majesty: A History of Mount Greylock*. A resident of Williamstown and an avid hiker, he is also author of *Hikes & Walks in the Berkshire Hills* and of *Skiing in the Berkshire Hills*. Founder in 1981 of *The Advocate*, a county-wide weekly newspaper, he is now a freelancer who has written on the environment for most Berkshire periodicals, as well as several longer studies as an environmental consultant. His novel, *The Double Axe*, was published by Scribner's.